THE IMAGE
OF CHILDHOOD

*The Individual and Society: a Study of the
Theme in English Literature*

PETER COVENEY

REVISED EDITION
WITH AN INTRODUCTION BY
F. R. LEAVIS

PENGUIN BOOKS

Penguin Books Ltd, Harmondsworth, Middlesex, England
Penguin Books Inc., 3300 Clipper Mill Road, Baltimore, Md 21211, U.S.A.
Penguin Books Australia Ltd, Ringwood, Victoria, Australia

—

First published by Rockliff as *Poor Monkey*, 1957
This revised edition published in Peregrine Books 1967

—

Copyright © Peter Coveney, 1957, 1967

—

Made and printed in Great Britain by
Cox & Wyman Ltd,
London, Fakenham and Reading
Set in Monotype Bembo

TO MY MOTHER

Contents

	ACKNOWLEDGEMENTS	9
	PREFACE TO THE FIRST EDITION	11
	PREFACE TO THE PEREGRINE EDITION	13
	INTRODUCTION BY F. R. LEAVIS	15
	AUTHOR'S INTRODUCTION	29
1	The 'Cult of Sensibility' and the 'Romantic Child'	37
2	Blake's *Innocence* and *Experience*	52
3	Wordsworth and Coleridge	68
	Wordsworth's 'Father of the Man'	
	Coleridge and the 'Imaginative Child'	
4	From Coleridge to Dickens	91
5	The Child in Dickens	111
6	George Eliot and Maggie Tulliver	162
7	Reduction to Absurdity	179
8	Innocence in Henry James	194
9	Mark Twain and Richard Jefferies	215
10	Escape	240
11	The End of the Victorian Child	280
	Butler's *Way of All Flesh*	
	Freud's Essay on Infantile Sexuality	
12	Joyce: Virginia Woolf: D. H. Lawrence	303
	EPILOGUE	337
	BIBLIOGRAPHY	343
	INDEX	349

Acknowledgements

The author's thanks are due to the proprietors of the copyrights in the following works quoted in the text:

Some Versions of Pastoral by William Empson; *The Great Tradition* by F. R. Leavis; *The Eighteenth Century Background* by Basil Willey (Chatto & Windus).

The Liberal Imagination by Lionel Trilling (Secker & Warburg).

The Triple Thinkers by Edmund Wilson (Oxford University Press).

The Wound and the Bow by Edmund Wilson (Houghton Mifflin Co.).

The Victorians and After, 1830–1914 by Edith Batho and Bonamy Dobrée (Cresset Press).

The Portrait of a Lady by Henry James (Oxford University Press).

The Wings of a Dove by Henry James (Eyre & Spottiswoode).

The Princess Casamassima and *What Maisie Knew* by Henry James (John Lehmann).

The Awkward Age by Henry James (Hamish Hamilton).

The Turn of the Screw by Henry James (Dent).

The Ordeal of Mark Twain by Van Wyck Brooks (E. P. Dutton & Co.).

The Story of J. M. B. by Denis Mackail (Peter Davies).

Barrie and the Kailyard Novelists by George Blake (Arthur Barker).

Portrait of Forrest Reid by Russell Burlingham (Faber & Faber).

Apostate, Brian Westby, Following Darkness, Spring Song, Uncle Stephen and *Young Tom* by Forrest Reid (Faber & Faber).

The Garden God by Forrest Reid (David Nutt, London, 1905).

An Outline of Psycho-Analysis by Sigmund Freud; *Sigmund Freud: Life and Work* by Ernest Jones (Hogarth Press).

Common Reader, To the Lighthouse, Mrs Dalloway and *The Waves* by Virginia Woolf (Hogarth Press).

Principles of Psychology by William James (Macmillan).

Virginia Woolf: Her Art as a Novelist by Joan Bennett (Cambridge University Press).

Virginia Woolf by David Daiches (Editions Poetry London).

Dubliners and *A Portrait of the Artist as a Young Man* by James Joyce (Jonathan Cape).

Modern Man in Search of a Soul, The Integration of the Personality and *Psychology of the Unconscious* by C. G. Jung (Kegan Paul).

ACKNOWLEDGEMENTS

Freud or Jung by Edward Glover (Allen & Unwin).

St Mawr, Sons and Lovers, England my England, The Rainbow, Letters and *Lady Chatterley's Lover* by D. H. Lawrence (Heinemann).

'Henry James' by Stephen Spender (article in *Hound and Horn*).

The Crystal Box by Hugh Walpole (published privately 1924).

Roman Fountain, The Golden Scarecrow, Jeremy, Jeremy and Hamlet, Jeremy at Crale by Hugh Walpole (Macmillan).

The Little White Bird, Margaret Ogilvy, Peter Pan and *A Window in Thrums* by J. M. Barrie (Hodder & Stoughton).

Sentimental Tommy by J. M. Barrie (Cassell).

Abinger Harvest by E. M. Forster (Edward Arnold).

Barrie by Thomas Moult (Jonathan Cape).

Preface to the First Edition

THE feeling which led me to undertake this book was I suppose the simple enough and common one that such a study badly needed doing. It is a study of childhood as it has been presented in literature written for adults in, for the most part, the nineteenth and early twentieth centuries. It does not therefore deal with books written for children, except for those which, for various reasons, have attracted an adult readership. It is a survey rather than a work of scholarship, in the narrow sense of the word, and, for this reason, I have not aimed at covering everybody for inclusiveness' sake. It none the less, I hope, substantiates its judgements by close reference to the works under discussion. To some readers it may seem to leave out authors whom they themselves might have included, or wished to see discussed in such a study. It became clear to me, however, before very long, that I would have to select, and select fairly ruthlessly, both for reasons of space, and if I were to succeed in tracing the continuities which I initially suspected and set out to verify. The very immensity of the number of books about children in our literature, since the end of the eighteenth century, was one of the signals directing me to this study. It suggested that it would be useful to find out what it was about – if not all, at least, partly. For this reason I have kept for the most part to the major authors, those through whom the development of sensibility towards the child may be said to have moved. I have tried to place the point of the compass rather than to describe the whole extent of what proved to be a very wide circle. The only hope can be that I shall have at least suggested some of the criteria which may be brought to the assessment of authors who may appear to some to lie neglected on the circumference.

In placing the point, however, I have tried to be as circumspect as possible. I have approached most authors in a general way, relating what they have to say about children to themselves, their times, and their work as a whole. This method seemed best for two reasons:

because I did not wish to compile a catalogue of literary children; but more so, because of the nature of the subject. It became impossible to consider an author's attitude to childhood without very soon realizing that one was considering his attitude to something very closely synonymous with life. The references were therefore unavoidably the widest. The child had been the focus of so many authors' work that one wondered if one might not find, when all the focal interests were gathered together, a focus of one aspect of the general literary sensibility of the period.

To those who prefer to consider the art rather than the artist, my approach may seem at times too biographical. I risked, however, and I hope to some extent survived, the danger of biographical blurring, simply because it was a risk that had to be taken. The possibility that an author was carrying into his work merely a limiting response to his own childhood was something that could not be ignored. Reference to his own life, in so far as it could be ascertained, became an obligation. In any event, biographical references have not been made for their own sake. They have been directed to the art, with the hope that they might help to elucidate its meaning and suggest something of its worth.

I should like to thank the Librarian of the University of Hull, Mr Philip Larkin, and his staff, for their great assistance and long-suffering in obtaining for me the works I needed; Mr John Farrell for his great help with the proofs, and for his immeasurable kindness in compiling the index; and the many of my friends who have been patient enough to discuss this book with me, and especially Mr Donald Mitchell, Mrs Kathleen Mitchell, and Mr Philip Povey, for their very particular advice and aid. Any felicities the book may have are, I feel, largely owing to them. Other things should, and no doubt will, be placed at my own door.

P. J. C.

Needler Hall,
  University of Hull.
February, 1957.

Preface to the Peregrine Edition

I HAVE little to add by way of a preface to this edition, except to note the change of title. This change is made in the hope that the subject and intentions of the work will be more immediately evident to the reader. The new title suggests the central interests I had in making the study, especially when it is read in relation to the sub-title, *The Individual and Society: a Study of the Theme in English Literature.*

The text itself has, for the most part, only been revised stylistically.

I am indeed conscious of the honour accorded me by Professor Leavis, in his so generously writing an introduction to this edition.

P. J. C.

University of Nottingham, 1966.

Introduction by F. R. Leavis

MR COVENEY'S book is very unusual: it is original, it has an important theme, and the criticisms one makes as one reads amount in sum to a high tribute. I think that no reader intelligently interested in English literature will not find himself giving to *The Image of Childhood* the kind of attention I intimate here. It deals with facts and considerations such a reader will be pretty familiar with, and its treatment of these constitutes the definition of a theme he will recognize to be, so presented, both original and central for the critical understanding of English literature during the period of the great novel. The originality lies in the combination of firmness and sensitiveness with which, in the defining, the essential relations are grasped and the theme established in terms of given writers and actual history. The scholarship of the book, which proceeds more closely and scrupulously by the adducing of the relevant data than most literary studies praised as scholarly, is that of a student who, well equipped outside the immediate field of literary criticism, responds to what he rightly sees as his prime data, the works of creative writers, with the sensibility and judgement of a literary critic.

In so far as his theme admits of being given in a title, *The Image of Childhood* (with the cooperation of the sub-title) gives it. Mr Coveney's first major author is Blake. Of course, he refers with due emphasis and specificity to Rousseau and his immense part in the revulsion against Reason and conventional formalism that marks the latter half of the eighteenth century. More generally, Mr Coveney reminds us that Blake, as the great original genius will inevitably be, was very much a man of his own time.

Of course, he was, with unusual completeness and intensity, an individual, and his peculiar kind of insistence on the individual life and the authority of the individual experience was the way in which his distinctive genius manifested itself. 'Sensibility,' wrote Eliot, 'alters in us all from age to age whether we will or no, but expression

15

is only altered by a man of genius.' Blake was the man of genius; after generations of literary taste for which the only mode of expression was statement, and the 'virtues of good prose' were demanded of poetry, and these virtues were inescapably committed to the suggestion of manners and the social context, Blake achieved for himself the escape from prose and manners, and the expression of the intensely individual sensibility. '*Si je ne vaux pas mieux, au moins je suis autre*': everyone knows that sentence from the opening of Rousseau's *Confessions*. But Blake lies under no suspicion of being concerned to assert difference as such. His implicit insistence on the individual experience and sensibility is his inevitable demonstration against Locke and Newton; against the cultural ethos associated with their names – and, for Blake, with that of Sir Joshua Reynolds.

'To generalize is to be an Idiot.' Blake insists on the truth that life is 'there' only in the individual life, and that lives can't be aggregated, generalized or dealt with quantitatively in any way. It is a disastrous illusion that we can attain to the real by any abstracting process, or that perception is a matter of passive exposure to an objective world of which science gives a true report. The eye is part of the brain, and the brain is a representative of the living whole, an agent of the psyche: perception is creative. This truth, clear and indisputable for Blake, had for him its full context of significance. The elementary truth that can be demonstrated experimentally, and very simply, was for him a demonstration of the comprehensive truth that life is essentially and inescapably creative: perception is not an isolated and readily circumscribed function. There is a continuity from the inevitable everyday creativeness of the ordinary individual life to the creativeness of the artist.

Here we have Blake's conception of Art, surely the only sound one; one of which we may perhaps say that it has been recovered in our time in spite of the critical influence of T. S. Eliot, whose confusions were an inheritance from the late Victorian age. Blake's conception of Art was his answer to the Lockean universe and the ethos of Reason, decorum and mechanism. In an age in which a great creative genius had to insist, as Blake did, on the indispensableness of the artist to society it was natural that childhood should command that attention from him which gives him his key place in Mr Coveney's study. In the child, life asserts its spontaneity, without which there is nothing.

Mr Coveney discusses Innocence and Experience with characteristic tact and sensitiveness. He knows that the right kinds of scrupulousness and delicacy entail some boldness: one must be content not to establish necessary distinctions with final precision locally. He notes that when Blake wrote his *Songs of Innocence* the idea of an Original Innocence to be found in the child had already won some currency as a retort to Original Sin. It is a pregnant observation, and what Mr Coveney does with it in defining his theme historically and comparatively is admirable. Not having myself a whole study on my hands, I may perhaps allow myself to underline some distinctions in relation to Blake. One cannot then, I think, fairly extract from Blake's antithesis any coherent doctrine of Original Innocence, the spontaneous individual, cramped, blighted and corrupted by society. True, his poems that come under Experience, and his proverbs, convey a plain enough distaste for *Thou shalt nots* that offer to thwart desire and natural impulse, and there are well-known poetic indictments of social oppressions, callousnesses and cruelties. But 'experience' is not a narrowly definitive word, and Blake's *Songs of Experience* don't encourage the belief that all the disharmonies and sicknesses that trouble innocence and destroy the reign of joy are to be blamed on society in any ordinary sense of the word (wide as is the possibility of use that it covers). The theme of 'The Clod and the Pebble' is a major preoccupation for Blake. It is the theme – the usurping ego, possessive and destructive love, the lapse from the ego-free spontaneity of innocence – that has a supremely characteristic creative expression in 'The Sick Rose', one of the finest of the *Songs of Experience*.

Blake was a marvellous psychologist. With the intelligence, vitality and self-transcendence of genius, he had a sure insight into the conditions of health and sickness in the individual life. But I don't think we should hesitate to testify bluntly that there seem to be no good grounds for crediting him with a comprehensive human wisdom, and that he has no real answers to the questions prompted by his reports in the field of his clearly valid insight; questions that he wrestles with so pertinaciously in his mythopoeic works;

questions raised for him by the human drama enacted in contemporary France and becoming history as he contemplated it.

The claim to be made for Blake is a very impressive one. Mr Coveney makes it in distinguishing the sense in which Blake is a 'romantic'. The cult of Feeling, of Original Innocence, and of the child lends itself readily to egotism, irresponsibility, evasion of the real, and nostalgic reversion. That if 'romantic' means these tendencies Blake deserves to be called something else, Mr Coveney brings out very clearly. He also brings out how inevitably inclusive the term is ('romantic movement', 'romantic tradition'), and so how little in itself, to any unambiguous effect, definitive. Thus with good reason he calls Dickens a 'romantic novelist', knowing, though his main aim is to insist on Dickens's strength, that the general acceptance such a description can count on – or could have counted on till very recently – carries with it a pejorative or decidedly limiting implication. People think of Little Nell, and, at the best, of David Copperfield. And no one would deny that the sentimental, evasive and morbid tendencies associated with the romantic tradition are to be found in Dickens's *œuvre*; that he can exploit childhood in the interests of illicit emotional satisfactions, and, when at his subtlest in the sentimental vein, make a moving presentment of the child's experience too much an indulgence in self-pity. But, with a propriety that his book establishes, Mr Coveney intends with the term 'romantic' to emphasize all that strength which in the great Dickens relates him to Blake.

I take an especial interest in this part of the book. For, confronting the problem of getting the greatness of Dickens recognized as it ought to be, but certainly hasn't yet been at all generally, I have again and again thought how like Blake he is in his strongest work. The propriety of calling the ways in which Blake's genius, at its most impressive, expresses itself 'romantic' is fairly clear. The peculiar insistence on the individual spontaneous life, and on art as the typical manifestation of its creativeness – wonder being a characteristic expression, or sign, of fully human vitality – is the protest of genius against the world of Locke and Newton, Reason and reasonableness, 'weight and measure' and the Grand Style. The peculiar intensity, expressing itself in an extraordinary economy of art (the 'wiry bounding line'), with which Blake realizes the vital truths he vindicates, make him unmistakably a writer of the 'Romantic movement' – of the Romantic climate and inspiration. But the truths are not the less vital for that, and the vindication added something to the human heritage.

I say this, having, I realize, tacitly adduced the major work of Dickens as a proof. But, of course, it will be asked: what influence can Blake, who was so far from being a current author in his time and didn't come in with the Romantic poets, be supposed to have had? A study of the evidence may some day be written showing that Blake, his poetry, and his thought were well enough known to make him an 'influence' that academic literary historians can consider factually established. And if there were grounds for believing that Dickens had read Blake, that would make Blake (in my judgement) an 'influence' of certainly not less importance on the literature of the Victorian age than Wordsworth; for *Little Dorrit*, where the characteristics that make one think of Blake belong to the essential organic structure of the dramatic poem, is a much greater creative work than any in which Wordsworth may be seen as counting, and it is representative of the art that puts Dickens among the very greatest writers.

But I am not intending to commit myself to the belief that Dickens had read Blake. What is plain beyond question is that he was familiar with Wordsworth and with Romantic poetry in general, and that his interest and responsiveness were those of an originating genius who was equipped by nature to be himself a great poet. Further, a man of wonderfully quick intelligence, he mixed with the *élite* that shared the finest culture of the age and, when first frequented by him, was like himself pre-Victorian. One can say that his genius, entailing a completeness of interest in human life (Dickens was not a 'solemn and unsexual man'), cities and civilization that it was Wordsworth's peculiar genius not to have, spontaneously took those promptings of the romantic heritage which confirmed his response to early Victorian England; confirmed the intuitions and affirmations that, present organically in the structure and significance of *Hard Times* and *Little Dorrit*, make one think of Blake.

I have in mind, of course, the way in which the irrelevance of the

Benthamite calculus is exposed; the insistence that life, in so far as it *is* life, is spontaneous and creative, so that the appeal to self-interest as the essential motive is life-defeating; the vindication, in terms of childhood, of spontaneity, disinterestedness, love and wonder; and the significant place given to Art – a place entailing a conception of Art that is pure Blake.

In *Hard Times*, with its comparative simplicity as a damning critique of the hard ethos and the life-oppressing civilization, the identity of the affirmatives, or evoked and related manifestations of life and health and human normality, by which he condemns, with those of Blake is clear. *Little Dorrit*, his greatest work, is immensely more complex, and offers something like a comprehensive report upon mid-Victorian England – what is life, what are the possibilities of life, in this society and civilization, and what could life, in a better society, be? To elicit the convinced assent to the proposition that here too the underlying structure of value-affirmations (implicit, spontaneous and inevitable) upon which the form and significance depend is Blakean is not so easy. But the structure is there; for the book *has* organic form and essential economy: it is all significant. Recognizing this, and the close relation to *Hard Times*, one perhaps finds oneself commenting that *Little Dorrit* in its strength and abundance is so characteristic of the writer's genius that the Blakean in it is properly called the Dickensian.

What I have been implicitly granting is that Mr Coveney's phrase, 'the greatest of the romantic novelists', used for Dickens, has much point; it does, in the context he gives it, something very important. And in saying this I am recognizing incidentally that, among other things we owe his book, it impels us, and in a timely way, to make a fresh approach to the Romantic period. I have already intimated my agreement that the Romantic Movement 'added something' (my phrase); enriched the heritage, that is, in ways not as a rule fully recognized even in sympathetic uses of the adjective. This truth is manifest in the distinctive greatness of Dickens; the greatness we take stock of when, dismissing the time-honoured traffic in his claims as a 'social reformer', we contemplate the profoundly creative response to Victorian civilization that his strongest work, his classical 'criticism of life', is. His vindication of human dignity, his wholly unrhetorical and unposturing and essentially religious presentment of the inherent human claim, may be called anti-Flaubertian. It makes us look, if back to Blake, then forward with a clear perception of a direct vital relation, to D. H. Lawrence. And Lawrence's distinguished and influential contemporary was T. S. Eliot: my point is made there.

The ethos of Eliot's ideology (so far as he had one – and he certainly had attitudes and dispositions which his critical writings, and his influence in general, made current) is no longer fashionable. But his formulations, in an inert kind of way, regain their prestige in the academico-metropolitan literary world (that of the Sunday papers) where *Tradition and the Individual Talent* passes for a profound and classically final piece of critical thought. Did not Eliot say that Lawrence was 'incapable of what is ordinarily called thinking', and is that pronouncement a byword for its revealing absurdity?

A just and true respect towards Eliot entails this note. That is, he ranks among those writers one's sense of whose importance and distinction is associated inseparably with their having prompted, or compelled, a final and significant No – which, of course, in the nature of the case, will not be all there is to be said. The sufficient comment on Eliot's classicism came, appropriately, from Lawrence: 'This classiosity is bunkum, still more cowardice.' Eliot's classicism is, explicitly, anti-romanticism; when he identifies the 'romantic' it is always in traits that enforce the pejorative use of the word. And a way of defining the kind of vital strength one has in mind when one assents to Mr Coveney's calling Dickens a 'romantic' novelist is to say that it is what Eliot deliberately rules out from the creative process and the 'mind of the artist' in his account of 'impersonality'. The famous essay, in short, has for essential purpose to absolve the artist from responsibility towards life.

A distinctive sense of responsibility towards life – that is what the Romantic Movement brought to the human heritage; added (who doesn't hope?) as a permanent enrichment. To put things in this way is to pay a tribute to the felicity of Mr Coveney's approach to post-Augustan literary history. To study the new preoccupation with childhood is to define the new sense we contemplate as we pass from Blake to Dickens and Dickens to Lawrence. It is new in a central way; not something aberrant and eccentric to be corrected by the authority of a 'tradition' to which the artist 'sacrifices himself'.

There had been profoundly serious art before. But the 'human heritage' is not a hoard handed down from the past, though it carries an access to much in the past with it. The continuing life of the language that forms so essential a part of it gives the type of the way it lives if it is anything at all: it lives in the living creative response to the challenges of the changing present. The century of the American and French Revolutions and the opening Industrial Revolution, and of the inevitable reaction against 'Locke and Newton', produced changes and challenges enough to make the emergence of a 'new sense of responsibility towards life' comprehensible – to explain a notable development of 'language'. What my phrase portends in the field of creative writing is something sufficiently 'there' for contemplation when, in the context that Mr Coveney provides, we think of Blake, Dickens and Lawrence.

Though not one of optimism, neither is the spirit of it one of defeat. The sense in which it is positive, one of faith in life, comes out in the contrast between the two contemporaries, Lawrence and Eliot – or between Eliot and Dickens.

> A crowd flowed over London Bridge, so many,
> I had not thought death had undone so many

– Dickens hated the ugliness, squalor and oppressive inhumanity of the London he knew, but the hatred is positive, an expression of the undefeated and uncowed life in himself, and it is not in contradiction with his making the new railway that was being driven through the Camden Town of *Dombey and Son* to Euston the symbol of a hope and a promise residing in intelligent human energy. In *Little Dorrit* the same spirit, neither defeatist nor Shelleyan, makes the disinterested spontaneity of innocence, love and sympathetic perception in the heroine, the child, and – equally un-self-assertive – the indomitable vital disinterestedness of the Artist or creative mind, here (very significantly) personified in the inventor, Daniel Doyce, mutually reinforcing presences in the world as Dickens sees and judges it. They convey, and evoke – for, being wholly convincing, they can't be dismissed as sentimental foils to the general clear-sighted and discouraging realism, an element of faith in life sufficient to defy with some effect the worst suggestions of Dickens's inclusive testimony.

'Defy' seems the right word, for in Dickens (and in Lawrence) despair and defeat don't always seem to be mere impotent spectres. But there is nothing Shelleyan about the defiance. The high revolutionary ardour was a necessary constituent of the total romantic response; I mean, we see it as necessary when we consider what it is that makes the great Dickens a 'romantic novelist': he is not tragic or stoically resigned. But neither is he naïve: he can feel with intensity that the world begins again with every child, but if Blake was a great psychologist so was Dickens. The 'wonder' (one might with point say 'Laurentian wonder') he exemplified in the vitality of his art and knew to be the response and proof of the truly living ('You are not to wonder', said Gradgrind to his children) went with a robust and subtle realism about human nature; an intense questing and exacting sense for the real being prepotent in him.

Mr Coveney deals admirably with what I called the 'total romantic response'. He is good on Wordsworth, and brings out all the significance of his development, noting how even the nature of his interest in childhood suffers, in his Victorian phase, a falsifying change into something Victorian. He discusses illuminatingly how 'Victorian' came to get this pejorative force, the approach by way of the 'image of childhood' proving to be a peculiarly suitable one. Dickens himself, we know, didn't always and everywhere treat in that strong spirit of genius I have described the theme that so obviously lends itself to nostalgia, sentimentality, false idealism and drug-addictive evasion – to diverse forms of sick refusal to recognize unequivocally, not merely the actual, but the real.

Nor did the grosser and more consistent evasions of reality, the more deplorable perversions of what a sane adult must, even in spite of himself, know to be the truth, confine themselves to best-sellers of the Victorian age. And as for the equivocal child-cult in its subtler and more sophisticated forms, Mr Coveney, having discussed with insight and discriminatory sensitiveness the case of Lewis Carroll, traces the line that runs through Barrie and A. A. Milne. How nearly the considerations it raises may bear on the intellectual-literary culture of which an *élite* is custodian we realize when we recall (say) the interest taken by E. M. Forster in Forrest Reid (see Chapter 10, section 5 in *The Image of Childhood*).

Mr Coveney doesn't neglect to discuss the significance of Freud for his theme, or to bring out the ironies inherent in the history that moves from Original Innocence to Infantile Sexuality, and his discussion is as full of stimulus to thought as one could wish. He is always in the best of ways suggestive, not offering as a rule summarizable conclusions, the value of his enterprise being inseparable from its not lending itself to results of that kind. He drops an abundance of seeds; suggestions, that is, that, given an organic pregnancy by the context, strike root in the reader's mind and grow. And among such suggestions the reader will find a good many of a kind he will hardly have thought promised by the title. Anyone, for instance, committed to discussing in an essay – or a book – the significance of the development in the nineteenth century of 'aesthetic' ideas of Art and the Artist (Eliot and Pound and Joyce are involved, as well as writers with obvious affinities to Pater) would do well to turn a receptive mind on *The Image of Childhood*. And since it seems likely that, in university English, a paper on 'The Novel' may be instituted at more than one place, I will remark that the student taking it will, if intelligent study is in question, get more help from Mr Coveney's book than from most of the books with (for the innocent) promising titles. To enforce the practical spirit in which I say this, I will offer the hypothetical examiner an illustrative clutch of the useful quotations he might be glad to make questions of.

Middlemarch owed its undeniable strength to the balance George Eliot achieved between her psychological interests and the acute social awareness within which she contained it.

This nourishment of sensibility with social interests, and the nourishment of political interests with feeling, are perhaps some of the criteria of a really important literature; and literature may be felt to suffer a coarsening or emasculation whenever the balance is upset.

The social novel of Disraeli, Mrs Gaskell and Kingsley was not merely a coarse and unfortunate phenomenon. It represents something essential to the literary consciousness of the age, without which *Bleak House*, *Middlemarch* and *Felix Holt* would have been impossible.

From the establishment of the great Victorian novel, poetry suffered continuous enfeeblement.

The impact of the young sensibility and intelligence on the assumptions of a society can be the most suitable subject for a great literature, and one perhaps especially relevant to our own period.

And in this one sees the continuity of a tradition developed through Blake, Wordsworth, Coleridge, Dickens and Mark Twain. For them, as for Lawrence, the child was a symbol of their concern with the individual humanity of man in relation to the influences, most often the encroachments, of modern, industrial, urban society upon it.

It was, in fact, just this combination of his intense psychological insight with his social grasp which made of him [Lawrence] the very great novelist he was.

By way of emphasizing that Mr Coveney's book is of the kind that compels close attention and invites real discussion, entailing perhaps some disagreement on the reader's part about this and that, I will move towards a close by registering a disagreement or two of my own. About *What Maisie Knew* I have differed with Mr Marius Bewley (see his *The Complex Fate*, pp. 114–44) and now find myself differing with Mr Coveney. He writes (p. 205):

But, undeniably, the book does evoke a certain response; it skirts dangerously close to something akin to 'obscenity'. There is a vibration not entirely imported into the work by the misunderstanding of the reader. James's intention prevented his placing very much force on the normal moral disgust the adults evoke. To write so deliberately in contrary motion to the popular moral sense places an enormous burden on the morality he sought to convey through awareness and consciousness.

I think that Mr Coveney concedes too much to Mr Stephen Spender, for I think he should have conceded nothing at all. He may be right; one reports what one feels. I myself can only report that I feel no vibration such as he seems to suggest – no vibration that justifies in any way the thrill of the reader who feels himself responding to thrillingly skirted obscenity. The obscenity of the adult behaviour in one sense is plain enough – as it is obviously meant to be. But surely there is no thrill of the *risqué* for us, and none of which we can say that James must have, or ought to have, anticipated it, in the idea of gross sexual misconduct that, because of the innocence of childhood, is cognizable by Maisie, and thought of by her, only as unkindness, fickleness, brutal indifference to sensitive feelings, unlovingness, crass egotism. (What can be worse?) There is a thrill, no doubt, for poor conventionally moral Mrs Wix. But we, who also know what sexual misconduct is and know it is what the adults are practising, surely don't register any vibration of the morally hazardous or feel at all inclined to criticize James's delicacy or moral tact, because the moral disgust we know to be appropriate – and expected of us – doesn't much colour the totality of our response. We don't, because of the wonderful success with which James engages us in the innocence of the child, making it so real, unquestionable and immediate. The adults are vivid enough, but for Maisie they belong to another world. The effect of our knowing about them what Maisie doesn't is given in that question about what they are as she knows them which I have put, parenthetically, above: What can be worse? And what can?

The thrill I get is one of astonished admiration for the art that defines and conveys so salutary a moral significance. This is the line that runs through Blake and Dickens, and gives the theme of *The Image of Childhood* its central nerve. I suggested some years ago that the prompting for *What Maisie Knew* came from *David Copperfield*. It is now plain to me that *Little Dorrit* counts for at least as much.

Mr Coveney writes admirably about *Huckleberry Finn*. But here again he seems to me to make an unjust criticism. On p. 230 we read:

The intrusion of Tom Sawyer dissipates the moral intensity of the novel. The freeing of the nigger, which would have been the ultimate test of Huck's moral resolution, is solved by the arbitrary trick of Tom's knowing all along that Jim had been already freed.

– I hope that other readers, and Mr Coveney himself, will agree that there is an irony here that he has missed; one characteristic of the essential Mark Twain, and belonging to the deeper resonance of the book.

I will close by saying that the repulsion my own perusals of *The Way of All Flesh* have left me with demands a severer criticism of that morbidly egotistic, self-ignorant and Pharisaical performance than Mr Coveney, acute as his commentary is, actually comes out with. Small-minded, blind and odiously complacent, it has been a breeder and re-inforcer of small-mindedness, blindness and odious complacency since it was given to the world – in the formative years of the original Bloomsbury.

F. R. LEAVIS

Author's Introduction

UNTIL the last decades of the eighteenth century the child did not exist as an important and continuous theme in English literature. Childhood as a major theme came with the generation of Blake and Wordsworth. There were of course children in English literature before the Romantics. They were the subject of innumerable Elizabethan lyrics; and through Dryden, Pope and Prior there had been a whole tradition of minor, complimentary verses addressed to young 'children of quality'. But in the Elizabethan drama, in the main body of Augustan verse, in the major eighteenth-century novel, the child is absent, or the occasion of a passing reference; at the most a subsidiary element in an adult world.

With Blake's *The Chimney Sweeper* and Wordsworth's Ode on *Intimations of Immortality from recollections of Early Childhood*, we are confronted with something essentially new, the phenomenon of major poets expressing something they considered of great significance through the image of the child. Blake's 'Innocence' and Wordsworth's 'natural piety' had their easily distinguishable ancestry. But the fact remains that within the course of a few decades the child emerges from comparative unimportance to become the focus of an unprecedented literary interest, and, in time, the central figure of an increasingly significant proportion of our literature. The appearance of the child was indeed simultaneous with the changes in sensibility and thought which came with the end of the eighteenth century. The simultaneity of the changes and the appearance is too exact to be coincidental. It seems inescapable that the appearance of the modern literary child was closely related to the revolution in sensibility which we call the 'romantic revival'. The creation of the romantic child came from deep within the whole genesis of our modern literary culture.

To suggest a relation between literature and society might seem to imply that too much, perhaps, is to be explained too easily by too little. But without proposing anything rigid, it is generally acceptable that some relation of cause and effect lay between Elizabethan England and the preoccupations of Shakespearian tragedy. The world of Shakespeare was confronted with the problem of social, and, more narrowly, political disintegration. The sense of cosmic strain and social disorder in Shakespeare derived in some way from the dissolution of medieval society that was in process, and the discoveries of the new cosmology. The tensions of Renaissance individualism were translated into the central interests of the drama. The recurrent theme of 'Rome' was natural to an age concerned with the appearance of the 'nation-state' and the loyalties of the 'citizens' and 'statesmen' who served it. It is this sort of relation between a society and its literature which lies between modern society and the theme of childhood in nineteenth- and twentieth-century literature. There is a similar relation between theme and context.

The end of the eighteenth century saw the origins of the spiritual crisis against which so much of our modern literature has been written. The securities of the eighteenth-century peace dissolved in the era of the Revolution. The social and political ferment which had ended with the middle of the seventeenth century was renewed. The social, political, and, more especially, the intellectual problems arising from the French and Industrial Revolutions found no resolution. In a rapidly dissolving culture, the problem of the nineteenth-century artist was essentially new and inevitably complicated. The long artistic alienation had begun. The concern of the modern European intellect has been, in part, the maintenance of individual integrity within the search for the security of universal order. At no time, except perhaps in the early decades of the seventeenth century, has that maintenance and search been so pressing in its demand as in the century of Darwin, Marx and Freud.

The society created by the industrial developments of the late eighteenth and nineteenth centuries was increasingly unconcerned with and often inimical to art. The frequent fate of the later nineteenth-century artist was not only to find himself alienated and bewildered, but confronted by the rapid disintegration of his audience. The actual contraction of his audience may be debated – it is after all difficult to be precisely statistical about these things – but the proportion of the literate public to whom the serious artist could expect to address himself certainly diminished. For even if there were at the end of the century as many readers responsive to the best creative work as at the beginning, there was a new literate public who were most certainly not. A new mass literature supplied the demands of uninformed literacy; and the relative influence of the mature creative voice was proportionally diminished. The central problem of any culture in process of rapid development lies in cultural transmission, and there was as we know in the nineteenth century a serious, some would say disastrous, discontinuity. Whereas, for a few decades in the middle of the century, the Victorian middle class produced and respected literary figures who were public figures in the way Addison and Johnson had been, James at the end of the century was successively reduced (and it was not *wholly* his fault) to a private world of increasing irrelevance. Art for Art's sake was the aggressive defence of an art on the run; the ivory tower the substitute, *faute de mieux*, for the wished-for arena. Dickens was the last English man of letters to have a really successful public voice – something, for all that might be said, Wells and Shaw never achieved. After him the moat between literature and the literate public widens; and the impact of literature upon the real flow of public affairs becomes sporadic and occasional.

In this context of isolation, alienation, doubt and intellectual conflict, it is not difficult to see the attraction of the child as a literary theme. The child could serve as a symbol of the artist's dissatisfaction with the society which was in process of such harsh development about him. In a world given increasingly to utilitarian values and the Machine, the child could become the symbol of Imagination and Sensibility, a symbol of Nature set against the forces abroad in society actively de-naturing humanity. Through the child the artist could express his awareness of the conflict between human Innocence and the cumulative pressures of social Experience. If the central problem of the artist was in fact one of adjustment, one can see the possibilities for identification between the artist and the consciousness of the child whose difficulty and chief source of pain often lie in adjustment and accommodation to environment. In childhood lay the perfect image of insecurity and isolation, of fear and bewilderment, of vulnerability and potential violation. Professor Empson has spoken of the 'tap-root' which the nineteenth-century artist frequently kept for reference to his childhood. For some authors, the 'tap-root' became, *in extremis*, an habitual means of escape, a way of withdrawal from spiritual and emotional confusion in a tired culture. In an age when it became increasingly difficult to grow up, to find valid bearings in an adult world, the temptation seems to have been for certain authors to take the line of least emotional resistance, and to regress, quite literally, into a world of fantasy and nostalgia for childhood. Over one line of art, distinguishable at the end of the century, lay the seductive shadow of Peter Pan. If neurosis is the result of a fixation of the personality at an infantile stage of emotional development, there would often seem a neurotic connexion between some modern authors and their exclusive preoccupations with children. There may indeed have been an element of neurosis, to a greater or lesser extent, in the majority of authors concerned with the theme of childhood in the nineteenth and twentieth centuries.

But morbid involvement is a charge which can only be levelled at comparatively few. Nostalgia and regressing impulse, which were, in this sense, an artistic condition of the age, did not consume the genius of Blake, Wordsworth, Dickens and Mark Twain – though with Dickens and Mark Twain they were powerful and corrosive influences. The importance is that for them the child became a symbol of the greatest significance for the subjective investigation of the Self, and an expression of their romantic protest against the Experience of society. The nineteenth-century interest in the child was in fact no esoteric interest of minor writers existing on the eccentric peripheries of literature. The child lies at the heart of *The Prelude*, *Hard Times*, *Dombey and Son* and *Huckleberry Finn* – works which in any evaluation have undeniable significance as serious, one might say perhaps, adult art. To compare their strength with the sentimentalities of *David Copperfield* or *Peter Pan* is to see the extremes of interest to which the child could be put. Frequently, indeed, as in the case of Dickens, there was an amazing inconsistency within the work of the same author. The child is now a symbol of growth and development, and now a symbol of retreat into personal regression and self-pity. Increasingly isolated, and without the securities of a widely-accepted culture, the nineteenth-century artist was, it seems, impelled towards the subjective investigations and involvements which became the *raison*, and in some cases, the strength of his art. But, and the case of Wordsworth is specially relevant, with some the reference of their subjective interest is always towards outward development. The child became for Wordsworth the basis of a whole philosophy of human nature. For Dickens an interest in the child nourished the growth of a moral interest which he dramatized through the medium of his greatest fiction. The history of the child in nineteenth-century literature does in fact display both the weakness and the strength of all romantic art; how close together the morbid introversion and the objective awareness lay.

The concept of the child's nature which informed the work of Blake, Wordsworth and Dickens was of original innocence. Stemming most forcefully from Rousseau, and in contradiction to the long Christian tradition of original sin, it was this which gave the weight and edge to the general commentary of these authors as they expressed it through the symbol of the innocent child. But it was a symbol susceptible to continuous deterioration. The instrument became blunt through over-assertion and special pleading. The symbol which had such strength and richness in the poetry of Blake and some parts of the novels of Dickens became in time the static and moribund child-figure of the popular Victorian imagination; a residue only of a literary theme almost entirely evacuated of the significance it had earlier borne. The romantic assertion of innocence created a concept of the child's essential nature which for religious or psychological reasons might be considered either morally debilitating or emotionally false. It was against this conventionally innocent child that a revolution was effected at the turn of the nineteenth century. Just as the eighteenth century had turned from the Christian doctrine of original sin to the cult of original virtue in the child, so the nineteenth century turned from the assumption of original innocence to the scientific investigation of the infant and child consciousness. Literature, however, did not discover the child through the medium of psycho-analysis. The influence of Freud was to redirect, clarify, sometimes enrich (and in part, perhaps, explain) an interest which was already very clearly there. And in this the continuity of nineteenth-century interests becomes strikingly plain. The Romantic sensibility had often concerned itself with childhood as an agent in the quest for psychological insight and awareness. In the greatest authors, in Wordsworth and Dickens, say, subjective preoccupations had been balanced, if sometimes precariously, with the objective interests characteristic of a great literature. For them, childhood became part of the objective 'wisdom' which, through the power of their creative intelligence, they sought to convey. A major concern of Freudian analysis was to increase awareness of the child and objective appreciation of the importance of the childhood consciousness to the development of the adult mind. In this sense, it is not preposterous to suggest that across the century Wordsworth's *Prelude* and Freud's Essay on Infantile Sexuality may be said to join hands.

It is not easy to define the precise relationship between psycho-analysis and modern literature; but there can be no doubt that Freud's theories concerning human personality and motive, and especially his emphasis on the importance of the child's consciousness in the formation of adult personality, created an intellectual climate within which many authors have, if not always consciously, developed. Freud was a powerful agent in the ventilation of the sentimental atmosphere which had grown up around the Victorian child; a solvent too of the religious savagery towards the child, such as Butler described in his *Way of All Flesh*. Idealization of the child's nature and cruelty towards the 'children of Satan' existed side by side in nineteenth-century society – a phenomenon which justifies, perhaps, considerable investigation.

Cause and effect are difficult, however, to distinguish in the subtle field of artistic choice. Subjective and social factors are not easy to distinguish in discussing why any author should write about the particular themes he chooses. Less precise still may be the influence of intellectual ideas in directing the interests and motives of creative literature. Even so, the frequency of the treatment of childhood in modern literature suggests the presence of common and objective factors predisposing so many authors to their choice. A theme ceases to be personal or eccentric when it becomes the serious and deliberate choice of so many over so long a time. It becomes reasonable to speak in terms of a literary phenomenon, and, it is remarkable, a pheno-menon of our own culture, as distinct from every other before it. It is not only a matter of literature influenced by the intellectual climate created by the theories of Rousseau in the eighteenth and Freud in the twentieth century, but that so many authors should find the child so congenial an image, either of growth or regression, of potency or regret. From the last decades of the eighteenth century, the symbol of the child accumulated about itself a variety of responses, but among them one can always make the distinction between those authors who went to the child to express their involvement with life, and those who retreated towards the symbol from 'life's decay' – to use Lewis Carroll's expression. In writing of childhood, we find that in a very exact and significant sense the modern author is writing of life. In the literature of the child in the nineteenth and twentieth centuries we have a reflection of the situation of certain artists in modern times; their response, at a deep and significant level, to the condition in which they found themselves; and, if their feelings could achieve the projection, the condition in which they found humanity. Con-sidering the nature of that condition, it is perhaps not remarkable that through writing of childhood there should be those who wanted to go back to the beginning to begin again, and others who wanted just to go back.

CHAPTER I

The 'Cult of Sensibility' and the 'Romantic Child'

THE literary climate in which the Romantic child developed was prepared in the half-century from Rousseau's *Emile* to Wordsworth's *Prelude*. His appearance lay in the opposition of two centuries, the eighteenth and nineteenth; in the development of the 'cult of sensibility'; in the 'revolt', as J. S. Mill, in his *Essay on Coleridge*, called it, of the 'human mind against the philosophy of the eighteenth century'; in the whole movement of the late eighteenth century from Reason to Feeling.

Literary generalizations notoriously distort and underestimate the figures who go to make them. No period demands a minimum of generality and a maximum of particular reference more than the half-century from Rousseau to Wordsworth and Coleridge. The 'cult of sensibility' conjures the influence of Rousseauism, of Richardson and Sterne; and the 'revolt' of Mill's essay gives precisely the influence of Coleridge upon nineteenth-century thought; and it might be objected that to align the two is to invite confusion. But it is the continuity of interest, the intellectual focus which gives the character to the generation of the Pre-Romantics, and allows us to talk of a central conflict between Reason and Feeling, within which the romantic child was created.

The eighteenth century had seen a consolidation of the achievement of the closing decades of the seventeenth. Newton's *Principia* and Locke's *Essay Concerning the Human Understanding* initiated a period of wide intellectual acceptances and assurance. Addison's 'shining frame' and 'spacious firmament' proclaimed their 'great Original'. 'The works of Nature everywhere sufficiently evidence a Deity,' said Locke, and Shaftesbury declared the deity 'the best-natured Being in the world'. To another, Man lived in a 'spacious and well-furnished world', and to yet another, the 'Works of the

Lord' were 'incomparably contrived, and as admirably made, fitted up, and placed in the World'.

There was indeed a savour of a cosmic estate agency about the thought of the age; of tensions relaxed within the general frame of things. If a century before the fear had been that the 'frame of things' might 'disjoint', Newtonian science had provided, for those who wanted to accept it, a new frame, within which a rational universe was seen to pursue its natural laws in sensible assurance and peace. Tragic possibilities disappeared from literature; the nervous line of earlier seventeenth-century verse gave way to the measured Augustan cadence. The scope of literature became contained within the potentialities of satire, which in itself presupposes an order fundamentally accepted. Satire is an emanation from order itself, investigating such factors as 'bad taste', which would be likely to disrupt its underlying values; and the greatest Augustan literature is satirical.

But the cosmic peace, the 'cosmic Toryism', as Professor Willey has called one aspect of it, was short-lived. The imperfections of the social and political order of the old régime brought against itself inevitable ridicule. The wars, corruption, injustice, and brutality of eighteenth-century Europe suggested that the cosmic frame, orderly though it might be, contained a blurred and imperfect picture, and gave the edge to Voltaire's ironic ' *Tous les événements sont enchaînés dans le meilleur des mondes possibles*'. Order, Nature, and Reason remained; but they now became the basis of 'perfectibility', of Reason applied to human institutions. The rationalism of acceptance of the early century became by the middle the newer rationalism of discontent, which in time informed the optimisms of the French Enlightenment and the social engineering of the Revolution itself. If Newton had revealed the Divine Original Engineer in the universe, perfectibility would reveal the perfect engine of man in the body social and politic. It became a common acceptance of dissident thought by the middle of the century that social imperfections might be eradicated, and man's unruly superstition controlled, by the application of Reason and the human engineering made possible by the fundamental application of 'associationism'.

A passage from Mill is relevant:

Every consistent scheme of philosophy requires as its starting-point, a theory respecting the sources of human knowledge. . . . The prevailing theory in the eighteenth century . . . was that proclaimed by Locke, and commonly attributed to Aristotle – that all knowledge consists of generalizations from experience. Of nature, or anything whatever external to ourselves, we know, according to this theory, nothing, except the facts which present themselves to our senses, and such other facts as may, by analogy, be inferred from these. There is no knowledge *a priori*; no truths cognizable by the mind's inward light, and grounded on intuitive evidence. . . . From this doctrine, Coleridge, with the German philosophers since Kant . . . strongly dissents.

This account of the basic premise of the century stands as it did when Mill wrote it. A quotation from Locke serves to show it at its source:

Let us then suppose the mind to be, as we say, white paper, void of all characters, without any ideas: How comes it to be furnished? Whence comes it by that vast store which the busy and boundless fancy of man has painted on it with an almost endless variety? Whence has it all the materials of reason and knowledge? To this I answer, in one word, from EXPERI-ENCE.

The deliberately diminishing implications of 'busy and boundless fancy', 'painted', and 'endless variety' find their vanishing point in Locke's 'one word'.

This materialist determinism informed the thought of the whole generation of *philosophes* in France; and in England, Hartley, in his *Observations on Man* (1749), following the mechanics of Newtonian science, desired to explain the mind in terms of a mechanism. Knowledge for him, as for the whole school, proceeded by association between the senses and the external world; not from the intuitive sensibility, not from the Imagination of the Romantics, not from the Vision of Blake; but from the sense-perceptions only, by which men are linked to their physical environment. Remove their environment and all men are equal; determine the environment and you may contrive man's happiness.

It was this determinism which Priestley developed from Hartley, and Godwin vulgarized at the end of the century. It was through Bentham that it was transmitted into practical application in England in the nineteenth century. He acquired the first statement of the moral mathematics of the utilitarian calculus from Priestley's *First Principles of Government*:

It was from that pamphlet, and that page of it [that contained the phrase, the greatest happiness of the greatest number] that I drew the phrase, the words and import of which have been so widely diffused over the civilized world.

For morality itself, following the premise, was reducible to sensation. Values were not absolutes cognizable by man through his human nature, but a matter merely of pleasure and pain. The moral hedonism of Bentham derived essentially from the sensationalism of Locke.

It was, then, against this materialist, rationalist, perfectionist, and essentially secular eighteenth century that Rousseau, Blake, and pre-eminently Coleridge reacted. The thought of the century was abstract, intellectual, contemptuous of the past. 'How glorious, then, is the prospect, the reverse of all that is past, which is now opening upon us, and upon the world,' declared Priestley at the outbreak of the Revolution in France, and he was not untypical.

Rousseau's 'natural man', Blake's 'Vision', Coleridge's 'Imagination', and, in political thought, Burke's principle of 'human nature', were all solvents of the rationalist order of the *philosophes*. When Burke in his *Reflections on the Revolution in France* declared that 'politics ought to be adjusted, not to human reasonings, but to human nature; of which the reason is but a part, and by no means the greatest part', he was declaring himself on the side of those who reacted against the intellectualism of the century, on the side of those who glorified Feeling. He was, in fact, through an irony of misunderstanding, on the side of his anathematized Rousseau.

The establishment of the child as a literary theme was everywhere closely related to this reinstatement of Feeling. The rationalist school had itself been continually concerned with the theory of education. Locke's own *Thoughts Concerning Education* had in fact informed a whole tradition of educational theory. But the tradition was associationist; concerning itself with the swift creation, through controlled environment, of the rational adult man. It seldom considered the nature of the child as a child. Treated as a small adult, the child was to be trained out of his childish ways into the moral and rational perfection of regulated manhood. The child was the *tabula rasa* upon which, through education, sensation could work its beneficent influence. The tradition culminated in England in the work of Godwin, to be parodied in life in the education of J. S. Mill, and in fiction in the Gradgrindery of *Hard Times*. The cult of the child which informed the romantic literature of childhood lay with the opposing school, with the 'cult of sensibility' associated with Rousseau:

As the eighteenth century wore on [says Professor Willey], it was discovered that the 'Nature' of man was not his 'reason' at all, but his instincts, emotions, and 'sensibilities', and what was more, people began to glory in this discovery, and to regard Reason as an aberration from 'Nature'. *Cogito ergo sum* is superseded by *je sens, donc je suis,* associated with Rousseau.

About nothing did Rousseau *feel* more passionately than about childhood. His influence lies behind the whole progressive concentration of interest upon the child in the second half of the century. He more than any other created the climate in which Blake, Wordsworth, Lamb, Southey and Coleridge wrote.

Rousseau is an essentially ambiguous figure. Decried as an intellectual libertine by some (Dr Johnson thought him fit to be run from any civilized country), for others, he was the seminal authority of the Revolution which brought the triumph of Reason and Intellect in France. More than half the misunderstanding came from his own intellectual flamboyance; from his chronic inability to deny himself the extravagant pleasure of saying almost everything for the sake of effect.

If we associate with him the 'cult of sensibility', the 'noble savage', '*l'homme nouveau*', it is to be remembered that he wrote when there was already a growing predisposition to consider the 'Nature of Man' and 'Man in a state of Nature'. Hume, in his *Treatise of Human Nature* (1738), had through Reason declared the limits of Reason, and had, in Halévy's words, found that 'it is good to trust instinct, to give oneself up to Nature without being duped by any logical illusions'. Before Hume, Reason had been associated with Nature; after him, Nature became inextricably related to Feeling. In many ways he lay at the turning-point of the century.

Already, too, before Rousseau, there had been a reaction away from the pessimistic concept of human nature propagated by religion through its doctrine of original sin, and by the brutal strictures on human motive contained in Hobbes. A long tradition of Hebrew and Christian literature postulated the uncorrupted nature of the child, which had found expression in the verse of Vaughan and Traherne. The perfect 'pre-existent' state was an idea common to the Cambridge Platonists. Shaftesbury and Hutcheson had both declared man's benevolence in Nature. Shaftesbury speaks of 'that simplicity and innocence of behaviour which has been often known among mere savages, ere they were corrupted by our commerce . . . 'twould be an advantage to us to hear the causes of . . . our deviation from Nature'. Hutcheson described the natural state as one of 'Good-will, Humanity, Compassion, mutual aid, propagating and supporting off-spring'. Already the first impact on the strongholds of original sin were made on behalf of original innocence before Rousseau's *Emile*. The voyages of the sixteenth and seventeenth centuries had stimulated interest in primitive cultures; and it became an accepted formula for satire in the early century to contrast the original virtue of the savage with the debilitating corruptions of artificial society. The way of the tide was clear in La Drévetière's *Arlequin Sauvage* (1721), which was done into English in 1738 as *Art and Nature*. The last, significant word is given to the Indian:

Come with me then. I'll take you to a country where we shall have no need of money to make us happy, nor laws to make us wise; Our Friendship shall be our Riches. . . . No, no, let us go, and enjoy ourselves, and be happy as Nature and Common-Sense can make us![1]

'Nature' and 'Common-Sense' make a remarkable meeting-point for the two opposing cults of the century.

Rousseau's great contribution was to give authoritative expression to the new sensibility, and to direct its interest towards childhood as the period of life when man most closely approximated to the 'state of Nature'. His primary demand was, and it is perhaps difficult for us to see it as quite the revolutionary idea it was, that the child is important in himself, and not as a diminutive adult. For him the child was not the passive creature of external perception, but a self-active

1. Translated: Louis de Lisle de la Drévetière's *Arlequin Sauvage*, Paris, 1721.

soul, endowed with natural tendencies to virtue from birth, which in a state of nature could be developed, and, with extreme care, be nourished slowly towards the necessities of social existence. As early as his *First Discourse on the Arts and Sciences* he diagnosed a division between natural and social man. Society's ills derived, he declared, from man's departure from the state of natural grace: 'Our minds have been corrupted in proportion as the arts and sciences have improved.' He carried this anti-intellectualism further in his *Second Discourse*, in *La Nouvelle Héloïse* and in the great educational treatise, *Emile*.

Lord Morley in his work on Rousseau placed *Emile* well enough:

> [It is] one of the seminal books in the history of literature, and of such books the worth resides less in the parts than in the whole. It touched the deeper things of character. It filled parents with a sense of the dignity ... of their task. ... It admitted floods of light and air into the tightly closed nurseries and schoolrooms. ... It was the charter of youthful deliverance.

Rousseau was indeed so seminal that if anyone now bewails the relaxation of discipline in the schools, he pays hostile, if unconscious tribute to the latter-day influence of his theories.

The first, typical gesture of the book is well remembered: '*Tout est bien sortant des mains de l'Auteur des choses; tout dégénère entre les mains de l'homme.*' The public corruption of the day required this extravagant assertion. The secluded country life in which Emile was to be reared in the solitary company of his tutor was a condition in part forced on Rousseau, though it accorded well with the fashionable primitivism of the times. Although, in fact, he never made of it an absolute, it became the best remembered part of the whole educational romance. The popular climate any great thinker creates seldom reflects his own more subtle intentions. The importance of Rousseau lies as much in what became Rousseauism as in the gospel of *Emile* itself.

The central emphasis of the book lay on the assertion that the primary concern of all education should be the identity and peculiar nature of the child itself. The whole approach to childhood before Rousseau is nowhere better seen than in the fashionable dressing up of children as little adults. Art provides no more pathetic sight than the portraiture of this and the previous century with its little Dutch and English children starched into lace and taffeta before their time. But for Rousseau:

Nature wants children to be children before they are men. If we deliberately pervert this order, we shall get premature fruits which are neither ripe nor well-flavoured, and which soon decay. . . . Childhood has ways of seeing, thinking, and feeling peculiar to itself; nothing can be more foolish than to substitute our ways for them.

And again in the Preface:

We know nothing of childhood: and with our mistaken notions the further we advance the further we go astray. The wisest writers devote themselves to what a man ought to know, without asking what a child is capable of learning. They are always looking for the man in the child, without considering what he is before he becomes a man.

True education is simply the development of the original nature of the child.

And, for Rousseau, the 'original nature' of the child was innocence.

Let us lay it down as an incontrovertible rule that the first impulses of nature are always right; there is no original sin in the human heart; the how and why of the entrance of every vice can be traced.

This was different indeed from Watts's 'All the elect are born into this world, sinful and miserable', and from Janeway's *A Token for Children* (1671–2), in which he counselled parents to 'take some time daily to speak a little to your children one by one about their miserable condition by nature'. 'They are not too little to die,' he said, 'not too little to go to hell.'

Rousseau denied the whole solemn and substantial literature of the Christian 'fallen state'. For him all deviations from virtue derive from environment, from the ill-considered direction of parents and teachers. Previously moral education had lain in restraints imposed upon natural vice by rational virtue; and throughout medieval and Elizabethan times the chief restraint had been so often the actual sanction of corporal punishment – 'God's instrument to cure the evils of their condition'. For Rousseau, punishment, if there were to be any, should more justly fall on those who by their unwisdom corrupt the natural virtue of the child. Discipline he accepted; but its restraint should grow naturally from within, through the lessons of experience. If a child broke a window, he should be made to sleep in the draught caused thereby and thus learn natural wisdom. The method may have overlooked certain obvious possibilities; but religious exaggerations had often led to harsh repression. His theories removed the natural behaviour of children from an atmosphere of religious abomination and sin.

From these basic positions, Rousseau moved to the actual education of the child. At each stage he demanded that the child's particular nature should be respected. In infancy, everything should stimulate his senses and cultivate his body. His mind, his reasoning faculty, should be kept dormant for as long as possible. In childhood, his rational powers should be stimulated by activity only, and never by argument, never by words. Throughout his education the child should be confronted by the consequences of action, and never be deadened by the weight of abstract words. 'What do they teach? Words, words, words! To conceal their deficiencies teachers choose the dead languages.'

And then, from twelve to fifteen, the same anti-intellectual, anti-literary principle continues. 'Do, and don't say; only where it is necessary.' Books should be entirely forbidden, except for *Robinson Crusoe*, which alone could show the child how man in isolation might face his environment and subdue it. As for the rest: 'I detest books. . . . Reading is the scourge of childhood. They [books] merely teach us to talk about things we know nothing about.'

In adolescence, however, moral and social considerations must inevitably present themselves. Sexual passion could scarcely be contained experimentally. Here, indeed, the 'negative' method tended to break down. But, even so, the conscious 'teaching', the positive education he disliked so much, should be carefully withheld, even at this stage, until the child had acquired his first restraints for himself, naturally.

Later eighteenth-century educational theory became largely a gloss on the ideas conveyed so forcefully into the European consciousness through Rousseau's *Emile*. The vital genius of the book inspired the whole progressive school of educational thought in the nineteenth century. If original sin had informed the Christian centuries in their attitude to childhood, it is Rousseau's *Emile* that dominates the eighteenth and nineteenth centuries until Freud.

Hommes, soyez humains, c'est votre premier devoir. . . . Aimez l'enfance, favorisez ses jeux, ses plaisirs, son aimable instinct. Qui de vous n'a pas regretté cet âge où le rire est toujours sur les lèvres et où l'âme est toujours en paix? Pourquoi voulez-vous ôter à ces petits innocents la jouissance d'un temps si court qui leur échappe . . .? Pourquoi voulez-vous remplir d'amertume et de douleurs ces premiers ans si rapides, qui ne reviendront pas plus pour eux qu'ils ne peuvent revenir pour vous? Pères, savez-vous le moment où la mort attend vos enfants? . . . Faites qu'à quelque heure que Dieu les appelle, ils ne meurent point sans avoir goûté la vie.[1]

No one of Rousseau's stature and influence had written in this way of children before. This lyrical enthusiasm, this humanist rhetoric, which can only properly be sensed in its original, echoed throughout the romantic literature of the child; even, and, perhaps most significantly, its sentimental appeal to nostalgic regret.

The effect in England was immediate. The book was announced in August 1762 in the *Monthly Review*. The following month the *London Chronicle* published an article with extracts. Nugent's translation followed in 1763. M. Roddier, in his *Rousseau en Angleterre*, computes that at least 200 treatises were published before the end of the century, all in some way influenced by *Emile*. Some were no more than fashionable exercises on a theme. Many echoed Mrs Macaulay in her *Letters on Education* (1790):

There is not a virtue or a vice that belongs to humanity, which we do not make ourselves. . . There is not a wretch who ends his miserable being on a wheel, as the forfeit of his offences against society, who may not throw the whole blame of his misdemeanors on his education.

All were in sympathy with Lord Kames's *Loose Hints upon Education* when he declared himself chiefly concerned with the culture of the

1. 'Men, be human beings; this is your first duty. . . . Love childhood, indulge its games, its pleasures, and its lovable nature. Who has not looked back with regret on an age when laughter is always on the lips and when the spirit is always at peace? Why take from these little innocents the pleasure of a time so short which ever escapes them . . .? Why fill with bitterness and sorrow these first swift years which will never return for them any more than they can return for you? Fathers, do you know the moment when death awaits your children? . . . Make sure that whenever God calls them, they do not die without ever having tasted life.'

heart; since, as he thought, the heart was in great measure over-looked by writers upon education.

One of the most famous examples of Rousseau's direct influence was of course the education of Richard Lovell Edgeworth's son, Dick, who, through his father's youthful enthusiasms, was reared in the manner of Emile. Edgeworth wrote his *Memoirs* (1808) long after the first impulse of his optimism was spent. His account of the boy's education is half-sketched, and therefore the more tantalizing; one would like more detail of what actually happened. Evidently, left to his own freedom, the child became 'frank, generous, and courageous', but even before the father took him to Paris to present him to the author of *Emile*, the boy showed signs of too little 'defer-ence for others'. Walking the Paris streets for two hours with the philosopher, the child displayed excessive prejudice and enthusiasm for England; every horse and cart they saw being roundly declared by the boy to be 'English'. Unable to give the child continuous attention, Edgeworth delivered him over first to tutors and then to the care of an English public school. Disowned for his persistent waywardness, the boy went for the Navy, and after a period of service, settled in America, to die at the early age of thirty-two.

Edgeworth realized that he was as much to blame as the system he adopted. Disillusioned, he declared the system 'erroneous', but when he came to write, in collaboration with his more famous daughter, his *Essays on Practical Education* (1798), he could still write: '. . . we see many [children] whose temper and whose understanding have been materially injured by premature . . . instruction; we see many who are disgusted, perhaps irrevocably, with literature, whilst they are fluently reading books which they cannot comprehend. . . .'

Edgeworth's early enthusiasm had been greatly stimulated by his somewhat bizarre friend, Thomas Day, who in a letter of 1769 had written to him: 'If all the books in the world were destroyed, the first I should wish to save after the Bible would be Rousseau's *Emile*. . . . The more I read it, the more I admire it!' Day was a strange, unkempt youth, fearful of women, yet desperately searching for his own 'Sophie', his own perfect wife. Enthusiastically adopting two young orphan girls, he hoped in them to rear himself a wife. He reared them (until decency required their being sent away to school at Sutton Coldfield), performing endless experiments on their characters, so rumour had it, which included the firing of blank cartridges close to their ears, and the pouring of boiling wax on their arms, chastising them if they flinched for their lack of moral courage.

Not all of Rousseau's influence, however, lay in such diverting eccentricity. A whole flourish of 'Indian' plays, celebrating the cult of Nature, were in frequent production from the sixties until the turn of the century. Although the minor novels of 'sensibility' of Mrs Frances Brooke, Mrs Inchbald, Bage and Charlotte Smith may have derived their general character from Richardson and Sterne, their theme was often enough Rousseau's:

When I see the dumb creation, my dear Harry, pursuing steadily the purposes of their being ... I am astonished at the ... degeneracy of man. ... It has always appeared to me that our understandings are fettered by systems ... and that there needs no more to minds well disposed than to recover their native freedom. ... Convinced that the seeds of virtue are innate, I have only watched to cherish the rising shoot, and prune, but with a trembling hand, the too luxuriant branches.[1]

Mrs Brooke pursued the same polite enthusiasms in her next novel:[2]

I cannot help observing here, that the great aim of modern education seems to be, to eradicate the best impulses of the human heart, love, friendship, compassion, benevolence; to destroy the social, and increase the selfish principle. ... If my ideas are right, the human mind is naturally virtuous. ...

In her *Nature and Art* Mrs Inchbald rears her hero among the natives of 'Zocotora Island'; whilst the 'villain' is corrupted among people who 'taught him to walk, to ride, to talk, to think like a man – a foolish man, instead of a wise child, as nature designed him to be'. The most extravagant expression of the school perhaps came with Beaurieu's *Elève de la Nature*, which was done into English in 1773 as *The Man of Nature*. To preserve the hero from corruption, Beaurieu consigns him to the solitude of a wooden cage until he is fifteen, when he is transported to an uninhabited island, where his uncorrupted 'sensibility' is such that he weeps for the falling leaves.

1. Mrs Frances Brooke, *The History of Lady Julia Mandeville* (1763).
2. *The History of Emily Montague* (1769).

The increasing concern for childhood and education in the last decades of the eighteenth century is nowhere more significantly seen than in the literature actually written for children at that time. It was closely related to the general interest in education of the period, and often stemmed from the same enthusiasms as Methodist Non-conformacy. It was this perhaps which gave it frequently a moralizing quality entirely alien to the intentions of Rousseau, to whom, however, it frequently accorded superficial homage.

The condition of childhood of the time had aroused many religious consciences. Industrial development, together with the collapse of the public system for the relief of poverty, the decline of true craft apprenticeship, the exploitation of charity-school labour, especially in the industrial towns of the Midlands and North, created a situation that religious opinion could scarcely ignore. The miserable condition of so many children inspired some of Blake's greatest lyrics. Earlier if less indignant concern had resulted in the work of the Industrial and Sunday School Movements. The enthusiasm which created these also inspired the numberless tracts of varying moral weight which fell on the heads and shoulders of pauper and middle-class children in the last decades of the century.

One of the most popular of these moralizing books was Thomas Day's *Sandford and Merton*. Written between 1783 and 1789, it had nine editions before 1812. There are indeed forty-three editions of the work in the British Museum published before 1883. Influenced by Mrs Barbauld's *Early Lessons*, Day wished to continue her exhortations to juvenile virtue in a work of his own, and achieved one of the most famous of Victorian children's classics. Thousands of children in the nineteenth century were nurtured on the tale of Tommy Sandford, the poor farmer's son, reared under the care of the worthy vicar, Mr Barlow, and Harry Merton, the spoiled son of a rich West Indian merchant. The tale develops the simple theme of the regeneration of the one child by the other. Everywhere honesty has its due reward. The poor are ever honest; and the greater their poverty the nobler they prove. It was an odd (though perhaps not so odd) literary converse of the adult acquisitiveness which so distinguished the Age. The cult of poverty echoes throughout the pages of the children's literature of the time. Intended most especially for the sons and daughters of the middle class, these tales in the Sandford and Merton tradition frequently celebrate the ironic virtue of not laying up for yourselves treasures where thieves break through and steal.

Day's own moralizing was perhaps even exceeded by Mrs Trimmer, the 'mother' of children's literature, as Charlotte Yonge called her, and by Hannah More and John Aikin, pioneers of the Sunday School Movement. Maria Edgeworth began her literary career with moral tales for young people. Her *Parent's Assistant* (1800) continued to be issued by Macmillans as late as 1897.

In her criticism of Maria Edgeworth's *Moral* and *Popular Tales*, Madame de Staël saw the essentials of the situation clearly enough: '*Cette route rationelle et morne*,' she wrote, '*qui, par la science et la morale menait l'enfant au Dieu.*' The way, '*rationelle et morne*', was indeed leading to the savageries of Mrs Sherwood and her Fairchild children. Already the tormented shadow of the Fairchild children taken to see a murderer hanging at the gibbet, as a simple lesson not to quarrel among themselves in the nursery, lay before them.

All the sensuousness, the 'sensibility' of Rousseau and Madame de Genlis died in these harsh moralizing tracts of the Barbaulds and Trimmers. They are of that other 'eighteenth century'. For them Nature became something to 'dissect', to 'know'. Morality for little Tommy Sandford was essentially utilitarian and false, and essentially demoralizing therefore. Saved by the animals he had once taken care of, he declares: 'This proves to me that a good deed is never lost.'

Madame de Staël's acute strictures were echoed in England by Coleridge, who decried these 'prodigies of presumption, of arrogance, and insincerity ... these nurslings of perfected pedagogy'. Wordsworth ridiculed them in *The Prelude*, and Lamb, in a letter to Coleridge, declared: 'Hang them, I mean the accursed band of Barbaulds.... Think what you would be now, if, instead of having been nourished by good wives' stories, one had stuffed your head with geography and natural history.' 'Give me,' said Coleridge in reply, 'the works which charmed my youth, give me the *Thousand and One Nights*.'

The Barbaulds, even Day himself, had in fact taken Rousseau and denied his central premise of 'negative' education. They created the Enlightened *'vieux savants'* and *'jeunes docteurs'* he had so much detested. Madame de Staël, Lamb, Wordsworth and Coleridge, however, stood in Romantic opposition, on the side of fancy and the imaginative nourishment of make-believe, for the tradition of old wives' tales and the earlier chapbooks. Already in Coleridge's denunciations of 'Enlightened' education we hear the later strictures of Dickens on the 'forcing-system', in *Dombey and Son* and *Hard Times*.

The Romantic reaction against moralizing, utilitarian literature for children was part of its whole reaction against the child of the associationist eighteenth century; which in turn was part of its whole reaction against the central intellectual traditions of the Enlightenment. The literary tide was full set towards the shores of Feeling, and bore with it the fragile craft of the Romantic child. Helen Maria Williams could declare that : 'However dull the faculties of my head . . . when a proposition is addressed to my heart I have some quickness of perception.' For Mackenzie: 'The decisions' of the feelings 'will be always right'. Keats had a certainty of 'nothing, but the Holiness of the Heart's affections, and the Truth of the Imagination'. Within this assertion of Feeling, of the nineteenth century against the eighteenth, Blake entered with his own assertion that 'everything that lives is Holy', castigating the whole achievement of English rationalism for its 'Single Vision and Newton's sleep'. It was Blake who declared the 'vast majority' of children to be on the 'side of Imagination or Spiritual Sensation'. With Blake we have the first coordinated utterance of the Romantic Imaginative and spiritually sensitive child.

CHAPTER 2

Blake's Innocence *and* Experience

BLAKE was the first casualty of our modern sensibility; just as, in a very similar way, of the major talents, D. H. Lawrence was the last. His work was a triumph of indignation, an affirmation of the salvation open to spiritually awakened Man; his voice at once a counterpoint of disharmony across the general burden of his time, and an expression of the newer harmony that might be achieved through spiritual re-creation. His work was in essence a literature of human salvation. For Blake, children were no occasional interest, no vehicle for a mere personal nostalgia. They were for him a symbol of innocence, without which, as a religious artist, he could not have worked.

The movement towards interest in the child had created something of a minor tradition of eighteenth-century verse about children before Blake. Bruce, Lovibond, Gray, Scott, Beattie and Cowper had pointed the direction which Blake and Wordsworth took at the end of the century. Cowper, on receiving his 'Mother's Picture out of Norfolk', expressed an acute nostalgia for the 'joys that once were mine'; and in *The Task*, he remembered, 'not without regret', boyhood's 'hours that sorrow since has much endeared'. Scott, in his *To Childhood*, recalled the 'joy' which 'once was mine'. He 'mourned' the 'long-lost hours' of childhood, 'never, never to return'. Gray's *Ode on a Distant Prospect of Eton College* was instinct with the same nostalgia:

> Ah, fields belov'd in vain,
> Where once my careless childhood strayed,
> A stranger yet to pain!

Southey, in *To Margaret Hill*, hoped that:

> . . . in such a blessed isle
> We might renew the days of infancy,
> And life, like a long childhood, pass away
> Without one care . . .

Children in 'Nature' were frequent in the verses of Bruce, Lovibond and Thomson. The creative influences of Nature upon childhood were celebrated, a generation before *The Prelude*, in Beattie's *The Minstrel*, and in Bruce's *Lochleven*. Wordsworth would indeed have seen a monument erected to the 'memory of the innocent and tender-hearted Michael Bruce' who died in 1767, at the early age of twenty-one.

The 'romantic child' of Blake's *Songs of Innocence* may have been already there in embryo in the generation before him; but even if his own *Songs* are only to be fully understood by reference to the minor tradition which preceded him, in which were broached the themes of Nature and primitivism which came to full expression at the close of the century, his achievement is only to be measured by comparison with it. The *Songs of Innocence and of Experience* reveal the undeniable impact of a major talent upon the currencies of a minor literary convention.

Blake wrote against the fundamentals of English rationalism. The 'Idiot Reasoner', he declared, laughs at the 'Man of Imagination'. For him, Bacon, Newton and Locke were a malignant brood. Bacon's experimental method, Newton's materialist physics, and Locke's sensationalism came under his complete anathema. Together they represented the baneful influence of Reason, the power of the abstracted Intellect as a force against Life. Throughout society he denounced the institutions into which their materialism had been translated; in politics, religion, industry, and education. Blake's was, if nothing else, a coherent testimony; and the symbol of innocent childhood is central to that coherence.

In all the accepted philosophies, secular and religious, he saw the degeneration of the human soul through the denial of Man's individuality and his 'Imaginative Vision'. Men lay enslaved beneath 'systems', and their enfranchisement could only come through a renewed awareness of their original innocence, and their capacity for 'Vision' which through 'Experience' they had lost. Men might live, he asserted, in each 'minute particular' as children, live, in the moment of their imaginative joy. Religious creeds, philosophies, codes of law he saw as mere impediments. Considering himself a Christian, he deplored the abuses of Christ's teaching in the form of organized creeds. He was a Christian because Christ himself was a man who lived 'from impulse and not from rules'; and, in no small way, because he had said, 'except ye become as a little child; except ye be born again'.

This was the coherent weight behind his denial of Newtonian physics in the famous phrase that it was a system 'to educate a Fool how to build a Universe of Farthing Balls'. Against Locke's associationism he wrote: 'Man's Perceptions are not bounded by organs of perception; he perceives more than sense (tho' ever so acute) can discover.'

'Perception' was an important word for Blake. 'If the doors of perception were cleansed everything would appear to man as it is, infinite.' From the perception of the 'infinite', rationalism imprisoned the soul of man. 'May God us keep from Single Vision, and Newton's sleep.' Against the 'single vision' of rationalism, he posited his own 'double vision':

> For double vision my eyes do see,
> And a double vision is always with me.
> With my inward eye, 'tis an old man grey,
> With my outward, a thistle across my way.

His was the approach to external reality of the assured mystic. It was the 'inward eye', the 'inward vision', that concerned him; not the outward 'vegetative' Nature of Wordsworth's physical world. Crabb Robinson testified to his dislike for Wordsworth's 'naturalism'. Visiting him in his last days he read aloud the *Intimations Ode*, on the 'supposed pre-existent state'. Blake was in evident 'hysterical rapture' with the stanza beginning: 'But there's a tree of many one . . .':

His delight in W[ordsworth]'s poetry was intense. Nor did it seem less notwithstanding the reproaches he continually cast on W[ordsworth] for his imputed worship of Nature, which in the mind of Blake constituted Atheism.

For Blake 'Natural objects always did and now do weaken, deaden and obliterate Imagination in me. W[ordsworth] must know that what he writes valuable is not to be found in Nature.' For him the 'outward creation' was a 'hindrance . . . it is as the dirt upon my feet, No part of me'. If he were questioned as to what he saw when the sun rises; was it a 'round Disk of Fire somewhat like a Guinea?', he would reply: 'Oh no, no, no, I see an Innumerable company of the Heavenly Host crying, "Holy, Holy, Holy, is the Lord God Almighty".'

This was the 'Vision' which he himself had possessed as a child, and which he considered all children possessed. At seven his father sternly reproved him for declaring that he saw a tree with angels sitting in its branches; and later when entering Westminster Abbey as a young apprentice under Basire, he knew that he saw the twelve apostles advancing towards him down the aisles.

In his famous letter of 23 August 1799, to Dr Trusler, he asserted his belief in the Imagination, and, significantly, related it to the perceptions of the child:

I feel that a Man may be happy in This World. And I know that This World Is a World of Imagination and Vision. I see Every thing I paint In This World, but Every Body does not see alike. . . . As a man is, so he sees. . . . You certainly mistake, when you say that the Visions of Fancy are not to be found in This World. To Me This World is all One continued Vision of Fancy or Imagination. . . . I am happy to find a Great Majority of Fellow Mortals who can Elucidate My Visions, & Particularly they have been Elucidated by Children, who have taken a greater delight in contemplating my Pictures than I even hoped. Neither Youth nor Childhood is Folly or Incapacity. Some Children are Fools & so are some Old Men. But there is a vast Majority on the side of Imagination or Spiritual Sensation.

The stress lies on 'This World'. Blake was essentially a humanist. 'I feel that a Man may be happy in This World.' His was not the humanism of perfectionist rationalism, although that too was of 'This World'; but the humanism of intuitive joy:

> Thou art a man; God is no more;
> Thy own humanity learn to adore.

Through 'Vision' man might perceive the divinity in himself. The Creator and the universe are not separate from Man; but humanized and contained in his Vision. 'Everything that lives is Holy'; and to be respected in its 'minute particulars'. 'Deduct from a rose', he declared ironically, 'its redness, from a lily its whiteness . . . from a daisy its lowness, and rectify everything in Nature as the philosophers do. . . .' For Blake, society and its institutions were indeed one whole 'deduction' from the innocence, the capacity for uninhibited joy that, he asserted, men were born for.

The *Songs of Innocence* are, then, the affirmation of human life in children; the *Songs of Experience* the comparative denunciation of the forces in society which deny to both child and adult the expression of their imaginative joy, their essential humanity. His lyrics are no statement of fragile innocence, of pessimistic regret. Samuel Palmer declared him a 'man without a mask'; and society itself had no mask for him; least of all one of sentimentality. Everywhere in his work we are reminded of T. S. Eliot's remark about his 'naked vision'. Innocence and Experience were the 'two Contrary States of the Human Soul'; and through 'contraries' for Blake arose 'progression'. The force of his Innocence is in fact charged with the intensity of his Experience. His attitude to children was in no way regretful, nostalgic, static, and deadening. His sensibility was not caught within regret for itself. There is no echo of Lamb's: 'In my poor mind it is most sweet to muse Upon the days gone by', to be 'again a child'. In Blake there are none of Lamb's 'playmates':

> I have had playmates, I have had companions,
> In my days of childhood, in my joyful schooldays –
> All, all are gone, the old familiar faces . . .

There is none of this sort of thing in Blake; and considering the intensity of his emotion, the objectivity of his lyrics is an amazing achievement. He first affirms what Innocence is, as a reality felt in the experience of the poetry; and follows this with an unregretful perception of Experience. Through knowledge, acceptance, lay the reconciliation and power to 'be born again'. There is no 'romantic' nightmare, no cul-de-sac of debilitating regret; but awareness and indignation, tempered by a powerfully objective vision. There is a reminiscence of Traherne's *Centuries*:

Boyes and Girles Tumbling in the street, and playing, were moving jewels. . . . The people were mine . . . their Sparkling Eyes, Fair skins and ruddy faces. The skies were mine. . . . So that with much adoe I was corrupted and made to learn the Dirty Devices of this World. Which now I unlearn, and become, as it were, a little Child again that I may enter into the King-dom of God.

Blake's Innocence and Experience are very close to this unlearning of the 'Dirty Devices of this World'.

The subjective impulse behind the lyrics was of course there. The pastoral beauties of *Innocence* must have been in some way a reminis-cence of his own experience as a boy wandering the fields of Middle-sex. The fields, hills, and streams of eighteenth-century London reappear in *Jerusalem*:

> The fields from Islington to Marybone,
> To Primrose Hill and Saint John's Wood,
> Were builded over with pillars of gold;
> And there Jerusalem's pillars stood.

> Her little ones ran on the fields . . .

Not only the intensity of his own experience as a child, but the early contact he made with the Mathews family in Rathbone Place must have directed his interest towards children. In the Mathews's salon he doubtless met Mrs Trimmer, Mrs Barbauld herself, and Mrs Montagu, who gave the annual dinner to the climbing-boys of London. Significantly he broke with them; but their concern for children probably left a lasting impression. Most important perhaps of all the predisposing influences was his own childless marriage. Married in 1784, he had been five years without children of his own when he came to the *Songs of Innocence*.

It is the joy of the child in Nature that the *Songs* first celebrate:

> Old John, with white hair,
> Does laugh away care,
> Sitting under the oak,
> Among the old folk.
> They laugh at our play,
> And soon they all say:
> 'Such, such were the joys
> When we all, girls and boys,
> In our youth-time were seen,
> On the Echoing Green'. . . .

> Round the laps of their mothers
> Many sisters and brothers,
> Like birds in their nest,
> Are ready for rest,
> And sport no more seen,
> On the darkening Green.

The Shepherd, The Laughing Song, Spring, The Nurse's Song all echo this uninhibited joy of the child in Nature. *The Lamb, A Dream*, and *Night* celebrate his oneness with that Nature. *A Dream* makes the point with particular intensity. A child lying in grass sees a wandering emmet. No barriers in the child's consciousness lie between himself and the ant; merely a synthesizing compassion. The ant, 'troubled, 'wildered, and forlorn', cries out for its lost children:

> Pitying, I dropp'd a tear:
> But I saw a glow-worm near,
> Who replied: 'What wailing wight
> Calls the watchman of the night?
>
> 'I am set to light the ground,
> While the beetle goes his round:
> Follow now the beetle's hum;
> Little wanderer, hie thee home.'

The *Little Black Boy* carries the same compassion into the human sphere. The poem ends with the little black child declaring his love for the white:

> And then I'll stand and stroke his silver hair,
> And be like him, and he will then love me.

Love and compassion, however, lie not only between human souls but come finally from God:

> Sweet babe, in thy face,
> Holy image I can trace.
> Sweet babe, once like thee,
> Thy Maker lay and wept for me ...

But there is no duality between God and Man, between Creator and created. *The Divine Image* proclaims the central statement of his work:

58

> For Mercy, Pity, Peace, and Love
> Is God, our Father dear,
> And Mercy, Pity, Peace, and Love
> Is man, his child and care.
>
> For Mercy has a human heart;
> Pity a human face. . . .
>
> And all must love the human form,
> In heathen, Turk, or Jew;
> Where Mercy, Love, and Pity dwell,
> There God is dwelling too.

Blake's sense of the compassion between men finds expression in the 'social poems', *Holy Thursday* and *The Chimney Sweeper*. Each year on the Thursday of Whitweek, the charity-children of London attended divine service in St Paul's. Blake must surely have witnessed one of these occasions:

> 'Twas on a Holy Thursday, their innocent faces clean,
> The children walking two and two, in red and blue and green. . . .
>
> O what a multitude they seem'd, these flowers of London town!
> Seated in companies they sit with radiance all their own.
> The hum of multitudes was there, but multitudes of lambs,
> Thousands of little boys and girls raising their innocent hands.

The Chimney Sweeper realizes more closely the misery of many of these charity-children; especially the miserable condition and exploitation of the London climbing-boys. But, instead of the bitterness and indignation of its companion poem in *Experience*, here the child triumphs over his material squalor. He realizes his own 'white hair' in spite of his cruelly cropped head. Seeing an angel in his sleep, he is saved from his material miseries:

> And the Angel told Tom, if he'd be a good boy,
> He'd have God for his Father, and never want joy.

The themes, therefore, of *Innocence* are the celebration of childhood's joy in Nature, and the child's original sympathy for all created things. Even so, in *The Little Girl Lost* and *The Little Girl Found* he treats of sensual passion, which becomes the central theme of

Experience. They were subsequently transferred to the second collection, and they are best considered in their ultimate position. *Infant Joy* and *The Blossom* were, however, retained in *Innocence*, and they clearly celebrate the joy of human passion and conception. Mr Wicksteed maintains this in his analysis of the poems, and there is no reason to question his conclusion; the illustrations depict their sexual meanings clearly enough.

With the *Songs of Experience* we enter a different world. The pastoral gives place to the urban. Experience lives among the 'charter'd streets' of London. The taut rhythms of the verse convey the anxiety and indignation of its content; but the method of the poetry remains the same. The extraordinary vision of the poet is conveyed in visualized and concrete terms. The ease with which the poet maintains his intensity has surely seldom been equalled; the simple intensity of these lyrics proceeds with never a sense of strain. Their theory is never sought after or applied. Their feeling and thought are fused into the form, rhythm, and imagery of the verse. Poetry seldom gives this sense of completion and sufficiency.

Whereas the child had been the subject of all but one poem in *Innocence*, only half the poems of *Experience* deal specifically with children. Their innocence, once established, gives the force to Blake's progression into the adult world of *Experience*. Experience for Blake was the power of human nature and society to negate the enjoyment of the soul's Innocence. Love, in all its connotations, is at the heart of that innocence. The 'voice of the Bard' of the *Introduction* calls the 'lapsed soul' to renewal. The Miltonic conventions, which were to vitiate so much of his later verse, are comparatively new in Blake:

> Earth rais'd up her head,
> From the darkness dread and drear.

Earth's Answer gives the reason for the soul's imprisonment explicitly enough:

> 'Can delight,
> Chain'd in night,
> The virgins of youth and morning bear?

'Break this heavy chain
That does freeze my bones around.
Selfish! vain!
Eternal bane!
That free Love with bondage bound.'

'Free love' for Blake lay not only in its sensual manifestation. Love was the absolute expression of human life; its rejection, the rejection of life itself. To deny its physical expression was to deny the power of life against death. Love was the state of grace into which the child should continuously grow; an extension of the universal compassion which the child enjoys in his innocence; the fulfilment and continuity, in fact, of that innocence. The antithesis between Innocence and Experience in Blake is not the antithesis between sexual ignorance and sexual knowledge. There is no myth of Eden's tree of knowledge. The child's innocence is continuous. The corrupting serpent lies in the impediments of society, frustrating the enjoyment of his innocence. But again, in Blake, there is no duality between society and the individual. His psychological insight was acute enough to discern the impediments to the physical expression of love in the human heart itself. The discontinuity between Innocence and Experience, the impediments to sexual fulfilment, lay as much in the fear and the possessive character of human love, as in the inhibitions imposed by a Puritan society. In the developing child, fear and the jealousies of his lover complete the corruption of love, so effectively started by the prohibitions imposed by parents, Law, and puritanical religion.

It is often suggested that Blake's continual emphasis on the corrupting possessiveness of human love must have had some special reference to his own marriage. Certainly *My Pretty Rose-Tree* seems to suggest some unhappy episode. In any event, *The Clod and the Pebble* makes the point acutely enough:

Love seeketh only Self to please,
To bind another to its delight,
Joys in another's loss of ease,
And builds a Hell in Heaven's despite.

Some have gratuitously defended Blake from the implications of his

61

own creed – that his advocacy of 'free love' lay more in the word than the deed. But to burk at Blake's concept of innocent sexual love is to burk at everything he seriously intended. There can be little doubt that he had small sympathy for the possessiveness he thought inherent in the institution of Christian marriage.

The Little Girl Lost and *The Little Girl Found*, the poems he himself transferred from *Innocence*, are the most extensive account he gives of the child waking to the passions of sensual love. They are the account of innocent passion endangered by fear and prohibition. In *The Little Girl Lost*, he foresees a time when the 'desert wild', the symbol of sensual love, shall become a 'garden mild'. Adolescent desire, in the form of 'sleep', engulfs the young girl, while her parents fearfully weep for her. 'Beasts of prey' encircle her as she sleeps. The lioness 'loos'd her slender dress', and 'naked', they conveyed 'to caves the sleeping maid'. Searching for her in vain, the parents are led to their daughter by the 'lion old':

> 'Follow me,' he said;
> 'Weep not for the maid;
> In my palace deep,
> Lyca lies asleep.'

The parents' fears are reconciled:

> To this day they dwell
> In a lonely dell,
> Nor fear the wolvish howl,
> Nor the lions' growl.

This reconciliation, this fearless acceptance of sexual love is not found in *A Little Girl Lost*; its pessimistic intention is clear from its inscription:

> Children of the future age
> Reading this indignant page,
> Know that in a former time
> Love, Sweet Love, was thought a crime.

Coleridge took exception to the verses that followed, fearing their influence over ignorant minds. Their meaning is entirely unequivocal:

Once a youthful pair,
Fill'd with softest care,
Met in garden bright
Where the holy light
Had just removed the curtains of the night.

There, in rising day,
On the grass they play;
Parents were afar,
Strangers came not near,
And the maiden soon forgot her fear. ...

To her father white
Came the maiden bright;
But his loving look,
Like the holy book,
All her tender limbs with terror shook.

The 'holy book' conjures the whole code of prohibition implicit in Puritan religion. This was indeed Blake's chief case against religion. In *A Little Boy Lost* he castigates clerical intolerance; in *The Chimney Sweeper* he decries the indifference of the Church to the sufferings of little children. But in *The Garden of Love* and *The Little Vagabond* he comes to the crux of his case. It was the cold, inhuman, joyless Christianity which he was ultimately attacking:

I went to the Garden of Love,
And saw what I never had seen:
A Chapel was built in the midst,
Where I used to play on the green.

And the gates of this Chapel were shut,
And 'Thou shalt not' writ over the door;
So I turned to the Garden of Love. ...

And I saw it was filled with graves,
And tombstones where flowers should be;
And Priests in black gowns were walking their rounds,
And binding with briars my joys and desires.

In the 'social poems' of *Experience* Blake extends his indignation beyond the 'Garden of Love'. There had been earlier verse indignant at the sufferings of children. Cowper had pitied the poor 'shivering urchin' farmed out to the service of an old maid; and Crabbe had conveyed acutely the sufferings of the children in the rural slums of Aldeburgh. But Blake's account is altogether wider. He lived through, and felt closely, the first main phase of the Industrial Revolution. He was fundamentally alienated from its consequences. 'A Machine,' he declared, 'is not a Man nor a Work of Art; it is destructive of humanity and art.' In the prophetic poem *Jerusalem*, he denounced the whole shift of society in which the natural organic rhythm of craft work and development was broken, superimposing the artificial rhythm of the machine:

And all the Arts of Life they chang'd into the Arts of Death in Albion;
The hour-glass contemn'd because its simple workmanship
Was like the workmanship of the plowman, and the water wheel
That raises water into the cisterns, broken and burn'd with fire
Because its workmanship was like the workmanship of the shepherd;
And in their stead, intricate wheels invented . . .
To perplex youth in their outgoings and bind to labours in Albion . . . that
    they may grind
And polish brass and iron hour after hour . . . that they might spend the days
    of wisdom
In sorrowful drudgery . . .

Blake attacks the inhumanity of this society and especially its inhumanity to children. We have remarkably little evidence of Blake's relations with children in his own life; except for the Tatham account of the episode with Astley's circus-boy. The account squares fully with the indignation expressed in *Experience* on the miserable condition of so many children of the time:

Blake was standing at one of his windows, which looked into Astley's premises . . . and saw a boy hobbling along with a log tied to his foot, such an one as is put on a horse or ass to prevent their straying. . . . Blake's blood boiled, and his indignation surpassed his forbearance. He sallied forth, and demanded in no quiescent terms that the boy should be loosed, and that no Englishman should be subjected to those miseries, which he thought inexcusable even towards a slave. After having succeeded in obtaining the boy's release in some way or other, he returned home. Astley . . . having heard of

Blake's interference, came to his house and demanded, in an equally per-
emptory manner, by what authority he dare come athwart his method of
jurisdiction.

The two men quarrelled and almost resorted to blows; finally, however, Blake persuaded Astley of the justice of his 'humane sensibility',
and the men were reconciled.

It is this 'humane sensibility' which lies behind the indignation of
The Chimney Sweeper: 'Because I was happy upon the heath. . . .
They clothed me in the clothes of death.' The charity-children
appear again, going to their Divine Service on Holy Thursday, and
evoke the same urgent indignation:

> Is this a holy thing to see
> In a rich and fruitful land,
> Babes reduc'd to misery,
> Fed with cold and usurous hand? . . .
>
> And their sun does never shine,
> And their fields are bleak and bare,
> And their ways are fill'd with thorns:
> It is eternal winter there.

At one of these charity-services in 1706, the Archdeacon of Hunting-
don declared: '. . . the greatest disorders in any neighbourhood do
most commonly proceed from the folly of children'. Without
charity-schools, he went on, 'the poor, ragged children would
swarm like locusts in our streets, and by playing about with lies, and
oaths, and filthy language in their mouths, they would corrupt the
children of the better sort'. There is little reason to suppose that the
sentiments expressed on these occasions had changed very much by
Blake's own time.

Blake's social indignation was, however, not only particular;
particular instances of cruelty and inhumanity merely exemplified
the corruptions of a whole society. *London* is perhaps the most
vehement and inclusive outcry that any city or society has had
levelled against it. He produced many sketches of this poem which
became the summation of his case against late eighteenth-century
England:

I wander thro' each charter'd street,
Near where the charter'd Thames does flow,
And mark in every face I meet
Marks of weakness, marks of woe.

In every cry of every Man,
In every Infant's cry of fear,
In every voice, in every ban,
The mind-forg'd manacles I hear.

How the Chimney-Sweeper's cry
Every black'ning Church appals;
And the hapless soldier's sigh
Runs in blood down palace walls.

But most thro' midnight streets I hear
How the youthful harlot's curse
Blasts the new-born infant's tear,
And blights with plagues the marriage hearse.

Both *Innocence* and *Experience* are concerned with education in the widest sense of the word; with the nature of the child, and the corruptions he is exposed to by men and the agents of their society. It is interesting that Blake habitually ended the second collection of poems with the poem taken over from *Innocence* and placed last in the *Songs of Experience* – *The Schoolboy*. 'There is no use in education. Thank God I never was sent to school', he once declared. The poem gives the case against the education he was, so acutely, grateful to have missed:

I love to rise in a summer morn
When the birds sing on every tree;
The distant huntsman winds his horn,
And the sky-lark sings with me.
O! what sweet company!

But to go to school in a summer morn,
O! it drives all joy away;
Under a cruel eye outworn,
The little ones spend the day
In sighing and dismay . . .

> How can the bird that is born for joy
> Sit in a cage and sing? . . .

> O! father and mother, if buds are nipp'd
> And blossoms blown away. . . .

> How shall the summer arise in joy,
> Or the summer fruits appear?

'The bird that is born for joy' is the child of Blake's *Songs of Innocence*; his 'cage' the late eighteenth-century England of the *Songs of Experience*.

CHAPTER 3

Wordsworth and Coleridge

Wordsworth's 'Father of the Man'

If Blake developed his feelings about childhood from his times – and in writing of the child in Blake, there is a remarkable lack of necessity to refer to the man himself – *The Prelude* places the emphasis squarely on Wordsworth himself. The significance of the child to Wordsworth is a common acceptance:

> ... our childhood sits,
> Our simple childhood, sits upon a throne
> That hath more power than all the elements ...
> That twilight when we first begin to see
> This dawning earth ...

The reference, immediate and sure, to Nature recalls:

> The Child is father of the man,
> And I could wish my days to be
> Bound each to each by natural piety.

Even so early as 1899, James Fotheringham, in his study of *The Prelude*, remarked on Wordsworth's importance to the nineteenth century's interest in the child: 'It is owing to the movement he so well interpreted, and in good part owing to him, that we have studied the child-nature so much, and so carefully, as we have lately been doing.'

The initial facts at least are clear. For Wordsworth, childhood was the 'seed-time' of the 'soul'. He saw the development of the human mind as organic through infancy and youth to maturity. The relationship between the Child and Nature was fundamental to his concept of the growth of the moral personality. The child was in fact an essential part of the 'wisdom' he sought to convey.

With Wordsworth we are faced at once with this question of his 'wisdom', his 'philosophy'; with the 'illusion' as Arnold called it.

Dr Leavis has spoken of a 'critical blur'. How far were his philosophical intentions proper to his art; how far were they derived from Hartley; how much, in fact, was Coleridge saying when he declared his friend 'possessed more of the genius of a great philosophic poet than any man ...'; that he was 'capable of producing ... the first genuine philosophic poem'? This was the fulfilment Coleridge certainly wished upon him, a wish which may indeed have come from a mind whose own genius was more particularly intellectual than poetic. It was certainly the intention Wordsworth took for himself, if it remained an intention never truly fulfilled, or capable of fulfilment.

His philosophic interest does, however, suggest very much the character and quality of his sensibility. His greatest poetry is philosophic in the sense that it is the poetry of a man involved seriously with his art and the central problems of human existence. The 'philosophy' testifies to his own conception of his intellectual predicament, and to the anxious and acutely contemporary feelings with which he faced it. His attitude to childhood lay within his serious philosophic purpose of formulating a concept of the moral consciousness based on the relation between Nature and the poetic self.

If, as we have said, Wordsworth's attitude to the child begins with himself – the reference with him is always to his own childhood and adolescent experience – this is not to suggest anything like a self-seriousness with him. It is not, with him, a romantic assertion that 'I felt this, and therefore it is significant', but rather 'I felt this, and this is its general significance'. His concern with his own childhood became the means of establishing general truths about childhood itself, and that, in turn, only for establishing truths about the whole nature of Man. If he translated this interest into the system of Hartleian associationism, the initial significance lies in the interest rather than the degree of his involvement with Hartley, in what he wanted to do in his art, rather than the method he adopted for effecting it.

It was this prescription of seriousness for himself – the 'Mind of Man' was after all the 'haunt' and the 'main region' of his 'song' – which made him write in the following terms to John Wilson:

You have given me praise for having reflected faithfully in my Poems the feelings of human nature. I would fain hope that I have done so. But a great Poet ought to do more than this; he ought, to a certain degree, to rectify men's feelings, to give them new compositions of feelings, to render their feelings more sane, pure, and permanent . . .

The care of 'to a certain degree' points up something which cannot of course be said too often about him, the balance with which he defined his poetic intentions. He lived at the turning-point of two worlds in direct antithesis, which through the balance of his creative intelligence he sought to integrate, at – and there are many signs of it – considerable emotional pains to himself. Apply what descriptive terms to the antithesis we will – 'eighteenth-century' and 'romantic', 'reason' and 'feeling' – Wordsworth felt the emotional inadequacy of eighteenth-century intelligence, and at the same time foresaw, with his eighteenth-century sense, the emotional anarchy of the romantic subjective 'agony'. His awareness of the crisis in sensibility, which purely by chronological coincidence happened to occur at the turn of two centuries, was the cause of his reaction against both the dominant traditions of the eighteenth century, against its Intellect as exemplified in Godwin, and against its Sensibility as exemplified in the more exuberant disciples of Rousseauism. An atmosphere of crisis is of course the last thing we associate with Wordsworth's art. Its balance is so very sure. His achievement conceals rather than displays the acute tensions which nourished it. The frequently encountered suggestion of tameness and self-sufficient smugness in his poetry is most often an ironic measure of his success, or perhaps a misunderstanding of his intention to effect an equilibrium between intelligence and feeling, between sensibility and thought:

For all good poetry is the spontaneous overflow of powerful feelings: and though this be true, Poems to which any value can be attached were never produced on any variety of subjects, but by a man who, being possessed of more than usual organic sensibility had also thought long and deeply.

And again:

But habits of meditation have, I trust, so prompted and regulated my feelings, that my descriptions of such objects as strongly excite those feelings, will be found to carry along with them a *purpose*.[1]

It was, we may suspect, just this '*purpose*', this didactic impulse, and his nourishment of feeling with thought, which brought him neglect in the middle decades of the nineteenth century.

The two accounts of Wordsworth most frequently met with are therefore both partially right. Some, A. N. Whitehead among them, have seen him as a protagonist of Romantic feeling, consciously reacting against 'the mentality of the eighteenth century'; in the Enlightenment, he says, Wordsworth 'felt that something had been left out'. Arthur Beatty, however, saw him as a poet rigidly Hartleian, an exponent of the central associationist philosophy of the century. If Wordsworth is to be believed, neither is wholly, but both partially right. Both views point up the respective sides of the poet's sensibility.

In Hartley, he clearly considered himself possessed of the means to effect a fusion of emotion and thought, by displaying the organic growth of human consciousness from infancy and childhood according to the principles of associationism. It is important that he came to the formulation of his philosophic interest in Hartley as the result of an acute personal crisis. Many suggestions have been made to interpret this crisis in the lesser sense of the word personal. Mr Bateson has laid stress on Wordsworth's unhappy childhood. His mother died when he was eight, and he lived the rest of his childhood with harsh and unaccommodating grandparents. His father seems to have meant nothing to him; his place in Wordsworth's account of himself is an ominous silence. 'Many a time have William . . . and myself', wrote Dorothy in a letter to Jane Pollard, 'shed tears together, tears of bitterest sorrow. . . . We always finish our conversations, which generally take a melancholy turn, with wishing we had a father and a home. . . .' Professor Empson has said that Wordsworth used Nature as a father-totem; qualifying this with the further suggestion that

1. It is perhaps interesting to note that Jane Austen's *Sense and Sensibility* is an exercise on the same theme. The novel is not so much concerned with asserting an antithesis as with establishing an integration of 'sense' *and* 'sensibility', in the character of Elinor, in contradistinction to Marianne's uncivilized 'sensibility' alone.

both father and mother elements occupy an important place in Wordsworth's attitude to Nature. Emphasizing Wordsworth's cult of inanimate Nature, Sir Herbert Read has suggested the unhappy affair with Annette Vallon as the psychic impulse behind Wordsworth's 'retreat' to 'rocks, and stones, and trees'. Although, however, there is something of the cold, self-gratifying recluse in much of Wordsworth's poetry, unless we are to accept that he was astonishingly self-deceived, that his own testimony may be analysed away into nothingness, it seems reasonable to place the emphasis altogether otherwise; to see the 'retreat' as much cultural as precisely personal, and to suggest that in Wordsworth we have an essentially representative sensibility.

His own experience had been closely involved with the whole intellectual development of the century. The search for the elusive psychological details about 'what really happened to him in France' merely suggests that his 'seriousness' fell upon him suddenly, some time in the middle nineties. It would be more reasonable to assume that his early involvement with the Enlightenment was an intellectual attitude not lightly adopted, and that when confronted suddenly with doubt as to the moral truth of a philosophy he had so enthusiastically held to, the serious Wordsworth faced absolute spiritual disintegration. We know that as a youth he assumed the prevailing enthusiasm for Godwinian Enlightenment; and when the Revolution broke, we know his unqualified enthusiasm for it. His subsequent experience of disillusionment was no more nor less than the experience of a serious sensibility growing up intellectually. His passionate revulsion from his previous ethical and intellectual involvement with the eighteenth century suggests indeed the degree of passion with which his previous opinions had been held. In a mood of absolute moral and intellectual disintegration, all things for Wordsworth became 'meagre and stale'. For him, even the radical sanctions were gone. In isolation and alienation from everything he had previously stood for, he was thrust back upon himself, seriously experiencing what was to become a common 'romantic' predicament.

It may be, of course, that he then had recourse to 'Nature', as the all-supplying 'mother'; that his personal deprivations were suddenly aligned with his intellectual deprivations; that, in fact, a mixture of motives impelled him towards Nature as the universal Comforter (as others, perhaps, in later times have found religion or politics, in comparable intellectual situations). But if the impulse towards the massive introspections which were to form the basis of the great decade of his poetry were even initially escapist, their importance lies, as so often in romantic art, in the discipline which he brought to his 'escape'.

His poetic intention became, clearly, a reintegration of his self, for purposes that were in essence social. His concern for Nature and his own childhood contains, at its best, nothing of intellectual retreat, and none of the self-gratification of the affrighted, withdrawn 'romantic'. In the Preface to the second edition of the *Lyrical Ballads*, he defined his poetic purpose as 'religious', as a regard for the 'essential passions of the heart', for the 'sacred simplicities of life'. In a letter to John Wilson, he speaks of 'stripping our own hearts naked'. By a ruthless investigation of his self, he sought spiritual reintegration; to 'illustrate the manner in which our feelings and ideas are associated in a state of excitement'; to 'reconcile ... discordant elements'. It was not perhaps so much the purely philosophical content of Hartley's thought which attracted him, but the idea of 'association' itself, the means for emotional integration that he thought he could avail himself of in Hartley's system.

> Dust as we are, the immortal spirit grows
> Like harmony in music; there is a dark
> Inscrutable workmanship, that reconciles
> Discordant elements, makes them cling together
> In one society. How strange that all
> The terrors, pains, and early miseries,
> Regrets, vexations, lassitudes interfused
> Within my mind, should e'er have borne a part,
> And that a needful part, in making up
> The calm existence that is mine when I
> Am worthy of myself!

In the presence of the poetry, one may perhaps be excused for feeling that the unhappy liaison with Annette Vallon was not of really very much importance.

Here we have the equipoise; the subjective 'terrors, pains, and early miseries', the 'discordant elements' are 'reconciled' and made to 'cling together in one society'. Both *The Prelude* and the earlier *Lines Written above Tintern Abbey* (1798), are an investigation of the method by which, through Nature and the association of its experiences, the 'immortal spirit grows like harmony in music'. His investigation returned to childhood, to the 'seed-time' of the 'soul'. He begins his story 'early', in the attempt to 'understand himself'. The reference to Hartley is close and unmistakable. Infancy, a time of absolute sensation, is the first of the Hartleian 'three ages of Man'. In *Tintern Abbey*, a short prospectus of the longer work, he refers, parenthetically only, to infancy as the 'coarser pleasures of my boyish days, And their glad animal movements'. In *The Prelude*, he returns to:

> Those recollected hours that have the charm
> Of visionary things . . . that throw back our life
> And almost make our Infancy itself
> A visible scene, on which the sun is shining.

He recounts the vivid details of his infancy; but the reference is always general, and towards growth and development, towards the 'passions which build up our human soul'. All the time there is an 'intertwining', an 'intercourse', a 'building-up'. The second age is one of Feeling rather than pure sensation. *Tintern Abbey* gives what Nature had been to him in adolescence:

> . . . when like a roe
> I bounded o'er the mountains. . . . For nature then . . .
> To me was all in all.

Nature had become 'a feeling and a love'; it had no need of 'a remoter charm, By thought supplied'. This spontaneous, passionate response to Nature passes with maturity. But for the 'loss', there is 'abundant recompense'.

> . . . For I have learned
> To look on nature, not as in the hour
> Of thoughtless youth; but hearing oftentimes
> The still sad music of humanity,

74

> Nor harsh nor grating, though of ample power
> To chasten and subdue. And I have felt
> A presence that disturbs me with the joy
> Of elevated thoughts; a sense sublime. . . .

This 'sense sublime' received in the course of his poetry many definitions. In *The Prelude* it becomes the Reason, in a very particular sense of the word, by which he intended that supreme power of the human mind to fuse and synthesize experience, to find 'harmony' and the 'deep power of joy', tracing its organic growth in his own experience from its 'natal murmur'. He allowed the 'days gone by' to 'come back upon him', from the 'dawn almost of life', and thus the 'hiding-places of his power' seemed 'open'.

Until the Ode on *Intimations of Immortality*, where, for poetic purposes, he made use of the Platonic myth of the child's immortal nature, Wordsworth adhered strictly to the Hartleian concept of the child as a *tabula rasa*, impressed, and only impressed by the informing, 'intertwining' influences of Nature. Virtue for Wordsworth was not innate, in Rousseau's sense. He followed neither Blake nor Coleridge into transcendentalist intuition. In his important reply to Mathetes' letter in the *Friend* of 1809, he wrote: '. . . our eyes have not been fixed upon virtue which lies apart from human nature, or transcends it. . . . In Fact, there is no such virtue.'

But if the consistently intellectual character of his sensibility led him to couch his 'wisdom' in the Hartleian frame of the 'three ages', the poetry in fact is far removed from the sympathies of the philosopher himself, who could declare upon the poetic imagination in these terms: 'The pleasures of imagination . . . are generated from the sensible ones by association, come to their height early in life, and decline in old age.' Only ironically, in the light of the poet's decline, does this bear any relation to Wordsworth's poetic achievements. The poetry breaks out from its philosophical enclosure. One can speak of enclosure, the restricting influences of his philosophical tendencies, since they are everywhere apparent in his work:

> And I have felt . . . a sense sublime
> Of something far more deeply interfused,
> Whose dwelling is the light of setting suns,
> And the round ocean and the living air. . . .

... Therefore am I still
A lover of the meadows and the woods
And mountains; and of all that we behold
From this green earth; of all the mighty world
Of eye and ear, – both what they half create,
And what perceive; well pleased to recognize
In nature and the language of the sense,
The anchor of my purest thoughts, the nurse,
The guide, the guardian of my heart, and soul
Of all my moral being.

It is not difficult to detect here the encroachment of the philosophy. It would not be difficult to say – *here* the damaging intrusion occurs ('well pleased to recognize in nature and the language of the sense', perhaps), which leads inevitably to the metaphorical dryness of 'anchor', 'nurse', 'guide', and 'soul of all my moral being'. In seeking an equipoise between feeling and thought, the balance can be clearly felt to be upset towards the philosophy. The damage of his intellectual preoccupations is felt whenever he turns from conveying the experience and feelings illustrating the truths of his philosophy to the statement of the truths themselves. The imaginative lowering occurs when he turns from the feeling of his experiences in Nature to the statement of philosophical generalities. The intellectual habit of course grew upon him. The strength of his early poetry lay in the fact that Hartleian philosophy allowed him recourse to his infancy, youth, and early maturity, when the 'hiding-places of his power' were still 'open'. The later 'philosophies' of Anglicanism, duty, and mid-century patriotism, allowed him none of this recourse to the feeling of his childhood, and their harmful effects are everywhere displayed in the hardening, mechanical textures of his later verse.

The decline of his poetic spontaneity was a problem he himself admitted. Already in *Tintern Abbey* and *The Prelude*, there is some suspicion that recourse to the Hartleian concept of the third age of Man might become something of a wish-fulfilment. The suspicion is perhaps confirmed when we come to the celebrated Ode on *Intimations of Immortality from recollections of Early Childhood*, in which he confronted himself with the feelings of his poetic decline. More than anything else he wrote, the Ode conveys his awareness of the significance of childhood. In the Fenwick note he wrote: 'the visionary qualities of children have often been noted, and have been interpreted as intimations of immortality: I took hold of the notion of pre-existence as having sufficient foundation in humanity for authorizing me to make for my purpose the best use of it I could as a poet.'

On 26 March 1802, he wrote the verse in which he made the famous assertion about the child's fatherhood of the Man. Immediately after, he composed the first four stanzas of the Ode, which convey his intense awareness of a sense of loss at the level of his spontaneous appreciation of natural stimuli. He discontinued the poem at the unanswered question:

> Whither is fled the visionary gleam?
> Where is it now, the glory and the dream?

Resuming the Ode in 1806, he turned for explanation of his early spontaneity to the theory of the immortality of the child's nature; and for compensation, when its visionary character fades 'into the light of common day', he once more finds solace in the maturity of the 'philosophic mind', a further synonymous expression for the 'sense sublime' of the *Lines Written above Tintern Abbey*.

Professor Trilling in *The Liberal Imagination* has recently expressed the view that, 'so far from agreeing' with the common acceptance that the Ode is a conscious farewell on the poet's part to his creative powers, he sees it as 'actually a dedication to new powers'. This indeed expresses Wordsworth's own conscious intention. In the 'philosophic mind' we may be sure Wordsworth saw no prospect of deterioration. And yet his hope of finding nourishment from it was belied in the event, and I think within the poetry of the Ode itself, in distinction from its dedicatory statements, the diminishing of the poet's powers is already apparent. The first four stanzas give with every immediacy the sense of the poet's loss, through the immediacy of the verse. Against the perception that:

> The Rainbow comes and goes,
> And lovely is the Rose,

lies the irritant sense of loss – 'whither' was fled the 'visionary gleam'? Resuming the poem, he answers first by stating the pre-existent, visionary character of childhood:

> Our birth is but a sleep and a forgetting:
> The Soul that rises with us, our life's Star,
> Hath had elsewhere its setting,
> And cometh from afar:
> Not in entire forgetfulness,
> And not in utter nakedness,
> But trailing clouds of glory do we come
> From God who is our home:
> Heaven lies about us in our infancy!

It is a *locus classicus* indeed for the whole literature of childhood in the nineteenth century; and no less so its regretful, pessimistic continuation:

> Shades of the prison-house begin to close
> Upon the growing Boy,

The vision splendid dies:

> At length the Man perceives it die away,
> And fade into the light of common day.

The regret, the sense of loss, is once more the most vividly conveyed emotion:

> Thou little Child . . .
> Why with such earnest pains dost thou provoke
> The Years to bring the inevitable yoke, . . .
> Full soon thy Soul shall have her earthly freight,
> And custom lie upon thee with a weight,
> Heavy as frost, and deep almost as life!

It is at this point that the poem turns to its climactic assertion about the compensations of maturity:

> O joy! that in our embers
> Is something that doth live,
> That nature yet remembers
> What was so fugitive!
> The thought of our past years in me doth breed
> Perpetual benedictions . . .

> We will grieve not, rather find
> Strength in what remains behind;
> In the primal sympathy
> Which having been must ever be; ...
> In the faith that looks through death,
> In years that bring the philosophic mind.

The transition to this assertiveness is wholly awkward. A sonority takes over. The progression in *Tintern Abbey* to a comparable position evolves with the organic development of the feeling within the poem. In the Ode, the feeling seems to turn upon its tracks, in essence to contradict itself. Richness of metaphor succumbs to bald, rhythmic assertion. The feeling never recovers its ease and sureness without recourse to purely verbal ease of metre and rhyme. The sense of loss in the early stanzas is conveyed *through* the technique; there is no distraction from the immediacy of the emotion:

> There was a time when meadow, grove, and stream,
> The earth, and every common sight,
> To me did seem
> Apparell'd in celestial light,
> The glory and the freshness of a dream.

The rightness of:

> The Rainbow comes and goes,
> And lovely is the Rose ...
> Waters on a starry night
> Are beautiful and fair;
> The sunshine is a glorious birth

comes, we feel, from the integrity of the emotion which immediately follows:

> But yet I know, where'er I go,
> That there hath past away a glory from the earth.

There is of course in the whole Ode a certain tone which many have found not entirely agreeable, a certain artificiality of movement, which may in part derive from the over-conscious mechanics of the form – one's attention is continually distracted by some emphasis of rhyme, accent, or rhythm not essential to the movement of the poem's feeling. But this is altogether less evident in the early stanzas; and the assumption seems fair that in the first stanzas the intensity of the emotion subdues the artificiality of the form. The case is quite otherwise in the final stanzas of the Ode:

> O joy! that in our embers
> Is something that doth live,
> That nature yet remembers
> What was so fugitive! . . .
>
> We will grieve not, rather find
> Strength in what remains behind;
> In the primal sympathy
> Which having been must ever be . . .

It is almost as if the poet is seeking reassurance from the facility of his own expression.

The Ode became undoubtedly one of the central references for the whole nineteenth century in its attitude to the child. It is indeed of the utmost significance that the most intense emotion of the poem is one of regretful loss. The weight of the poetry falls so clearly on the poet's sense of his own loss of childhood's spontaneous enthusiasm in Nature. Throughout the first stanzas, vitality of response is everywhere equated with the 'Child of Joy', the 'happy shepherd-boy!' And the 'explanation' of the child's immortal nature adds further poetic weight to the regret. With every poetic justification, the nineteenth century remembered the 'shades of the prison-house', and the 'earthly freight', and the 'custom' which fell on Wordsworth's 'Child of Joy' – 'heavy as frost, and deep almost as life!' One remembers the poetically immediate, rather than the metrical assertions about the compensations of the 'philosophic mind'. The metrical facility of the closing stanzas do of course convey an impression of emotional adequacy. The heavy insistence of the rhymes deceives the reader, as perhaps Wordsworth himself, as to the intensity of feeling behind them. Attention to the metaphorical thinness and the awkward movement of the verse, however, suggests something altogether different from adequacy. The blurring as to the force of these final stanzas arises partly perhaps from the closing lines, which, although not in any way integral to the last section of the poem as a whole, are some of the most beautiful he ever wrote.

The reasons why this dedication to new powers was belied, lie outside our discussion. We need only suggest that the philosophic and moral compensations he acquired with age blunted the immediacy of his poetic experience. He moved very clearly away from the 'natural piety' which informed the great lyrics:

> Three years she grew in sun and shower;
> Then Nature said, 'A lovelier flower
>   On earth was never sown;
> This child I to myself will take;
> She shall be mine, and I will make
>   A Lady of my own.
>
> Myself will to my darling be
> Both law and impulse; and with me
>   The Girl, . . .
> Shall feel an overseeing power
>   To kindle or restrain. . . .'

The whole Wordsworthian equipoise lies in the power of Nature to 'kindle or restrain', to be 'both law and impulse'. By 1845, however, he writes of another girl:

> Left among her native mountains
>   With wild Nature to run wild. . . .

He poses the question as to what she needs to 'temper in her breast unruly fire' – and this is his answer, in 1845:

> Easily a pious training
> And a steadfast outward power.

Wordsworth confronted the moral problems of the early Victorian period with an Anglican orthodoxy. As Professor Willey has said of him: 'there is a steady retreat towards the religious sources of his mysticism, and grace supplants the visionary gleam'. But for those who consider poetry to have some significance within its life for the spiritual well-being of its creators and its audience, this 'becoming a better man' if a 'worse poet' contains an irony within it, if nothing more, and says something, emotionally, about the orthodoxy he adopted.

The consistency in Wordsworth is, however, the consistency of his seriousness. And this is evidenced in his interest in education which remained with him throughout his life. *The Prelude* is, in one sense, an educational treatise. There are throughout his work echoes of the whole eighteenth-century 'sentimentalist' movement in education. His debt to Rousseau was in general, rather than in particulars. Even though he demurred at the concept of Rousseau's 'original virtue' (the Ode is eccentric to his work as a whole), he adopted the reverential Rousseauist tone towards the child. His statements upon education lie close to *Emile*. *The Prelude* ridicules the Enlightened schoolmasters who know:

> The inside of the earth, and spell the stars. . . .
> Can string you names of districts, cities, towns . . .
> . . . he sifts, he weighs; . . . .
> All things are put to question.

Imprisoned within education, Wordsworth's child, no less than Blake's, was deprived of the influences of Nature and fancy:

> . . . in their woodland beds the flowers
> Weep, and the river sides are all forlorn. . . .
> Oh! give us once again the Wishing-Cap
> Of Fortunatus, and the invisible coat
> Of Jack the Giant-Killer, Robin Hood. . . .

Instead the 'guides and wardens of our faculties' confine the children down 'like engines'. In answer to education's 'intellectual' corruption, he cites immediately the story of the boy who, many a time,

> At evening, when the stars had just begun
> To move along the edges of the hills. . . .
> Blew mimic hootings to the silent owls
> That they might answer him. And they would shout
> Across the watery Vale, and shout again,
> Responsive to his call, with quivering peals,
> And long halloos, and screams. . . .

These 'mimic hootings to the silent owls' stand with Blake's child of Innocence against the desiccations of the eighteenth century's educational intellect. Even in the letter he wrote in later life to the inspectors appointed by a committee of the Council on Education, his opinions had not changed:

Let me ask you, dear Sir, whether throughout the Minutes too little value is not set upon the occupations of Children out of doors, under the direction, or by permission, of their parents, comparatively with what they do or acquire in school? Is not the knowledge inculcated by the Teacher, or derived under his management, from books, too exclusively dwelt upon, so as almost to put out of sight that which comes, without being sought for, from intercourse with nature. . . . It struck me also that from the same cause, too little attention is paid to books of imagination. . . . We must not only have knowledge but the means of wielding it, and that is done infinitely more thro' the imaginative faculty assisting both in the collection and application of facts than is generally believed.

These almost Jamesian periphrases testify to the residue of Rousseauism in Wordsworth. These cotton-wool utterances of a man seeming almost to be talking in his sleep, recall through the haze of intervening experience the enthusiasms of his first maturity.

There is no doubt of Wordsworth's spiritual influence in the nineteenth century. Mill, Leslie Stephen, and Rutherford considered him a power in their lives. His antithesis of town and country became of increasing importance to a century disfigured by the urban outrage of the Industrial Revolution. His plea for a sensuous relation between Man and Nature became a force among a whole generation of intellectuals at the end of the century dissatisfied with the human sterilities of the vulgarizers of Benthamite utilitarianism. His assertion for the power of the imaginative life, and especially the imaginative life of the child, became a potent romantic influence. Considering his assertion of childhood's visionary quality, and that in the child's consciousness lay powers of social and personal revitalization, it is not surprising that George Eliot, when she came to the tale of the regeneration of crabbed age through the agency of a child, in *Silas Marner*, should have placed at its head the following from Wordsworth:

> A child, more than all other gifts
> That earth can offer to declining man,
> Brings hope with it, and forward-looking thoughts.

Coleridge and the 'Imaginative Child'

If men laugh at the falsehoods that were imposed on themselves during their childhood, it is because they are not good and wise enough to contemplate the Past in the Present, and so to produce by a virtuous and thoughtful sensibility that continuity in their self-consciousness, which nature has made the law of their animal life. Ingratitude, sensuality, and hardness of heart all flow from this source. Men are ungrateful to others only when they have ceased to look back on their former selves with joy and tenderness. They exist in fragments, annihilated as to the Past, they are dead to the future, or seek for the proofs of it everywhere, only not (where alone they can be found) in themselves. A contemporary poet has exprest and illustrated this sentiment with equal firmness of thought and feeling.

Writing this in the *Friend* of 3 August 1809, Coleridge followed it by quoting Wordsworth's *Rainbow*. It is an exact appreciation of Wordsworth's doctrine of the child's relation to the organic development of the human consciousness. The emphasis lies, justly enough, on Wordsworth's 'thoughtful sensibility' and his firmness of 'thought and feeling'.

The friendship between the two men derived largely from the similarity of their intellectual interests, from their mutual desire to formulate a philosophy of man's whole consciousness. By effecting a harmony of thought and feeling they wished to move away from human 'fragmentation', and establish a philosophy of the total Self. Wordsworth translated his desire into the structure of associationism. Coleridge, however, in a letter to Poole of 1801 speaks of the 'overthrow of the doctrine of association as taught by Hartley'. It was this break with Hartley's philosophy which Mill in his *Essay* termed his 'revolt . . . against the philosophy of the eighteenth century'. Coleridge himself speaks indeed of his 'victory' over Hartleian philosophy; but although in this he broke with Wordsworth's own enthusiasm, it is nevertheless significant that he adds 'deep thinking is attainable only by a man of deep feeling'; and that 'all truth is a species of revelation'. Wordsworth's own statement of the relation between thought and feeling has been inverted. With Coleridge, 'deep thinking' is to be nourished by 'deep feeling'. The intention is effectively the same. Coleridge, however, discards associationism entirely. He breaks with the 'fragmentation' of human personality, caused, he thought, so disastrously, by the Intellectualism of the eighteenth century. His revolt was no less fundamental than Blake's. His essentially romantic assertion was that 'all truth is a species of revelation'. And within this lay his whole attitude to the child.

The philosophy of the eighteenth century was for Coleridge a philosophy of human 'death'. Descartes and Locke had 'untenanted Creation of its God', and substituted 'a universe of death', for 'that which moves with light and life informed'. 'We have', he said, 'purchased a few brilliant inventions at the loss of all communion with life and the spirit of nature'. 'The modern mind' had 'become infected with the contagion of its mechanic philosophy'. In contrast, he posits a theory of the human Reason, that supreme, intuitive faculty of the mind whereby spiritual reality, as Professor Willey has said, is spiritually discerned. Its synthesizing quality bears relation to Wordsworth's 'sense sublime'; except that for Wordsworth its origin lies in the process of association, and for Coleridge it is intuitive, innate. It is a faculty to be distinguished absolutely from man's lower faculty of Understanding, by which he classifies, analyses, and performs the functions of experimental science; valid in themselves, but dangerous if usurping the functions of the intuitive Reason. The ironic triumph of the eighteenth century had been, in Coleridge's words, to 'explode' moral science as 'mystic jargon'. The 'mysteries of religion' had been 'cut and squared for the comprehension of the understanding'. 'Imagination' had been 'excluded from poesy':

The groundwork therefore of all true philosophy is the full apprehension of the difference between the contemplation of reason, namely that intuition of things which arises when we possess ourselves as one with the whole ... and that which presents itself when ... we think of ourselves as separated beings, and place nature in antithesis to the mind, as object to subject, thing to thought, death to life.

Fusing Platonism, Christianity, and German idealist thought, he declared an enmity between the living organic whole, and what he conceived to be the eighteenth-century philosophy of dead parts. In Wordsworth himself indeed he had hoped to see the 'substitution' of 'life and intelligence' for the 'philosophy of mechanism, which strikes DEATH'.

The life of the organic human consciousness in poetry was the Imagination, and in religion and ethics, Reason. The 'Primary Imagination' he defined as the 'living power and prime Agent of all human Perception'; the 'Secondary Imagination' was that quality of the mind's imaginative activity which 'dissolves, diffuses, dissipates, in order to recreate . . . it struggles to unify. It is essentially vital'. It was the capacity of the poetic sensibility to fuse the perceptions of everyday life, to 'dissolve, diffuse, and dissipate' them and then 'unify' them into a new organic, vital whole. In religion and ethics, the absolute truth could be intuitively perceived, as with imagination in poetry, by the power of the organic Reason. It is this theory of the intuitive 'soul' which he expresses in the *Ode to Dejection*:

> Ah! from the soul itself must issue forth
> A light, a glory, a fair luminous cloud
> Enveloping the Earth.

and again, in precise contradiction of Locke and Hartley:

> I may not hope from outward forms to win
> The passion and the life, whose fountains are within.

He continues to assert the reality of:

> This light, this glory, this fair luminous mist,
> This beautiful and beauty-making power.

And, as indeed with Blake and Wordsworth, it is a concept close to the spirit of human 'Joy',

> Joy, Lady! is the spirit and the power
> Which wedding Nature to us gives in dower,
> A new Earth and new Heaven. . . .

It was this intuitive, imaginative quality of the soul which Coleridge saw in the child, and which he anxiously wished to preserve: the power of the intuitive soul could only survive if the discontinuity between childhood and maturity were avoided; if indeed the development of self-consciousness were continuous, organic; if there were wholeness. The 'feelings' of childhood should be carried 'into the powers of manhood' – feelings of freshness, wonder, and spontaneous joy in existence – the 'sense of wonder and novelty with the appearances, which every day for perhaps forty years had rendered familiar'. It was the 'character and privilege of genius' to retain the 'sense of novelty with old and familiar objects'; as of course it was the essential character and privilege of the child.

His strictures on the more exaggerated stanzas of the *Intimations Ode* reveal, however, the essential good sense of his attitude to childhood: 'In what sense does he [the child] read "the eternal deep"? In what sense is he declared to be "for ever haunted" by the Superior Being, or so inspired as to deserve the splendid title of a mighty prophet, a blessed seer?' He had little time also for the negative education of Rousseau. To his friend Thelwall, who declared that children must not be influenced before they reach years of discretion, he caustically showed his own weedy garden. To Thelwall's innocent inquiry why he kept it so: '"Oh," I replied, "*that* is only because it has not yet come to its age of discretion and choice. The weeds, you see, have taken the liberty to grow, and I thought it unfair in me to prejudice the soil towards roses and strawberries."' But this should not suggest its contrary. His attitude to children is perhaps best given in his description of his own son, Hartley:

Hartley is a spirit that dances on an aspen leaf – the air that yonder sallow-faced and yawning tourist is breathing is to my babe a perpetual nitrous oxide ... I look at my doted-on Hartley – he moves, he lives, he finds impulses from within and without ... he looks at the clouds and mountains ... and vaults and jubilates. ... Hartley whirling round for joy, Derwent eddying, ... shouting his little hymn of joy.

Perhaps though, even more than this capacity for joy, it is the integrity of the child that he wished most to enforce and preserve:

Two things we may learn from little children from three to six years old; that it is a characteristic, an instinct of our human nature to pass out of self. ... And not to suffer any one form to pass into me and become a usurping self.

It was the maintenance of this integrity of the child which Coleridge asserted as the chief aim of education, which should be essentially a process of educing the innate qualities of the human soul, by preserving the wonder, joy, imagination, and integrity of the child, so that its 'feelings' should be carried 'into the powers of manhood'. Education should be to educe, 'to call forth; as the blossom is educed from the bud, the vital excellencies are within; the acorn is but educed or brought forth from the bud'. If it should be an active process of 'educing', it should above all be a gentle one:

Touch a door a little ajar, or half-open, and it will yield to the push of your finger. Fire a cannon-ball at it, and the door stirs not an inch: you make a hole through it, the door is spoilt for ever, but not *moved*. Apply this moral to Education.

And again:

What are you crying for? said an Angry Parent to a Child, whom he had sharply and harshly rebuked. You have snuffed the candle too close, replied I – and can you wonder, that it gutters.

Commenting on the educational practice of his day, he sees:

. . . how many examples of . . . young men the most anxiously and expensively be-schoolmastered, be-tutored, be-lectured, anything but *educated*; who have received arms and ammunition, instead of skill, strength, and courage; varnished rather than polished; perilously over-civilized, and most pitiably uncultivated! And all from inattention to the method dictated by nature herself . . . that as the forms in all organized existence, so must all true and living knowledge proceed from within; that it may be trained, supported, fed, excited, but can never be infused or impressed.

It was a great error to cram the young mind with so much knowledge as made the child talk much and fluently: what was more ridiculous than to hear a child questioned, what it thought of the last poem of Walter Scott? A child should be child-like, and possess no other idea than what was loving and admiring.

Coleridge does indeed assert a distinction between Education and Knowledge closely resembling his famous distinctions between Imagination and Fancy, and between Reason and Understanding. Writing of Plato's educational theory in the *Friend* he says:

The EDUCATION of the intellect, by awakening the principle and *method* of self-development, was his proposed object, not any specific information that can be *conveyed* into it from without. Not to assist in storing the passive mind with the various sorts of knowledge most in request, as if the human soul were a mere repository ... but to place it in such relations of circumstance as should gradually excite the germinal power that craves no knowledge but what it can take up into itself, what it can appropriate and re-produce in fruits of its own. To shape, to dye, to paint over, and to mechanize the mind, he resigned as their proper trade to the sophists.

'Reading and writing', he declared, in illustration, should be considered among the *'means* of education', and never the *'end'*; for 'knowledge' could never be made the 'prime object' of life without 'injury to the understanding' and 'perversion' of men's 'moral institutions'.

For Coleridge, then, education should be the cultivation of those 'moral institutions'; the 'excitement' of the child's 'germinal powers'; an act of careful excitement and preservation. For him, no less than for Wordsworth, the child was an integral part of his whole philosophy. Only by the preservation of the child's wonder, joy, and spontaneous imagination could Man's moral nature develop into Reason and Imagination, the two sovereigns of his mature existence. Coleridge's sensuous appreciation of childhood, and its significance to him, are made entirely clear in the report of his lecture on *The New System of Education* appearing in the *Bristol Gazette* for 18 November 1813:

Returning to general education of children, Mr Coleridge observed there was scarce any being who looked upon the beautiful face of an infant, that did not feel a strong sensation – it was not pity, it was not the attraction of mere loveliness; it was a sense of melancholy; for himself, he always when viewing an infant, found a tear a candidate for his eye. What could be the cause of this? It was not that its innocency, its perfectness, like a flower, all perfume and all loveliness, was like a flower to pass away. [It was rather the] thought, doubtlessly felt by everyone – if he could begin his career again, if he could recover that innocency once possessed, and connect it with virtue. With these thoughts, who could avoid feeling an enthusiasm for the education of mankind. Suppose it possible that there was a country, where a great part of its population had one arm rendered useless; who would not be desirous of relieving their distress; but what was a right arm withered, in comparison of having all the faculties shut out from the good and wise of past ages.

The Lecturer concluded with recommending an observance of the laws of nature in Education of Children; the ideas of a child were cheerful and playful; they should not be palsied by obliging it to utter sentences which the head could not comprehend nor the heart echo; our nature was in every sense a *progress*; both body and mind.

CHAPTER 4

From Coleridge to Dickens

BY the early decades of the nineteenth century, then, the symbol of the romantic child was established; and it was, primarily, a poetic symbol. It was not until the establishment of the nineteenth-century novel in the thirties, and more especially in the forties, that the child found another major vehicle. Almost a generation lay between the revolution in poetry and the novel. Jane Austen, and Scott even, had their roots clearly in the past. The eighteenth-century novel (one is thinking of Fielding and Smollett rather than of Richardson and Sterne) was one of event rather than of analysis of personality and motive, and the tradition died slowly. When the greatest of the English 'romantic' novelists came first to the novel, he chose in *The Pickwick Papers*, and not only by the chance of his early reading, an eighteenth-century formula for his work.

A revolution in the novel occurred in *Oliver Twist* (1838), *Jane Eyre* (1847), *Wuthering Heights* (1847), and *Dombey and Son* (1848). It was not only a revolution within the novel itself, however; but a revolution as between poetry and prose. The energies revitalizing literature at the close of the eighteenth century had been directed into poetry. At some point in the main flow of literary feeling, those energies were deflected into the novel. The novel, as we have known it, as a vehicle for psychological analysis rather than the recounting of events, became the major literary form in the mid-nineteenth century. As novels, in this sense, the works of Fielding and Smollett are unrecognizable.[1] From the establishment of the great Victorian

---

1. The tradition of the novel of 'events' continued, of course, throughout the nineteenth century, and into our own. It is the continuity of it in Trollope which does most to make him a minor figure. The culture of the eighteenth century was substantial enough to support a novel of picaresque event. That of the Victorian *bourgeoisie* was less substantial; our own even less so – which is perhaps why efforts to revive the picaresque tradition in our own time seem so irrelevant.

novel, poetry suffered continuous enfeeblement. The sphere of poetry became more and more peripheral, and it has really remained so ever since. The representative mid-Victorian literary mind lay in Dickens and George Eliot rather than, say, Tennyson; just as in the twentieth century the representative mind has been D. H. Lawrence. It is sobering to reflect that a case could be made out for the judgement that the last extensive exercise of the English poetic sensibility was Wordsworth's *Prelude*. *The Waste Land* was in part impressive for its sheer improbability, for its spectacular reversal of the main flow of literary events; a fact which may, in time, have some effect on its lasting appraisal.

In this central transference towards prose, the flow carried within itself the characteristics of the romantic sensibility – the self-awareness, the heightened sense of individual personality, the social protest, and, too, the increased awareness of the child, as a vehicle for social commentary, as a symbol of innocence and the life of the imagination, as an expression also of nostalgia, insecurity, and, one can just detect it, introspective self-pity. The sensibility is continuous; time was the only intervening factor. The reflection in the prose mirror is in fact almost exact.

Dickens is of course the focus for any study of the establishment of the child in the nineteenth-century novel. But in the same decade as *Oliver Twist* (1838), Marryat wrote *Peter Simple* (1834); and in the same decade as *The Old Curiosity Shop* (1841) and *Dombey and Son* (1848), we have Frances Trollope's *Michael Armstrong* (1840), Charlotte Yonge's *Abbeychurch* (1844), and Charlotte Brontë's *Jane Eyre* (1847). *Alton Locke* was published in the same year as *David Copperfield* (1850). Dickens's achievement lying across three decades was to summate themes which were widely exercising the whole literary sensibility. The novelists of the middle century echoed his own intense concern with English childhood.

The factor governing the literature of the child from the 1830s was the condition of children in society. The romantic period had asserted the innocence and frailty of the child. The victimized condition of the child in early Victorian England did not square with the image of childhood that had been created. The tension between innocence and experience, sounded initially by Blake, became the main *motif* of early and mid-Victorian literature of the child. The revelations of successive Royal Commissions on industry, and particularly the findings of the Commission on the Employment of Young Persons and Children of 1842, astounded and affronted the public conscience. *Oliver Twist* represented the feelings of an age anxious about the miserable condition of its children, and inspired others to similar protest. Mrs Trollope's *Michael Armstrong* and Charlotte Elizabeth's *Helen Fleetwood*, though both only mediocre in achievement, took the theme of the defenceless orphan, and added further witness to the literary concern with the pathos of the child.

One of the great strengths of nineteenth-century fiction was its close concern with society. If this contributed to a degree of coarsening, easily remarkable, novels of the early and mid-century suffered none of the introverted attenuations we find in the work of many later novelists. If coarsening is the defect of a too close concern with specifically social problems, over-refinement and irrelevance are the defects consequent upon its reverse. *Middlemarch* owed its undeniable strength to the balance George Eliot achieved between her psychological interests and the acute social awareness within which she contained it. Its achievement would perhaps have been impossible had the general literary awareness not been so socially involved. This nourishment of sensibility with social interests, and the nourishment of political intelligence with feeling, are perhaps some of the criteria of a really important literature; and literature may be felt to suffer coarsening or emasculation whenever the balance is upset. The decadence of English fiction is closely involved in this dissociation of the novelist from his society – a condition to some extent forced upon him; a condition against which a few, however, have attempted to struggle. The intensity of the struggle has often been the central criterion of a novelist's art – one thinks of Dickens, Lawrence and Scott Fitzgerald.

The social novel of Disraeli, Mrs Gaskell and Kingsley was not merely a coarse and unfortunate phenomenon. It represents something essential to the literary consciousness of the age, without which *Bleak House, Middlemarch* and *Felix Holt* (the political excellence of which has suffered quite unjustifiable lack of appreciation) would have been impossible. *Felix Holt* is in fact refreshing because it is the work of a sensibility concerning itself with precisely political themes. It is depressingly unusual (remembering *1984* and *Brave New World*) to meet with so intelligent and sensitive a political interest in the novel. And the same may be claimed for Disraeli and Mrs Gaskell, as of course for Dickens himself. In them we find the full flourishing of the Victorian political awareness directed into the novel. *Sybil* and *Mary Barton* present as poignantly as Dickens the condition of industrial England, and, within it, the condition of the English industrial child.

Disraeli's power lies in his range, and the intellectual focus he brings to integrate that range into a coherent analysis of early Victorian society. His weakness comes when he focuses that analysis for the purposes of a political idealism, the revival of a feudal paternal aristocracy, manifestly irrelevant to the political possibilities of his times. Then he betrays the distortion arising from deliberate selection of events.

Sybil was inspired by the Report of the Commission on the Employment of Young Persons and Children of 1842, and, like the novels of Mrs Gaskell and Kingsley, it must be read against the background of its evidence:

I'm a trapper in the Gamber pit. I have to trap without a light, and I'm scared. I never go to sleep. Sometimes I sing when I've a light, but not in the dark; I dare not sing then.

This was the testimony of a girl of eight. The Report gave the condition of the children in the mines in these terms:

Chained, belted, harnessed like dogs in a go-cart, black, saturated with wet, and more than half-naked – crawling upon their hands and feet, and dragging their heavy loads behind them – they present an appearance undescribably disgusting and unnatural.

In 1843 and 1844, Disraeli travelled extensively in the industrial areas. Thomas Duncombe, a fellow Member of Parliament, helped him to collect the information he needed of the conditions which were encouraging so effectively the spread of Chartism and trade unionism. *Sybil* analyses these conditions and the moral corruptions consequent upon them.

The interest of the novel ranges over the rural slums of the Marney estates, where a 'virtuous mother in the sacred pangs of childbirth gives forth another victim to our thoughtless civilization'. In Mowbray, the booming industrial town, interest immediately centres on the factory adolescents, no more than children in age, but artificially aged and corrupted by their condition. The first English Teddy boy appears in the character of Dandy Mick – 'he was about sixteen, with a lithe figure, and a handsome, faded, impudent face' – who cheeks the 'old-fashioned' Mother Carey. Confronted with not caring for his dying mother, he declares her only to be drunk:

'And if she is only drunk?' said Mother Carey. 'What makes her drink but toil?'

'That's a good one,' said the youth; 'I should like to know what my mother ever did for me, but give me treacle and laudanum when I was a baby to stop my tongue and fill my stomach.'

His female companions enter the scene; girls who had given up work at 'Trafford's Mill', where they had been offered education, because they 'couldn't stand the country', and needed 'company' – 'so many schools at Trafford's; couldn't stand it'.

There is no despair about these children, because times are good. The 'gaily-dressed' girls spend their leisure at the local palais, called evidently in those days 'The Temple'. They drink their expensive tea and keep their own households. *Mutatis mutandis* there is a strangely modern atmosphere about Disraeli's analysis:

'I think the world is turned upside downwards in these parts,' said Mother Carey. 'A brat like Mick Radley to live in a two-pair, with a wife and family, or as good, as he says. . . . Fathers and mothers goes for nothing.'

But these girls and Dandy Mick are scenery; with the creation of Devilsdust we are brought to the front of the drama. Devilsdust is the case of an industrial society bringing upon itself the nemesis of juvenile corruption and the destruction of itself through rabid radicalism in the form of 'physical force' Chartism. Devilsdust is the quintessentially deprived industrial child:

About a fortnight after his mother had introduced him into the world, she returned to her factory, and put her infant out to nurse – that is to say, she paid threepence a week to an old woman, who takes charge of these new-born babes for the day, and gives them back at night to their mothers, as they hurriedly return . . . to the dungeon or the den, which is still by courtesy called 'home'. The expense is not great: laudanum and treacle . . . affords these innocents a brief taste of the sweets of existence. . . . Infanticide is practised as extensively and as legally in England, as it is on the banks of the Ganges; a circumstance which apparently has not yet engaged the attention of the Society for the Propagation of the Gospel in Foreign Parts. . . . We cannot say he [Devildust] thrived; but he would not die. So, at two years of age, his mother being lost sight of . . . he was sent out in the street to 'play', in order to be run over. . . . They gave him no food; he foraged for himself, and shared with the dogs the garbage of the streets. . . . [He slept] with a dungheap at his head, and a cess-pool at his feet. . . .'

'Wandering' into a factory, to a job in a 'wadding hole' he becomes 'dark and melancholy, ambitious and discontented. . . . [He] never murmured, but read and pondered on the rights of labour, and sighed to vindicate his order.'

It is of course a mental characterization. There is an atmosphere of selective unreality. The politically-intended realism takes on the inevitable emotional unreality of a political *roman à thèse*. But Disraeli's political intention derives from an intense social perception. The following is in fact taken almost verbatim from the Report of the Royal Commission:

See, too, these emerge from the bowels of the earth! Infants of four and five years of age, many of them girls, pretty and still soft and timid; en-trusted with the fulfilment of most responsible duties. . . . Their labour indeed is not severe, for that would be impossible, but it is passed in darkness and solitude. They endure that punishment which philosophical philanthropy has invented for the direst criminals, and which those criminals deem more terrible than . . . death. . . . Hour after hour elapses, and all that reminds the infant trappers of the world they have quitted and that which they have joined, is the passage of the coal-wagons for which they open the air-doors of the galleries.

The mordant comment follows:

Sir Joshua, a man of genius and a courtly artist, struck by the seraphic countenance of Lady Alice Gordon, when a child of very tender years, painted the celestial visage in various attitudes on the same canvas, and styled the group of heavenly faces – guardian angels! We would say to some great master of the pencil, Mr Landseer, or Mr Etty, go thou to the little trappers and do likewise!

The theme of the book is the moral destruction of the labouring classes, through the corrupting influences of class-war, and the distortion of relationships throughout society arising from the dereliction of the aristocracy from their social duty. Wholesome, serious working men, like the handloom weaver Warner, are compelled towards the moral corruption (for Disraeli) of radical politics: 'No food, no fuel, no furniture, and four human beings dependent on him, and lying in their wretched beds, because they had no clothes.' The loom, he declares, had 'gathered my children round my hearth with plenteousness and peace'. This image of childhood, lived in wholesomeness about the hearth, among the toil of the loom, is the essential antithesis of the childhood and youth depicted in Devilsdust and Dandy Mick, fictions materializing from the pages of the Report of the Royal Commission.

In *Mary Barton* (1848) Mrs Gaskell takes the same England. But, this time, it is a social novel by a religious novelist, and not by a politician. With Disraeli's *Sybil* we had a sequence of ideas, and the factual evidence to substantiate them. With *Mary Barton* the interest lies in the misery of the victims of an uncharitable and therefore immoral society. *Mary Barton* is the commentary of socially-conscious Nonconformacy. It draws no political conclusions. Its remedies are moral. Only by a renewal of human charity could the sufferings of an industrial society be relieved. Those sufferings are given as most acute when they involve the hunger, starvation and death of little children.

Mrs Gaskell's protest on their behalf was that of the Nonconformist conscience faced with a society in which the ethics of the Christian religion were so notoriously ignored. Living in Manchester, among philanthropists such as Thomas Wright and Travers Madge, she herself continually ministered to the needs of the industrial poor. Her account in *Mary Barton* of the slums of Ancoats and Ardwick rival for their realism the account of Engels himself. It is not surprising when we remember that she came to the writing of *Mary Barton* with its description of the infants and children of the Manchester slums in an effort to contain her grief at the death of her own infant son.

The inscription of the first chapter, reminiscent indeed of Blake, sets the theme:

> There's Richard he carries his baby,
> And Mary takes little Jane,
> And lovingly they'll be wandering
> Through field and briery lane.

It becomes an ironic comment indeed on the families who wander through the first chapter, carrying their children on their walks through the rural penumbra of industrial Lancashire. A sense of social loss is conveyed in the sharp juxtaposition of town and country. The industrial poor, 'couples with three or four toddlers', roam the alien countryside.

The central figure, Barton, is a 'thorough specimen of Manchester man'. He is physically stunted, since 'in his childhood he had suffered from the scanty living consequent upon bad times, and improvident habits'. His 'wan, colourless' features point up the youth of his daughter, Mary. His shadow falls across the image of the young girl picking her 'buds of hawthorn', and taking her infant brother into her arms with 'a girl's fondness for infants'. For the moment, the times are good. There is just a chance of survival for youth and the pleasures of family life. The opening chapters create a sense of life precariously surviving its industrial environment.

But social tragedy comes with the decline of trade, and personal tragedy when Barton's wife dies in childbirth. Embittered, Barton turns to sour social complaint. In company with the other unemployed of the Manchester slums he thinks of the rich living well, and of their own 'pale, uncomplaining wives at home', and of their 'wailing children asking in vain for food'. Barton remembers his own experience in the past when:

His little son, the apple of his eye . . . fell ill of the scarlet fever. Everything, the doctor said, depended on good nourishment, on generous living, to keep up the little fellow's strength. . . . Mocking words! when the commonest food in the house would not furnish one little meal. . . . Hungry himself, almost to an animal pitch of ravenousness, but with the bodily pain swallowed up in anxiety for his little sinking lad, he stood at one of the shop windows. . . . And out of this shop came Mrs Hunter! She crossed to her carriage, followed by the shopman loaded with purchases for a party. . . . Barton returned home with a bitter spirit of wrath in his heart, to see his only boy a corpse!

The novel turns to the 'terrible years' of 1839–41. Chapter VI is inscribed in this way:

> How little can the rich man know
> Of what the poor man feels. . . .
>
> *He* never saw his darlings lie,
>   Shivering, the flags his bed;
> *He* never heard that maddening cry,
>   'Daddy, a bit of bread'.

The gestures are crude indeed. But somehow *Mary Barton* convinces by its absolute sincerity. It has no sense whatever of writing for sensational effect, as you sometimes get, for example, with Zola. There is with Mrs Gaskell no sentimentality of the squalid.

Carson's Mill burns down, throwing its 'hands' into unemployment. The mothers of Ancoats are reduced to opium 'to still the hungry little ones. . . . It was mother's mercy'. Barton visits a friend dying of typhoid fever, and finds: 'three or four little children rolling on the damp, nay wet brick floor, through which the stagnant filthy moisture of the street oozed up'. The mother lies senseless on the floor: 'her little child crawled to her, and wiped with its fingers the thick-coming tears'. Starvation, disease, and death itself pervade the novel. Everywhere hatred and 'vindictive feelings exhibited themselves in rabid politics'. Out of misery came Chartism; and out of Chartism rejected, only further hatred and violence. The quotation of Samuel Bamford's hymn gives the religious motive of the work:

> God help the poor! An infant's feeble wail
>   Comes from yon narrow gateway, and behold!
> A female crouching there, so deathly pale,
>   Huddling her child, to screen it from the cold; . . .
>
> God help the poor! Behold yon famished lad,
> No shoes, nor hose, his wounded feet protect;
> . . . God help thee child forlorn!
> God help the poor!

For Mrs Gaskell the forlorn children of *Mary Barton* are the pathetic victims of a society in which the feelings of common human brotherhood are denied. Her complaint was not economic; it was not the inefficiency of *laiser aller* capitalist society which roused her anger; but the setting of selfish gain above the common good, especially when times were bad. Trouble should be shared by rich and poor; and those more fortunate should come to the aid of those in need. She was aware enough, however, to realize that often the poor were their own worst enemies. The ignorant Mrs Davenport, briefing Barton for his journey to London to petition the Queen, reminds him 'what a sore trial it is, this law o' theirs keeping children fra' factory work'. Barton turns on her, and undertakes to tell the Queen only that there are children 'born on wet flags, without a rag t'cover 'em'.

Mrs Gaskell never returned exactly to this industrial theme. Six years later, in *North and South*, she turned to the moral and emotional problems of a young woman offered the love of a man, an industrialist, with whom morally she is out of sympathy. The centre of interest now lies in the middle class; the working class functions outside the central interest of the novel. The nations of *North and South* are not the Two Nations of *Sybil*; but the two nations of rural, southern, ecclesiastical England and the mercantile, industrial North.

With Disraeli the child had been presented as a factor of his political analysis; with Mrs Gaskell it had been presented in the terms of an outraged Manchester Nonconformist conscience. With Charles Kingsley the child is presented from the indignation of radical Anglicanism. In both Disraeli and Mrs Gaskell the child was part only of the general portrayal of early Victorian England; with *Alton Locke* the whole interest is directed towards the case of a child and his later development, at the mercy of sweated labouring conditions and the severities of Puritan morality. Coming three years after *Jane Eyre* (1847), and in the same year as *David Copperfield*, it adopts the subjective form of narrative; it is in fact a fictitious autobiography of a boy who through the bitterness of his experience becomes a Chartist.

Alton Locke burns with unmistakable class-consciousness, through Kingsley's awareness of the horror to humanity perpetrated in the

slums and factories of the Industrial Revolution. A southern writer,
like Dickens, he had little direct contact with the heavy industries of
the North. He knew intimately, however, the artisan and trader
classes of London, and he took their miserable condition as symptomatic of a whole society given to the god of industrial progress without consideration for the human misery that might result. Fanny
Kingsley testified to the 'state of nervous prostration to which the
writing of the book reduced him'. He wrote against the background
of an appalling cholera epidemic in Bermondsey. His visits among
the sick there almost demented him. He sought interviews with
members of the Whig Government, and travelled specially to
Oxford to inform the Bishop of what he had seen, and to recruit his
sympathy. *Alton Locke* issued from the frenzy of his intense moral
and nervous tension.

It is therefore essentially a tract. Kingsley's own humanitarian
religion speaks through the voice of Locke himself. It is not so much
a novel as a vituperative tract, a magnificent diatribe, closely regulated, however, by Kingsley's acute intelligence. Even in its depiction
of the worst scenes of human horror there is a sharp reality, a definite
control. Its brutalities are not measured for their sensational literary
effect. If it loses aesthetically from its subjective vehemence, it is a
loss caused by Kingsley's conscience. It has all the naïve anger of the
desperately injured and enraged animal. Kingsley was neither
novelist nor artist. He assumed the technique of the novel to convey a
sermon, a social morality.

The child, Alton, is born into the urban prison of London:

My earliest recollections are of a suburban street; of its jumble of little shops
and little terraces, each exhibiting some fresh variety of capricious ugliness
... dusty stunted lilacs and balsam poplars ... little scraps of garden. ...

As a child he sits:

in the little dingy, foul, reeking, twelve foot square back-yard where huge
smoky party-walls shut out every breath of air, and almost all the light of
heaven ... all of a sudden the horror of the place came over me; those grim
prison-walls above ... the dreary, sloppy, broken pavement; the horrible
stench of the stagnant cesspools; the utter want of form, colour, life, in the
whole place.

The selected realism ('dusty stunted lilacs ... little scraps of gardens') is reminiscent of Dickens himself; and the 'utter want of form, colour, life, in the whole place' seems to point directly on to Lawrence – 'the utter negation of the gladness of life, the utter absence of the instinct for shapely beauty which every bird and beast has ... all went by ugly, ugly, ugly. . . .'

Obsessed with the squalor, the boy dreams of Pacific Islands, wondering also at the life of the wagoners who passed the house nightly for the London markets. There is a sure echo of Wordsworth and Coleridge in the image of the child deprived of joy and wonder in his urban prison; the tension between urban restraint and the child's wonder and delight in Nature is essentially of the Romantics: 'I knew every leaf and flower of the little front garden; every cabbage and rhubarb plant ... was wonderful to me ... I brought home wild-flowers, and chance beetles and butterflies. . . .'

But although the novel is so consciously *à thèse*, Kingsley obtains something of the child's-eye view. His mother walks the boy along the urban streets 'holding my hand tight the whole way' to keep him from temptation. When his mother is visited by missionaries, the child asks his own cogently awkward questions, wanting passionately to believe in the wonder and mystery of the mission-field. His disenchantment is real as he watches the 'squat, red-faced, pig-eyed, low-browed man, with great soft lips' greedily help himself so generously to the sugar the child knew was so hardly come by. The child's 'instinct true, about human character' comes into play; the quality of the morality of overseas missionary work is judged by the child from the quality, in terms of sensitivity, of those who propagated it. In these small episodes, Kingsley obtains something of a dramatization for his theme and achieves something close in kind to Dickens's own major achievement in a similar genre.

The child's mother is a central interest of the early chapters: 'My mother moved by rule and method; by God's law. . . . She seldom smiled. . . . She never commanded twice, without punishing.' She had no affection for her children, because they 'were still "children of wrath and of the devil". . . . Our God, or gods, were hell, the rod, and the ten commandments, and public opinion.'

Kingsley's attack upon the severities of the Puritan treatment of children falls within the tradition of romantic indignation against the Trimmers and Barbaulds. Speaking as 'a Christian – an orthodox Churchman (if you require that shibboleth)', he analyses the 'terrible strugglings of this great, awful, blessed time'. And the essential struggle was to release Christianity from the deadening negativity of Puritan morality: 'Oh, those "Sabbaths"! days, not of rest, but utter weariness, when the beetles and flowers were put by, and there was nothing to fill up the long vacuity, but books of which I could not understand a word; when play, laughter . . . were all forbidden.'

For Kingsley, this kind of religion had little relevance to mid-Victorian society. He did not see its miseries deriving from the original vice of man's nature. For him, sin was the 'will of the world and the devil, of man's avarice and laziness and ignorance'. The 'contempt' into which Christianity had fallen in the 'minds of thinking workmen' arose from its essential irrelevance to a 'generation to whom God's love shines out in every tree and flower and hedge-side bird'. To the working-man, children were not 'children of wrath and of the devil'; but rather 'in the smiles of their innocent children', men 'see the heaven they have lost – the messages of baby-cherubs, made in God's own image'.

In Kingsley the concept of the romantic child merges with Christianity to become a theology of childhood Innocence. *Alton Locke* is an interesting fusion of Wordsworthian naturalism with Christian humanitarianism, a fusion of the secular romantic tradition about the child with Anglican compassion for human nature; a fusion which Kingsley perhaps best expressed in his *Water Babies*.

His revolt against the Puritan doctrine of the child's 'fallen nature' is conveyed in *Alton Locke* through the boy, Alton's, own revolt: 'he revolts instinctively' against the religion of his mother; Kingsley believes, 'by a divine inspiration'. And the child's 'instinct', his intuitive knowledge of his own divine nature, leads him to write his first hymn, denying the doctrine of Calvinist 'particular redemption'.

> Jesus, He loves one and all;
> Jesus, He loves children small;
> Their souls are sitting round His feet,
> On high, before His mercy-seat.

This Christian Rousseauism was of course open to the sentimentalities of secular Rousseauism itself. With Kingsley's hymn we are not far removed from the whole ethos of 'All things bright and beautiful', and of 'Gentle Jesus, meek and mild'.

Following this initial assertion of Alton's innocent nature, Kingsley then proceeds to recount the child's initiation into 'experience'. The 'pale, consumptive, rickety, weakly boy, all forehead and no muscle' shambles along at his mother's side, 'with a beating heart', into his life as an 'apprentice' in a tailor's workshop. Sent out from an 'unconscious paradise into an evil world', the child is overawed by the horror of his working conditions and the bawdiness of his fellow-workers. The re-creation of the life of the workshop is as authentic as the comparable scenes in *David Copperfield*. A sense of deprivation grows on the boy; with adolescence he becomes a free-thinking Chartist. He breaks with his mother's religion, and is turned from home, because she refused to see him as a 'child', but as an 'incarnate fiend' a 'child of wrath and the devil'. Through reading, through his friendship with an old Scottish bookseller, and most especially through a visit to the Dulwich Art Gallery, the boy finally awakes 'out of the narrow dullness of Puritanism'.

The drama of the novel centres upon the tension between the youth's social conscience and the demands of personal love. It is enacted against a finely described social background, in which Kingsley continues to express his central concern with the condition of childhood. Chartists, he declares, were goaded by 'seeing possible heaven' in the shape of children 'slipping away':

While our little children die around us, like lambs beneath the knife, of cholera and typhus and consumption, and all the diseases which the good time can and will prevent; which, as science has proved, and you the rich confess, might be prevented at once, if you dared to bring in one bold and comprehensive measure, and not sacrifice yearly the lives of thousands to the idol of vested interests, and a majority in the House. Is it not hard to men who smart beneath such things to help crying aloud – 'Thou cursed Moloch-Mammon, take my life if you wilt; let me die in the wilderness, for I have deserved it; but these little ones in mines and factories, in typhus-cellars, and Tooting pandemoniums, what have they done? If not in their fathers' cause, yet still in theirs, were it so great a sin to die upon a barricade?'

The point is dramatized when Locke goes to Bermondsey to visit the house of a 'sweated tailor', Downes. He finds the man's family dead:

There was his little Irish wife: – dead – and naked; the wasted white limbs gleamed in the lurid light; the unclosed eyes stared . . . and on each side of her a little, shrivelled, impish child-corpse – the wretched man had laid their arms round the dead mother's neck – and there they slept, their hungering and wailing over at last for ever; the rats had been busy already with them – but what matter to them now?

This passage gives the strength of Kingsley's particular clarity. But in *Alton Locke*, as in *Sybil* and *Mary Barton*, the interest is seldom psychological. Even so the character of the young Alton conveys something closer to the consciousness of a young child than anything in Disraeli or Mrs Gaskell. For the social novel as a whole, however, children were agents in a moral or political thesis. It was essentially a propagandist literature, employing feelings about the child established a generation before. There is already a feeling that the image of the romantic child has become to some extent external and applied.

In Marryat's *Peter Simple* (1834) and Charlotte Brontë's *Jane Eyre* (1847) there is, however, an interest which is recognizably 'psychological'. Even though the Marryat is much more a tale of youth and adventure than a novel of childhood, it deals sensitively with the situation of boyhood confronted with the cruelties of a harsh environment. With *Jane Eyre* we have something much more significant, an account of a child, conveyed from within its consciousness. The choice of the autobiographical form, and the sensationalism of the emotion, increase its impression of vivid 'reality'. Charlotte Brontë seeks a complete identity of feeling between her 'victim' and the reader, and nothing intrudes, least of all the writer's judgement, between the reader and the heroine's psyche, as it is displayed. A sympathy for the heroine is continuously cultivated, and the pathetic experiences of her childhood plainly contribute to the calculated effect. Jane Eyre is perhaps the first heroine in English fiction to be given, chronologically at least, as a psychic whole. Nothing, in fact, quite like *Jane Eyre* had ever been attempted before.

But if sympathy, and emotional realism, are the effects intended, everything depends upon the quality of the sympathy and experience evoked. It is clearly not the sort of sympathy, for example, created for Fanny in *Mansfield Park*, whose situation as an unwanted child in a 'superior' household is factually very similar. Jane Austen, however, was clearly not so much concerned with the potentialities for pathos in Fanny's situation, as with developing through her a means for intelligent and sensitive commentary upon the irresponsible, self-indulgent behaviour of the Bertram children and the Crawfords. *Mansfield Park* is as much a novel about education as any in the language, and for this reason it was necessary for the story to begin with Fanny's childhood. But the pathos of her situation is continuously disciplined by the comedy of Lady Bertram and Mrs Norris. There is no feeling that the writer wishes to attract the reader's vicarious self-pity.

And this, it seems, is exactly what *Jane Eyre* sets out to do; perhaps because everything in its author herself had been similarly attracted towards the situation of her heroine. The situation of the cruelly-deprived orphan and, by extension, the cruelly-deprived adult very clearly sets Charlotte Brontë's imagination aflame. The reader scarcely ever escapes the pressure of that omnipresent 'I'.

I now stood in the empty hall; before me was the breakfast-room door, and I stopped, intimidated and trembling. What a miserable little poltroon had fear, engendered of unjust punishment, made of me in those days! I feared to return to the nursery, and feared to go forward to the parlour; ten minutes I stood in agitated hesitation: the vehement ringing of the breakfast-room bell decided me; I *must* enter.

'Who could want me?' I asked inwardly, as with both hands I turned the stiff door-handle. . . . The handle turned, the door unclosed, and passing through and curtseying low, I looked up at – a black pillar! such, at least, appeared to me, at first sight, the straight, narrow, sable-clad shape standing erect on the rug: the grim face at the top was like a carved mask, placed above the shaft by way of capital.

The passage is typical. Its intimidation, fear, 'agitated hesitation', set the emotional key. It catches of course, in a way very close to Dickens's *Oliver Twist* and *David Copperfield*, the child's view of the world, grotesque, and magnifying, both physically and emotionally, the impressions of its environment. But whereas with Dickens the method evokes a feeling of reality, and an attitude to Oliver Twist, say, as a child, the purpose of the emotional realism in the account of the childhood of Jane Eyre is used to establish certain basic attitudes towards the heroine, sympathies which are transferred to Jane Eyre the 'adult'. Something akin to this partially spoils *David Copperfield*, which never quite extricates itself from the self-pitying motive of its early chapters, brilliantly done as they undoubtedly are.

The early chapters of *Jane Eyre* establish the heroine as the victim. They insist on her victimization, her loneliness, her isolation. The autobiographical form itself serves to create this sense of an isolated, trapped psyche, at the mercy of an unsympathetic and actively cruel environment. Its active cruelty is indeed a powerful concomitant. There is a disturbing relish about the account of the physical and moral tortures she endures. It is as if she enjoys, masochistically, the experiences of her persecution. She seems almost to provoke her self-torment. There is no end to the spiral of deprivation, and its continuously intensifying craving for love. Every twist of the knife intensifies the expectation of gratification. Everything is carefully prepared for the extended sado-masochistic relation between Jane and Rochester which lies, of course, at the heart of the novel. Jane's whole childhood and life are an extension of that initial: '. . . dreadful to me was the coming home in the raw twilight, with nipped fingers and toes, and a heart saddened by the chidings of Bessie, the nurse, and humbled by the consciousness of my physical inferiority to Eliza, John, and Georgiana Reed'.

Unconsciously perhaps, the novel portrays the psychic condition of deprived childhood, with its incipient 'persecution mania' compelling her to behave delinquently to justify her sense of persecution and thus obtain satisfaction. Jane Eyre is very much Dickens's Miss Wade of *Little Dorrit*; but that is an altogether other account of an adult's continuing to live a childhood's deprivation and consequent sense of inferiority. Miss Wade evokes no 'sympathy' beyond that usually felt for the emotionally ill. With *Jane Eyre* there is none of Dickens's distance between author and his creation, and the force of the prose is such as to narrow any distance of intelligent criticism which might lie between the reader's appreciation and the heroine's feelings. We are borne along on the crest of the mania:

Habitually obedient to John, I came up to his chair: he spent some three minutes in thrusting out his tongue at me ... I knew he would soon strike, and while dreading the blow, I mused on the disgusting and ugly appearance of him who would presently deal it ... all at once, without speaking, he struck suddenly and strongly. I tottered. ...

... I saw him lift and poise the book and stand in act to hurl it ... the volume was flung, it hit me, and I fell, striking my head against the door and cutting it. The cut bled, the pain was sharp. ...

Why was I always suffering, always browbeaten, always accused, for ever condemned? Why could I never please? Why was it useless to try to win any one's favour? ... I dared commit no fault: I strove to fulfil every duty; and I was termed naughty and tiresome, sullen and sneaking, from morning to noon, and from noon to night.

The episode in the 'red-room', with all its intense 'realism' of childhood's claustrophobia, heightens the portrayal of the persecution. But a moment's extrication from the pressure of the very powerfully neurotic prose brings the suspicion that the 'facts' of the child's experiences with the Reed family have been carefully selected as instruments of an emotional torture.

The situation continues at Lowood:

As yet I had spoken to no one, nor did anybody seem to take notice of me; I stood lonely enough: but to that feeling of isolation I was accustomed; it did not oppress me much.

'... I sank prostrate with my face to the ground. Now I wept: Helen Burns was not here; nothing sustained me; left to myself I abandoned myself, and my tears watered the boards. I had meant to be so good, and to do so much at Lowood: to make so many friends, to earn respect, and win affection ... now, here I lay again crushed and trodden on; and could I ever rise more?

'... if others don't love me, I would rather die than live – I cannot bear to be solitary and hated, Helen. Look here; to gain some real affection from you, or Miss Temple, or any other whom I truly love, I would willingly submit to have the bone of my arm broken, or to let a bull toss me, or to stand behind a kicking horse, and let it dash its hoof at my chest.'

The masochism has further definition when, eight years later, she decides to leave Lowood:

I desired liberty; for liberty I gasped; for liberty I uttered a prayer ... I abandoned it and framed a humbler supplication; for change, stimulus: that petition, too, seemed swept off into vague space: 'Then,' I cried, half desperate, 'grant me at least a new servitude! ... A new servitude! There is something in that,' I soliloquized ... 'I know there is, because it does not sound too sweet; it is not like such words as Liberty, Excitement, Enjoyment: delightful sounds truly; but no more than sounds for me; and so hollow and fleeting that it is mere waste of time to listen to them. But Servitude! ... Any one may serve. ...'

A 'new servitude' precisely defines her subsequent relation with Rochester, with all its extended self-hurting, frustrating eroticism. To see the psychological realism of Jane Eyre's childhood for what it is, is to be prepared for this:

'Why are you silent, Jane?'
I was experiencing an ordeal: a hand of fiery iron grasped my vitals. Terrible moment: full of struggle, blackness, burning! ... One dear word comprised my intolerable duty – 'Depart!'
'Jane, you understand what I want of you? Just this promise – "I will be yours, Mr Rochester."'
'Mr Rochester, I will *not* be yours.'
Another long silence.
'Jane,' recommenced he, with a gentleness that broke me down with grief, and turned me stone-cold with ominous terror – for this still voice was the pant of a lion rising –
'Jane, do you mean to go one way in the world, and to let me go another?'
'I do.'
'Jane' (bending towards and embracing me), 'do you mean it now?'

The insistence of Mr Rochester's 'Jane' certainly tightens the 'grasp' of the 'hand of fiery iron'. The disordered, disjointed movement of the prose through colons, semi-colons, ejaculations, and simple sentences, is perhaps one of the most immediately striking things about *Jane Eyre*, expressing the disorder of its heroine's emotions. There is the pressure of a neurotic speech-rhythm in the autobiographical prose:

That kind master, who could not sleep now, was waiting with impatience for day. He would send for me in the morning; I should be gone. He would have me sought for: vainly. He would feel himself forsaken; his love rejected: he would suffer; perhaps grow desperate. I thought of this too. My hand moved towards the lock; I caught it back, and glided on.

The account of Jane Eyre's childhood would be moving enough if it were the intentional account of a child's delusional mania resulting from the deprivation of family love. Its intention is, however, otherwise. Jane Eyre is indeed pathetic, a victim – but not quite in the way Charlotte Brontë intended us to sympathize with her. As a portrayal of childhood, it certainly made its impact. It is interesting to note Sidney Dobell's appreciation:

Who that remembers early childhood, can read without emotion the little Jane Eyre's night journey to Lowood? How firmly, yet how unconsciously, are those peculiar aspects of things which cease with childhood developed in this simple history! . . . That feeling of unlimited vastness in the world around. . . . This 'I' that seems to have no inheritance in the earth, is an eternity with a heritage in all heavens . . . a kind of veiled divinity – in all these 'I's' and 'me's'.

A contemporary reviewer of *David Copperfield* drew comparisons between the two novels. Its portrayal of childhood leads inevitably to comparison with Dickens; even though it is a comparison which suggests differences rather than similarities. Dickens is the central figure in the transference of the romantic child into the Victorian novel.

CHAPTER 5

The Child in Dickens

I

To write of the child in Dickens is not only to survey Victorian childhood; it is to write of Dickens himself, both as man and artist. The child was at the heart of his interest; at the centre of the Dickens world. There is perhaps no other major English novelist whose achievement was so closely regulated by a feeling for childhood. And yet, Dr Batho and Professor Dobrée, in their *Victorians and After*, put it this way:

The pity is that this giant never grew up intellectually; he could not enter into the minds of grown men as Browning could; but he could, and most brilliantly did, into the minds of youths up to about twenty. David Copperfield is without a possible rival. But where Dickens touched upon social reform, anywhere in fact where he began to think, he falls below the level of second-rate, though the generous indignation that he shows is worthy of a full and complete man.

But the case to be made about Dickens is not that there was any dissociation between his feelings for childhood and youth and the understanding he brought to adults and their relation to Victorian society; it is not that his constant interest in children prevented his entering 'into the minds of grown men as Browning could'; but rather that his feeling for childhood enriched his imaginative responses as a whole. His own experience as a child, and his awareness of children in the society about him, served to create a basis of feeling from which he launched the fundamental criticism of life for which his mature art is so remarkable. It is within the context of this criticism that the child in Dickens is to be considered.

It has become accepted that Dickens went beyond the mere description of the surface comedy of life, for which in the past he has earned so much misleading, if justifiable praise. His superficial achievements in fact often conceal the deeper intentions of his mature art. Dickens's continuous interest lay in the life of the feelings.

Society for him is an emanation from the world of human feeling, upon which, in rebound, it had in turn its deepest influence. He set his art in the world of creative or destructive sensibility. In his work, the external world materializes from the feelings of the individuals who compose it. It is upon the feelings of its victims that for him the external world has its most significant effect. The drama of his work lies so frequently within the theme of the oppressor and the oppressed. His own childhood, and the fate of so many children of his time, were the symbol of the crimes perpetrated by a harsh society upon its victims; and the significant area of those crimes lay within their victims' inmost feelings. The child in Dickens lives at the point of impact between the world of innocent awareness and the world of man's insensitivity to man.

This experience of Dickens in his own childhood worked for both strength and weakness. Where he failed to extricate his feelings from a too close identification between his own past misery as a child and the general miseries of children in early Victorian England, where he failed to control his experience sufficiently, where feeling outran sense, he blurred and undermined his art. But where he exerted that control, his achievement goes beyond the reach of criticism which talks of 'giants' who never 'grew up intellectually'.

To stress the achievement, however, is not to deny the weakness. It requires no special acuteness to discover his major weakness, that his uncontrolled fertility made him often more of an 'entertainer' than an artist 'seriously involved'. It needs only half an eye to detect the sentimentalities, especially towards children, to discern the poor little drudge of the blacking factory, corroding his feelings in torments of self-pity. He is there on almost every other page. But it is the other page, between, that deserves its due attention.

It has been perhaps disastrous for Dickens's general reputation that he became so swiftly and so indiscriminately a 'classic'. His comparatively early works, issuing in a stream of youthful invention scarcely equalled at any time elsewhere, were quickly created into a popular world of Dickens in which his more serious, and less easily assimilated achievement was neglected. It is as relevant to take *Pickwick* and *The Old Curiosity Shop* as representative Dickens, as to take the tedious vulgarities of *The Taming of the Shrew* as significant

Shakespeare, or to attend as seriously to *The Trespasser* as, say, to *St Mawr*.

The relevance of Dickens's childhood to his art is indeed reminiscent of Lawrence, whose response to civilized life was no less insistent, and whose childhood and youth at Eastwood similarly informed his creative work as a whole. So with Dickens, the loss of his childhood security at Chatham, and the episode of the blacking warehouse, the rub between what the ideal might have been and the realities of what so depressingly was, can be discerned throughout the novels. As a child Dickens experienced that initial irritation of spirit and deprivation which can frequently be the source of either neurosis and criminality, or of a passionate but valid social criticism. With both novelists there was indeed the tendency to ineffectual and often irresponsible outcry, the same ever-present danger of over-statement, of squandering emotion in self-pity and social recrimination. With both men there was an inability to exorcize, perhaps to forgive the past. It is of course the quality and intensity of this first awareness which often controls the quality of the whole creative life of an author, and his greatness may in some way depend upon his capacity to sustain the continuity of his initial response, to escape the shades of the 'prison-house' of 'maturity', and sit outside, as Dickens did so successfully in *Little Dorrit*, and, with the free imaginative responses of the child, consider the lives of the prisoners within.

Dickens's mature interest lay in conveying through the medium of a dramatized morality the impact of the conflict between goodness and evil upon the feelings of his characters. To discuss him as a realist, to discuss the exactitude of his social commentary, is to confuse the essential purposes of his art. His account of the world was continuously moral.

In the early novels, evil is expressed through the characters of particular individuals, in Fagin and Monks, and Ralph Nickleby. Later he came to see evil as embodied in society itself and its institutions, of which individual men are either innocent victims or culpable agents. But whether evil is expressed through individuals, or through the institutions of a corrupt society, goodness is always characterized through individuals remarkable for their generous flow of human feeling. The quality of the characterization may change, the account become more subtle, but the warm-hearted, generous, kindly individual is always there, suffering the oppressions of evil, or combating the influences of an inhuman and corrupt society.

But to talk of goodness and evil is to talk in abstractions of an art which is never abstracted. The morality is conveyed, and again one is reminded of Lawrence, through the immediate experience of the characters in the drama. There is nothing in Dickens so abstracted as Eliot's:

> Unreal City,
> Under the brown fog of a winter dawn,
> A crowd flowed over London Bridge, so many,
> I had not thought death had undone so many.

The 'fog everywhere' in the opening pages of *Bleak House* is experienced in the lives of the individuals who endure it. It cruelly pinched 'the toes and fingers' of the 'shivering little 'prentice boy' on the deck of the Thames' skipper; and 'chance people on the bridges' were 'peeping over the parapets into a nether sky of fog, with fog all round them, as if they were up in a balloon, and hanging in the misty clouds'. With Dickens there are people in the fog, individualized, experiencing the fog. There is a fundamental difference between Dickens's human perception and Eliot's abstraction.

The conflict of Life with the forces of Experience brings us close to the central interest of romantic art, and places Dickens as heir to the romantic poets. It is part of his considerable achievement that he used the technique of the novel to express a moral and symbolic reality only previously expressed through the medium of poetry. When faced with this sort of interest in Dickens it is possible to talk of a common nineteenth-century sensibility, which contains Blake, Wordsworth, Dickens, and one would say Matthew Arnold. Their unifying factor was a certain dissatisfaction, a humanist concern. Their singularity was a matter of the solutions they proposed and the individuality of their techniques. The difference between the *Songs of Innocence and Experience* and *Dombey and Son*, or between *Culture and Anarchy* and *Hard Times*, is more a question of method than of intention. In a disintegrating culture it is the common factors which are easily missed, and which it is sometimes valuable to distinguish.

At some point in his career, Dickens saw his own childhood experience as part of the general experience of his time. From that awareness came his determination to convey the struggle of innocence with evil, which became the pivot of his mature art. The child became for him the symbol of sensitive feelings anywhere in a society maddened with the pursuit of material progress. The novels of Dickens are an account of the plight of human sensibility under the cast-iron shackles of the Victorian world.

This central enthusiasm which Dickens felt for Life as opposed to the forces of human misery and death is strikingly given in a passage in *Nicholas Nickleby*, where he describes the people of Hampton racecourse. The theatre, the circus, the travelling showman, Punch and Judy players, were often identified with the idea of human joy in his work. In them the play of emotion and imagination was free. They lay outside the Benthamite and Malthusian prospectus, outside the regulations of a money-economy. He is writing here as a young man of twenty-six:

It was one of those scenes of life and animation, caught in its very brightest and freshest moments, which can scarcely fail to please: for if the eye be tired of show and glare, or the ear be weary with a ceaseless round of noise, the one may repose, turn almost where it will, on eager, happy, and expectant faces, and the other deaden all consciousness of more annoying sounds in those of mirth and exhilaration. Even the sunburnt faces of gipsy children, half naked though they be, suggest a drop of comfort. It is a pleasant thing to see that the sun has been there; to know that the air and light are on them every day; to feel that they *are* children, and lead children's lives; that if their pillows be damp, it is with the dews of Heaven, and not with tears; that the limbs of their girls are free, and that they are not crippled by distortions, imposing an unnatural and horrible penance upon their sex; that their lives are spent from day to day at least among the waving trees, and not in the midst of dreadful engines which make young children old before they know what childhood is, and give them the exhaustion and infirmity of age, without, like age, the privilege to die. God send that old nursery tales were true, and that gipsies stole such children by the score!

It is a remarkable passage. Its enthusiasm is its own commentary. Its emotions lie deep within the romantic ethos. Might it be that these children of Hampton racecourse, with their sunlight, were consciously opposed to the 'writing ghosts', as Gissing calls them, of the world of Squeers?

II

'A not very robust child'   *Preface to Nicholas Nickleby*
'A not-over-particularly-taken-care-of boy'
Dickens: *Letter to Washington Irving*

The facts of Dickens's childhood are clear. Living first at Portsea and London, and then at Chatham, he was a happy child until he was ten. Returning to London in 1822, the Dickens family came upon hard times, and the rest of his childhood is a tale of neglect and deeply-felt misery.

The Chatham days are a very ordinary story of a vital, if 'not very robust child', absorbing his first experience of life. They would hold no special interest, if they were not the story of the boyhood of a genius, and if they had not become, by comparison with what came after, one of the major influences of Dickens's emotional life. It is a simple tale of curiosities aroused and affection requited, of excursions into the Kentish countryside, of amateur theatricals and visits to London for the pantomime, of jaunts with his father of a Sunday morning to sing comic songs to the admiring frequenters of the dockyard taverns.

All in fact went happily, normally, and well, until John Dickens was recalled to London. Already, perhaps unknown to the boy, there had been increasing financial worry. Matters became worse upon the return of the family to London. For a time the boy was left at Chatham to complete his school term; but, at length, one very wet morning, he was put on the coach, the Blue-Eyed Maid, for London. Later he recalled the 'damp straw' in which he had been packed 'like game, and forwarded carriage-paid, to the Cross Keys, Wood Street, Cheapside'. There was no other 'inside passenger, and I consumed my sandwiches in solitude and dreariness, and it rained hard all the way, and I thought that life was sloppier than I had expected to find it'.

It is a turning-point of the utmost importance in Dickens's life. It continued to rain for him 'all the way' throughout the rest of his childhood, and indeed for so many of the multitude of children who haunt his fiction.

He found his family in Bayham Street, Camden Town, 'about the poorest part of the London suburbs then', as Forster put it, 'and the house was a mean small tenement, with a wretched little back garden abutting on a squalid court'. Beset by financial worry, the family neglected the child:

As I thought in the little back garret in Bayham Street, of all I had lost in losing Chatham, what would I have given, if I had had anything to give, to have been sent back to any other school, to have been taught something anywhere.

The family's fortunes declined pathetically. 'I know that we got on very badly with the butcher and the baker, and that very often we had not too much for dinner.' Tradesmen bawled in the passageway of the house, while his father cowered in a room above. Little by little the furniture went, and, with it, the eighteenth-century novels he had read at Chatham. Sent to sell them to a bookseller on the Hampstead Road, this must have seemed to him the saddest thing of all.

Worse, however, followed. A relation, James Lamert, suggested to the impoverished parents that their son might be usefully employed in his blacking warehouse at Hungerford Stairs on the riverside. For an extra six valuable shillings a week, the family was willing, as presumably were so many others of the time, to forget the degradation of the work involved, especially for a boy of ability and painful sensibility:

It is wonderful to me [he said later, in the autobiographical fragment he wrote before coming to *David Copperfield*], how I could have been so easily cast away at such an age. It is wonderful to me, that, even after my descent into the poor little drudge I had been since we came to London, no one had compassion enough on me, a child of singular abilities, quick, eager, delicate, and soon hurt, bodily or mentally, to suggest that something might have been spared, as certainly it might have been, to place me at any common school. . . . No one made any sign. My mother and father were quite satisfied. They could hardly have been more so, if I had been twenty years of age, distinguished at a grammar school, and going to Cambridge.

The world of the warehouse was ugly; his new companions raw and uncultivated:

No words can express the secret agony of my soul, as I sank into this companionship; compared these everyday associates with those of my happier childhood; and felt my early hopes of growing up to be a learned and distinguished man, crushed in my breast. . . . My whole nature was so penetrated with the grief and humiliation of such considerations, that, even now – famous and caressed and happy – I often forget in my dreams that I have a dear wife and children – even that I am a man – and wander desolately back to that time of my life.

Eleven days after he began work at the warehouse, his father was arrested at a suit for £40, and after a few days found himself in the Marshalsea. In a few weeks the family followed him there. The boy was boarded out however to a certain Mrs Roylance, and continued to work at Mr Lamert's.

The fortunes of the family improved. John Dickens's mother died, and his debts were settled out of the old lady's savings. Released from the Marshalsea, he settled with his family in an even poorer district of Camden Town. But nothing was said of releasing the boy from his wretched employment, until upon a quarrel between Lamert and his father the boy was withdrawn. Even so, his mother went to the pains of visiting Lamert in an effort to compose the quarrel. This 'warmth', as he put it, on his mother's part for him to go back, he never forgot: 'I do not write resentfully or angrily, for I know how all these things have worked together to make me what I am; but I never afterwards forgot, I never shall forget, I never can forget, that my mother was warm for my being sent back.'

If it is suggested that Dickens's reaction to his five months' experience at the blacking warehouse was obsessive and morbid, it should be remembered that the boy was in a state of complete despair and bewilderment during this time. An adult sees through and around his predicament. To the child, despair is a total experience. Humanity only learns slowly perhaps that bad things usually come to an end. For an intelligent and imaginative child to have affection and sympathy unaccountably withdrawn will cause a trauma from which he will suffer throughout life. There is no doubt of the deep psychological wounding which Dickens suffered at the hands of his parents, and of the inevitable conclusions he drew as to the power of money in a society which devoted so much energy to the creation of wealth, and was so specially blind to the privations of the poor. As a child, Dickens undoubtedly received the wound from which so much of his sentimentality springs. But the experience was not only traumatic; for he gained no less an awareness of society and 'experience' which served him throughout his creative life.

III

'The work of Dickens's whole career was an attempt to digest these early shocks and hardships, to explain them to himself, to justify himself in relation to them, to give an intelligible and tolerable picture of a world in which such things could occur.'

Edmund Wilson: *The Wound and the Bow*

Without Dickens the Victorian awareness would have been different; England would have felt differently, if indeed in certain ways at all, and most surely differently about children. In his *Dickens World*, Humphry House recounts the development of Dickens's awareness of his society. The nostalgic, antiquated atmosphere of the early novels did not survive into the forties. The lack of social immediacy of *Pickwick* and *Nicholas Nickleby* may have derived in part from the eighteenth-century novels Dickens read at Chatham; but more significantly from the fact that by living in London, he was insulated from the effect, and more especially from the sight of the industrial and social changes that were in process in the Midlands and North a generation before.

With the development of the railways, however – in 1846 alone some 4,500 miles of new track were authorized by Parliament – the exact state of the country became revealed. The metal roads laid bare the true anatomy of the new society. They both revealed the change and accelerated it. The physical realities of the change were brought sharply home to Dickens when he returned to Chatham in later life, and found everything so altered. He went back to the old house in Ordnance Terrace, but, as Forster describes the visit, the playing-field had been 'swallowed' by a railway station. 'It was gone, with its two beautiful trees of hawthorn; and where the hedge, the turf, and all the buttercups and daisies had been, there was nothing but the stoniest of jolting roads.'

The sense of physical change is strikingly conveyed in the novels. In *Dombey and Son*, when Susan Nipper makes that last desperate journey to the area north of Somers Town, to find the old nurse who would have brought warmth of affection to the dying Paul, she finds the house had vanished:

There was no such place as Staggs's Gardens. It had vanished from the earth. Where the old rotten summer-houses once had stood, palaces now reared their heads, and granite columns of gigantic girth opened a vista to the railway world beyond. The miserable waste-ground, where the refuse-matter had been heaped of yore, was swallowed up and gone. . . . Bridges that had led to nothing, led to villas, gardens, churches, healthy public walks. . . . There were railway hotels, coffee-houses . . . railway plans, maps, views, wrappers, bottles, sandwich-boxes, and time-tables. . . . Railway omnibuses, railway streets. . . . There was even railway time, observed in clocks, as if the sun itself had given in . . .

The whole passage (which should be read in its entirety) expresses that attraction and distaste that so many of the time must have felt. The 'wholesome comforts and conveniences . . . the villas, gardens, churches' are balanced against the 'monster train' and the passage ends significantly with: 'But Staggs's Gardens had been cut up root and branch. Oh woe the day, when "not a rood of English ground" – laid out in Staggs's Gardens – is secure!'

From the same novel, *Dombey and Son* (it is very much the turning-point of his art), we have the following description of the northern suburbs where the great iron roads drove relentlessly through an area where he himself had lived, to the heart of the capital:

The second home is on the other side of London, near to where the busy great north road of bygone days is silent and almost deserted, except by wayfarers who toil along on foot. . . . The neighbourhood in which it stands has as little of the country to recommend it, as it has of the town. It is neither of the town nor country. The former, like the giant in his travelling boots, has made a stride and passed it, and has set his brick and mortar heel a long way in advance; but the intermediate space between the giant's feet, as yet, is only blighted country and not town. .... She stood at the door looking after him ... as he made his way over the frowzy and uneven patch of ground which lay before the house, which had once (and not long ago) been a pleasant meadow, and was now a very waste, with a disorderly crop of beginnings of mean houses rising out of the rubbish, as if they had been unskilfully sown there.

It might very well, and very closely, describe any urban development anywhere, at any time since then and the age of the town-planners. It is almost incredible in its contemporary awareness of *laisser-aller* urban development.

But the physical landscape change was merely the surface of change throughout the whole structure of mid-nineteenth-century society. The homogeneities of the world of the eighteenth-century aristocrat, London merchant and small-time industrialist, controlled by the unreformed politics of the old régime, and dominated by the aristocratic-bourgeois culture of the metropolis and the watering-places, was collapsing under the pressures of the new industrialism. The newer leaders of early Victorian society were buttressed in power by the philosophies of the new age, the economic thought of Adam Smith and Malthus and the political reform of Bentham and James Mill. The citadels of political power had at least been breached in 1832. The budgets of Peel and Gladstone in the forties and fifties practised the convenient economics of Cobdenite Free Trade. The first major encounter of capital and labour, however, on the political front came with the Chartist agitations of the forties. Beyond the victories of the middle class lay earnest of further enfranchisement to come. The Victorian middle class never attained a period of stability equal to that in which, following the Restoration, the aristocracy achieved the order of the eighteenth century. The problem of cultural transmission was bedevilled by the sheer rate of social change. To take up a position at all was to pitch camp on a cultural landslide.

The mid-century predicament was the central theme of Dickens's maturity. For him the danger lay in the new society seeking a solution to its predicament among the values of the momentarily triumphant middle classes; and the fear that under the world of progress and industrial development the generous impulses of human life would be submerged. A society obsessed with the practicalities of the Benthamite calculus would very likely be careless of the emotional and imaginative life of the individuals within it, and especially careless of the child.

Within this context of bewilderment and anxiety Dickens viewed his own childhood and translated it into the account of the children he gives us in the novels. An insistent characteristic of Dickens's work is its sense of isolation and solitude. Loneliness for Dickens was the essential concomitant of the megalopolitan age. It was a general plight, which, in *Dombey and Son*, he gives in this way:

She often looked with compassion, at such a time, upon the stragglers who came wandering into London, by the great highway hard by, and who, footsore and weary, and gazing fearfully at the huge town before them, as if foreboding that their misery there would be but as a drop of water in the sea, or as a grain of sea-sand on the shore, went shrinking on, cowering before the angry weather, and looking as if the very elements rejected them. Day after day, such travellers crept past, but always, as she thought, in one direction, always towards the town. Swallowed up in one phase or other of its immensity, towards which they seemed impelled by a desperate fascination, they never returned. Food for the hospitals, the churchyards, the prisons, the river, fever, madness, vice, and death – they passed on to the monster, roaring in the distance, and were lost.

And this isolation, which is general, he finds particularized in the child. The theme is insistent in *The Old Curiosity Shop*. On her first entry, Little Nell is lost. The whole novel is indeed an account of the nightmare pilgrimage of Nell and her grandfather through the wide sad world, hounded on mercilessly by the evil genius of Quilp, one of Dickens's most terrifying creations. Little Nell enters the novel in this way:

I turned hastily round, and found at my elbow a pretty little girl, who begged to be directed to a certain street . . .
'It is a very long way from here,' said I, 'my child.'
'I know that, sir,' she replied timidly, 'I am afraid it is a very long way, for I came from there tonight.'
'Alone,' I said, in some surprise.
'Oh yes, I don't mind that, but I am a little frightened now, for I have lost my road.'

The theme of isolation has its utmost expression when Little Nell and her grandfather come to an industrial town in the Midlands. It is, presumably, Birmingham:

Evening came on. They were still wandering up and down, with fewer people about them, but with the same sense of solitude in their own breasts, and the same indifference from all around. The lights in the streets and shops made them feel yet more desolate, for with their help night and darkness seemed to come on faster. . . . Why had they ever come to this noisy town. . . . They were but an atom, here, in a mountain heap of misery . . .

One is reminded of the child Dickens saw in the Edinburgh slum, a sick child, lying in an old box for a cradle, seeming to 'wonder what it was a' aboot'. Society for the victimized Stephen Blackpool of *Hard Times* was 'aw a muddle'. It was indeed the chaos of mid-nineteenth-century England, the plight of the individual in the bewilderment and flux of the times which led Dickens to his interest in social reform, and especially in the reform of the condition of the child. Industrial society had for long been developing faster than political institutions and public morality could contain. Looking back from the comparative securities of our welfare society, it is perhaps difficult to understand Dickens's passionate outcry for the oppressed children of the poor. His equation of evil with material squalor, and his optimism about the moral improvements likely to follow from social reform may seem altogether too facile. Our own interests are more inward, because in a sense our social reforms have driven them there. The condition of nineteenth-century England scarcely permitted the metaphysical sophistications which perhaps Dr Batho and Professor Dobrée were thinking of when in social matters they found Dickens less than second-rate.

His speech at the dinner given on behalf of the Children's Hospital in Great Ormond Street in February, 1858, reveals his special concern for the children of the poor:

But ladies and gentlemen, the spoilt children whom I must show you are the spoilt children of the poor in this great city, the children who are, every year, for ever and ever irrevocably spoilt out of this breathing life of ours by tens of thousands. . . . I shall not ask you to observe how good they are. . . . I shall only ask you to observe how weak they are, and how like death they are. . . . This is the pathetic case which I have to put to you . . . on behalf of the thousands of children who live half-developed, racked with preventible pain, shorn of their natural capacity for health and enjoyment. . . . If these innocent creatures cannot move you for themselves, how can I possibly hope to move you in their name.

The character of the crossing-sweeper in *Bleak House* shows the close relation between his creative work and his social interest. The idea for Jo came from a Law Report, printed in the *Household Narrative* for January 1850.

Alderman Humphrey: Do you know what an oath is?
Boy: No.
Alderman: Can you read?
Boy: No.
Alderman: Do you ever say your prayers?
Boy: No.
Alderman: Do you know what prayers are?
Boy: No.
Alderman: Do you know what God is?
Boy: No. . . .
Alderman: What do you know?
Boy: I knows how to sweep a crossing.
Alderman: And that's all?
Boy: That's all. I sweeps a crossing.

The scene is given almost verbatim in the novel.

'One of the problems', says Humphry House, 'with which he was concerned in one way or another in nearly all his novels was the influence of environment, especially in childhood, upon habits and character.' Dickens was neither philosopher nor theologian. He contains no consistent account of the origin of sin or its expiation. He worked within the romantic assumptions. Virtue was the natural state of man, and happiness its environment. For Dickens, as for Rousseau and Blake, man was born of a good father. The evil conditions of society prevented his entering into his kingdom, his inheritance by nature:

Look round upon the world of odious sights . . . at the lightest mention of which humanity revolts, and dainty delicacy living in the next street, stops her ears, and lisps, 'I don't believe it!' Breathe the polluted air, foul with every impurity that is poisonous to health and life. . . . Vainly attempt to think of any simple plant, or flower, or wholesome weed, that, set in this foetid bed, could have its natural growth, or put its little leaves forth to the sun as God designed it. And then, calling up some ghastly child, with stunted form and wicked face, hold forth on its unnatural sinfulness, and lament its being, so early, far away from Heaven – but think a little of its having been conceived ... in Hell! ... Then should we stand appalled to know, that where we generate disease to strike our children down and entail itself on unborn generations, there also we breed ... infancy that knows no innocence, youth without modesty or shame, maturity that is mature in nothing but in suffering and guilt. ... Oh for a good spirit who would take the house-tops off, with a more potent and benignant hand ... and show a Christian people what dark shapes issue from amidst their homes.

The values of this passage from *Dombey and Son* are, in a very simple way, Christian. But his statement of the relation between environment and criminality became more subtle as he developed. The slum becomes the outward expression of inward spiritual decay throughout society, embracing every class:

But he [Tom-All-Alone's] has his revenge. Even the winds are his messengers, and they serve him in these hours of darkness. There is not a drop of Tom's corrupted blood but propagates infection and contagion somewhere. ... There is not an atom of Tom's slime, not a cubic inch of any pestilential gas in which he lives, not one obscenity or degradation about him, not an ignorance, not a wickedness, not a brutality of his committing, but shall work its retribution, through every order of society, up to the proudest of the proud, and to the highest of the high.

The great works of Dickens's major phase are peopled with characters dominated by their environment, and especially by their childhood. *Hard Times* and *Great Expectations* are in their entirety but variations on this theme; and in *Hard Times* the central interest is in a particular agency of environment, in education.

Dickens was not an educational theorist. He was not concerned with matters of the curriculum, or with the class problem of the public schools. He devoted himself significantly to the emotional effect of education upon the children exposed to its influence. In school the innocent and helpless child was most vulnerable to misery and corruption. School-teachers in Dickens are legion, from Squeers, through Blimber, to Creakle and Mrs Wopsle – a savage tally of brutality, ignorance, and hypocrisy, of mental, physical, and emotional bludgeoning. For the most part it is a negative account. He gives few alternatives to the evils he savaged and lampooned. His chief target was the private school which throve on the inactivity of the State. Of the large grammar or public school there is scarcely a mention. Dr Strong's Academy in *David Copperfield* is perhaps the nearest he came to a positive account of what he would have liked:

Dr Strong's was an excellent school; as different from Mr Creakle's as good is from evil. It was very gravely and decorously ordered, and on a sound system; with an appeal, in everything, to the honour and good faith of the boys, and an avowed intention to rely on their possession of those qualities unless they proved themselves unworthy of it, which worked wonders. We all felt that we had a part in the management of the place, and in sustaining its character and dignity. Hence we soon became warmly attached to it . . . and learnt with a good will, desiring to do it credit . . . the Doctor himself was the idol of the whole school . . . for he was the kindest of men. . . . He would have taken his gaiters off his legs to give away . . .

There is no word of the curriculum. The values of the passage are those of trust, order, kindness, and freedom.

Religion, like education, was a determining agency of the child's environment. Although not theologically concerned, Dickens displayed a continuous interest in religion and its emotional influence on society and in particular on the young. One of his earliest adventures into the world of polemical journalism was an attack on the Sabbatarians who were trying to curtail the Sunday pleasures of the new industrial masses by Act of Parliament. The doctrines of Puritan Christianity did not concern him, but rather the constriction of feeling from which it derived. The 'Murdstone religion' was for him as much a force against life as the industrial slums and the world of Dombey and Gradgrind:

It was a Sunday evening in London, gloomy, close, and stale. Maddening church bells of all degrees of dissonance. . . . Melancholy streets in a penitential garb. . . .

Arthur Clennam in *Little Dorrit* then recalls the 'dreary Sunday of his childhood':

when he sat with his hands before him, scared out of his senses by a horrible tract which commenced business with the poor child by asking him in its title, why was he going to Perdition? . . . and which, for the further attraction of his infant mind, had a parenthesis in every other line with some hiccupping reference as 2 Ep. Thess. c. iii. v. 6 and 7. There was the sleepy Sunday of his boyhood, when, like a military deserter, he was marched to chapel by a picquet of teachers three times a day, morally handcuffed to another boy.

It is reminiscent of the Murdstones in *David Copperfield*:

As to any recreation with other children of my age, I had very little of that; for the gloomy theology of the Murdstones made all children out to be a swarm of little vipers (though there *was* a child once set in the midst of the disciples) and held that they contaminated one another. The natural result of this treatment . . . was to make me sullen, dull and dogged . . .

The Murdstones with their 'gloomy taint', with their 'austere and wrathful' religion, are particular villains of the Dickens world. They purveyed a special villainy. Agents of corruption, like Creakle, Dombey, M'Choakumchild, and Bounderby, they all worked their particular blight in the world of the human spirit; for they were all 'at enmity with joy'.

IV

Oliver Twist is the first novel in the language with its true centre of focus on a child. Although it came after *Sketches by Boz* and *Pickwick*, in a sense it was Dickens's first novel. It was a startling innovation. *Pickwick* had been created by the deflection of a publisher's intention to suit the convenience of genius. With *Oliver Twist*, it was as if, his triumph established, he was declaring that *Pickwick* was not all he might do in the way of more serious entertainment. From the first *Oliver Twist* was a *roman à thèse*. For the first time Dickens's comic powers were turned towards the serious severities of satire. Written in 1838, the novel is an indignant commentary on the Poor Law Amendment Act passed by the Whig Parliament four years before. The miseries consequent upon the cold, harsh logic of the Amendment are sufficiently known. With its intention that the condition of the 'pauper should cease to be really or apparently so eligible as the situation of the independent labourer of the lowest class', the Act for Dickens was a symbol of the new age of Malthusian economics and Benthamite reform. *Oliver Twist* was written as part of the case against the inhumanity of the 'well-regulated' workhouses. Its significance lies, however, not in the exactness of its social commentary, but in the fact of its indignation, and that at the heart of it lay a child.

Dickens's historical sense has been much debated. There seems little doubt of his carelessness about the time sequences of his novels. *Oliver Twist* was not a piece of accurate research; but, rather, the expression of what Dickens *felt* would happen to a child in a society which could conceive of the 1834 Act. It is to miss the essential point to suggest that if the novel were written in 1838, and that Oliver was nine, the account of his infancy would have occurred before the Amendment went through the Whig Parliament.

As a novel *Oliver Twist* is unachieved. Its intentions are not fully clarified. High spirits are not always fused into the wider purposes of satire. The picaresque method of the construction jars continuously with the mechanism of the unifying, but grotesque, plot. Sustaining the suspense by the crude device of retaining the identity of his villain, the dénouement with Monks is no more than the perfunctory lifting of a pantomime backcloth to disclose the sunset cyclorama beyond. The interest of the piece, however, lies in the establishment of Dickens's themes, and in the development of his technique.

The central theme is clear enough: 'Oliver Twist's ninth birthday found him a pale, thin child, somewhat diminutive in stature, and decidedly small in circumference.' Dressed in his Poor Law clothes: 'He was enveloped in the old calico robes which had grown yellow in the same service, he was badged and ticketed, and fell into his place at once – a parish child – the orphan of a workhouse – the humble, half-starved drudge – to be cuffed and buffeted through the world – despised by all, and pitied by none.'

The insistence is on helplessness and isolation. When Oliver leaves the baby farm, to go into the workhouse proper, he misses the 'little companions in misery he was leaving behind, they were the only friends he had ever known; and a sense of his loneliness in the great wide world sank into the child's heart for the first time'.

After committing the famous offence of 'asking for more', Oliver was kept a close prisoner:

He only cried bitterly all day; and, when the long, dismal night came on, spread his little hands before his eyes to shut out the darkness . . . drawing himself closer and closer to the wall, as if to feel even its cold hard surface were a protection in the gloom and loneliness which surrounded him.

Farmed out to the coffin-maker, Oliver is given a bed beneath the counter: 'He was alone in a strange place. . . . The boy had no friends to care for, or to care for him.' In desperation, he runs away. The wide world of loneliness opens before him. Creeping 'close under a hayrick' he listens to the wind which 'moaned dismally over the empty fields; and he was cold and hungry, and more alone than he had ever felt before'. When, seven mornings later, he creeps into Barnet; he finds the 'street was empty; not a soul had awakened to the business of the day. The sun was rising in all its splendid beauty; but the light only served to show the boy his own lonesomeness and desolation, as he sat, with bleeding feet and covered with dust, upon a door-step.' The condition of the child's 'lonesomeness' is indeed tellingly established.

In his isolation, he falls prey to the environment of cruelty and corruption of the world of Fagin and Sikes. Dickens conveys the evil of the London slum world by endowing his material description with moral significance. In *Oliver Twist* we have the first appearance of the symbolic technique which he brought to such achievement in his later work. The moral intention of the novel is conveyed through the selection of concrete imagery. The whole of the first phase of the novel, until the point where Oliver goes to live with the Maylies near Chertsey, is of winter:

The night was very dark. A damp mist rose from the river. . . . It was piercing cold, too; all was gloomy and black.

The night was bitter cold. The snow lay on the ground, frozen into a hard thick crust. . . . Bleak, dark, and piercing cold, it was a night for the well-housed and fed . . .

At last, when Oliver lies wounded and deserted by Sikes, evil and isolation come side by side:

The air grew colder, as day came slowly on; and the mist rolled along the ground like a dense cloud of smoke . . . the damp breath of an unwholesome wind went languidly by, with a hollow moaning. Still, Oliver lay motionless and insensible on the spot where Sikes had left him.

It is the hard wintry décor of the child who had cried out to Bumble on his way to the undertaker's:

'No, no, sir!' sobbed Oliver, clinging to the hand which held the well-known cane; 'no, no, sir; I will be good indeed; indeed, indeed I will, sir! I am a very little boy, sir; and it is – so – so –'
'So what?' enquired Bumble in amazement.
'So lonely, sir! So very lonely!' cried the child.

The symbolic technique conveys the world of Sikes, who lives, tellingly enough, bereft of the wholesome influence of sunlight:

In the obscure parlour of a low public-house . . . a dark and gloomy den, where a flaring gas-light burnt all day in the winter-time; and where no ray of sun ever shone in the summer . . .

This has its sequel after the murder of Nancy:

The sun – the bright sun, that brings back, not light alone, but new life, and hope and freshness to man – burst upon the crowded city in clear and radiant glory. . . . It lighted up the room where the murdered woman lay. It did. He tried to shut it out, but it would stream in.

With Fagin, perhaps, the material world and the sense of implicit evil are most remarkably fused:

The mud lay thick upon the stones, and a black mist hung over the streets; the rain fell sluggishly down, and everything felt cold and clammy to the touch. It seemed just the night when it befitted such a being as the Jew to be abroad. As he glided stealthily along, creeping beneath the shelter of the walls and doorways, the hideous old man seemed like some loathsome reptile, engendered in the slime and darkness through which he moved: crawling forth by night, in search of some rich offal for a meal.

The images are crude; the technique as yet unsubtle. Even so *Oliver Twist* reveals the centre of Dickens's moral interest, and the method through which he was to express it. He conveys the world of the Brownlows and the Maylies, the world of 'life' and 'sunlight', with exactly the same technique. But with them the achievement is limited. A more immediate sense of evil pervades *Oliver Twist* than of goodness. The sense of goodness conveyed is altogether too facile:

In a handsome room; though its furniture had rather the air of old-fashioned comfort, than of modern elegance; there sat two ladies at a well-spread breakfast table ...

This is the suburban paradise of the Maylies, and the same trivializing cosiness infects even the natural surroundings of the villa near Chertsey:

Who can describe the pleasure and delight ... the sickly boy felt in the balmy air, and among the green hills and rich woods, of an inland village! ... It was a lovely spot to which they repaired. ... The rose and honeysuckle clung to the cottage walls ... and the garden-flowers perfumed the air with delicious odours.

The lost Chatham days obtrude themselves here. The language is loose; the image unclear. There is a sentimental sweetening:

And when Sunday came, how differently the day was spent ... and how happily too. ... There was the little church, in the morning, with the green leaves fluttering at the windows; the birds singing without. ... The poor people were so neat and clean ...

This sudden declension into cliché bears no comparison with the image of the corrupt world of Fagin against which it is set. The ending is unconvincing because the language itself is unconvincing. The 'balmy air' and 'little church' do not stand against the world of Monks:

In the heart of this cluster of huts ... stood a large building, formerly used as a manufactory. ... But it had long since gone to ruin. The rats and the worm, and the action of damp, had weakened, and rotted the piles on which it stood.

The 'rot', the 'damp', and the 'rats' are felt within Monks's own collapsing soul. There is no comparable immediacy in the image of the Chertsey villa.

But one impressiveness the novel has: in the remarkable account it gives of the world seen through the eyes of a child. Dickens catches that acute visual awareness of children; that grotesque other dimension of reality which children have:

He soon fell into a gentle doze, from which he was awakened by the light of a candle: which, being brought near the bed, showed him a gentleman with a very large and loud-ticking gold watch in his hand, who felt his pulse, and said he was a great deal better.

Earlier, when Oliver stands before the Guardians to be apprenticed to the chimney-sweep, the same eye is at work:

'Oh, is this the boy?' said the old gentleman.
'This, is him, sir,' replied Mr Bumble. 'Bow to the magistrate, my dear.'
Oliver roused himself, and made his best obeisance. He had been wondering, with his eyes fixed on the magistrates' powder, whether all boards were born with that white stuff on their heads, and were boards from thenceforth, on that account.

It is the horror of Oliver's childhood that is perhaps caught most convincingly of all:

'What's your name?' Oliver tried to reply, but his tongue failed him. He was deadly pale; and the whole place seemed to be turning round and round.
'What's your name, you hardened scoundrel?' demanded Mr Fang. 'Officer, what's his name?' This was addressed to a bluff, old fellow . . . who was standing by the bar. He bent over Oliver, and repeated the enquiry; but finding him really incapable of understanding the question . . . he hazarded a guess.

And again, when Oliver is pursued by the crowd, the fantasy takes on the reality of nightmare:

'Stop thief! Stop thief!' There is a passion *for hunting things* deeply implanted in the human breast. One wretched breathless child, panting with exhaustion; terror in his looks; agony in his eyes; large drops of perspiration streaming down his face . . . they hail his decreasing strength with still louder shouts, and whoop and scream with joy. . . . Stopped at last. A clever blow. He is down upon the pavement, and the crowd eagerly gather round him; each newcomer jostling and struggling with the others to catch a glimpse. . . . Oliver lay, covered with mud and dust, and bleeding from the mouth, looking wildly round upon the heap of faces that surrounded him.

And later, when Oliver is recaptured by Sikes:

Weak with recent illness; stupefied by the blows and the suddenness of the attack; terrified by the fierce growling of the dog, and the brutality of the man; overpowered by the conviction of the bystanders that he really was the hardened little wretch he was described to be; what could one poor child do! Darkness had set in; it was a low neighbourhood; no help was near; resistance was useless. In another moment, he was dragged into a labyrinth of dark, narrow courts. . . .

This is the world of *Oliver Twist*. It is essentially the world of the Dickens child.

V

With *Nicholas Nickleby*, Dickens takes another institution and another boy. But the theme is the same. Oliver becomes Smike, and the workhouse, Dotheboys Hall. Dickens gives his own account of the novel's origin in the Preface:

Of the monstrous neglect of education in England . . . private schools long afforded a notable example . . . any man who had proved his unfitness for any other occupation . . . was free . . . to open a school anywhere . . . these Yorkshire schoolmasters were the lowest and most rotten round in the whole ladder. Traders in the avarice, indifference, or imbecility of parents, and the helplessness of children; ignorant, sordid, brutal men. . . .

His first impressions of the Yorkshire schools came from a tale he had heard of 'a suppurated abscess that some boy had come home with, in consequence of his Yorkshire guide, philosopher and friend having ripped it open with an inky penknife. The impression made upon me, however made, never left me.'

'At last having an audience,' he resolved to write about them. On the pretence that he was anxious to place a boy in one of the schools, he went into Yorkshire, incognito, visiting the area of Greta Bridge and Bowes, where there may have been as many as 800 pupils at that time. Lawsuits in the 1820s had exposed their notoriety. T. P.

Cooper, in his *With Dickens in Yorkshire*, cites the evidence of a case of 1823. One of the poor unfortunates testified:

I felt a weakness in my eyes, and could not write my copy; Mr Shaw said he would beat me; on the next day I could not see at all, and I told Mr Shaw, who sent me and three others to the washhouse. I staid in the washhouse about a month . . . there were nine boys totally blind.

Whilst at Bowes, Dickens visited the graveyard. He most probably saw 'on that dreary afternoon' the graves of twenty-four boys between seven and eighteen, who had died at the Academy between 1810 and 1834. The 'first gravestone' he 'stumbled on was placed above the grave of a boy, eighteen long years old . . . I suppose his heart broke . . . I think his ghost put poor Smike in my mind, upon the spot. . . .'

The new novel did not, however, repeat the procedure of *Oliver Twist*. Dotheboys Hall is seen within a wider social context. The early chapters establish the values of a society in which Dotheboys can exist. Again, as with Fagin and the Maylies, there are two worlds in opposition, characterized this time in the lives of two brothers:

These two brothers had been brought up together in a school at Exeter, and being accustomed to go home once a week, had often heard . . . long accounts of their father's sufferings in his days of poverty, and of their deceased uncle's importance in his days of affluence; which recitals produced a very different impression on the two: for while the younger . . . gleaned from thence nothing but forewarnings to shun the great world and attach himself to the quiet routine of a country life; Ralph, the elder, deduced . . . the two great morals that riches are the only true source of happiness and power, and that it is lawful and just to compass their acquisition by all means short of felony. . . . Ralph always wound up . . . by arriving at the conclusion, that there was nothing like money.

The action of the novel begins with the death of the younger brother, who had 'attached himself to the quiet routine of a country life'. His impoverished family come to London to ask assistance from the brother, who 'always wound up . . . by arriving at the conclusion, that there was nothing like money'. Confronted with his widowed sister-in-law Ralph only evinces:

'Husbands die every day, ma'am, and wives too.'
'And brothers also, sir,' said Nicholas, with a glance of indignation.

Mrs Nickleby vaguely suggests that her husband died from a broken heart:

'Pooh,' said Ralph, 'there's no such thing. I can understand a man's dying of a broken neck ... but a broken heart – nonsense, it's the cant of the day. ...'
'Some people, I believe, have no hearts to break,' observed Nicholas, quietly.
'How old is this boy, for God's sake?' enquired Ralph.

The conflict between the nephew and his uncle is the developed conflict of the book. Nicholas is introduced in this way: 'There was an emanation from the warm young heart in his look and bearing which kept the old man down.'

The 'warm young heart' keeping the 'old man down' is the significance of the novel: and within this conflict the fate of Smike is enacted. He lies at the heart of the novel. Squeers, Dotheboys Hall, and Smike, its most pathetic victim, are the dramatized symbol of the usurer's world; and to appreciate the force of the final revelation that Smike is in fact Ralph Nickleby's son, whose identity had been concealed for his father's mercenary purposes, is to be aware of the world the usurer represents.

It is often suggested that the 'case against money' in *Nicholas Nickleby* is in part vitiated by the fact that Ralph was essentially dated, a figure of a passing, if not already past phase of economic development; whereas, in his different way, Dombey was essentially 'modern'. To some extent, of course, the point is valid. But the interest of both lies in the continuity of Dickens's intention to express the emotional consequences of the pursuit of wealth. In *Dombey and Son* he certainly found a vehicle more apposite to the society in which he was writing.

The structure of *Nicholas Nickleby* is of a sort characteristic of Dickens. It is a structure of concentric circles, and there is always reference outward and inward; in this case outward to the extremities of Ralph Nickleby's world of money, the world of Sir

Mulberry Hawk, Lord Verisopht, the Mantellinis, and Alfred Gride; and inward towards the pivotal centre, which, as so often, is the fate of a child.

The inmost circle of *Nicholas Nickleby* is the world of Dotheboys Hall. Comprising only one hundred pages of the novel, the comment is so minutely dramatized that to extract from it, to convey its real texture, is almost impossible. The life of the Hall is given with grotesque savagery:

Pale and haggard faces, lank and bony figures, children with the countenances of old men, deformities with irons upon their limbs, boys of stunted growth, and others whose long meagre legs would hardly bear their stooping bodies, all crowded on the view together. . . . There were little faces which should have been handsome, darkened with the scowl of sullen dogged suffering; there was childhood with the light of its eye quenched, its beauty gone, and its helplessness alone remaining; there were vicious-faced boys brooding, with leaden eyes, like malefactors in a jail . . . what an incipient Hell was breeding there!

And this is how Squeers's children slept:

It needed a quick eye to detect from among the huddled mass of sleepers . . . As they lay closely packed together, covered, for warmth's sake, with their patched and ragged clothes, little could be distinguished but the sharp outlines of their pale faces. . . . There were some who, lying on their backs with upturned faces and clenched hands . . . bore more the aspect of dead bodies. . . . A few – and these were among the youngest of the children – slept peacefully on with smiles upon their faces, dreaming perhaps of home; but ever and again a deep and heavy sigh . . . announced that some new sleeper had awakened to the misery of another day.

At the heart of Dotheboys is the ghost of the boy who died, eighteen 'long years old', whose grave Dickens had seen on his visit to Yorkshire. But in many ways the characterization of Smike is less satisfactory than that of Oliver Twist; perhaps because, in its development, the drama does not centre on him. He is a described figure, and Dickens's own self-pity is scarcely ever absent. He is a creation of continuous pathos:

After the lapse of a minute or two, the noise of somebody unlocking the yard gate was heard, and presently a tall lean boy, with a lantern in his hand, issued forth.

He shuffles into, and through the pages of the novel, the merest sound of a key in a lock. His fate is simple enough. The source of his fees having dried up, he is kept on by Squeers as too valuable an asset to be left to die – too quickly. In desperation he leaves Dotheboys with Nicholas, for whom, from the first, he conceives a deep attachment. He trails through the novel, constant in his pathetic devotion to Nicholas, Kate, and Mrs Nickleby, There is a fatalism about him. It is in the nature of his creation that he should die young:

'Oh dear, oh dear!' he cried, covering his face with his cracked and horny hands. 'My heart will break. It will, it will!'

The Cheerybles send him into Devonshire, in an effort to restore him; but he cannot even summon the energy to rise and wave farewell to Kate whom he loved:

'I cannot make it!' he cried, falling back in his seat, covering his eyes. . . . He raised his withered hands and clasped them fervently together.

He prays that he will meet Kate again in Heaven:

'In Heaven – I humbly pray to God – in Heaven!' It sounded like the prayer of a broken heart.

Dickens's sense of pathos has gone far beyond his control here. But the ailment from which Smike dies – a broken heart – has ironic reference to his father's outburst earlier in the novel. It is necessary to the central theme of the novel that Smike should in fact die in this way. Secretly married to a woman whose inheritance depended on her not marrying, Ralph had been willing to conceal the birth of his son, until by a trick of an enemy he is told the boy is dead; whereas in fact he had been taken to Squeers's Academy. In the 'mist' which 'gold conjures up' about a man, 'destructive of all his old senses', Smike had been forsaken and had perished.

The weakness of *Nicholas Nickleby* lies, as with *Oliver Twist*, in the characterization of goodness. There is no real counterbalance to the world of Ralph Nickleby and Squeers in the characters of Nicholas, Kate, Mrs Nickleby, and the Cheeryble Brothers. The Cheeryble fraternity in fact never survives its astonishing name. The name works its own unconscious parody. As with *Oliver Twist* human kindness prevails through the arbitrary contriving of the plot. Both artistically and morally the resolution of the novel is entirely unacceptable.

Nevertheless, no matter how inadequate the characterization of the Cheerybles, there is, in *Nicholas Nickleby*, a development of Dickens's portrayal of 'life', which has its significance for his later work. The Crummles episode is essentially a portrayal of a society in which life is free from the restraints of a utilitarian philosophy. Its significance can be missed in the generally picaresque construction of the work. Nicholas's experience with the company of actors is essentially something that happened to him on the road. Its relevance to the development of Dickens's central values is, however, unmistakable:

Nicholas was prepared for something odd, but not for something quite so odd as the sight he encountered. At the upper end of the room were a couple of boys, one of them very tall and the other very short, both dressed as sailors – or at least as theatrical sailors, with belts, buckles, pigtails . . . fighting what is called in play-bills a terrific combat . . .

The subsequent descriptions of this bizarre company are the most enthusiastic of the book:

As Mrs Vincent Crummles recrossed back to the table, there bounded on to the stage from some mysterious inlet, a little girl in a dirty white frock with tucks up to the knees, short trousers, sandalled shoes, white spencer, pink gauze bonnet, green veil and curl-papers, who turned a pirouette, cut twice in the air . . . then, looking off at the opposite wing, shrieked, bounded forward to within six inches of the footlights, and fell into a beautiful attitude of terror. . . .

The immediate reminiscence is of the Natcha – Kee – Tawara sections of Lawrence's *Lost Girl*.

Too much could be made of all this. The Crummles are used to give vitality to several instalments, we may be sure. But it is interesting to see the world he goes to for life and animation. There is a deeply intended implicit comparison between the world of Vincent Crummles and the world of Squeers.

But the main strength of the opposition to Ralph Nickleby must of course lie in Nicholas and Kate; and there, very precisely, is the weakness. The plot contrives the exposure of Ralph Nickleby, and the deportation of Squeers on the count of falsifying a will. Dotheboys breaks up:

For some days afterwards the neighbouring country was overrun with boys. . . . There were a few timid young children, who, miserable as they had been . . . still knew no other home. . . . Of these, some were found crying under hedges and in such places, frightened at the solitude. One had a dead bird in a little cage; he had wandered nearly twenty miles, and when his poor favourite died, lost courage, and lay down beside him.

Both Kate and Nicholas marry, and settle near one another. Again as in *Oliver Twist*, there is the same thinning out of moral texture:

The money which Nicholas acquired in right of his wife he invested in the firm of Cheeryble Brothers, in which Frank had become a partner. . . .

The first act of Nicholas when he became a rich and prosperous merchant was to buy his father's old house.

In short, Nicholas attains to the sort of ambition which in *Great Expectations*, Dickens takes as the power of corruption in the character of Pip. At this stage, it seems, Dickens was unready to draw the conclusions of the premises of the early chapters; conclusions which would have brought him to a fundamental anatomy of nineteenth-century society, for which, as yet, he was evidently unprepared. Nevertheless, the importance of *Nicholas Nickleby*, no less than of *Oliver Twist*, lies in its establishment of his interests in fiction, in gaining his perspective of the world.

The grass was green above the dead boy's grave, and trodden by feet so small and light, that not a daisy drooped its head beneath their pressure. Through all the spring and summer-time, garlands of fresh flowers wreathed by infant hands rested upon the stone, and, when the children came to change them lest they should wither and be pleasant to him no longer, their eyes filled with tears, and they spoke low and softly of their poor dead cousin.

We are very near in this to the image of the romantic child. There is an echo of Blake, though the expression is less precise. There is a selection of images to evoke a calculated response. It is clear that Dickens was at work within a widely established sensibility about children. His own influence, however, upon the sensibility, is none the less clear. There is a resonance in this – sentimental, even morbid perhaps – which is essentially *not* of Blake or Wordsworth. The vividly new concomitant is death.

VI

With *Dombey and Son* we are indeed confronted with the death of another child. With the first emergence of Dickens's really achieved technique, he gives the account of the psychic murder of a son by his father. *Dombey and Son* is an account of the pursuit of wealth and power, and the consequent denial of love and the expression of imagination and feeling by the pursuer in the lives of his children. Obsessed by his ambition to forward the fortunes of his business, Dombey withdraws from his children the normal affection of a father. He destroys his son; and would have destroyed his daughter, had not his obsession been broken through by his moral and financial ruin. He is saved by opening his feelings to receive the affection of his daughter. The novel is contained within the implicit irony of the title, that, in the words of Miss Tox, 'Dombey and Son is a daughter after all!'

The account of Paul Dombey's destruction is an amazing performance. It is, without question, one of the great imaginative triumphs of English fiction. Imaginative, because that is very precisely what it is. It displays an imaginative intensity which without the assurance of seeing it in the text, one might think impossible to the novel as a form. It contains a metaphorical organization which continually astounds in the way only the greatest dramatic poetry astounds.

It is no account this time of a workhouse orphan, or an unwanted child; but rather the favoured son of a prosperous merchant. The analysis shifts from the periphery of social outrage to the heart of the Victorian matter itself. *Oliver Twist* was a tale of cruelty and corruption by the sin of social omission. Dombey's offence is of the nature of wilful commission.

Dombey's universe – the context is of the widest – is evacuated of wonder. He embodies the society which Blake and Coleridge saw in theoretical gestation:

The earth was made for Dombey and Son to trade in, and the sun and moon were made to give them light . . . rainbows gave them promise of fair weather; winds blew for or against their enterprises; stars and planets circled in their orbits, to preserve inviolate a system of which they were the centre.

The point, once established, is immediately dramatized into the world of individual feeling. There is no abstraction away from the human beings involved within this air-tight universe of mercantile regimentation. Paul is born:

'Florence, you may go and look at your pretty brother, if you like, I dare say. Don't touch him!'
The child glanced keenly at the blue coat and stiff white cravat, which, with a pair of creaking boots and a very loud ticking watch, embodied her idea of a father.

When Dombey is faced with the danger of his wife's death in child-birth:

He had a sense within him that . . . he would be very sorry, and that he would find a something gone from among his plate and furniture, and other household possessions.

And when the poor unfortunate woman dies, muttering in her delirium, there was 'no word or sound in answer. Mr Dombey's watch and Dr Parker Peps's watch seemed to be racing faster.' The dry mechanical symbolism of the watch continues throughout the novel. Deciding to recruit a nurse to take charge of the motherless Paul, Dombey briefs the woman accordingly:

I desire to make it a question of wages, altogether. You will receive a liberal stipend for the discharge of certain duties. . . . When those duties cease to be . . . rendered . . . there is an end of all relations between us. . . . When you go away from here, you will have concluded what is a mere matter of bargain and sale, hiring and letting. . . . The child will cease to remember you; and you will cease, if you please, to remember the child.

The woman, Polly Toodles, and her family are in fact immediately introduced as partisans of that other world of humanity and feeling. With them, in alliance, is the orphan Walter Gay who works in Dombey's office. Throughout, Walter is contrasted with Paul, as the creation of a warm, affectionate world from which Paul himself is excluded. Walter is the 'cheerful-looking, merry boy, fresh with running home in the rain; fair-faced, bright-eyed, and curly-haired'. The two worlds are confronted:

The boy with his open face, and flowing hair, and sparkling eyes, panting with pleasure and excitement, was wonderfully opposed to Mr Dombey, as he sat confronting him in his library chair.

The point is made; but Walter Gay is an over-idealized creation. With Dickens there is always this weakening at the centre of goodness. For all the wealth of the enthusiastic description, for all his being 'fair-faced, bright-eyed, and curly-haired', we are no further towards knowing anything really essential about him, as an active moralizing figure. In the terms of the moral fable, he is an applied failure.

But the Dombey world is wonderfully given, within the close texture of its imagery:

It was a corner house, with great wide areas containing cellars frowned upon by barred windows. . . . It was a house of dismal state, with a circular back to it, containing a whole suit of drawing-rooms looking upon a gravelled yard, where two gaunt trees, with blackened trunks and branches, rattled rather than rustled, their leaves were so smoke-dried.

It was as blank a house inside as outside. . . . Every chandelier or lustre, muffled in holland, looked like a monstrous tear depending from the ceiling's eye.

The sterility of the 'two gaunt trees' rattling their 'smoke-dried' leaves is instinct in the book. Paul himself withers like a flower bereft of the wholesome nourishment of sunlight.

The insistence of the novel's theme is nowhere better given than at the child's christening, which, in a wholly fantastic way, becomes, in meaning, his funeral:

It happened to be an iron-grey autumnal day, with a shrewd east wind blowing – a day in keeping with the proceedings. Mr Dombey represented in himself the wind, the shade, and the autumn of the christening . . . when he looked out through the glass room, at the trees in the little garden, their brown and yellow leaves came fluttering down, as if he blighted them.

On setting out for the ceremony, 'the chief difference between the christening party and a party in a mourning coach, consisted in the colours of the carriage and horses'. On arrival at the church, 'little Paul might have asked with Hamlet, "Into my grave?" – so chill and earthy was the place'.

With a richness of reference, all three fundamental ceremonies of the Church are thrust side by side. 'The very wedding looked dismal as they passed in front of the altar.' In a damp corner there were black trestles for funerals, and a coil or two of deadly rope. And all the time:

It was a dull, grey, autumn day indeed, and in a minute's pause and silence that took place, the leaves fell sorrowfully.

The image returns after the christening:

It was a bleak autumnal afternoon indeed; and as she walked, and hushed, and ... pressed the little fellow closer to her breast, the withered leaves came showering down.

A certain impression of over-statement might be suggested perhaps by this selective extraction of the imagery. But in context there is an absolute rightness about these passages. Their effect is cumulative rather than repetitive. Their whole significance focuses upon the following:

The chill of Paul's christening had struck home, perhaps, to some sensitive part of his nature ... he was an unfortunate child from that day.

The blight is indeed in 'some sensitive part of his nature'. It is an ailment of the boy's psyche. The boy's illness is nowhere specified. There are symptoms of tuberculosis; but whereas Smike's own disease is mentioned, it is left tellingly inexplicit with Paul Dombey. His death is inward, a thing of the boy's heart.

The corruption of Paul's nature is given through the portrayal of his precocious madness. There is a deep sense of infant lunacy about the child, which by insistence becomes truly frightening:

He was childish and sportive enough at times, and not of a sullen disposition; but he had a strange, old-fashioned, thoughtful way, at other times, of sitting brooding in his miniature armchair, when he looked (and talked) like one of those terrible little beings in the fairy tales. . . . He would frequently be stricken with this precocious mood. . . . But at no time did he fall into it so surely, as when, his little chair being carried down into his father's room, he sat there with him after dinner, by the fire.

The fire is a recurrent image, casting a weird, non-life-giving light on the Dombey household. 'The bright fire was sparkling like a jewel' in the young boy's eyes – when he said (and the passage is central):

'Papa! What's money?' . . .
'What is money, Paul?' he answered. 'Money?'
'Yes,' said the child, laying his hands upon the elbows of his little chair, and turning the old face up towards Mr Dombey's, 'What is money?'
Mr Dombey was in a difficulty. He would have liked to give him some explanation involving the terms circulating-medium, currency . . . but looking down at the little chair, and seeing what a long way down it was, he answered,
'Gold and silver and copper. . . . You know what they are.'
'Oh yes, I know what they are,' said Paul, 'I don't mean that, papa. I mean, what's money after all.' . . .
'What is money after all?' said Mr Dombey. . . .
'I mean, papa, what can it do?' returned Paul, folding his arms (they were hardly long enough to fold) and looking at the fire, and up at him, and at the fire, and up at him again.
'Money, Paul, can do anything. . . .'
'Anything, papa?'
'Yes. Anything – almost,' said Mr Dombey.
'Anything means everything, don't it, papa?' asked his son.
'It includes it; yes,' said Mr Dombey. . . .
'Why didn't money save me my mamma,' returned the child. 'It isn't cruel, is it?'
'Cruel!' said Mr Dombey. . . . 'No. A good thing can't be cruel.'
'If it's a good thing, and can do anything,' said the little fellow, thoughtfully, as he looked back at the fire, 'I wonder why it didn't save me my mamma.' He didn't ask the question of his father this time. Perhaps he had seen with a child's quickness, that it had already made his father uncomfortable.

But the discomfiture is only momentary. Dombey is soon explaining:

How that money causes us to be honoured, feared, respected, courted . . .
and how it could do all, that could be done. . . .

'It can't make me strong and well, either, papa; can it?' asked Paul,
after a short silence; rubbing his tiny hands.

'Why you *are* strong and quite well . . . are you not?'

Oh! the age of the face that was turned up again, with an expression half
of melancholy, half of slyness, on it. . . .

'I am so tired sometimes,' said little Paul, warming his hands, and looking
in between the bars of the grate, as if some ghostly puppet-show were performing there.

The puppet-show raises the ghost indeed of one of Dickens's
favourite images of life. It is an image strikingly inverted.

With the child already ailing, Dombey decides that he should be
placed at an 'infantine Boarding-House of a very select description'.
Paul goes to Brighton, into the world of Mrs Pipchin. The shade,
sterility, and death of the 'infantine Boarding-House' is vividly
given through the imagery:

The Castle of this ogress and child-queller was in a steep bye-street, at
Brighton; where the soil was more than usually chalky, flinty, and sterile,
and the houses were more than usually brittle and thin . . .

Inside the house Mrs Pipchin kept 'half a dozen specimens of cactus,
writhing round bits of lath, like hairy serpents', and 'several creeping
vegetables, possessed of sticky and adhesive leaves . . .'

The whole account of Paul Dombey is related to Dickens's interest
in education. But the account is never in intellectual terms. Mrs Pipchin, and later Dr Blimber, are further agents in the spiritual torture
of the dying boy.

The compulsive insanity of the child comes through when a
carriage is bought for him:

. . . in which he could lie at his ease . . . and be wheeled down to the seaside. Consistent in his odd tastes, the child set aside a ruddy-faced lad who
was proposed as the drawer of this carriage, and selected, instead, his grandfather – a weazen old, crab-faced man. . . . His favourite spot was quite a
lonely one, far away from most loungers; and with Florence sitting by his
side . . . and the wind blowing on his face, and the water coming up among
the wheels of his bed, he wanted nothing more.

The sea is an image of Paul's death, just as for Walter Gay it is an image of wonder and life. For Paul, death itself is coming up 'among the wheels of the bed'. For one brief moment, however, for Paul too, the sea becomes a symbol of life. He talks to Dr Blimber of the tales the old crab-faced man had told him in his carriage by the sea.

'He knows all about the deep sea, and the fish that are in it, and the great monsters that come and lie on rocks in the sun . . .'

'Ha!' said the Doctor, shaking his head; 'This is bad, but study will do much!'

Paul is moved to the Doctor's Academy when he is six. Dr Blimber and his daughter are the next agents in the child's destruction. Once again there is the same insistence on the distortion of natural growth: 'In fact Dr Blimber's establishment was a great hothouse, in which there was a forcing apparatus incessantly at work. All the boys blew before their time . . . nature was of no consequence.' The house 'fronts the sea' with 'sad-coloured curtains'. Tables and chairs were set in rows 'like figures in a sum'. There was no sound 'through all the house but the ticking of a great clock in the hall'. Miss Blimber, who taught Latin and Greek, 'kept her hair short and crisp, and wore spectacles. She was dry and sandy with working in the graves of deceased languages . . . Miss Blimber dug them up like a ghoul.' Mr Feeder, B.A., the Doctor's assistant, was a 'kind of human barrel-organ, with a little list of tunes at which he was continually working'. Here indeed we have a foreshadowing of the educational theme worked out most fully in *Hard Times*. Paul is introduced to Dr Blimber, who receives him with the patronage of: 'How is my little friend?' The clock in the hall takes up the refrain of this quintessential phrase of all unfelt phrases that adults have ever thrown at children:

'How, is, my, lit,tle friend? How, is, my, lit,tle friend?' over and over again. . . .

'Ha,' said Dr Blimber, 'shall we make a man of him?'

'Do you hear, Paul?' added Mr Dombey, Paul being silent.

'Shall we make a man of him?' repeated Dr Blimber.

'I had rather be a child,' replied Paul.

'Indeed,' said the Doctor. 'Why?'

The child sat on the table looking at him, with a curious expression of suppressed emotion in his face, and beating one hand proudly on his knee as if he had the rising tears beneath it, and crushed them. But his other hand strayed a little way the while, a little farther – farther from him yet – until it lighted on the neck of Florence.

It is mistaken to castigate this sort of thing for its sentimentality. The meaning is too insistent. Sentimentality only occurs where the meaning is inadequate to the emotions into which it is translated. The emotion here seems in exact keeping with the meaning conveyed.

Sitting on his pedestal Paul listens to the clock in the hall – 'How, is, my, lit,tle friend?'

He might have answered 'weary, weary; very lonely, very sad.' And there, with an aching void in his young heart, and all outside so cold, and bare, and strange, Paul sat as if he had taken life unfurnished, and the upholsterer were never coming.

Subjected to Dr Blimber's forcing-system the boy rapidly succumbs:

[He] liked nothing so well as wandering about the house by himself, or sitting on the stairs, listening to the great clock in the hall. He was intimate with all the paperhanging in the house; saw things no-one else saw in the patterns; found miniature tigers and lions running up the bedroom walls, and squinting faces leering. ... The solitary child lived on, surrounded by this strange arabesque work of his musing fancy, and no one understood him.

It is the morbidity of fancy given no healthy nourishment of expression. The morbidity is essential to Dickens's meaning. Dombey waits for his son 'qualifying to be a man':

Could he have but seen ... the slight spare boy above, watching the waves and clouds at twilight ... breasting the window of his solitary cage when birds flew by, as if he would have emulated them, and soared away.

Before he can return home, the boy collapses. His illness and death are conveyed through his own eyes. In a sense the world is dying round him. He hears the ominous phrases about his condition, more frightening in that they were but half-understood:

Lying down again with his eyes shut, he heard the apothecary say, out of the room and quite a long way off – or he dreamed it – that there was a want of vital power (what was that, Paul wondered) . . .

Again and again he hears them say he is 'an old-fashioned boy'. 'Floy,' said Paul, 'do you think I have grown old-fashioned? I want to know what they mean, Floy.'

The climax comes with the relation of the father and his child, on Paul's death-bed. When Dombey comes down to see his son at Brighton, the boy is not sure 'whether that had been his father in the room, or a tall shadow on the wall'. Their relation is reduced to its essence, to its final reality:

But this figure with its head upon its hand returned so often, and remained so long and sat so still and solemn, never speaking, never being spoken to, and rarely lifting up its face, that Paul began to wonder languidly, if it were real; and in the night-time saw it sitting there, with fear.

'Floy,' he said, 'what *is* that?'

'Where, dearest?'

'There! at the bottom of the bed.'

'There's nothing there, except papa.'

The figure lifted up its head, and rose, and coming to the bedside said: 'My own boy, don't you know me?'

Paul looked it in the face, and thought, was this his father?

The declension to the impersonal pronoun is the last – terrible – commentary on their relationship. It is a stroke of consummate genius.

Paul's death occurs only one quarter way through the novel. The rest of the tale is of Florence's continued rejection, of Dombey's ruin, and of his ultimate salvation by accepting her love. The account of Dombey's ruin lies close to Dickens's interest in the determining influences of environment during childhood. Visiting Cheltenham soon after the death of Paul, Dombey falls in with a certain Mrs Skewton, who blatantly proceeds to sell him her recently widowed daughter for a second wife. Mrs Skewton is in fact one of Dickens's great strokes; one of the great things in English imaginative literature. She is a grotesque creature of disgusting falsity:

Slightly settling her false curls and false eye-brows with her fan, and showing her false-teeth, set off by her false complexion . . . 'What I want,' drawled

Mrs Skewton, pinching her shrivelled throat, 'is heart.' It was frightfully true in one sense, if not in that in which she used the phrase. . . . 'In short . . . I want Nature everywhere. It would be so extremely charming.'

This fantastic and horrible creature sells her daughter to Dombey as a profitable financial transaction. The significance of this to Dickens's theme is given when the mother and daughter are alone:

The very voice was changed as it addressed Edith, when they were alone again.

'Why don't you tell me,' it said, sharply, 'that he is coming here tomorrow by appointment?'

'Because you know it,' returned Edith, 'Mother.'

The mocking emphasis she laid on that one word!

'You know he has bought me,' she resumed . . .

'What do you mean?' returned the angry mother, 'Haven't you from a child —'

'A child,' said Edith, looking at her, 'When was I a child! . . . What childhood did you ever leave to me? I was a woman – artful, designing, mercenary, laying snares for men – before I knew myself. . . . You gave birth to a woman. Look upon her. She is in her pride tonight. . . . Look at me . . . who have never known what it is to have an honest heart, and love. . . . Look at me, taught to scheme and plot when children play. . . .'

Without the moral energy to resist the marriage, she takes Dombey. In her passionate self-disgust she ruins him by appearing to the world to have accepted seduction at the hands of his chief clerk, Carker. The horror of the situation is conveyed through the description of the woman who had made it, through the corruption of her child. Struck down by paralysis, we have this, as the final comment on Mrs Skewton:

Edith hurried . . . to her mother's room. Cleopatra was arrayed in full dress, with the diamonds, short-sleeves, rouge, curls, teeth, and other juvenility all complete; but Paralysis was not to be deceived, had known her for the object of its errand, and had struck her at her glass, where she lay like a horrible doll that had tumbled down.

Dombey's ruin becomes his redemption. He is at last aware of his crime, and the novel ends with a reconciliation between father and daughter:

Autumn days are shining, and on the sea-beach there are often a young lady, and a white-haired gentleman. With them, or near them, are two children; boy and girl. . . . The white-haired gentleman walks with the little boy . . . helps him in his play. Sometimes when the child is sitting by his side and looks up in his face, asking him questions, he takes the tiny hand in his, and holding it, forgets to answer. Then the child says: 'What, Grandpapa, am I so like my poor little uncle again?'

'Yes, Paul; but he was weak and you are very strong.'

'Oh, yes, I am very strong.'

'And he lay on a little bed beside the sea, and you can run about.' And so they range away again busily, for the white-haired gentleman likes best to see the child free and stirring.

Dombey's atonement is made. The crime against Paul is expiated in the 'free and stirring' romantic child.

VII

Hard Times is a tract about and against the age. Nowhere did Dickens give more explicitly the morality he conceived against mid-Victorian society. But it is not a tract in the limiting sense that *Alton Locke* is. The morality is fused absolutely with the drama. It is one of his greatest *novels*; as fine as anything he achieved within the intentions and methods he set himself. Its very success and single-mindedness perhaps, its lack of superficial complications, account for its comparative neglect.

Dickens wrote the 100,000 words of the novel in five months. He prepared for it with characteristic thoroughness. At the end of January 1854, he journeyed north to Preston, where the textile workers had been out on strike for twenty-three weeks. The town was orderly, sullen, resigned. Embittered mill-hands stood debating their sad condition. Dickens surveyed the scene from the 'old, grubby, smoky, mean, intensely formal red-brick' of the Bull Hotel. Preston was metamorphosed into the Coketown of *Hard Times*. Scarcely any other of his major works came from him so urgently. After finishing it, he felt 'appallingly used up', 'stunned with work'. 'I am three parts mad, and the fourth delirious, with perpetual rushing at *Hard Times*.'

It is difficult now to conceive of the effort of creative awareness required to give such a synthesized account of a society only then newly emerging. The novel is the account of an industrial society, and the philosophies of those who created and sustained it. Significantly the account centres on the point where that social philosophy made its corrupting contact with children. Gradgrindery is a summation of everything utilitarianism meant in the life of the spirit for Dickens. The novel is essentially an educational drama. Gradgrind's salvation only comes through awareness of the blight he has commissioned in the lives of his children. The intention and resolution are identical to those of *Dombey and Son*; except that here the impulse to self-identification and self-pity is rigorously controlled. The theme of the novel is nowhere marred by the intrusion of self-sentimentality.

The book opens in the schoolroom. The cruelty is no longer the cruelty of Squeers. As with Blimber and Mr Feeder, the cruelty is psychic:

'Now, what I want is Facts. Teach these boys and girls nothing but Facts. Facts alone are wanted in life. Plant nothing else, and root out everything else. ...' The speaker, and the schoolmaster, and the third grown person present, all backed a little, and swept with their eyes the inclined plane of little vessels then and there arranged in order. ... Mr Gradgrind ... seemed a galvanizing apparatus; ... charged with a grim, mechanical substitute for the tender young imaginations that were to be stormed away. ... 'Girl number Twenty,' said Mr Gradgrind ... 'I don't know that girl. Who is that girl?'

'Girl number Twenty' does not know the definition of a horse. She is enlightened by Bitzer, a boy 'so unwholesomely deficient in the natural tinge, that he looked as though, if he were cut, he would bleed white'. Bitzer gives his definition of a horse:

Quadruped. Graminivorous. Forty teeth, namely twenty-four grinders, four eye-teeth, and twelve incisive. Sheds coat in the spring; in marshy countries, sheds hoofs too. ... Thus (and much more) – Bitzer.

The government officer – 'a mighty man at cutting and drying' – steps forth to explain, there being some natural doubt among the children, why rooms should never be papered with representations of horses:

Do you ever see horses walking up and down the sides of rooms in reality – in fact? . . . Why, then, you're not to see anywhere what you don't see in fact. What is called Taste, is only another name for Fact.

This crushing of the intuitive fancy, of 'everything that was not susceptible of proof and demonstration' is the central romantic theme of the novel. Cecilia Jupe, 'girl number Twenty', the girl from Sleary's Horse-riding, is unbreakable at the wheel of Fact. She stands outside the world of Gradgrind, like the children of Hampton race-course, and the Crummles family in *Nicholas Nickleby*. Through her the Gradgrind family find their salvation.

Mr Gradgrind achieves his initial triumph and finds his ultimate tragedy in his own children:

It was his school, and he intended it to be a model. He intended every child in it to be a model, just as the young Gradgrinds were all models. . . . No little Gradgrind had ever seen a face in the moon. . . . No little Gradgrind had ever known wonder on the subject . . .

With the world of the Gradgrind schoolroom established, the wider Gradgrind world opens around it. Content with his morning's instruction, Mr Gradgrind makes his way home:

to his matter-of-fact home, which was called Stone Lodge. . . . He had virtually retired from the wholesale hardware trade before he built Stone Lodge . . . a very regular feature on the face of the country, Stone Lodge was . . . a great square house . . . a calculated, cast-up, balanced, and proved house . . .

Pursuing his way, he is suddenly and disconcertingly confronted with that other world of life and animation: 'He had reached the neutral ground upon the outskirts of the town, which was neither town, nor country, but yet was either spoiled, when his ears were invaded by the sound of music. The clashing and banging band attached to the horse-riding establishment . . . was in full bray.'

He finds his own Louisa and Tom actually peeping in:

'Wanted to see what it was like,' returned Louisa shortly.
'What it was like?'
'Yes, father.'
There was an air of jaded sullenness in them both, and particularly in the

girl; yet, struggling through the dissatisfaction of her face, there was a light with nothing to rest upon, a fire with nothing to burn, a starved imagination keeping life in itself somehow.

With the appearance of Bounderby the world opens more widely about the children:

He was a rich man; banker, merchant, manufacturer. . . . A big, loud man, with a stare, and a metallic laugh. A man made out of a coarse material . . .

Together, Bounderby and Gradgrind proceed to confront Mr Sleary with the corruption he had introduced into the school in the person of 'girl number Twenty'. The keynote is struck:

Coketown, to which Messrs Bounderby and Gradgrind now walked, was a triumph of fact. . . . It was a town of machinery and tall chimneys, out of which interminable serpents of smoke trailed themselves for ever and ever, and never got uncoiled. . . . It contained several large streets all very like one another, inhabited by people equally like one another, who all went in and out at the same hours, with the same sound upon the same pavements, to do the same work, and to whom every day was the same as yesterday and tomorrow, and every year the counterpart of the last and next.

The deprived condition of the Gradgrind children is seen now to represent the sterilities of the whole Coketown society:

Is it possible, I wonder, that there was any analogy between the case of the Coketown population and the case of the little Gradgrinds? . . . That, exactly in the ratio as they worked long and monotonously, the craving grew within them for some physical relief – some relaxation, encouraging good humour and good spirits, and giving them a vent – some recognized holiday, though it were but for an honest dance to a stirring band of music – which craving must and would be satisfied aright, or must and would inevitably go wrong, until the laws of the Creation were repealed.

This, the central moral assertion of the work, is dramatized through the fate of the Gradgrind children themselves. The boy becomes sullen, heartless, and ultimately a thief. Louisa succumbs to frustration and bewilderment, wondering incessantly about her life, yet without the 'education' to control its natural emotions. Sitting in the room which had 'much of the genial aspect of a room devoted to haircutting', she gazes, in a way reminiscent of Paul Dombey, interminably into the falling ashes:

'I don't see anything in it, Tom, particularly. But since I have been looking at it, I have been wondering about you and me, grown up.'

'Wondering again!' said Tom.

'I have such unmanageable thoughts,' returned his sister, 'that they *will* wonder.'

Time passes mechanically in Coketown, and the children grow up:

Time went on in Coketown like its own machinery, so much material wrought up, so much fuel consumed, so many powers worn out, so much money made . . .

'Louisa is becoming,' said Mr Gradgrind, 'almost a young woman.'

Time with 'innumerable horse-power' also 'worked away' with Tom, and he became 'that not unprecedented triumph of calculation which is usually at work on number one'.

Louisa bestows on him, with all his worthlessness, all the capacity for affection she possesses. Emotion will have its outlet somewhere. For his advancement she accepts marriage with Bounderby. She has no moral will to resist something she knows intuitively as a degradation. Set within Stone Lodge, and against the whole panorama of Coketown, Mr Gradgrind conveys Bounderby's proposal. She contains her despair beneath a surface of resignation:

[She went to the] stern room, with a deadly statistical clock in it, which measured every second with a beat like a rap upon a coffin-lid. A window looked towards Coketown. . . . she saw the high chimneys and the long tracts of smoke looming in the heavy distance gloomily.

In this setting, the Gradgrind world has its final triumph, of 'fact' over Louisa's feeling:

'Louisa, my dear, you are the subject of a proposal of marriage that has been made to me.'

Again he waited, and again she answered not one word. This so far surprised him, as to induce him gently to repeat,

'A proposal of marriage, my dear.' To which she returned, without any visible emotion whatever –

'I hear you father. I am attending I assure you. . . . Father . . . do you

think I love Mr Bounderby? ... Father ... do you ask me to love Mr
Bounderby? ... Father,' she still pursued, 'does Mr Bounderby ask me to
love him?'

Gradgrind finds 'love', 'the expression itself', perhaps a 'little mis-
placed'.

'What would you advise me to use in its stead, father?'

The barriers between their sympathy, however, are too high, and her
energy expires:

'Are you consulting the chimneys of the Coketown works, Louisa?'
'There seems to be nothing there, but languid and monotonous smoke.
Yet when the night comes, fire bursts out, father!' she answered, turning
quickly. ...
'Father, I have often thought that life is very short.' This was so distinctly
one of his subjects, that he interposed –
'It is short, no doubt, my dear. Still, the average duration of human life is
proved to have increased of late years ...'
'I speak of my own life, father.'
'Oh indeed? Still,' said Mr Gradgrind, 'I need not point out to you,
Louisa, that it is governed by the laws which govern lives in the aggregate.'
'While it lasts, I would wish to do the little I can, and the little I am fit for.
What does it matter!'

She struggles wearily to convey to her father the reality of her fate:

'What do I know, father,' said Louisa, in her quiet manner, 'of tastes and
fancies; of aspirations and affections ... what escape have I had from problems that could be demonstrated, and realities that could be grasped?'
'My dear ... quite true, quite true!'
'Why father ... the baby-preference that even I have heard as common
among children, has never had its innocent resting-place in my heart. You
have been so careful of me, that I never had a child's heart ...'
'My dear Louisa,' said he, 'you abundantly repay my care. Kiss me, my
dear girl.'

The degradation of the marriage works itself through in Louisa's
near-seduction by Harthouse, the 'politician' from London, who
manages to attract her feelings by playing on her affection for her
brother. The plight of the young woman, in face of their intrigue, is

conveyed in a remarkable passage. The two men converse in a rose-garden. Tom Gradgrind stands 'plucking buds and picking them to pieces'. Finally when they reach agreement we have:

'Now you see, Tom,' said Mr Harthouse, in conclusion – himself tossing over a rose or two, as a contribution to the island [of rose-petals which Tom had thrown into the ornamental pond below them] which was always drifting to the wall as if it wanted to become part of the mainland. . . .

The relation of the imagery to Louisa's own predicament needs no emphasis. It is an astonishing example of Dickens's method. The reference of the flowers, the 'island', the 'ornamental pond', and the 'drifting', and the wanting to 'become part' of the 'mainland', are an amazing correlation between the image and the psychic reality he wishes to convey.

Terrified of herself, the girl returns to her father. She lies 'the triumph of his system', an 'insensible heap at his feet':

Father if you had known . . . what even I feared while I strove against it . . . that there lingered in my breast, sensibilities, affections, weaknesses, capable of being cherished into strength . . . would you have doomed me . . . to the frost and blight that have hardened and spoiled me? . . . With a hunger and thirst upon me, father, which have never for a moment been appeased; with an ardent impulse towards some region where rules, and figures, and definitions were not quite absolute; I have grown up, battling every inch of my way.

Louisa's corruption is mirrored in her brother, who becomes first gamester, and then, unable to pay his debts, a thief. He robs Bounderby's bank, and in a desperate effort to conceal his crime, implicates the innocent worker, Stephen Blackpool. In the world of Bounderby and Gradgrind, Blackpool represents the isolated 'good' individual, hounded by both master and fellow-men. Cast out of Coketown, he is forced to return, however, to clear his name. On his way back across the moors, he falls down a disused mine-shaft, is fatally injured and dies with the truth of the robbery on his lips.

In an effort to get him from the country, out of the reach of justice, Tom is secreted to Sleary's Horse-riding. The circus 'villains' become Dickens's agents of salvation. The significance of the situation is suggested by the fact that the scheme is almost foiled by the irrepressible Bitzer. The tables are poignantly turned on Gradgrind by the boy who had known, only too well, his 'definition of a horse':

'Bitzer,' said Mr Gradgrind, broken down, and miserably submissive to him, 'Have you a heart?'
'The circulation, sir . . . couldn't be carried on without one.'

Gradgrind pleads with him; only to receive his own philosophies returned, with interest, in his face:

'I am sure you know that the whole social system is a question of self-interest. . . . I was brought up in that catechism when I was very young, sir, as you are aware.'

The arch which sprang up from the first educational chapters reaches down now into the bitter ground of Gradgrind's defeat. It is left to Sleary, in his lisping way, to express the meaning of the work:

'that there ith a love in the world, not all Thelf-intereth after all, but thome-thing very different. . . .'

Extracted, this might seem almost ludicrous as the statement of a novel's theme. Within its context, however, it is a measure of Dickens's art, that he can with every ease fuse his morality with his characters, enabling him to place this weight on Sleary, to express the fundamental Dickensian antithesis, between the sensibilities of life and the sensibilities of death. The Maylies and Fagin; Nicholas Nickleby and Squeers; Walter Gay and Mr Dombey; Edith Dombey and Mr Carker; Sleary and Mr Gradgrind – these are the essential characters of Dickens's moral drama, and within their conflict his children have their significant existence.

VIII

The stress has been laid on this aspect of Dickens's work, because I think it the most important aspect. His children are not only closely related to what he had to say as a writer, but, for that reason perhaps, exemplify the kind of interests he brought to the novel, and the methods within which he worked. It seemed more important to lay the stress there rather than to show him as a great creator of child characters – superb as of course he was in this. David Copperfield, and Pip in *Great Expectations*, are among the most remarkable evocations of childhood in the whole range of the century's literature, and scarcely pale before the more consciously psychological creations of our own.

It might, however, be objected that to place the emphasis on his strength, on the children who clearly function within his morality, is to conceal the very thing which perhaps one remembers first about his children – their sentimentality. Sentimentality does indeed serve to describe the feeling one frequently has with Dickens's children, that he has directed towards the child exaggerated emotions of pathos, deriving from his self-pitying attitude to his own experience as a child. By indulging his own emotion, he clearly provided an image of childhood through which his audience could only too easily indulge itself. Sentimentality is, however, to be very carefully distinguished from deep feeling. Sometimes his apparent sentimentality is merely the depth of the emotional requirement of the situation he is dealing with, as it very clearly is in the case of Paul Dombey. It is not so much the depth as the motive of the feeling which matters. Sentimentality seems most often to derive from some self-indulgence in the author, when his feelings are motivated by a desire to emphasize some emotion unassimilated into his mature consciousness, some feeling uncontained within the integrating influence of his whole sensibility. There is the sentimentality of sadness which indulges the pathetic; and there is the sentimentality of optimism which idealizes. There is, of course, that other sentimentality of the squalid with which we have become so familiar in modern literature, which, for no very evident purpose, makes things – life, sex, industrialism, society – seem absolutely, by sentimentalizing selection, squalid, and 'worse than they are'. It is precisely for this reason that one might consider *Germinal* sentimental, or some, though by no means all, of Hemingway's work; or, and this time I think it would be all, of Mr Tennessee Williams's. Through overemphasis and selection, sentimentality exaggerates and disorders;

and although it does not always consume a sensibility, it always flaws. The difficulty is that sentimentality is most often sincere (except for the commercial artist who knows his audience and its weaknesses) – and this is its power.

With Dickens's children, we find both the pathos and the idealization – and sometimes, perhaps, the squalid as well. We feel his emotions rush towards the image and accumulate about it, until his children become sometimes no more than the accumulated presence of his own self-pity, idealizing the happiness and security he had lost, proving to himself and the world at large his subsequent 'victimization'. In his sentimentalized children there seems no doubt that he was creating an image, at once pathetic and idealized, of himself. It so happened that his personal experience coincided with the general experience, and that he was able to bring to his experience the discipline of his intelligence, his humour, and the general awareness of his social sympathy, and by so doing transmuted his weakness, if not always, at least sometimes, into his strength.

It is the conscious self-identity of *David Copperfield* which makes the whole tone of the novel in some way distasteful. But the death of the schoolboy in *The Old Curiosity Shop* springs from the same self-identifying motive:

He was a very young boy; quite a little child. His hair still hung in curls about his face, and his eyes were very bright; but their light was of Heaven, not earth. The schoolmaster took a seat beside him, and stooping over the pillow, whispered his name. The boy sprang up, stroked his face with his hand, and threw his wasted arms round his neck, crying out that he was his dear kind friend.

'I hope I always was. I meant to be, God knows,' said the poor schoolmaster.

'Who is that?' said the boy, seeing Nell. 'I am afraid to kiss her, lest I should make her ill. Ask her to shake hands with me.'

The sobbing child came closer up, and took the little languid hand in hers. Releasing his again after a time, the sick boy laid him gently down.

'You remember the garden, Harry,' whispered the schoolmaster, anxious to rouse him, for a dulness seemed gathering upon the child, 'and how pleasant it used to be in the evening time? You must make haste to visit it again, for I think the very flowers have missed you. . . . You will come soon, my dear, very soon now – won't you?'

The boy smiled faintly – so very, very faintly – and put his hand upon his friend's grey head.

It is interesting to compare this (with its 'so very, very faintly') with the death of Paul in *Dombey and Son*. The point to be made is that Paul's death is not sentimentalized, since it is contained within the meaning of the work as a whole – although those who read it, without taking the intention of the whole, may easily have taken it sentimentally. Paul Dombey's death moved the nation as much as Little Nell's, and we can have a fair idea of the quality of some of the 'movement' involved. Here in *The Old Curiosity Shop*, however, the death of the schoolboy has no meaning within the work. It is merely an occasion for Dickens's impulse towards self-pity to focus and reach its logical emotional conclusion in the morbidity of the child's death.

David Copperfield lays the finger on the origins of the sentiment-ality of *The Old Curiosity Shop*, and the flaw which predisposed him to see children as frail, sickly, oppressed, and, frequently, moribund. Dickens's children tend to move in a world of terror, fantasy, melo-drama, and death. In one sense, he continued, throughout his life, to see the world with children's eyes. This may have been the source of his love for the fantastic, and the basis of his comedy in the grotesque, of his seeing his characters as just that little larger than life. The scene in the churchyard at the opening of *Great Expectations* is, in this sense, quintessential Dickens. This may perhaps account for a certain crudeness in his ideas, for his tendency towards over-simplification, especially of moral issues. Sometimes in the novels things are pre-sented as too much a matter of pure black and white. His characters sometimes exist in a too straightforward world of innocence and villainy. His 'innocence' and 'experience' have not always the rich-ness of emotional definition we find in Blake's. His women are, if they are young, too virtuous; his older women too often comic. Even Gradgrind is something of a mechanical creation not fully *felt* into the novel. Even with *Hard Times* one feels the breath of creative life stop; its idea is not completely fulfilled in terms of feeling.

But, even so, it still seems important to point up the strength, rather than simply to catalogue his creations, or to reiterate the com-plaints against him; and, by so doing, to lay the stress on the continuity between his art and the romantic, in tracing the continuity between the romantic and the mid-Victorian. Even so the weakening of the romantic image of the child in Dickens was a major influence in the development of the child in nineteenth-century fiction. The sentimentality was a new major concomitant; and it was added by a major voice – perhaps *the* major voice of the middle century. It was a phenomenon of nineteenth-century literature for popularizing authors to take over the debilitating characteristics of the major authors, and to exercise their whole sensibility within their sentimentalizing extremities. Dickens's introduction of morbidity – which was only one aspect, though a significant one, of his own image of the child – became the central focus of the popular idea of Dickens's children. Paul Dombey *dying*, not *why* he died, became the focus of interest. The irony was that some of the great authors, such as Dickens and George Eliot, but especially Dickens, were fated to leave a legacy of powerful attitudes to childhood which only represent a minor aspect of their own art.

CHAPTER 6

George Eliot and Maggie Tulliver

I

IF Dickens's self-involvement with his own childhood led to his sentimentalizing of the romantic image, the same factor led George Eliot into a comparable sentimentality. The children of *The Mill on the Floss* are as important to the development of the Victorian world-picture of the child as Little Nell, Jo, and David Copperfield. Hers is another case of the weakness becoming an unfortunate legacy. Her failure fully to control the subjective interests which she brought to her fiction until after *Silas Marner* moulded the children of her earlier novels.

Children as such were never of course so important to her as they were to Dickens. But where they occur, and they occur frequently enough to assume significance, there is, almost always, a subjective resonance, an idealizing sentimentality towards them. A subjective interest informed as we have seen the work of Wordsworth and Dickens in writing of childhood. But whereas for them the child became part of their 'wisdom', with George Eliot there is no comparable assimilation. She never attempted a *Prelude* or a *Hard Times*. She turned away from childhood almost altogether in her later works. Her portrayal of childhood in *Middlemarch* is of the same nature as its portrayal in *Mansfield Park*. It would seem that once she was able to rid herself artistically of the need to write of children, she left them, significantly enough, alone. And for this reason, the children of her early novels were perhaps even more debilitating than Dickens's; since her prestige swiftly covered her entire work, and her memorable children were not creations of her maturity.

She brought to her work an intense recollection of an England she intimately associated with her own childhood in the Midlands, and this as we know worked for strength in her early novels. But the recollection carried within it personal responses to her own childhood, its affections and its emotional difficulties. In the children which she placed within her social recollection, I think we see very clearly the personal responses to her own situation as a child working themselves through. Her own physical plainness, her wish that she herself might have been beautiful, her intellectual yearnings, her sense of personal vitality unfulfilled, the loss of her childhood intimacy with her father and brother descend into the ugly and beautiful, high-spirited and unrequited children of her early novels. They are both the creation of what she was, and more especially of what she might have been. It is not so much a matter that she wrote out of her own experience, and her experience as a child; but that she mingled her own aspirations and regrets, uncritically, with her characters, and especially with her children. Her great strength and significance for the novel may have been, to use Lawrence's perceptive remark about her, that she put 'all the action inside'. But in the early novels, it was very often she herself who was 'inside'; there was no controlling intelligence working in the round; no external criteria of intelligent feeling; no guiding hand. To write from 'inside' is to exercise the greatest self-discipline, to maintain the control from 'without'.

The first *Scenes of Clerical Life* raise the warning sufficiently. The imagination doing a 'little Toryism by the sly, revelling in regret' sets their theme. The object of the regretful 'sly' Toryism, Shepperton church, is significantly enough presented through her own childhood vision of it. Within its 'charm', the Barton children are presented:

But by this time Mr Barton has finished his pipe . . . Nanny is at that moment putting him [Walter] in the little cot by his mother's bedside; the head, with its thin wavelets of brown hair, indents the pillow; and a tiny, waxen, dimpled fist hides the rosy lips, for baby is given to the infantine peccadillo of thumb-sucking.

and again:

Nearest her mother sits the nine-year-old Patty, the eldest child, whose sweet fair face is already rather grave sometimes, and who always wants to run up-stairs to save mamma's legs. . . . Then there are four other blond heads – two boys and two girls, gradually decreasing in size down to Chubby . . .

The children's names always set the tone so tellingly: Chubby,

Dickey, Patty, Sophy. She seldom gives a child its name except by a revealing diminutive:

While this conversation was going forward, Dickey had been furtively stroking and kissing the [his mother's] soft white hand . . .
   'Why are you kissing my hand, Dickey?'
   'It id *to* yovely,' answered Dickey.

All the children until *Middlemarch* talk this baby-talk. Extracted in this way, it becomes astonishing to see the weakness to which so supremely intelligent a mind could be reduced.

Even in the *Scenes*, however, there are signs of the later psychological strength. Acutely observed, the Barton children show that disconcerting inability of the young to involve themselves in adult sorrow. They refuse to be encumbered with the whole adult paraphernalia of death:

They leaned towards her, and she stroked their fair heads, and kissed their tear-stained cheeks. They cried because mamma was ill and papa looked so unhappy; but they thought, perhaps next week things would be as they used to be again . . .

And after their mother's death:

Dickey had rebelled against his black clothes, until he was told that it would be naughty to mamma not to put them on, when he at once submitted; and now, though he had heard Nanny say that mamma was in heaven, he had a vague notion that she would come home again tomorrow, and say he had been a good boy and let him empty her work-box. He stood close to his father, with great rosy cheeks, and wide open blue eyes, looking first up at Mr Cleves and then down at the coffin, and thinking he and Chubby would play at that when they got home . . .

In the midst of all the 'fair heads' and 'rosy cheeks', the ironic distance is almost achieved, the unswerving eye for psychological reality. The same idealization and perception jostle together in the picture of Caterina in *Mr Gilfil's Love Story*. The little girl plays by the bed where her father lies dead:

Her large dark eyes shone from out her queer little face. . . . She held an empty medicine-bottle in her hand, and was amusing herself with putting the cork in and drawing it out again, to hear how it would pop.

Antony Wybrow in the same story, however, is merely a 'beautiful boy with brown curls and splendid clothes'. 'Beautiful' and 'splendid' convey well enough the idealizing atmosphere of the story.

The *Scenes* are admittedly 'prentice-work. But the weakening factors are everywhere at work in the next novel, *Adam Bede*. The craftsmanship is more developed; but the impulse remains. The re-creation of the 'old' England through personal recollection, expressed in the Poyser family, is wonderfully done. The children are in their way essential to the portrayal of the Poysers. But one wonders what Totty, Tommy, and Marty really contribute:

'Munny, my iron's twite told; p'ease put it down to warm.'
The small chirruping voice that uttered this request came from a little sunny-haired girl between three and four ...
'Munny, I tould 'ike to do into de barn to Tommy ...'

Tommy and Marty are equally idealized:

Mrs Poyser ... peeped into the room where her two boys lay, just to see their ruddy round cheeks on the pillow, and to hear for a moment their light regular breathing.

Later they are given as dressed in 'little fustian tailed coats and knee breeches, relieved by rosy cheeks and black eyes'. In such descriptions, the use of 'little' is never merely factual, but serves to add an emotional sweetening. For the children in *Adam Bede*, quaintness is all. Their sweetness mingles with an endearing naughtiness. Their naughtiness is nothing if not engaging:

'We began with calling her Lotty, and now it's got to Totty. To be sure it's more like a name for a dog than a Christian child.'
'Totty's a capital name. Why she looks like a Totty. Has she got a pocket on?' said the Captain. ...
'It's dot notin' in it,' she said. ...
'Oh, she's a funny little fatty ...'[1]

There is a detectable murmur of intelligent discontent with this sort of thing, however, in the ironic comment which follows, that

1. It is not inappropriate perhaps to suggest that the same emotional attitude is applied to her children as to her dogs – that other pervasive sentimentalizing element in so many of her novels.

'people who love downy peaches are apt not to think of the stones' –
typical indeed of her later manner.

But with *Adam Bede*, as with the *Scenes*, there are passages of remarkable vitality and strength. There is an unmistakable rightness
about such things as this: one feels the enrichment her own childhood brought to her work:

The fact was that this Sunday walk through the fields was fraught with
great excitement to Marty and Tommy, who saw a perpetual drama going
on in the hedgerows, and could no more refrain from stopping and peeping
than if they had been a couple of spaniels or terriers. Marty was quite sure
that he saw a yellowhammer on the boughs of the great ash, and while he
was peeping, he missed the sight of a white-throated stoat. . . . Then there
was a little greenfinch, just fledged, fluttering along the ground, and it
seemed quite possible to catch it, till it managed to flutter under the black-
berry bush . . .

There is no intervention here between the facts and their recollection
– even though later we have, inevitably, 'the three pairs of small legs
trotted on'.

II

The Mill on the Floss was unequivocally autobiographical in a sense
that the earlier novels were not. With Maggie Tulliver the self-
identification is very nearly complete. The story of Tom and
Maggie at Dorlcote Mill is essentially that of Mary Ann Evans and
her brother Isaac at Griff. One says unequivocally; but in fact there is
an equivocal blurring as to the identity of the narrator right from
the outset. There is an inexplicitness about her identity which
suggests something of the confusion of the author's emotional
impulse which one detects throughout the work. The reader is not
sure when the events are happening, or who is precisely involved.
The blurring is deliberately courted. There is the vagueness of a
dream, and, inevitably enough, the word itself is used:

That little girl is watching too: she has been standing on just the same spot
at the edge of the water ever since I paused on the bridge. And that queer
white cur . . . perhaps he is jealous, because his playfellow in the beaver
bonnet is so rapt. . . . It is time the little playfellow went in, I think; and there

is a very bright fire to tempt her. . . . It is time, too, for me to leave off resting my arms on the cold stone of this bridge. . . . I have been . . . dreaming that I was standing on the bridge . . . as it looked one February afternoon many years ago. Before I dozed off, I was going to tell you what Mr and Mrs Tulliver were talking about . . . on that very afternoon I have been dreaming of . . .

The novel proceeds from this ambiguous relation between the author and its heroine. The strict bounds between subjective and objective feeling, essential to successful art, are not drawn.

The stress of *The Mill on the Floss* lies at the end of Book II, and in the final chapter preceding the Epilogue. At these points the meaning of the work is drawn into focus. The intention behind the re-creation of Maggie's childhood becomes clear when it is brought to its full close at the end of Book II with:

They had gone forth together into their new life of sorrow, and they would never more see the sunshine undimmed by remembered cares. They had entered the thorny wilderness, and the golden gates of their childhood had for ever closed behind them.

The subsequent theme of the novel lies in a regretful contrast between the joy of Maggie's infancy and childhood and the sorrows of her 'maturity'. Maggie and Tom are to experience the tribulation of their 'thorny wilderness' until the arbitrary dénouement of their drowning:

The boat reappeared – but brother and sister had gone down in an embrace never to be parted; living through again in one supreme moment the days when they clasped their little hands in love, and roamed the daisied fields together.

The novel is held within this structure of regret for childhood, with its 'golden gates', and those conclusive 'daisied fields'. Maggie Tulliver is not, intentionally, presented as a young woman who could not successfully extricate herself from the affections of her childhood. It is not the kind of tragic analysis, such as we might have expected from the George Eliot of the later novels. Tragedy presents us with the unfulfilment of human emotion; but it is an emotion which we are left convinced that the victim should never have sought. It is altogether otherwise with *The Mill on the Floss*. The image of the brother and sister going down in an embrace 'never to be parted; living through again in one supreme moment the days when they clasped their little hands in love' justifies the feelings which had in fact ruined Maggie. Her flaw, her inability to come to terms with her life after the 'golden gates' of childhood closed, which might have been conveyed in tragic terms, is justified, and we are left with the conviction, wholly enervating, that it is life that is wrong – whereas, one would have thought that a mature analysis of her fate would have seen her childhood itself as her delusion, and, ironically, her 'thorny wilderness'.

It may be objected that this is to say no more than that *The Mill on the Floss* is not what it was never intended to be, a tragedy. But the feeling remains that a mature sensibility dealing with the fate of Maggie Tulliver might have translated it into tragic terms; for it contains all the essential concomitants of tragedy. The tragic hero is most often the victim of circumstance or of his own feelings. Whether in ignorance or with intent, he offends against the inexorable requirements of a religious or social order, and finally his subversive individualism stands condemned. In the final analysis, the tragic hero is always wrong. Tragedy is a catharsis of the self, as much as it is a catharsis of anything. It is after all the refreshment of feeling obtained from witnessing great tragedy that the selfish impulse should be seen to be finally unjustified. Its poignancy rests on the sympathies attracted towards a victim who in the final resolution is shown to be wrong. We do not after all take from *Lear* the feeling that paternal love should be allowed the indiscipline of hate. The final discipline of tragedy perhaps lies in its arousing sympathies which are finally purified through the inevitable calamity which falls, and by falling condemns. It dramatizes the harshest reality of the human condition, that what is inexorable is right.

If romanticism is the justification of the self against order, it is perhaps why one cannot really have romantic tragedy. One can only have romantic pathos, which again is why *The Mill on the Floss*, and, say, *Madame Bovary*, are essentially non-tragic works. They both leave too strong a residue of pathos with the reader, and pathos, unresolved, is perhaps the most corrosive feeling which literature can convey. This is to say why, in the last resort, one finds *The Mill on the Floss* demoralizing. Its definition of life as a matter of 'golden gates' closing, its nostalgic turning away from life towards the 'daisied fields' of its conclusion, is not the comment on human existence one might expect from an author whose later work centres so much upon the various definitions of the idea of responsibility.

This is not, of course, to ignore the strength of *The Mill on the Floss* in its parts. The recollected life of Griff is done through the agency of a superb craftsmanship. We are certainly made to feel, through all the resources of a great writer, the poignant reality of Maggie and Tom's 'golden' childhood. The life of Dorlcote Mill has an accumulated presence in the novel, a presence of something very much experienced in the feelings of its author, and we may find ourselves fully acknowledging the values she attaches to the life of the Mill:

There is no sense of ease like the ease we felt in those scenes where we were born, where objects became dear to us before we had known the labour of choice, and where the outer world seemed only an extension of our own personality: we accepted and loved it as we accepted our own sense of existence and our own limbs ... and is not the striving after something better and better in our surroundings, the grand characteristic that distinguishes man from the brute. ... But heaven knows where that striving might lead us, if our affections had not a trick of twining round those old inferior things – if the loves and sanctities of our life had no deep immovable roots in memory.

The Wordsworthian values become even clearer in those passages following the famous expedition of the two children, fishing in their 'own little river':

The wood I walk in on this mild May day, with the young yellow-brown foliage of the oaks between me and the blue sky, the white star-flowers and the blue-eyed speedwell. ... These familiar flowers, these well-remembered bird-notes, this sky, with all its fitful brightness ... such things as these are the mother tongue of our imagination, the language that is laden with all the subtle inextricable associations the fleeting hours of our childhood left behind them.

This is very much Wordsworth's 'natural piety'. The tone, the cadence, the vocabulary and, above all, the meaning, are Words-worth's own: 'such things as these are the mother tongue of our imagination, the language that is laden with all the subtle inextricable associations . . .'. There is no sense, however, of the meaning being 'applied'. There is no discontinuity between drama and comment; the commentary grows out of the life of Tom and Maggie's child-hood. The two children live within the whole texture of life at Dorlcote Mill; and when misfortune descends on the Tullivers, part of the poignancy lies in the consequent dissolution of everything that their life there had intended, the disruption of life's own organic continuity. Mr Tulliver himself 'couldn't bear to think of himself living on any other spot than this, where he knew the sound of every gate and door'. He wanted to 'die in th'old place, where I was born and my father was born'. In presenting the life of Dorlcote Mill, George Eliot was presenting the feelings of an 'old-fashioned man' and his children; and by forcefully contrasting them with latter-day 'instructed vagrancy', she was commenting on the rootless culture of a *laisser-aller* society. This is the heart of Maggie's outcry, when everything that Dorlcote meant to her, in its accumulation of the 'old inferior things', was swept away:

Maggie went on, half sobbing as she turned over the few books. 'I thought we should never part with that while we lived – everything is going away from us – the end of our lives will have nothing in it like the beginning.'

The nostalgia in *The Mill on the Floss* functions therefore on two levels; the regretful nostalgia for Maggie's 'golden' childhood, and this other carefully felt social nostalgia, conveying its sense of loss, and containing what George Eliot conceived to be its 'wisdom' for life. That the two are mingled inextricably is suggested in the following:

It was one of their happy mornings. They trotted along and sat down together, with no thought that life would ever change much for them: they would only get bigger and not go to school, and it would always be like the holidays; they would always live together and be fond of each other.

The wish-fulfilment is immediately audible. It is a significant passage. Nevertheless, it may be relevant to wonder whether without this intense personal involvement, the strength of the presentation of the life of the Mill could ever have been achieved.

There is a remarkable continuity in the novel's characterization. A contrast is sustained between the impulsive, imaginative, passionately affectionate Maggie, both as child and adult, and the obverse character of the practical Tom. In this continuity lies the failure of Maggie's relation with Stephen Guest, and, unwittingly, the spoiling of the novel. The 'charm', the unreproved wilfulness of Maggie the child is carried into her adult life. The disciplines applied to Gwendolen Harleth are entirely lacking. Maggie's fate is whatever happens to her providentially in a world where the 'golden gates of childhood' close, and where affectionate nature is confronted with the disillusionment of the 'thorny wilderness'. She is provided with no disciplines except that of family duty which in itself is a matter for suspicion – there is something almost unpleasant about the harping on the love between the girl and her father and Tom – and the disciplines suggested to her by her devotional reading. But at the centre of her characterization there is a lack of self-knowledge, with its consequent self-indulgence. She is the poignant victim of her fate; and in a very real sense we feel the author breaking her own heart. *The Mill on the Floss* reveals something of the weakness inherent in the whole romantic concept of the innocent victimized child. The charm of 'innocence' conveyed in Maggie's life at the Mill serves to exonerate the irresponsibilities of Maggie as an adult. The childhood episode when Maggie runs away to the gipsies is clearly paralleled to her later flight with Stephen Guest. They are both the flight of frustrated emotion seeking its imaginative indulgence – a flight wholly admissible in a child, but which raises certain questions of responsibility in the behaviour of an adult.

But as with *Adam Bede*, the psychological perceptions are everywhere apparent in the particulars of the novel. Tom is inevitably idealized by the general flavour – 'a lad with light-brown hair, cheeks of cream and roses, full lips. . . .' But his schooling under the 'thumbscrew' methods of the Rev. Stelling is excellently drawn. Even with him there is a distance, which is still more marked in the account of Philip Wakem. It is an accurate account of the mind of a crippled child, whose strength can be judged perhaps by thinking of what Dickens might have made of a similar creation. Wherever she extricated herself, George Eliot allowed her supremely intelligent sensibility to operate.

III

Silas Marner was the last of the novels inspired by her own childhood. The famous conversations in the Rainbow, the finely-drawn accounts of early nineteenth-century religion in Lantern's Yard and Raveloe, derive directly from the sources which enriched the 'life' of *Adam Bede* and *The Mill on the Floss*. Once again, this time even more explicitly, she draws her Wordsworthian conclusions. The poet's influence was plain enough in the values she attached to the society of Dorlcote Mill. It was not surprising therefore that, when she came to *Silas Marner*, she should have seriously considered rendering its morality in verse; and that, deciding on a prose form, she should have prefaced it with a quotation from Wordsworth himself:

> A child, more than all other gifts
> That earth can offer to declining man,
> Brings hope with it, and forward-looking thoughts.

The force of the book lies in the presentation of Silas Marner, the 'declining man' in question, and the redemptive influence of a young child. Marner himself is excellently drawn. The psychology of hoarding, following upon the deprivation of affection in his youth, with its consequent sense of injustice and alienation, is brilliantly done. His presence is truly created. The weight, however, of the moral must fall on its protagonist, on the agency of Marner's redemption, on the child who bestows the 'forward-looking thoughts'.

We are warned perhaps of what to expect, in the presentation of little Aaron Winthrop. He is an 'apple-cheeked youngster of seven'. It is all very reminiscent. Even so, with Aaron, we have a brilliant instance of her power to dramatize her moral theme:

She [Mrs Winthrop] stroked Aaron's brown head, and thought it must do Master Marner good to see such a 'pictur of a child'. But Marner on the other side of the hearth, saw the neat-featured rosy face as a mere dim round, with two dark spots in it.

Marner's physical blindness is an extraordinarily dramatic commentary on his spiritual blindness towards the boy. With the appearance of the 'child' of the novel, we are in no doubt as to her significance: the sight of her for Marner 'stirred fibres that had never been moved in Raveloe – old quiverings of tenderness – old impressions of awe at the presentiment of some Power presiding over his life'. One cannot mistake the Wordsworthian reminiscence:

She was perfectly quiet now, but not asleep – only soothed by sweet porridge and warmth into that wide-gazing calm which makes us older human beings, with our inward turmoil, feel a certain awe in the presence of a little child, such as we feel before some quiet majesty or beauty in the earth or sky – before a steady glowing planet, or a full-flowered eglantine, or the bending trees over a silent pathway . . .

The influence of this 'presence' over Marner is quite explicit:

Eppie was a creature . . . seeking and loving sunshine, and living sounds, and living movements; making trial of everything, with trust in new joy. . . . The gold had kept his thoughts in an ever-repeated circle, leading to nothing beyond itself. . . . but Eppie was an object compacted of changes and hopes that forced his thoughts onwards. . . . Eppie called him away from his weaving . . . re-awakening his senses with her fresh life, even to the old winter-flies that came crawling forth in the early spring sunshine, and warming him into joy, because *she* had joy.

Eppie has then the sort of significance that Miranda or Perdita has. This is the sort of analysis evidently intended; for what is the meaning of *Silas Marner* if it is not it? But the object called upon to sustain the poetic weight staggers beneath it, totters, in fact 'toddles' beneath it. There is a failure in the characterization of the central image:

And the little one, rising on its legs, toddled through the snow, the old grimy shawl in which it was wrapped trailing behind it, and the queer little bonnet dangling at its back – toddled on to the open door of Silas Marner's cottage . . .

And once inside Marner sees it:

It was a sleeping child – a round, fair thing, with soft yellow rings all over its head. Could this be his little sister come back to him in a dream – his little sister whom he had carried about in his arms for a year before she died, when he was a small boy without shoes or stockings.

With George Eliot's children we are never very far from 'brothers and sisters' (one remembers her early collection of verse). The child is in fact named Hepzibah, after Marner's mother and sister. The name is immediately sugared into one of those unfortunate abbreviations – Eppie.

In idea, the meaning of Romantic childhood is well enough conveyed:

No child was afraid of approaching Silas when Eppie was near him: there was no repulsion around him now, either for young or old; for the little child had come to link him once more with the whole world. There was love between him and the child that blent them into one, and there was love between the child and the world . . . to the red lady-birds and the round pebbles.

But as a character of the novel, the child is presented to us in this way, and one has an immediate sense of inadequacy:

This was the introduction to a great ceremony with soap and water, from which baby came out in new beauty, and sat on Dolly's knee, handling her toes and chuckling and patting her palms together with an air of having made several discoveries about herself, which she communicated by alternate sounds of 'gug-gug-gug' and 'mammy'.

He turned round again, and was going to place her in her little chair near the loom, when she peeped out at him with black face and hands again, and said, 'Eppie in de toal-hole'.

The strengthening which succeeded the historical adventure of *Romola* is everywhere apparent in *Felix Holt*, both in general and in particular, in the presentation of its children. The significance is that children now fade from George Eliot's work, except as part of a general *milieu*, or as a reference backward in the lives of her characters. Her children are no longer used as symbols upon which her subjective interests focus. They take their place within the general texture of her mature interests. The new objectivity is seen in the portrayal of Job Tudge in *Felix Holt*. He was a 'small fellow about five, with a germinal nose, large round blue eyes, and red hair that curled . . . a tiny, red-haired boy, scantily-attired'. Reminiscent as this is, there is a difference of tone from what had gone before (although even he evinces an admonition to Esther at one point – 'zoo soodn't kuy').

In *Middlemarch*, the children never obtrude. They play their subsidiary part. The Vincy and Garth children are different in kind from the Poyser and Tulliver households. Ben Garth is 'an energetic young male with a heavy brow', and Letty Garth (perhaps the last of Mary Ann Evans) snatches at her father's letter seals like a 'young terrier'. The image is exact; and it does not sweeten either the child, or, even more significantly, the terrier. The echoes of course persist. Letty Garth had had 'her life much checkered by resistance to her depreciation as a girl'. But the echoes are an almost inaudible murmur among the voice of her mature genius. There is no blurring of her psychological interest as her eye travels down the age-scale.

In *Daniel Deronda*, she is in fact able to contain references to the childhood of her heroine within the whole psychology of her characterization. Maggie Tulliver and Gwendolen Harleth are worth continuous comparison. The new objectivity becomes clear in the title of the first book of *Daniel Deronda* – 'The Spoiled Child'. Maggie was in fact no less spoiled, though the agencies were different. The description of her heroine in these terms would have been inconceivable to the author of *The Mill on the Floss*. Maggie is a 'naughty gell', and not a 'spoiled child'. She was excusably 'borne along on the tide'. She did not, like Gwendolen Harleth, escape her emotional responsibilities by fleeing to the very precise decadence of foreign gaming-houses. The theme of 'continuity' of the earlier book is returned to:

Pity that Offendene was not the home of Miss Harleth's childhood, or endeared to her by family memories. A human life, I think, should be well rooted in some spot of a native land, where it may get the love of tender kinship for the face of earth.

The difference of approach is very clear in that 'Miss Harleth' – it has the distance necessary to the investigation of a 'spoiled' heroine's situation, and reminds one of Jane Austen's:

Emma Woodhouse, handsome, clever, and rich, with a comfortable home and happy disposition, seemed to unite some of the best blessings of existence. ... The real evils indeed of Emma's situation were the power of having rather too much her own way. ...

and Lawrence's:

Lou Witt had had her own way so long, that by the age of twenty-five she didn't know where she was. Having one's own way landed one completely at sea.

The rootlessness of Gwendolen conveyed in the opening sequence when Deronda sees her in the 'dull, gas-poisoned absorption' of the gaming-house, is a testimony to her inadequacy. In face of Mrs Glasher's disclosures, Gwendolen has fled abroad. The point is impressed quite clearly; and this inadequacy, this rootlessness, this modernity if you like, is seen as part of the rootlessness to which she had become used in her childhood:

She had disliked their former way of life, roving from one foreign watering-place or Parisian apartment to another, always feeling new antipathies to new suites of hired furniture.

It is the interest of *The Mill on the Floss* transposed into an entirely different key. In adult life, Gwendolen assumes the impulse to escape she had earlier learned from her parents; and, significantly, she had been thoroughly spoiled at school: she passed 'two years at a showy school where on all occasions of display she had been put foremost', and this had only 'deepened her sense that so exceptional a person as herself could hardly remain in ordinary circumstances or in a social position less than advantageous'.

The central egotism of Gwendolen's character had its explicit origins in her childhood. The references are continuous. Refusing to rise from bed to fetch her mother medicine, she made good her fault next day by caresses which 'cost her no effort. . . . Having always been the pet and pride of the household. . . .' For pride, indeed, in face of her family's ruin, she undertakes the disastrous marriage with Grandcourt, and in the final phrase of Book III, the 'spoiled child', now grown into a young woman, speaks – 'everything is to be as I like'. It is a phrase of superlative ironic genius, summing up in itself the preceding three books, and casting its ironic shadow before it. It can be compared, in its strength, with the 'golden gates' of the earlier novel, which were no less conclusive in their own weakness.

The other children of the book, Gwendolen's sisters, are given in this way:

Of the girls, from Alice in his sixteenth year to Isabel in her tenth, hardly anything could be said on a first view, but that they were girlish, and that their black dresses were getting shabby.

The George Eliot voice, poised and articulate, has assumed control. It is very much the voice of *Sense and Sensibility* and *Mansfield Park*. The children are now securely fixed within the frame of the author's mature interest and perception. Deronda himself, however, is as idealized in childhood as he is throughout the novel:

Still he was handsomer than any of them, and when he was thirteen might have served as model for any painter who wanted to image the most memorable of boys: you could hardly have seen his face thoroughly meeting yours without believing that human creatures had done nobly in times past. . . . The finest childlike faces have this consecrating power.

The tone is ominous and familiar:

Daniel had not only one of those thrilling boy voices which seem to bring an idyllic heaven and earth before our eyes, but a fine musical instinct. . . .

In the conversations with his uncle there is almost the tone of *Little Lord Fauntleroy*:

'All changes are painful when people have been happy, you know,' said Sir Hugo, lifting his hand from the boy's shoulder to his dark curls and rubbing them gently . . .
'I should like to be a gentleman,' said Daniel, with firm distinctness, 'and go to school, if that is what a gentleman's son must do . . .'

Even so, in Deronda, we have further evidence of her special perceptions about children:

Daniel then straining to discern something in that early twilight, had a dim sense of having been kissed very much, and surrounded by thin, cloudy, scented drapery, till his fingers caught in something hard, which hurt him, and he began to cry.

Again the embarrassment of the child in face of suspicions about his legitimacy is sensitively conveyed. He broods on these suspicions, and she declares:

It is in such experiences of boy or girlhood, while elders are debating whether most education lies in science or literature, that the main lines of character are often laid down.

Daniel had trusted his uncle, and was horrified at the possibility of his betrayal by him:

Who cannot imagine the bitterness of a first suspicion that something in this object of complete love was *not* quite right? Children demand that their heroes should be fleckless, and easily believe them so: perhaps a first discovery to the contrary is hardly a less revolutionary shock to a passionate child than the threatened downfall of habitual beliefs which makes the world seem to totter for us in maturer life.

The strength, however, of her attitude to the child in her last phase may be seen best perhaps in her description of the Meyrick children:

Everything about them was compact, from the firm coils of their hair, fastened back *à la Chinoise*, to their grey skirts in puritan nonconformity with the fashion. . . . All four, if they had been waxwork, might have been packed easily in a fashionable lady's travelling trunk. Their faces seemed full of speech, as if their minds had been shelled, after the manner of horse-chestnuts, and become brightly visible.

This would have been impossible to the George Eliot of the *Scenes*, *Adam Bede*, *The Mill on the Floss*, and *Silas Marner*. It is so very much assured. Taking the Meyrick children in contrast with the Bartons, the Poysers, and the Tullivers, it becomes clear that the presentation of her children went exactly, and significantly, *pari passu* with the whole presentation of her genius as she revealed it. She bestowed on the Child her subjective weakness; but also her abiding strength.

CHAPTER 7

Reduction to Absurdity

IN the same year as *Silas Marner* (1861), *East Lynne* was published. That both should have attracted a wide readership is an interesting curiosity. Both contained a significant child. William Carlyle of *East Lynne* is perhaps the most notorious of the Victorian 'dying' children, whose ancestry lay in Little Nell and Paul Dombey. With Mrs Henry Wood we see the force of Dickens as a bridge between the romantic child and the child of the popular Victorian novel. In her we have all the lurid deteriorations the romantic image was heir to.

Paul Dombey, and Eppie in *Silas Marner*, were, however, presented within a seriously-intended context. William Carlyle's context on the other hand is no more than a moralizing melodrama, declaring the inevitable retributions of carnal sin. William's death is merely one more bitter pill for the heroine, the sinful Lady Isabel, who deserts her husband and children for the sake of 'passion'. William's death is the one last, careful, twist of the knife of the sadist masquerading as moralist. The prefacing quotation from Longfellow gives the idea:

> Truly the heart is deceitful, and out of its depths of corruption
> Rise ... the misty phantoms of passion;
> Angels of light they seem, but are only delusions of Satan.

At the moment when Lady Isabel succumbs to this deceit of passion, we have this from Mrs Henry Wood:

> Oh, reader, believe me! Lady – wife – mother! should you ever be tempted to abandon your home, so will you awaken! Whatever trials may be the lot of your married life ... *resolve* to bear them; fall down upon your knees and pray to be enabled to bear them ... bear unto death, rather than forfeit your fair name and your good conscience ...

The priorities of the last sentence are by no means accidental and untypical of the whole book. Everywhere its morality, its belief in the moral responsibilities of the marriage tie, is confused with the claims of social respectability. The fear of the social stigma of illegitimacy resulting from Lady Isabel's elopement is more important to the novel than the reality of her sin. Everything would have been right for Mrs Henry Wood if only Captain Levison had had the decency to regularize matters by marrying the woman he had 'dishonoured'. Her Satan is very much the sort of undesirable person who doesn't leave his moral visiting-cards. Lady Isabel's crime is felt as much more of a social *faux pas* than a downright sin.

The power of the book lies in its recruitment of all the horrors of hell to enforce the confusion. Although one is never really sure whether Lady Isabel has offended God or the decencies of society, poor lady! she gets it unmercifully just the same. Her fate is contrived with every sadistic device at the command of ingenious and morbid fancy. She is crucified on the 'cross' Mrs Henry Wood's morality contrives for her. The goads are applied with relish. *East Lynne* is very much the propaganda of the fear of physical love, and it contains, significantly enough, its attendant hysteria.

That it should find apotheosis in the parodies of later generations is not remarkable. It sounds funny enough today. Its snobbism suggests the kind of class audience it was intended to attract. It assures the reader that he 'need not be reminded that we speak of women in the higher positions of life', and Lady Isabel at a moment of utmost misery remembers to exclaim: 'If you have put me beyond the pale of the world, I am still Lord Mount Severn's daughter!' It seems almost to have intended to impress its morality on the middle orders by its aristocratic flavouring. Its snobbism was perhaps a calculated part of its spiritual uplift. Its morality has 'tone'. But no matter how we may look down our literary noses at it today, it *was* a best-seller; and reading it as a contemporary, seriously-intended piece (which is the effort one has to make with all literature), horror is not too strong to evince at its intentions, and more so, its best-selling acceptance. The fact that it treats itself as a great novel is perhaps its most insidious quality. We may be consoled by the feeling that nothing quite so essentially nasty could ever pass itself off as serious literature again.[1]

Since, basically, it is a tale of corruption by sin, we have Lady Isabel's innocence given in these terms:

A light, girlish form, a face of surpassing beauty, beauty that is rarely seen, save from the imagination of a painter, dark shining curls falling on her neck and shoulders smooth as a child's. . . . Altogether the vision did indeed look . . . as one from a fairer world than this. . . .

The 'shoulders smooth as a child' fall within the general procedure by cliché. It has, significantly, become, by the mid-century, a stock image. Anything pleasant for Mrs Henry Wood had associations with a 'fairer world than this'. She was not, it seems, very much enamoured of Blake's 'this world', and children, being one of the most pleasant things within the compass of her cliché, exist with more than half a foot in the longed-for grave. The book suggests very forcefully that they would be very much better off in the 'fairer world than this'. Wherever they appear, children are heavily idealized. It is a literature of stock superlatives. William Carlyle is a 'little fellow . . . open-tempered, generous-hearted, earnest-spirited'. One detects perhaps more of George Eliot than Dickens in this sort of thing:

'Come hither, my darlings,' she [Lady Isabel] cried.
Isabel and William ran to her. . . .
'Would my little dears like to go a great way with mamma? . . .'

or again:

'Would my baby like mamma to go away and leave him?' she asked, the tears falling fast on his fair curls.

The real *use* of the children, however, is to increase the sadistic tension of the second part of the novel, when Lady Isabel, in disgrace, returns to East Lynne to be her own children's governess. Her husband believing her dead in a railway accident (Mrs Henry Wood had all the journalist's flair for things contemporary) had married

1. In the light of certain literary developments, since this was written, this sentence now seems to me somewhat depressingly optimistic.

again – and not only that, but had indeed married Lady Isabel's former rival. Mrs Henry Wood's knife was nothing if not meticulous. William Carlyle's death is the last blow the book contrives with astonishing imaginative cruelty for the sinful Lady Isabel. In his dying in the presence of his mother whom he does not recognize, and who cannot disclose herself, one can see limitless provision for frustration.

His death is not only this, however. It is part also of what might be called the 'death-wish' of the whole work: 'She didn't pray to die; but she did wish that death might come to her.' It is an odd, self-deceiving, ambiguous 'death-wish'. But wished-for, if not exactly prayed-for, the whole impulse of the book is towards death. 'There will be a blessed rest for the weary, when this toilsome life is ended', it declares. It would be a very complex, but not unrewarding, study to investigate the relation between the severely repressive morality of Victorian society and the satisfactions it sought in such works as *East Lynne* in the prospect of dying. It seems almost that if roses could not be gathered in this 'toilsome life', there was always the 'land, as Mrs Barbauld says, where the roses are without thorns, where the flowers are not mixed with brambles'. The imagery is almost too exactly 'psychological' to be believed – but nevertheless believable.

The true luxury of the book comes with the death of the child, the culminating pleasure of Lady Isabel's frustration. The real frustration lies, one senses, in the relation between the 'governess' and her 'husband'. The book is full of physical titillations, such as when, on one of their walks, Mr Carlyle helps the 'governess' over a stile, and she feels her 'husband's' fingers in her palm. The physical frustration of the woman in face of her husband seems indeed to be transferred very clearly to her erotic feelings towards the dying boy:

She glided down upon her knees and let her face rest on the bolster beside him, her breath in contact with his. .... She leaned over him, her breath mingling with his; she took his little hand in hers.

And again:

Lady Isabel gazed down at William, as if she would have devoured him, a yearning, famished sort of expression upon her features.

There are, quite clearly, some strange emotions entangled within this convenient image of the 'dying son'. *East Lynne* is very much a case for the literary psychiatrist.

But, if these are the realities of the emotional situation, the death itself is overlaid with Mrs Henry Wood's purposeful morality:

'It's nothing to die when God loves us,' the child declares.

'But whether we live or die, we are in the hands of God: you know that, William, and whatever God wills is always for the best,' his father replies.

By the side of William Carlyle's dying bed knelt the Lady Isabel. The time was at hand, and the boy was quite reconciled to his fate. Merciful indeed is God to dying children! It is astonishing how very readily, where the right means are taken, they may be brought to look with pleasure, rather than fear, upon their unknown journey.

The child is morbidly consoled that it will not be long for him to wait for the whole family to die, and he ponders on the prospect of Paradise:

'I wonder how it will be?' pondered he, aloud. 'There will be the beautiful city, with its gates of pearl, and its shining precious stones, and its streets of gold. . . . Madame Vane [his mother] will Jesus come for me? . . . It will be so pleasant to be there; never to be tired or ill again. . . . Don't cry papa,' whispered William, raising his feeble hand caressingly, to his father's cheek. 'I am not afraid to go. Jesus is coming for me.'

The death-luxury reaches finality in Lady Isabel's:

'We *can* bear death; it is not the worst parting that the earth knows. He will be quit of this cruel world: sheltered in heaven. I wish we were all there!'

Bathos, however, is never far away:

'I am going to heaven. Where's Archie? . . . Archie, good-bye; good-bye dear. I am going to heaven: to that bright blue sky, you know. I shall see mamma there, and I'll tell her that you and Lucy are coming soon.'

In the psychic relaxations of our own time, we can only guess at the morbid tensions this kind of self-flagellation satisfied. *East Lynne* was of course consciously a 'tear-jerker'. But the significant thing is that the tears were there for clever jerking. One may assume that Mrs

Henry Wood knew her audience well enough never to miss a single opportunity. Criticism cannot debate her morality; but only, through the literary evidence, display the quality of its expression. To discuss the relation between the morality and its expression would be to cross the narrow and attractively undefended frontier between literary criticism and moral philosophy itself. One can only suggest that the quality of a literary sensibility is never a poor guide to the quality of what is being said. Emotionally *East Lynne* expresses a barbarism more remote from the sensibility of our own time than anything in the whole range of English literature before it. One might excusably feel more kinship with the mutterings of savagery than with Mrs Henry Wood's: '. . . it is astonishing how very readily, where the right means are taken, they [children] may be brought to look with pleasure, rather than fear, upon their unknown journey.'

Pleasure? Resignation perhaps. Pleasure is an active state of anticipation. 'Pleasure' gives the whole emotional façade away. One feels that, for once, Mrs Henry Wood has perhaps said too much.

II

Whereas with *East Lynne* the 'child' is an instrument in a much wider morality, at the end of the century Marie Corelli took the romantic child itself as her theme in both *The Mighty Atom* (1896), and *Boy* (1900), and in a quite remarkable way we have hit off the final bathos of the romantic concept. Marie Corelli was an *ex officio* member of the commercial literary world. She was the popularizing, reader's digest novelist, reduced to its essentials. With an infinite capacity for intellectual mauling, she laid waste in her novels about childhood the whole romantic tradition. Everything was dragged into her intellectual rag-bag. Everything was fair game; convenient grist to the commercial mill. Her range was wide; and her targets well-calculated. It testifies to the wide acceptance of the romantic image of the child that she should have deemed it profitable to level it so carefully within her sights.

The Mighty Atom has a tabloid indignation. Its thesis is directed against 'those self-styled "Progressivists" who by precept and example assist the Infamous Cause of Education Without Religion'.

Borrowing from 'French Atheism', these 'self-styled "Progressivists"' denied 'the Knowledge and Love of God' to children in
'board-schools and elsewhere'. With Marie Corelli we hear already
the first stirring of the propaganda didacticism of the tabloid newspaper. It is a novel of anger and 'exposure' done with consummate
vulgarity.

The theme is explicitly romantic. Nature is bluntly juxtaposed to
civilization. Freedom is opposed to learning. Childhood lies shackled
with education. We can smell the corpse of Blake's *Schoolboy* in this:

A little brown bird fluttering joyously out of a bush ... piped a gentle
roundelay for the cheering and encouragement of those within ... in the
room beyond it a small boy sat at a school-desk reading ... he turned
quickly at the sound of the bird's song ... his deep thoughtful eyes darkening and softening with a liquid look as of unshed tears ... an almost appalling
expression of premature wisdom on his pale wistful features ... the bird ...
had come to reassure him ... that fine bright weather – such weather as
boys love – might be expected tomorrow.

The bird seems to say '... here is a living creature shut up with a
book which surely God never had the making of. ...'

It is perhaps more of Dickens than Blake. There is in fact a continuous, and one feels not exactly unconscious, reminiscence of *Hard
Times* and *Dombey and Son*. The novel is replete with *papier mâché*
impersonations of Dickens's villains. Mr Gradgrind, in the person of
Mr Valliscourt, takes a house in the country near the sea so that his
little son, Lionel, 'will be able to continue his holiday tasks under an
efficient tutor'. He speaks 'in a dry methodical way, cracking walnuts
between whiles'. The effects of her imagery have always the air of
being drawn from a well-thumbed literary card-index. She evokes
the image of Dr Blimber's Academy, sweetened by softening
references to Blake's *Songs of Innocence*. Negatively, she gives expression to the residue of the romantic tradition; but the 'possible
other case' to what she abhors, the humanism and life of Blake and
Dickens, she translates into positives all her own. In the character of
Mr Montrose, the muscular child-salvationist, we have Marie
Corelli's 'life':

'Still at it, Lionel! ... Look here, drop it all for today! ... I'll take you for a pull on the water. . . . You look fagged-out . . . what do you say to a first-class Devonshire tea at Miss Payne's?'

And later, during the 'pull on the water':

'I say, Mr Montrose,' he [Lionel] shouted – 'This is glorious!'
'Aye, aye,' responded Montrose, B.A. . . . 'Life's a fine thing when you get it in big doses!'

The 'big doses' are later defined:

'You'll find plenty of boys to fight with – and to conquer! – fighting is the rule of this world, my boy, and to those who fight well, so is conquering . . . go to a public school – Eton, Harrow, Winchester, – any of them can turn out men.'

Marie Corelli digresses liberally on what might be considered an entirely evil theme:

The young truant whom Mother Nature coaxes out in the woods . . . when he should be at his books . . . and has an innate comic sense of the uselessness of learning dead languages . . . is probably the very destined man who, in time of battle, will prove himself a hero of the first-rank, or who, planted solitary in an unexplored country, will become one of the leading pioneers of modern progress and discovery. Over-study is fatal to originality of character; and both clearness of brain and strength of physique are denied to the victims of 'cram' . . .

To such muscularities she reduces Wordsworth's 'one impulse from a vernal wood' and Dickens's whole case against the utilitarian education of Gradgrind and Dr Blimber. The romantic case for 'wonder', 'imagination', and 'joy' becomes in Marie Corelli the anti-intellectualism of public-school philistinism. One hears in this novel of 1896 the ominous murmurings of the England of Bottomley and the 'white feathers' of 1914–18.

The quality of the 'life' she is asserting is everywhere exposed in the emotions of the prose. We have already heard Montrose, B.A. defining the meaning of life in fourth-form slang. This, in the bric-à-brac phrases of the gossip-column wedding, is Wordsworth 'done into' Marie Corelli:

The burning bars of saffron widened in the western heavens, – shafts of turquoise-blue, pale rose, and chrysoprase flashed down towards the sea like reflections from the glory of some unbarred gate of Paradise.

It is not only education, however, which she deplores; but more particularly the education of the 'self-styled "Progressivists"'. The book is a cantankerous denunciation of Frederic Harrison's materialist positivism, and everything which Harrison stood for. The type of 'intellectual' discussion she conducts requires the introduction of personal invective. The 'mighty atom' is religion itself, the soul of Man, which annihilates Mr Harrison. The case for religion is characterized in the persons of Mr Reuben Dale and his little daughter Jessamine. Reuben Dale, 'drawn from life', as she declares, is the 'simple-hearted, God-fearing', West Country man. He had never heard 'of the feverish and foolish discussions held in over-populated cities where deluded men shut out God from their consciences.' He is, quite clearly, Wordsworth's 'Michael' reduced to absurdity. It is in conversation with him that Lionel receives initiation into the religion he had so far been denied:

'Please, Mr – Mr Dale, what do you mean by your soul?' . . .
'I mean . . . the "vital spark o' heavenly flame" in all of us, that our dear Lord died to save.'

The quality of the religious discussion involved becomes apparent when the boy sees a beggar and cogently inquires why a beneficent deity should allow such suffering to exist. 'So it must seem', declares the author, 'to anyone who leaves God out.' The problem is resolved by a 'good' maid explaining to the boy that God 'looks after the beggar'. Later in the novel, when Lionel stands watching the old grave-digger at work on his own daughter Jessamine's grave, he asks:

'You are going to cover up her beautiful curls and blue eyes in all that red-brown earth?'

Reuben Dale replies:

'. . . 'tis all for the best. He'll gi' me grace to see 'twas for the best.'

Jessamine serves as the symbol of a child brought up in fear of God.

She is a fusion of both the romantic, and Marie Corelli's 'religious' child.

> Jessamine's eyes had such heavenly sweetness in their liquid depths, and something moreover beyond mere sweetness, – the untroubled light of a spotless innocence such as sometimes makes the softly-tinted cup of a wood-land flower remind one involuntarily of a child's eyes ... the child-look is in such blossoms, and we often recognize it when we come suddenly upon them peering heavenwards out of the green tangles of grass and fern. Jessamine's eyes were a mixture of grave pansy-hues and laughing forget-me-nots.

We hear this fusion of the romantic and the religious when the children go out of the church into the sun, which shone as if to say 'Suffer them to come unto me and forbid them not, for of such is the kingdom of heaven'. Wordsworth's Nature and the residues of an undoctrinal Christianity have fused into Marie Corelli's Christian romanticism. The cults of 'innocence' and 'rusticity' combine to form the religion of the following. Jessamine declares to Lionel that her mother is an angel:

> 'Feyther says she often flies doon ... an' kisses 'im, an' me too, when we'se asleep ...'
> 'Then she is dead?' queried Lionel.
> 'Nowt o' that. ... Hasn't I told 'ee she's an angel?'

In contrast to this child of sure Corellian faith, Lionel sighs the sighs of a 'tired young thing overweighted with thought, and longing for rest and tenderness'. The echo is continuously Dickensian. Like Paul Dombey, the boy sits in his window at night in a state of cosmic wondering. Hearing an owl, he ponders: 'Perhaps it is like me, wondering why it was ever made.' Only in sleep, in a semblance of death, does he take on the 'heavenly sweetness' of Jessamine. In sleep, his face takes on that 'divine half-wondering, half-solemn smile, which is never seen save on the lips of sleeping children, and the newly dead'.

With Marie Corelli, as with Mrs Henry Wood, death is never very far removed from her image of the child. Paul Dombey is recreated in Lionel Valliscourt. The logic of the book is that he too should die, the victim of his father and of the atheism of his education, and, ingeniously, the plot thus resolves. The boy is taken to Clovelly to recover his failing energies. Tormented already by his new tutor, Professor Cadman Gore, who succeeds the unacceptable Montrose, B.A. ('I don't like fads or fancies of any kind. Stick to facts, – master them thoroughly'), the boy is deserted by his mother, who could no longer sustain the hardness of her husband's heart. Alone, the child experiences the torments of his soul's growing awareness. 'He clenches' his small 'hot hands hard', and questions the 'facts' of Professor Cadman Gore's education, who, perhaps worse than anything for Marie Corelli, was a believer in the emancipation of women. The Professor had nearly married 'one such Christ-scorning female, with short hair and spectacles, who had taken high honours at Girton, and who was eminently fitted to become the mother of a brood of atheists'.

Bereft of Montrose, B.A., his mother, and little Jessamine, the boy descends the carefully prepared stairway towards suicide. Whilst in Clovelly, he hears of a suicide by hanging. Conveniently enough, his mother left with him her sash, which he uses to discover the answer to the question his education had denied to him – as to his soul's immortality. He decides to discover the answer on a basis of trial and error. The suicide comes as a shock in the novel – perhaps because one could never expect such a feat of contrived literary morbidity. Innocent of the ways of this species of literary mind, one misses perhaps all the carefully laid signals. Kneeling at his window, the child prays to God, in the person of the 'Almighty Atom'. 'This world,' he says, 'frightens me . . . but of You I am not afraid.' With the words of 'Gentle Jesus' on his lips, he takes the sash and hangs himself.

Marie Corelli assures us that his suicide reflects the influence of French atheism in English schools. With the convincingness of newspaper exposure, she adduces her incontestable evidence. The circulation of Edgar Monteuil's *Catéchisme du Libre-Penseur* in French schools had caused, she declares, a wave of child-suicides throughout France; so much so that the *Conseil de Nantes* had decided to reintroduce religion into their schools. Like his little French brothers, Lionel had died to find the God 'denied him by the cruelty and arrogance of man'.

If *The Mighty Atom* were not evidence enough of the truly terrifying thing mental mediocrity is when gifted with verbal ease and the assurance of an audience, Marie Corelli re-emphasized the matter when she returned to childhood as her theme for *Boy*. Published in 1900, it ran through thirteen editions before 1913, when it was first issued cheap. This time romantic 'Nature' is jettisoned. Instead, she trawls another theme close to the romantic tradition into her philosophical net. *Boy* is the tale of 'innocence' corrupted by the power of environment. At the outset we are at once in the presence of concentrated 'innocence':

Lifting a pair of large, angelic blue eyes upwards, till their limpid light seemed to meet and mix with the gold-glint of his tangled curls, he murmured pathetically, – 'Oh, Poo Sing! Does 'oo fee ill? . . . Oh, Poo Sing!'

Boy is seated in his high-chair surveying and addressing the 'poor thing', his father. But it is not in any cheap tenement, as one might have supposed, but the 'town house' of the 'Honourable James D'Arcy-Muir'. To strike up the contrast between childhood's innocence and drunken corruption, the *Intimations Ode* is drawn in, paraphrased:

It is impossible not to see, in the eyes of many of these little human creatures, a look of infinite perplexity, sorrow and enquiry, – a look which gradually fades away as they grow older and more accustomed to the ordinary commonplace business of natural existence, while the delicate and dim memories of the Soul in a former state wax faint and distant.

Wordsworth's 'Imperial palace' becomes 'a time, set far away among rainbow eternities'. The 'halo of divine things was still about' Marie Corelli's Boy. Given an engraved Doré edition of the *Paradiso* (there could be no doubt that Marie Corelli was well-read, if she read nothing well), the child asserts his celestial origin: 'Boy seen f'owers and boo'full people'. 'Boy *may* remember where he came from', sighs Miss Letty, his would-be saviour from the vice of his parents. The book preaches the moral responsibility of parenthood; and it is a tale of the 'tragic' corruption of Boy at the hands of his selfish parents. Miss Letty, a 'rustling glittering dream', with 'small hands with big diamonds flashing on their dainty whiteness', fails to persuade his parents to allow her to adopt him. Instead he goes with his parents to their new home in the West Country. Allowed to run wild with the vulgar boys of the village, he imbibes the blasphemous cynicism of the fishermen. He becomes indifferent, coarsened, cynical; and when he goes on holiday to Miss Letty, she finds the 'far-off beautiful angel look of his countenance had all but vanished'. With devastating lunacy, the author intrudes:

We may ask whether for many a child it would not have been happiest never to have grown up at all. Honestly speaking, we cannot grieve for the fair legions of beloved children who have passed away in their childhood, – we know, even without the aid of Gospel comfort, that it is 'far better' with them so.

The death-escape of *East Lynne* returns with Marie Corelli. With them both the 'Gospel of Life' becomes, disturbingly, a gospel of death.

As in *The Mighty Atom*, Marie Corelli now brings forth her own positives. She defines the moral guidance Miss Letty would have bestowed on Boy. They play at cards, and Boy cheats. Miss Letty pleads with him to grow up a 'brave, honest man, and a gentleman!' If only, she thought, she could get 'Boy away from his home surroundings and place him at a good English preparatory school, she would perhaps be the saving of him'. Instead, however, of all horrors, Boy is sent to a *French* school. Like *The Mighty Atom*, the book is redolent with anti-French prejudice. She knew exactly the key to pitch her drum. At an English school, she declares:

'. . . he would have been taught there that death is preferable to dishonour. But at a foreign school he'll learn that to tell lies prettily and to cheat with elegance, are cardinal points in a gentleman's conduct. . . . They spy on boys in foreign schools.'

Miss Letty's military friend opines:

'It's a d—d shame to try and turn an upright-standing Briton into a French frog.'

Boy himself declares to his unrepentant mother:

'Oh, mother, mother!' he said, at last giving way to his sobs, 'I did want to be a real English boy! – a real, *real* English boy.'

Returning to England, Boy is sent to Sandhurst, which, surprisingly, comes in for a little by the way criticism. Almost as if it were St Cyr, and remembering her 'romantics', she declares: 'Modern education' is intent on 'checking all natural emotion – killing enthusiasm'.

Expelled from Sandhurst for drunkenness, Boy gambles, and, to pay his debts, falsifies a cheque (one of Miss Letty's own). Repentant, he joins up for the Transvaal War. Within the space of four pages, we are regaled with a set-piece on the virtues of patriotism, and a set-piece on the lunacies of war. With an ardent desire to please everybody, Marie Corelli always wore her moral hat at a variety of rakish angles. Boy dies in action; but is saved, however, for a long 'moving' death-scene, by his boyhood friend, Alister McDonald, whom in distant days Miss Letty had known would grow up a 'warm-blooded courageous man'.

III

Boy represents, on the most vicious level perhaps, the absolute decadence of the romantic idea of innocence. Its annual editions throughout the Edwardian period suggest their own disturbing commentary as to its wide acceptability. Innocence for Blake had been a symbol of rich definition, containing within it Blake's own positive assertion of 'life'. By the middle century, however, innocence had become closely associated with pathos; and once the symbol had become pathetic, it became the convenient vehicle for the expression of regret and withdrawal. In talking of childhood, the great Romantics were, in a very real sense, talking of the whole condition of Man. For Blake, Wordsworth, and in some of Dickens, the child was an active image, an expression of human potency in face of human experience. Innocence for them was valuable for what it might become, if it could survive the power of corrupting experience. We can see how, in its origin, the symbol of romantic innocence was very much a symbol of a secular humanist religion. And this is the distinction to be made between the original romantic and the debased-romantic, Victorian concepts of innocence. From the middle century, the emphasis shifts towards the state of innocence itself, not as a resilient expression of man's potential integrity, but as something statically juxtaposed to experience, and, ultimately, indeed quite quickly, something not so much static as actually in retreat. At best, in its widespread dissemination, the romantic image was sweetened into the vacuities of *Little Lord Fauntleroy*; at worst, the positive assertion of life became a negative assertion of withdrawal and death. The conflict between innocence and experience was felt to be lost before it began; its only resolution lay in the defeat of death itself. After Dickens, the romantic child of innocence exists very close indeed to the fact of early death. Children no longer grow up and develop into the maturities of Wordsworth's *Prelude*. The child dies, as Smike and Paul Dombey die, and as William Carlyle and Lionel Valliscourt die. The Victorians seem to have taken to themselves the romantic image of childhood, and negated its power. The image is transfigured into the image of an innocence which dies. It is as if so many placed on the image the weight of their own disquiet and dissatisfaction, their impulse to withdrawal, and, in extremity, their own wish for death. These are not exaggerated conclusions to draw when a society possesses for popular reference the image of a purity which must die before it is corrupted. It is a remarkable phenomenon, surely, when a society takes the child (with all its potential significance as a symbol of fertility and growth) and creates of it a literary image, not only of frailty, but of life extinguished, of life that is better extinguished, of life, so to say, rejected, negated at its very root.

CHAPTER 8

Innocence in Henry James

S o far, we have been for the most part concerned with tracing a continuity, if indeed a continuous deterioration. It is perhaps part of Henry James's distinction that he could take both innocence and childhood as major interests at the end of the century, and create a successful literature separate altogether from the tradition we have been discussing. In the light of what had happened to the romantic image of the child, it is not surprising that a serious writer should have perhaps felt that *there*, there wasn't very much left. In this matter of his treatment of childhood, more than in anything perhaps, we feel just how far he was from becoming an *English* writer. Dickens's child came from his very special English awareness. The fate of Dickens's child is very much his commentary on the fate of English humanity in the middle century. The child in Henry James is very much the child of an expatriate American, intimately concerned with the problems of the influence of an 'old' culture upon the 'innocent' new, the product of a sensibility functioning in the society of a wealthy expatriate. The symbol of the sensitive child developing into an awareness of the complexities of life seems to have been specially attractive to him, perhaps as a reflection of his developing awareness of the complexities of his own European initiation.

Most of the greater James novels are in fact an inquiry into the fate of innocence, an investigation of the dramatic and moral possibilities of innocence confronted with life. His central figure in so many novels was some young person, either child, adolescent or young adult, someone, often an American, on the edge of life, capable of receiving life to its fullest, capable too of finding it only to have it ruthlessly withdrawn. We remember in *The Portrait of a Lady* Isabel Archer's 'fixed determination to regard the world as a place of brightness, of free expansion, of irresistible action'. We remember too, however, that although she took 'the first steps in the purest confidence', she had suddenly found the infinite vista of a multiplied life to be a dark, narrow alley with a dead wall at the end:

Instead of leading to the high places of happiness, from which the world would seem to lie below one, so that one could look down with a sense of exaltation and advantage, and judge and choose and pity, it led rather downward and earthward, into realms of restriction and depression where the sound of other lives, easier and freer, was heard as from above.

The recurrent situation in Henry James is of this sense of potential innocent life, and its frustration, either through the ruthless egotism of his villains, or, as he developed, through the agency of his hero's, or more usually his heroine's fate.

It was an easy transference to express this theme in terms of the child. Or, to put it the other way, we see how he tended to conceive his central characters very often as 'children'. They share just those characteristics of the child which provide an opportunity to discuss the values of the adult world – its innocence, its painful capacity for impression and sensation, for corruption, for, above all, becoming the victim. So that in Maisie of *What Maisie Knew* and in Nanda Brookenham of *The Awkward Age*, we have the consistent Jamesian heroine.

And in this respect, it is unfortunate that the most famous children in Henry James should be the corrupted Miles and Flora of *The Turn of the Screw*. This unrepresentative short novel might easily give the misleading impression that James was mainly concerned with innocence assailed with the horrors of sexual depravity. There can be no doubt, of course, that *The Turn of the Screw* is very intimately relevant to a discussion of the 'case' of Henry James – it has a personal, subjective resonance. But it is precisely for that reason that it should be very clearly distinguished from the other works, closely surrounding it in date of composition, in which childhood is the central theme. *What Maisie Knew* and *The Awkward Age* display James the moral artist treating seriously of childhood and adolescence, and they lead inevitably, in a way in which *The Turn of the Screw* does not, to a discussion of his interests and methods as an artist. He wrote of Hawthorne that he was 'perpetually looking for images which shall place themselves in picturesque correspondence with the spiritual facts with which he is concerned'. In Maisie and Nanda Brookenham, James himself found exact characterization for the 'spiritual facts' which so intensely concerned him.

Returning to the novel after his disastrous adventures into the drama, in a mood of acute self-doubt as an artist, he wrote in consecutive years, beginning in 1897, *What Maisie Knew, The Turn of the Screw,* and *The Awkward Age.* Their consecutiveness suggests forcibly enough a close concern with childhood. But to turn to these novels of the nineties from *The Portrait of a Lady* and *The Bostonians,* is to discover almost the work of another man. The characteristics which vitiated so much of his later work have already encroached. The success of his early work had depended on the truth of the dictum he laid down in the Preface he ultimately wrote to *The Portrait of a Lady,* where he speaks of the 'perfect dependence of the "moral" sense of a work of art on the amount of felt life concerned in producing it'. The strength of *The Portrait of a Lady* lies in the feeling it creates of the 'life' of Isabel Archer, and the contrast established in terms of feeling between her freely discriminating responses and the restricting egotism of Osmond and Madame Merle. Her discriminating criteria – 'to judge and choose and pity' – live in the novel, and we feel intensely their frustration. The force of the novel lies in the sense it evokes of the moralizing power of human sensitive awareness in the character of Isabel Archer.

But with James's development, the emphasis shifts from this personal drama of life in conflict with human egotism, to an impersonal drama of life frustrated by circumstance, by fate. Milly Theale in *The Wings of the Dove* consummates what was to become an obsession with James. She was to be:

... a young person conscious of great capacity for life, but early stricken and doomed, condemned to death under short respite, while also enamoured of the world; aware moreover of the condemnation, and passionately desiring to 'put in' before extinction as many of the finer vibrations as possible, and so to achieve, however briefly and brokenly, the sense of having lived.

The 'strange bitter fate' of the hero of *The Princess Casamassima* was to look 'at the good things of life only through the glass of the pastry-cook's window'. The phrase recurs almost verbatim in *What*

Maisie Knew. Maisie has that 'odd air of being present at her history, in as separate a manner as if she could only get at experience by flattening her nose against a pane of glass'.

Every commentator on James has been brought to the question of his singular development. Dr Leavis speaks of 'some failure about the roots and at the lower levels of life' . . . 'that is, he did not live enough'. Mr Edmund Wilson has found 'something incomplete and unexplained about James's emotional life' which 'seems to appear unmistakably from his novels'. In the later novels he considers that James was often dramatizing his own 'frustrations'.

Almost every circumstance of James's life led to 'incompleteness' and the habit of withdrawal. His own account of his childhood points to a child thrown back passively on his own 'lucid consciousness':

I lived and wriggled, floundered and failed, lost the clue of everything but a general lucid consciousness . . . which I clutched with a sense of its value.

Within the confines of New England, James speaks of his family's 'almost distressfully uninvolved and unconnected state'. They were 'disconnected from business' and could 'only be connected with the negation of it, which had as yet no affirmative . . . side'. The Genteel Tradition was entirely inimical to serious art. We remember the advice of James T. Fields, the influential editor of the *Atlantic* – 'what we want is short, *cheerful* stories'. It was as much the failure of American literary culture as of European which finally reduced him to the groping for the refinements of civilized intercourse, which, tragically, he was never to find.

His reception as a novelist in both England and America contributed to his withdrawal. The Prefaces which he wrote for his novels towards the end of his life were 'in general, a sort of plea for Criticism, for Discrimination, for Appreciation on other than infantile lines – as against the so almost universal Anglo-Saxon absence of these things'. Edith Wharton, who knew him perhaps more intimately than most, spoke of his 'deep consciousness of his powers, combined with a bitter, a lifelong disappointment at his lack of popular recognition'.

Everything, then, the circumstances of his youth, his expatriation, his reception as an artist, tends to explain his 'case'. And yet, in face of this, there remains the suspicion of something in James himself, some personal factor, in some way working to make him so uncongenial to his audience, reducing him, in Dr Leavis's words, to that 'inability to state, to tackle his themes, or to get anything out clearly and finally'. Whatever the disrespect he met with, Conrad faced a comparable lack of real recognition and survived. At the time of James's death, Lawrence was in the process of that investigation of civilized values which became *The Rainbow*. Everything points to some original factor in James himself, of which his life was both a symptom and an aggravation. One can only feel some initial deficiency which fed the artistic disaster.

Disaster, however, suggests something altogether too strong; unless it is taken as a justifiable word to use to lament the deficiencies of genius. With James, more than with any other of the great novelists, one is left with a sense of powers never fully brought to effect. But the child novels reveal, in a brilliant way, the power of his genius to circumvent his disability by using it. The child's psyche, claustrophobic, contained, gazing out upon the mysteries of adult life, had particular relevance to the kind of sensibility he was so often concerned to convey. The moral perceptions of *What Maisie Knew* are in fact the perceptions of a unique sensibility. On the other hand, *The Turn of the Screw* only too strongly reveals, in an almost painful way, the fine edge on which his sensibility functioned. In treating of childhood in *The Turn of the Screw*, we see how closely, for patently neurotic reasons, he came to complete artistic disaster.

The character of Pansy in *The Portrait of a Lady* suggests James's distinctive image of childhood. She is the innocent 'blank page', as much the victim as Isabel herself of her father's egotism. She is involved with Isabel, therefore, in the whole moral texture of the novel. Osmond's wilfulness in attempting to sacrifice her to the convenient marriage with Lord Warburton is part of the novel's general theme. That there is more than mere victimized innocence about her, that she is more than just a convenient article of the novel's furniture is, however, conveyed in the following. She is a victim, with a frank, and very wide-eyed awareness. It is a forecast of a characteristic which he developed so brilliantly in *What Maisie Knew*:

'Your father would like you to make a better marriage,' said Isabel. 'Mr Rosier's fortune is not at all large.'

'How do you mean better – if that would be good enough? And I have so little money; why should I look for a fortune?'

'Your having so little is a reason for looking for more.'

With which Isabel was grateful for the dimness of the room; she felt as if her face were hideously insincere. . . . Pansy's solemn eyes, fixed on her own, almost embarrassed her. . . .

'What should you like me to do?' her companion softly demanded.

The question was a terrible one. . . .

'To remember all the pleasure it's in your power to give your father.'

'To marry someone else you mean – if he should ask me?' . . .

The child's eyes grew more penetrating. . . . She stood there a moment with her small hands unclasped and then quavered out:

'Well, I hope no one will ask me!'

Later in the novel we have:

Isabel was touched with wonder at the depths of perception of which this submissive little person was capable; she felt afraid of Pansy's wisdom – began almost to retreat before it . . .

Before coming to *What Maisie Knew*, James again displayed his interest in the child, in the short story, *The Pupil*. It is the tale of Morgan Moreen, a sensitive, intelligent boy, surrounded by the decadent squalor of an expatriate family living beyond its means. The child establishes a 'felt' relation with his tutor, only to meet death in the excited moment when he is to be given over to the young man's permanent charge. The world in which Morgan Moreen establishes his valid and sensitive relationship is essentially the squalid, vulgar, negative world of Maisie Farange.

The Preface makes quite clear James's intentions with *What Maisie Knew*. The situation was that of a young girl confronted with her parents' divorce, with their re-marriage, and then with the clandestine liaison between her step-parents, whilst her natural parents succumb to vicious promiscuity. And this is what James intended to make of this seemingly perverted fiction:

. . . it became rather quaintly clear that, not less than the chance of misery and of a degraded state, the chance of happiness and of an improved state might be here involved for the child, round about whom the complexity of life would thus turn to fineness, to richness.

... the small expanding consciousness would have to be saved ... rather than coarsened, blurred, sterilized, by ignorance and pain. .... No themes are so human as those that reflect for us, out of the confusion of life, the close connection of bliss and bale, of the things that help with the things that hurt. ... To live with all intensity and perplexity and felicity in its terribly mixed little world would thus be the part of my interesting small mortal ... really keeping the torch of virtue alive in an air tending infinitely to smother it ... by sowing on barren strands, through the mere fact of presence, the seed of the moral life ...

James does not manipulate the puppets of moral indignation however. His interest was to go further than the obvious moral comments on the Faranges, and the Brookenhams in *The Awkward Age*, and to show in fact the triumph of innocence through the freely developing consciousness of youth, and in this way to keep 'the torch of virtue alive'.

By setting Maisie in the midst of divorce and sexual depravities, James accepted the full challenge of the morality he wished to convey. He gives the finest edge to the positions he adopts, by divorcing them from the idea of immorality, which is so frequently confined to sexual irregularity. *What Maisie Knew* investigates the deeper morality of human sympathies, and the loyalties of sensitive human relationships. Its morality is that of a human consciousness enriched by 'innocent' acceptance of the squalid, developing an awareness of love and respect through their very absence and negation. The novel evokes a sense of the child's indestructible integrity.

James was, of course, concerned with the moral corruption, in the usual sense, of late nineteenth-century England. In the early chapters of the novel, he gives us this society, in the terms which interested him, of its personal relationships:

This was a society in which for the most part people were occupied only with chatter.

Everybody was always assuring everybody of something very shocking, and nobody would have been jolly if nobody had been outrageous.

In this context of malice, gossip, and brutal self-indulgence, the 'poor little monkey' is 'abandoned to her fate'. Promiscuous sexuality is not the central interest; it is symptomatic of the all-pervading selfishness. Her parents 'wanted her not for any good they could do her, but for the harm they could, with her unconscious aid, do each other'. She was indeed a 'ready vessel for bitterness, a deep little porcelain cup in which biting acids could be mixed'.

The immediacy of James's feeling is everywhere conveyed through the immediacy of the imagery. There is no gulf of contrivance between feeling and expression, such as one often finds in those long, exhausted images of the later novels. In *What Maisie Knew* the imagery contains a perfect psychic reality:

Maisie received in petrification the full force of her mother's huge painted eyes – they were like Japanese lanterns swung under festal arches.

The next moment she was on her mother's breast, where, amid a wilderness of trinkets, she felt as if she had suddenly been thrust, with a smash of glass, into a jeweller's shop-front.

and surpassingly:

She was taken into the confidence of passions on which she fixed just the stare she might have had for images bounding across the wall in the slide of a magic-lantern. Her little world was phantasmagoric – strange shadows dancing on a sheet . . . a mite of a half-scared infant in a great dim theatre . . .

Maisie's phantasmagoric world is given in a way reminiscent of *David Copperfield*, with its keenly felt and disconnected sensations of a child thrust into an adult environment, with its wilful, and casual, sadism towards children. Her father refuses her her mother's letters. The pathos and cruelty of this might so easily have been sentimentalized (one thinks of *Jane Eyre*). James presents it in terms of mordant comedy:

. . . he confined himself to holding them up at her and shaking them, while he showed his teeth, and then amusing her by the way he chucked them, across the room, bang into the fire.

The vulgarity and casual cruelty of her father's friends are felt through the child's own consciousness:

Some of these gentlemen made her strike matches and light their cigarettes; others, holding her on knees violently jolted, pinched the calves of her legs till she shrieked – her shriek was much admired – and reproached them with being toothpicks.

The whole texture of the child's artificial relation with her mother is given through her sensations, translated into the terms of the imagery:

... she was able to make allowances for her ladyship's remarkable appearance, her violent splendour, the wonderful colour of her lips and even the hard stare, the stare of some gorgeous idol described in a story-book. ... Her professions and explanations were mixed with eager challenges and sudden drops, in the midst of which Maisie recognized as a memory of other years the rattle of her trinkets and the scratch of her endearments, the odour of her clothes and the jumps of her conversation. She had all her old clever way ... of changing the subject as she might have slammed the door in your face.

In the narrow compass of a short novel, James gives us the development of a child from 'phantasmagoric' infancy to almost discretionary adulthood. The type of moral development in question is admirably given in the child's carrying messages of hatred between the parents: '"He said I was to tell you," she faithfully reported [to her mother], "that you're a nasty horrid pig!"'
The child protects herself by assuming stupidity. She had:

... the complete vision, private but final, of the strange office she filled. It was literally a moral revolution and accomplished in the depths of her nature. ... She had a new feeling ... of danger; on which a new remedy rose to meet it, the idea of an inner self or, in other words, of concealment.

This 'moral revolution' is achieved by Miss Overmore's 'rolling' her eyes at the child with all the force of vulgar adult innuendo. The moral result is the child's first awareness of her own integrity.
Perhaps the finest example of the moral method of the novel comes in the scene in Kensington Gardens, where, in the company of her step-father, she meets her mother accompanied by one of her 'men'. The situation is almost grotesque in its depravity. But Maisie sits and converses with the 'man', while at a distance her mother and her step-father were 'face to face in hatred'. Out of the 'bale', Maisie receives the central moral lesson of the book. The Captain tells the

child that her mother is 'true!' The fact is patently untrue; and yet
for the girl:

> She was fairly hushed with the sense that he spoke of her mother as she
> had never heard anyone speak. It came over her as she sat silent that, after all,
> this admiration and this respect were quite new words, which took a distinc-
> tion from the fact that nothing in the least resembling them in quality had on
> any occasion dropped from the lips of her father, of Mrs Beale, of Sir Claude,
> or even of Mrs Wix. . . .
> 'Oh do you love her?' she brought out with a gulp that was the effect of
> her trying not to make a noise. . . . 'Say you love her, Mr Captain; say it,
> say it!' she implored. . . . 'You *do* love her?'
> 'My dear child –' The Captain wanted words.
> 'Then don't do it only for just a little.'
> 'A little?'
> 'Like all the others.'
> 'All the others?' – he stood staring.
> She pulled away her hand. 'Do it always!'

Through the negative depravity of promiscuous love, the child is
brought to the moral awareness of the quality of lasting love and
respect. Love, loyalty, and respect are no longer concepts for her, but
lived realities, perfectly dramatized.

The passage has its sequel when later her mother, in an outburst of
self-pity and excusal, declares herself 'good'. Maisie, remembering
the Captain's expression of love, recalls it to her mother; merely to
discover that it had not been for 'always'.

> 'What business have you to speak to me of him?'
> Her daughter turned scarlet. 'I thought you liked him.'
> 'Him! – the biggest cad in London!' Her ladyship towered again, and in
> the gathering dusk the whites of her eyes were huge.
> Maisie's own, however, could by this time pretty well match them;
> and she had at least now, with the first flare of anger that had ever yet
> lighted her face for a foe, the sense of looking up quite as hard as anyone
> could look down.
> 'Well, he was kind about you then; he *was*, and it made me like him.
> He said things – they were beautiful, they were, they were!' . . . there rose
> in her a fear, a pain, a vision ominous, precocious, of what it might mean
> for her mother's fate to have forfeited such a loyalty as that. There was

literally an instant in which Maisie fully saw – saw madness and desolation, saw ruin and darkness and death.

The 'madness and desolation' are, however, immediately contained within the comedy of the mother's returning to her purse the money she had been on the point of giving to her daughter:

'You're a dreadful dismal deplorable little thing,' she murmured. And with this she turned back and rustled away over the lawn.

Ida Farange, on her final exit, gives exactly, with the exception of one small adjective, an accurate and devastating description of herself.

The 'filial hope' which Maisie felt for her mother raises the secondary theme of the novel. In an ironic way, Maisie has a corrective influence in the lives of the squalid adults. It is the loyalty she establishes with her step-father, Sir Claude, which finally makes him the chief agent in her freedom. He facilitates her freeing herself from a world in which she was used as the instrument of adult egotism. In face of her step-mother, Mrs Beale, who in the final chapters tries to assert her will over the child, Sir Claude relinquishes Maisie to her own choice of Mrs Wix. Respecting her freedom, Sir Claude rescues her from her step-mother's grasp and 'kept hold of her; he held her in front of him, resting his hands very lightly on her shoulders and facing the loud adversaries'. Maisie's freedom is at last safe under the hands of the man whose own 'development' she had 'promoted'. Earlier in the novel, there had been this:

'The great thing is that you and I are all right.'
'*We're* all right,' Maisie echoed devoutly. . . . It was as if she must somehow take care of him.

Her own care had been reciprocated; a mutual respect had been established. The moral reality can be felt under Sir Claude's hands 'resting . . . very lightly on her shoulders'.

The force of the novel rests therefore on the positive world which Maisie creates from the sympathy and loyalties of human relationships. But it was, nevertheless, a dangerous performance. One can – just – see what Mr Spender meant when he declared that 'there is something particularly obscene about *What Maisie Knew*, in which a small girl is, in a rather admiring way, exhibited as prying into the sexual lives of her very promiscuous elders'. It is of course exactly what James does not do. The 'admiration' is admiration for precisely those moral values which Mr Spender ignores.

But, undeniably, the book does evoke a certain response; it skirts dangerously close to something akin to 'obscenity'. There is a vibration not entirely imported into the work by the misunderstandings of the reader. James's intention prevented his placing very much force on the normal moral disgust the adults evoke. To write so deliberately in contrary motion to the popular moral sense places an enormous burden on the morality he sought to convey through awareness and consciousness. It so happens that *What Maisie Knew* succeeds, for the reason that there is enough 'felt life' in Maisie's consciousness to sustain the morality.

But even in *What Maisie Knew* we feel the precariousness of his emphasis on consciousness. There is an interesting episode where it becomes a mere verbalism, not dramatized into its context; where in fact the art fails, and a personal obsession with 'awareness' takes over. It is the description of Maisie's first experience abroad:

Her vocation was to see the world and to thrill with enjoyment of the picture; she had grown older in five minutes. ... Literally in the course of an hour she found her initiation ... she recognized, she understood, she adored ... feeling herself attuned to everything and laying her hand, right and left, on what had simply been waiting for her.

But the awareness of the child is concerned with the refinement of human intercourse; and not with this sense of feverish thrilling. The effect of the passage seems entirely incongruous when we realize that it is the description of a little girl parading the streets of a rather inexpensive French seaside resort. We feel James has imported an emotional element into the novel, which obsessed him elsewhere, his avidity for life. It is not surprising to find the intrusion of that other obsessive, and essentially complementary interest. Maisie not only responds to life excessively. She is also the excluded witness:

She was to feel henceforth as if she were flattening her nose upon the hard window-pane of the sweet-shop of knowledge.

It gave her an odd air of being present at her history . . . as if she could only get at experience by flattening her nose against a pane of glass.

If such had been Maisie's case, it is scarcely irrelevant to suggest that she could never have 'known' anything. The images, brilliant as they are, are not related to the central meaning of the novel. They evolve from some external, intrusive factor of James's sensibility.

There are other faults in *What Maisie Knew*. There is its manifest 'over-treatment', which James himself detected. There is too much 'doing', too much cerebral manipulation of the plot. The Preface, although written much later, seems to give the hint: 'I recollect, however, promptly thinking that for a proper symmetry the second parent should marry too – which . . . was in any case what the ideal of the situation required.' The relationships of the adults have indeed a slightly mechanical quality, of fitting in with the ideal require-ments. The adults operate in a psychological void. Their disastrous marriages and liaisons proliferate without any psychological ex-planations. The plot seems in fact something of a compulsive fantasy in James himself. He establishes his negative environment for Maisie by such a nexus of odd adult infidelities that the reader is brought to demand an explanation which is never given. It might have been impossible to contain such an investigation within the method of the book. But by using a method which in a sense forbids it, he requires us to accept an Ida Farange, say, who displays not merely moral squalor but something very akin to nymphomania.

If *What Maisie Knew* is a comedy of innocence triumphant, *The Awkward Age* is a tragedy on the same theme. Strictly *The Awkward Age* falls outside a discussion of childhood in Henry James, for although he calls the two girls of the novel 'children', they are in fact young girls in their teens, at the moment when their innocence becomes of interest to him, at the moment of their initiation into life. Its significance in this context lies in its demonstration of James's continuous interest in the problem of innocence in the face of a cor-rupting environment. There are obvious comparisons to be drawn between the Faranges and the Brookenhams; the Brookenhams are of the same 'elbowing, pushing, perspiring, chattering mob'. But their delineation is altogether more complex. Whereas, in *What Maisie Knew*, the integrity of Maisie is established without her participation in her corrupt environment, the tragedy of Nanda is to be so much a corrupt participant herself that she becomes unacceptable to the man she loves. Her sexual involvement with the depravities of the Brookenham set is dramatized in her reading and aiding the circulation of a yellow-backed 'French novel'. In *The Awkward Age* James attempts to establish an integrity of innocence quite distinct from the integrity of Maisie. Nanda Brookenham functions clearly enough within the *affaires* and lusts of her mother's set. The tragedy of the book lies in Nanda's poignant knowledge that her initiation spoils her for the man, Vanderbank, whom she loves. She loves the man who 'minds' her corruption, simply because he 'minds'. Her salvation lies in her own awareness of herself, in the residual sense she has of her own integrity:

'But you don't imagine what I know; I'm sure it's much more than you've a notion of. That's the kind of thing, now, one *is* . . .'

'Oh, it's all right,' breathed Mitchy, divinely pacific.

'I'm sure I don't know whether it is; I shouldn't wonder if it were in fact all wrong. But what at least is certainly right is for one not to pretend anything else.'

She is saved by establishing her corrupt identity in the knowledge of Mr Longdon. He enters the novel in sharp distinction from the Brookenham world. He had loved, and almost married Nanda's grandmother, and carried with him an image of girlhood entirely old-fashioned and irrelevant to the condition Nanda inevitably found herself in. At first he idealizes the girl; but slowly his own innocence is initiated; he sees the corruption that Nanda 'couldn't help', the 'knowledge' of 'everything': 'Everything, literally everything in London, in the world she lives in, is in the air she breathes. . . .' These words of Vanderbank express the reality which ultimately Longdon himself accepts about Nanda. Initiated himself, he retains his own clearly established values of friendship and love. Accepting Nanda's corruption, he finally removes her to his own world of Beccles, which he had earlier described to Nanda in these terms:

. . . 'if we sit close we shall see it through. But come down to Suffolk for sanity. . . . I want to show . . . what life *can* give. Not of course,' he subjoined, 'of this sort of thing [that is, a fashionable country-house party].'

'No, – you've told me. Of peace.'

'Of peace,' said Mr Longdon. 'Oh, you don't know – you haven't the least idea. That's just why I want to show you.'

It is only, however, when Nanda has convinced him of her own true personality that she consents to go with him. In the last chapter they are discussing Nanda's unacceptability to Vanderbank, whom earlier Longdon had contrived that she should marry:

'Because, you know,' the girl pursued, 'I *am* like that.'

'Like what?'

'Like what he thinks.' Then so gravely that it was almost a supplication. 'Don't tell me,' she added, 'that you don't *know* what he thinks. You do know.'

And then finally:

'But,' she continued . . . 'we're many of us, we're most of us – as you long ago saw and showed you felt – extraordinary now. We can't help it. It isn't really our fault. There's so much else that's extraordinary that if we're in it all so much *we* must naturally be.' It was all obviously clearer to her than it had ever been, and her sense of it found renewed expression; so that she might have been . . . a very much older person than her friend. 'Everything's different from what it used to be.'

'Yes, everything,' he returned with an air of final indoctrination. 'That's what he [Vanderbank] ought to have recognized.'

Thus with the relationship of the 'indoctrinated' two, with their mutual awareness of each other, the novel closes, with an atmosphere of acceptance and consummation.

The establishment of the girl's integrity, her preservation of a deeper innocence, joins the work to *What Maisie Knew*. But its similarity should not conceal its essential difference from the earlier novel. Maisie develops her own sense of her integrity in spite of and sometimes with the aid of her sexually depraved environment. She is never herself sexually initiated. She is never 'spoiled'. Nanda Brookenham's initiation and survival is of an altogether different sort.

Technically, *The Awkward Age* is one of the most daring innovations in the English novel. But the 'doing', the 'finish' – its astonishing exploitation of the dramatized conversation – should not distract from its moral intentions. James himself gloried in the 'quantity of finish it stows away'. For him it was a 'job' wonderfully 'amusing and delightfully difficult from the first'. In a remarkable way, he seems himself to ignore its obvious moral intensities. It is an excessively difficult novel to read, and its 'finish' tends almost to conceal the moral drama between the worlds of Mr Longdon and the Brookenham set, which makes it stand as one of the great James novels.

If *What Maisie Knew* and *The Awkward Age* are representative of James's art, *The Turn of the Screw* most certainly is not. It is to be distinguished very clearly from its surrounding works. It is of course a tale of innocence and corruption. It deals superficially, that is, in a Jamesian theme. But *What Maisie Knew* and *The Awkward Age* are both novels of moral conflict; they are concerned with the dramatic impact between a freely developing innocence in relation to a corrupting environment. Their interest lies in the organic development of an innocent consciousness. The drama of *The Turn of the Screw* (and it is 'dramatic' enough, in a limiting sense of the word) partakes of none of this.

Mr Edmund Wilson, in his famous effort to establish an eccentric reading of the text (centring James's interest in the frustrated psyche of the spinster Governess), declares that the story would be the only work of James without a more or less 'serious' interest, if his theory about the Governess is unacceptable. Precisely so. The theory about the Governess *is* unacceptable, and the story *is* without a 'serious' interest. For clearly the particular moral situation James dealt in so frequently is not present in this short story. The fort of innocence is taken before the story begins. There is no moralizing conflict between innocence and corruption. The depravity of the children is a given fact; the drama turns upon the appearance of the ghosts of the persons responsible for their corruption to the person who wishes to discover, with such an avid interest, the specifications of their corruption. Maisie is not poignant; she is a resilient figure. Miles and Flora are poignant, in the sense that they are, pathetically enough, the victims of Quint's and Miss Jessel's corruption. Their fate is accomplished before the novel begins.

To attempt to see the story as a variation on James's theme of the 'frustrated Anglo-Saxon spinster' is entirely unacceptable. To suggest that the appearance of the ghosts takes place merely in the neurotic imagination of the Governess requires the rejection of the one piece of evidence which entirely justifies her story, her unprompted description of Quint's appearance. Mr Wilson suggests that this description 'answers the description of one of the master's valets who had stayed down there and used to wear his clothes'. It so happens that it doesn't merely answer the description of one of the valets, but, in all its convincing accuracy, is the incontrovertible evidence for accepting the ghosts' reality.

This is not, however, to suggest that the attitude of the Governess is anything but neurotic. Mr Wilson's essay is useful indeed in putting the emphasis on the psychological quality of the story, in directing attention the right way. For *The Turn of the Screw* is not a significant work of James's art, but the product of a seriously disordered sensibility. It is not really a piece for literary analysis at all; but something patently for the psychiatrist.

One can of course take it at its face value; take the 'amusement' he himself suggested for its intention:

... this perfectly ... irresponsible little fiction is a piece of ingenuity pure and simple, of cold artistic calculation, an *amusette* to catch those not easily caught.

The ghosts would be 'agents, in fact; there would be laid on them the dire duty of causing the situation to reek with the air of Evil. . . . What in the last analysis, had I to give the sense of? Of their being the haunting pair, capable . . . of everything – that is, of exerting, in respect to the children, the very worst action small victims so conditioned might be conceived as subject to.'

And again:

Only make the reader's general vision of evil intense enough, I said to myself – and that already is a charming job – and his own imagination, his own sympathy (with the children) and horror (of their false friends) will supply him quite sufficiently with all the particulars. Make him *think* the evil, make him think it for himself, and you are released from weak specifications.

One feels the evasion of all this however. The artistic hands are being very carefully washed – this 'irresponsible little fiction' – 'this piece of ingenuity pure and simple'. It is as if in afterthought James wished to retract from the curious story – curious indeed to call it a 'charming job'. But of course the cajolery almost works. We feel inclined to accept the author's word, and take it as an *amusette*. And therefore miss the force of: 'Make him [the reader] *think* the evil, make him think it for himself, and you are released from weak specifications.'

What, in fact, we may ask, was it that James required 'release' from? What indeed were these 'specifications'?

The 'specifications' are – and the equivocation makes them all the more suggestive – sexual depravities, and, in particular in the case of Miles, homosexual specifications. Read once, the dramatic appearances of the ghosts keep the story alive, fix the reader's interest. Read several times, the ghosts become insignificant melodrama. What remains to sustain the impulse of the story is the Governess's avid curiosity to discover the specifications from Miles as to what he did to be expelled from school, what he did with Quint. The conflict of the story lies between Miles and the Governess; and it is essentially a conflict between repression and admission, between the repressed secret corruptions of the child and the hounding parent-like figure of the Governess. It is significant that the girl, Flora, disappears from the story, for no very good reason; the final quest for discovery lies between the Governess and the boy. Considering that superficially the two children are equal in their corruption, there would be no reason (if it were not for a very good one) that the conflict should not resolve into a dénouement between the Governess and Flora. The subconscious motivation turns the story inevitably towards that wholly distasteful last scene between the Governess and Miles, in which, so feverishly, we have the dramatized conflict at the heart of the little fiction.

The conflict is essentially between the woman and the boy; but James introduces an ambiguity as to the attitude he requires from us towards them. The boy is at once vicious and corrupt and yet pathetic, the victim of the Governess's cruel pursuit. The Governess herself is at once the virtuous agent of the child's salvation, and at the same time an executioner, a clumsy and deranged pursuer. There

seems in James a conflict in himself which he translated into the
ambiguities of this painful story – the pursuit of the admission of
guilt and resentment of the agent of discovery. It seems reasonable to
suggest that the story is the outcome of a deep psychological conflict
within himself, between his sense of guilt, his desire for confession,
and his self-justifying resentment of discovery. The two factors in
his psyche pursue each other throughout the story, the Governess
seeking those 'weak specifications' and the boy retaining them from
her.

It is, I think, the Miles factor in James's motive which presents the
Governess so often in such a disagreeable light. There can be no
doubt of her infatuation for the children's guardian. It seems almost
as if the Miles factor in James is finding its revenge on its pursuer by
the common defence of *tu quoque*. She talks of 'saving' the boy; she
talks of 'one last turn of the screw of ordinary human virtue', but
her own deranged behaviour and infatuation serve as a continual
recrimination; at heart she is no better than the child. She comes out
of the story, so strong perhaps was James's subconscious resentment
of her, as a wholly distasteful figure.

A quotation will serve to show the method of repression at work.
The Governess talks to the housekeeper, Mrs Grose:

> 'Then I went on: "At all events, while he [Miles] was with the man –"'
> 'Miss Flora was with the woman. It suited them all!'
> 'It suited me too, I felt, only too well; by which I meant that it suited
> exactly the particular deadly view I was in the very act of forbidding myself
> to entertain.'

The 'forbidding myself' of the last line is quite astonishing in its
equivocation. It at once suggests how 'deadly' the 'particular view'
was, and, in contrary motion, that the 'view' must be an incorrect
one. And really what is one to make of that explanation of: 'It suited
me too, I felt, only too well' – by which she 'means' that 'it suited
exactly the particular deadly view'? The passage proliferates ambiguities. Like many another in the book, it is quite impossible to say
precisely what it means. The story proceeds by a suggestiveness
(which was all part of the 'charming job' perhaps) which makes for
the sense of its psychic dishonesty.

The climax comes in the last scene between the Governess and the boy; ushered in with that singularly inappropriate, but so telling image about the Governess's feelings. At last everyone has left. She is alone with the child. A secret (every signal has been suggestively given that it is sexual) lies between them. Singularly then she feels that she and the child were 'as some young couple who, on their wedding-journey, at the inn, feel shy in the presence of the waiter. He [Miles] turned round only when the waiter had left us. "Well! – so we're alone!"' The image of the 'wedding-journey' is absolutely apposite to the sort of repressed factor which lay between the two characters at this point. In a wholly fantastic way (for many years I was completely puzzled by my sense of surprise when confronted with this image), it becomes clear that the 'discoverer' is in James's image the 'bride'. The text continues:

'Oh more or less [alone].' I imagine my smile was pale.
'Not absolutely. We shouldn't like that!' I went on.
'No, – I suppose we shouldn't. Of course, we've the others.'
'We've the others – we've indeed the others,' I concurred.

The 'others' – the 'haunting pair, capable . . . of everything . . . of exerting, in respect of the children, the very worst action small victims . . . might be conceived as subject to' – they lay between the bride and groom of James's imagery on this substitute 'wedding-journey'.

We need not refer further to the obsessive appetancy for discovery of the last scene. At length, at the moment of the boy's admission, he finds security in death. He dies, as one would have imagined, without admitting to anything, except to the identity of Peter Quint. Without the child's convenient death, the story could have gone no further without defining the 'weak specifications' James had spent over a hundred pages to conceal. Speculations could, of course, be pursued endlessly. But the main point is the sort of interest *The Turn of the Screw* evokes. Its interest is biographical, and not literary. It seems to bear a very intimate relation to James's famous 'case'. It may or it may not explain it. In any event, it seems to point convincingly enough to what one might consider a neurotic complication in James's sensibility, which may have been responsible for leading him into that withdrawal, which in turn had such a rarefying influence on his art. Art, however, has been defined as the 'controlled neurosis'; and it is precisely the element of control which makes the distinction between the art of *What Maisie Knew* and the disorderly fantasy of *The Turn of the Screw*. Even if there were psychological factors directing James's interest towards innocence and its corruption, in *What Maisie Knew* and *The Awkward Age*, that interest was controlled into objective art. In those novels, James said what he had to say of significance as an artist about the innocence of the child.

CHAPTER 9

Mark Twain and Richard Jefferies

'Who does not see in the extraordinary number of books about boys
and boyhood written by American authors the surest sign of the pre-
valence of that arrested moral development which is the result of the
business life, the universal repression in the American population of all
those impulses that conflict with commercial success.'

Van Wyck Brooks: *The Ordeal of Mark Twain*

I

MARK TWAIN's greatness is something beyond dispute; that he was
something much more than Arnold Bennett's diminishing 'divine
amateur'. *Huckleberry Finn* has the undeniable universality of a
classic. Like all great art, it assumes its own independence of author
and environment. But to look at the sensibility through which the
universality was achieved, detracts nothing from it. To understand
something of Mark Twain's life and the society in which he wrote is
to become more fully aware of the quality of his commentary and
to realize how precariously the objective strength of *Huckleberry
Finn* was sustained. Everything in his life suggested that he would
write a novel of childhood escape, with all the attendant weakness
that that has usually implied, and yet *Huckleberry Finn* is that literary
rarity, a significant novel of a boy's escape from society.

Mark Twain's famous 'despair', his reproachful self-contempt, his
acute nostalgia, the revelations of the unmailed correspondence,
suggest an uncomfortable, disturbed, and at times tormented man.
His despair insists. His maxims maintain an unmistakable burden.
'Pity is for the living, envy for the dead.' 'Each person is born to one
possession which outvalues all his others – his last breath.' 'Be weak,
be water, be characterless, be cheaply persuadable', was the command his Deity gave to Adam, the only command he considered
humanity incapable of disobeying. Taken by those, such as Howells,
who should have known him better, as a humorous 'pose', it is

inconceivable in the light of the evidence to see the despair as any-thing but the expression of a deeply negated personality. There is no murmur of anything remotely resembling 'pose' in his feelings on the death of his daughter:

... she has been enriched with the most precious of all gifts that makes all other gifts mean and poor – death. I have never wanted any released friend of mine restored to life since I reached manhood. I felt in this way when Susy passed away; and later my wife ...

In a life complete with every evidence of an assured public success, there was this insistent frustration and despair. He cherished a re-current fantasy that life should begin old and regress continuously towards youth. Within his nostalgia, we find the fixed symbol of the Mississippi, and his constant urge to re-acquire the life of his early piloting days on the river. In *Life on the Mississippi*, he wrote: 'leave me there to dream that the years had not slipped away; that there had been no war, no mining days, no literary adventures; that I was still a pilot, happy and carefree as I had been twenty years before.' And again he writes: 'I'd rather be a pilot than anything else I've ever done in my life.' 'I am a person who would quit authorizing in a minute to go piloting.' At the moment of his first literary success, he could only say: 'I do not know what to write; my life is so un-eventful. I wish I was back there piloting up and down the river again. Verily, all is vanity and little worth – save piloting.' His career as a young Mississippi pilot represented for him a period of free, creative activity, and his feelings, even in his greatest work, flowed incessantly back towards it.

It is generally understood, therefore, that when people in middle age occupy themselves with their childhood it is because some central instinct ... has been blocked by internal or external obstacles: their consciousness flows backward until it reaches a period in their memory when life still seemed to them open and fluid with possibilities.

In writing this, Mr Brooks suggests that Mark Twain's own obstacles were both internal and external.

Mark Twain's relation with his mother has been frequently dis-cussed. The mothering he received at her hands made him, when he returned home as a grown man of thirty-two, in turn 'pet', 'comfort', and 'tease' her, in Paine's account of their meeting. He doubtlessly acquired from her his compulsion to succeed. From the moment of his father's death, she deliberately instilled into the young, impressionable child his responsibilities towards herself and the necessity of his success. Was it because of her that he became so desperately concerned with establishing his success, and so tormented with the prospect of social and literary failure? Was it from her that he acquired his compulsion towards conformity, for which he so much despised himself? Was his continual self-dissatisfaction (which in time took on really pathological dimensions) the expression of some deeper conflict? Was the writing for a public, of which he was so self-contemptuous, something he both required to do, and equally required to struggle against?

Whether or not Mrs Clemens's influence may be traced so deeply, it was surely her influence which led him into that incredible marriage with a woman who so notoriously mothered him (he used himself the picturesque expression 'edited'), and that singular relation with his daughters, who in his old age would pin notices about the house, telling him what, but more particularly what *not*, to do. His lack of independence was testified to both by himself and his friends. Paine says: 'It was always Mark Twain's habit to rely on somebody.' As an old man in 1900, he himself confessed that 'there has always been somebody in authority over my manuscript'. Of his wife, he wrote: 'After my marriage, she edited everything I wrote. And what is more – she not only edited my works – she edited me.' He was, he declared, 'the most difficult child she had'. 'I have,' he said, 'been used to obeying my family all my life.' There is no doubt that the conforming, the 'editing', satisfied, and at the same time acted as a perpetual emotional irritant. Aunt Polly in *Tom Sawyer* is at once irritating and endearing. Mark Twain himself, we feel, lived through that irritation and endearment.

That his nostalgia was closely associated in his own mind with his literary conformity comes out in *Life on the Mississippi*:

A pilot in those days was the only unfettered and entirely independent human being that lived in the earth . . . writers of all kinds are manacled servants of the public. We write frankly and fearlessly, but then we 'modify' before we print. In truth, every man and woman and child has a master, and worries and frets in servitude; but in the day I write of, the Mississippi pilot had none.

It may be suspected that the freedom he celebrates here arose from the fact that for that short period of his life, he won some equilibrium between the free activity of his own will and the satisfaction of his compulsion towards success. As a pilot he was 'free', because he was doubly free; enjoying the freedom of the self-liberating adolescent and the conforming child.

The Civil War ended all this, however. We remember his own dream 'that there had been no war'. Determined 'never to see his mother's face again, except as a successful man', he went west to the frontier. He found an environment unlikely to accept a man of disruptive, artistic talent. Men living on the precarious edge of civilization defend the social *mores* with their lives. The only acceptable literature was humorous. Humour was not only safe, but served equally as a solvent of the tensions under which the men of the frontier lived. Unsuccessful as a miner, Mark Twain followed in the tracks of Artemus Ward and Bret Harte, and became the professional humorist. His genius was recruited to the only indigenous literary tradition of the American nineteenth century.

Turning east, Mark Twain became the national humorist, the comic spokesman for a whole generation of national pioneers. The victory of the North opened the whole American continent to the 'progress' of the North-Eastern States, and he became its spokesman. The literature of New England was dominated by the Genteel Tradition. His marriage brought him into direct and painful contact with its emasculating gentilities and taboos. It was the New England of *Little Women*; a society against which Henry James's whole career was a continuous protest. In retaining his irony and humour, Mark Twain achieved both conformity and success and a degree of artistic independence.

Becoming the national 'funny man' led to his acute artistic self-disgust. 'We write frankly and fearlessly, but then we "modify".' 'I wasn't going to touch a book, unless there was *money* in it, and a good deal of it.' 'You see I take a vile, mercenary view of things.' He became one of the 'Vanderbilt gang', the snob who could be ashamed of meeting a poorly-clad amanuensis on the deck of an Atlantic liner, because everyone 'could see he belonged to us'. He knew, moreover, exactly what he was doing. His comment on the editorial policy for the newspaper his wealthy father-in-law bought for him is clear enough:

I am not going to introduce any startling reforms, nor in any way attempt to make trouble. . . . Such is my platform. I do not see any use in it, but custom is law and must be obeyed.

The same self-knowing, suicidal irony could make him write towards the end of his life:

The silent, colossal National Lie that is the support and confederate of all the tyrannies . . . that is the one to throw bricks and sermons at. But let us be judicious and let somebody else begin.

'Letting somebody else begin' meant writing to Whitman on his seventieth birthday to congratulate him for having lived to see the development of coal-tar. For the conforming Mark Twain, the century was the 'plainest and sturdiest and infinitely greatest and worthiest of all the centuries the world has seen'. In keeping with it, he led the Gatsby existence of the 'wealthiest grandees of America'. 'There were *always* guests,' says Paine, 'they were coming and going constantly.'

That he deeply frustrated and hurt himself becomes painfully clear. We have the account of one revealing exchange between Mark Twain and the genteel *milieu* of his wife's friends, in the witness of Mrs James T. Fields:

His wife had told him to see how well we behaved (poor we!) and he knew he had everything to learn. He was so amusing about it that he left us in a storm of laughter. Yet at bottom I could see it was no laughing matter to him. He is in dead earnest.

One remembers Freud's definition of humour as 'an economy of expenditure in feeling'. Quite early on as a humorist he had cried out to one of his companions: 'Oh Cable, I am demeaning myself – I am allowing myself to be a mere buffoon. It's ghastly. I can't endure it any longer.' Continually he declared his writing 'bosh'. 'I must go on chasing' phantoms, he told his brother, 'until I marry, *then* I

am done with literature and all that bosh – that is, literature where-
with to please the general public. I shall write to please myself then.'
He pleaded constantly for someone to 'get' him 'out of business'.
He wanted, he told Howells, to 'throw the pot-boiling pen away'.

What exactly was it that he would write to 'please himself'? It was
indeed the exact truth about the 'National Lie' which his public
career served so brilliantly to sustain. For the private Mark Twain,
the 'plainest and sturdiest and infinitely greatest and worthiest of all
the centuries' was really this:

Well, the 19th century made progress – the first progress in 'ages and ages' –
colossal progress. In what? Materialities. Prodigious acquisitions were made
in things which add to the comfort of many and make life harder for as
many more. But the addition to righteousness? Is that discoverable? I think
not. The materialities were not invented in the interest of righteousness. . . .
In Europe and America there is a vast change . . . in ideals – do you admire
it? All Europe and all America are feverishly scrambling for money. Money
is the supreme ideal. . . . Money-lust has always existed, but not in the history
of the world was it ever a craze, a madness, until your time and mine. This
lust has rotted these nations; it has made them hard, sordid, ungentle, dis-
honest, oppressive.

'Civilization,' for this Mark Twain, was a 'shabby poor thing and
full of cruelties, vanities, arrogancies, meanness and hypocrisies. As
for the word, I hate the sound of it, for it conveys a lie.' Above all he
despised 'civilization' for its suppression of the natural instincts of
man 'We have no *real* morals, but the forced suppression of natural
and healthy instinct.' Benjamin Franklin (as significantly for D. H.
Lawrence[1]) represented the paltriness of the American commercial
tribal morality:

His maxims were full of animosity toward boys. Nowadays a boy cannot
follow out a single natural instinct without tumbling over some of those
everlasting aphorisms and hearing from Franklin on the spot. If he buys
two cents' worth of peanuts, his father says, 'Remember what Franklin has

1. Lawrence in his own essay on Franklin put it this way: 'I can remember
when I was a little boy, my father used to buy a scrubby yearly almanac . . .
crammed in corners it had little anecdotes and humorisms, with a moral tag . . .
probably I haven't got over those Poor Richard tags yet. I rankle still with
them. They are thorns in young flesh.'

said, my son, "A groat a day's a penny a year,"' and the comfort is all gone out of those peanuts.

Huckleberry Finn enacts the revolt of 'natural and healthy instinct' against its suppression by a 'moral' society. Everything in Mark Twain's youth and resentful maturity suggested that he would produce a work idealizing boyhood, that his sensibility would regress towards the past, and that within that nostalgia the Mississippi would serve as a focal interest. It was his genius to fuse his personal nostalgia and his social awareness into the universal commentary of *Huckleberry Finn*, even if, in a sense, it was America's tragedy that the talent of her greatest genius should have been squandered in putting back the 'comfort' into a bag of 'peanuts'.

With its subjective involvement, Mark Twain's art exists on that narrow frontier between creative fulfilment and neurotic destruction. One might cite Dickens as a comparable English case. In both writers a personal nostalgia, with an acute awareness of the past, created a dissatisfaction which they fused into the wider purposes of their art. The nineteenth century was perhaps the century of the neurotic masterpiece, through which a catharsis of emotional conflict might be achieved. How many people, troubled with the same repression as Mark Twain, with his regressing 'escapism', found purification and expansion of their feelings through the art of *Huckleberry Finn*. This may partially explain, perhaps, why he and Dickens both passed so effortlessly into the folk literature of their two nations.

Tom Sawyer and *Huckleberry Finn* are essentially complementary, and should be read closely together. The serious intentions of the first may be detected in his own statement in the Preface:

Although my book is intended mainly for the entertainment of boys and girls, I hope it will not be shunned by men and women on that account, for part of my plan has been to try pleasantly to remind adults of what they once were themselves, and of how they felt and thought and talked, and what queer enterprises they sometimes engaged in.

This was as much of a serious purpose as he would publicly admit. The unmailed letter to the theatrical manager who planned to dramatize the novel gives his attitude rather more clearly:

That is a book, dear sir, which cannot be dramatized. One might as well try to dramatize a hymn.

It is clear what the hymn was intended to celebrate:

Saturday morning was come, and all the summer world was bright and fresh, and brimming with life. There was a song in every heart, and if the heart was young the music issued at the lips.

Tom Sawyer is in fact Mark Twain's hymn to the 'child of Nature', born for Blake's 'joy'. It pursues the familiar romantic antitheses, especially between natural enjoyment and religious inhibition. In church, Tom is set, 'next the aisle, in order that he might be as far away from the open window and the seductive ... summer scenes as possible'. The 'seductive summer scenes' are given with unmistakable force:

It seemed glorious sport to be feasting in that wild free way in the virgin forest of an unexplored and uninhabited island far from the haunts of men, and they said they would never return to civilization. The climbing fire lit up their faces and threw its ruddy glare upon the pillared tree-trunks of their forest temple.

The image of 'Jackson's island' lies fully within the romantic tradition of the child:

The marvel of Nature shaking off sleep and going to work unfolded itself to the musing boy. A little green worm came crawling over a dewy leaf ... and when ... it came decisively down upon Tom's leg and began a journey over him, his whole heart was glad – for that meant that he was going to have a new suit of clothes ... a gaudy piratical uniform. Now a procession of ants appeared ... A brown spotted lady-bug climbed the dizzy height of a grass-blade, and Tom bent down close to it and said:

> 'Lady-bug, lady-bug, fly away home,
> Your house is on fire, your children's alone.'

The fusion of the natural and the human is as close indeed as in Blake's own *Songs*:

Tom stirred up the other pirates, and they all clattered away with a shout, and in a minute or two were stripped and chasing after and tumbling over each other in the shallow limpid water. ... They felt no longing for the little village sleeping in the distance ... A vagrant current ... had carried off their raft, but this only gratified them, since its going was something like burning the bridge between them and civilization.

The motive of escape is contained by the continuous awareness and definition of the civilization to which Nature is opposed. The negative civilization of St Petersburg is a presence in the novel. The 'little village' lies there 'sleeping in the distance', with the cant and hypocrisy of its religion and the 'captivity and fetters' of its school. A whole social commentary lies in the identification of Tom's feelings about religion with that of the dog lying in the aisle 'sad at heart, lazy with the summer softness and the quiet, weary of captivity, sighing for a change'. Tom, the dog, and the beetle, like all of God's natural creatures, were prisoners of St Petersburg's Calvinism.

But the case against civilization so easily becomes this sort of thing:

'It's just the life for me,' said Tom. 'You don't have to get up, mornings, and you don't have to go to school, and wash, and all that blame foolishness.'

The ambiguity of feeling behind Mark Twain's 'escape' is immediately felt. The adult revolt and the juvenile 'not having to wash' are in constant friction throughout the book. Tom's attitude to Aunt Polly reveals the tension. She is patently a re-creation of his own mother. She is at once the object of ridicule – 'Spare the rod and spile the child, as the good book says' – and a vehicle of endearing pathos:

Then her conscience reproached her, and she yearned to say something kind and loving; but she judged that this would be construed into a confession that she had been in the wrong. ... So she kept silence, and went about her affairs with a troubled heart.

In face of her, Tom's revolt becomes endearing 'naughtiness'. Tom becomes no more than the image of the universal 'naughty boy'. He breaks Aunt Polly's 'old heart' with his 'outrageousness'. Jackson's Island fades. The pangs of conforming conscience (in terms of boredom) drive Tom Sawyer back to society and home. For him the bridges were not burned.

But there were two small boys in Mark Twain's psyche; one other besides the conforming Tom:

Shortly Tom came upon the juvenile pariah of the village, Huckleberry Finn, son of the town drunkard . . . he was idle, and lawless, and vulgar, and bad. . . . Tom was like the rest of the respectable boys in that he envied Huckleberry his gaudy outcast condition. . . . Huckleberry came and went at his own free will . . . he did not have to go to school, or to church, or call any being master, or obey anybody; . . . he was always the first boy that went barefoot in the spring and the last to resume leather in the fall. . . . In a word, everything that goes to make life precious, that boy had. So thought every harassed, hampered, respectable boy in St Petersburg.

'Tom' – the conforming Mark Twain – 'envied Huckleberry.' In the character of Huckleberry Finn, he introduces into *Tom Sawyer* an element which is not assimilated into the total imagination of the work. There is an unmistakable difference in tone between Tom and Huck. Huck's revolt is absolute, uncompromised, except through the manipulation of the plot. The word 'pariah' sets Huck outside, and in so far as his characterization is felt, his revolt remains unresolved:

Huck Finn's wealth . . . introduced him into society – no, dragged him into it, hurled him into it – and his sufferings were almost more than he could bear. The widow's servants kept him clean and neat, combed and brushed, and they bedded him nightly in unsympathetic sheets that had not one little spot or stain which he could press to his heart and know for a friend . . . he had to go to church; he had to talk so properly that speech was become insipid in his mouth; whithersoever he turned, the bars and shackles of civilization shut him in and bound him hand and foot.

Remembering Mrs James T. Fields ('he was so amusing about it that he left us in a storm of laughter. Yet at bottom I could see it was no laughing matter to him'), we feel an exact personal reference to Mark Twain's own predicament.

Huck flees; only to be cajoled back by Tom, who tells him 'the trouble he had been causing', and 'urges him to go home'.

Don't talk about it, Tom. I've tried it, and it don't work; it don't work, Tom. It ain't for me; I ain't used to it. The widder's good to me, and friendly; but I can't stand them ways. She makes me git up just at the same time every morning . . . I got to wear them blamed clothes that just smothers me, Tom; they don't seem to git any air through 'em, somehow . . . I got to go to church, and sweat and sweat – I hate them ornery sermons! I can't ketch a fly in there, I can't chaw, I got to wear shoes all Sunday. The widder eats by a bell; she goes to bed by a bell; she gits up by a bell – everything's so awful reg'lar a body can't stand it.

The feelings which informed the early chapters of the book have been transferred to Huck, and all the conforming Tom can evince in face of them is the unconvincing: 'Well, everybody does that way, Huck.' The feelings prove unanswerable, and Mark Twain is left with no alternative but to bring the story to conclusion by deflecting Huck into a typical 'Tom Sawyer' adventure. Huck is cajoled from his awkward feelings by Tom's:

Tom saw his opportunity:
   'Looky here, Huck, being rich ain't going to keep me back from turning robber.'

Twain can only resolve the situation of the boy who 'whithersoever he turned, the bars and shackles of civilization shut him in and bound him hand and foot' by seducing him into the language of Tom Sawyer himself. The language of the two boys, significantly, coincides:

'Now that's something like! Why, it's a million times bullier than pirating . . . and if I git to be a reg'lar ripper of a robber, and everybody talking 'bout it, I reckon she'll be proud she snaked me in out of the wet.

The timing of this conflict between Tom and Huck, right at the close of *Tom Sawyer*, has its significance. At his entry, Huckleberry Finn is given unequivocally. He is stated, and undiscussed – 'everything that goes to make life precious, that boy had'. His image is then lost among the adventures of the book, until, just before the end, just before it is too late, the great rebellious utterances appear, pointing, as they do, all the way to *Huckleberry Finn* – only to be smudged over again by a return to the tone of the book's 'adventures'. Everything suggests that in the character of Huckleberry Finn, Mark Twain had approached in *Tom Sawyer* the truth of what he wished to say, and had retired in immaturity from its full expression. He had perhaps discovered in himself an element which he could not fully control, or dare to develop. It was not until 1883, after seven years of composition, that he brought to fulfilment what he had to say about Huckleberry Finn.

Huckleberry Finn was a work which Mrs Clemens was indifferent to, though, with as much as Mark Twain allowed her to know about it, she disliked it. It came out without any great amount of external 'editing', even though, as a whole, it was perhaps subject to the pressures of his own compulsions, to avoid the more serious implications of Huckleberry Finn's escape.

In *Huckleberry Finn* he now enacts what was only partially dramatized in the early chapters of *Tom Sawyer*, and stated by Huck towards its end. The same initial antagonisms between society and Nature are asserted:

She put me in them new clothes again, and I couldn't do nothing but sweat and sweat, and feel all cramped up. Well, then, the old thing commenced again. . . . The widow rung a bell for supper, and you had to come to time.

There is an exact continuity; and again the outer dramatized experiences reflect the inward constriction of human feelings. Nature again lies seductively outside:

Then I set down in a chair by the window and tried to think of something cheerful . . . The stars was shining, and the leaves rustled . . . and I heard an owl. . . . Pretty soon a spider went crawling up my shoulder . . . I used to slide out and sleep in the woods, sometimes, and so that was a rest to me.

Huck's irritations with society are the same as Tom's in the early chapters of the first novel. The differences are that Mark Twain has this time chosen to write in the first person, which establishes an undeniable intimacy, an identity between the author and his hero, and now develops through the symbol of the river the whole significance of the 'wild freedom' of the 'unexplored and uninhabited' Jackson's Island 'far from the haunts of men' which he broached in *Tom Sawyer*.

The Mississippi is of course the real presence of *Huckleberry Finn*. It is the all-containing reference:

I laid there [in a canoe on the river] and had a good rest and a smoke ...
looking away into the sky, not a cloud in it. The sky looks ever so deep
when you lay down on your back in the moonshine ...

It is the raft which, in such intimate and elemental contact with the
river, ultimately links the boy, in the serious way Mark Twain
intended, with the whole created universe:

It was kind of solemn, drifting down the big still river, laying on our backs
looking up at the stars, and we didn't ever feel like talking loud, and it
warn't often that we laughed, only a little kind of a low chuckle.

The book does in fact deal in the fundamental solemnities. It dramatizes the romantic antithesis between the wholeness and mystery of
the natural Creation and a 'sivilization' of broken human parts. The
solemnity is *there* in the book. There is no external philosophizing.
The meaning is wholly contained within the drama of the novel.
Mark Twain's own knowledge of the river, conveyed in the dramatic
experience of the work, adds its unmistakable strength:

... then the river softened up, away off, and warn't black any more, but
grey. .... Sometimes you could hear a sweep screaking ... and by-and-by
you could see a streak on the water which you know by the look of the
streak that there's a snag there in a swift current ...

The use of the vernacular is no device to give the charm of local
colour. There is an astonishing equation between what is to be said
and the means Mark Twain uses to say it. The language retains the
feelings within the protagonist of his idea; there is no superimposed
mental feeling upon the character of the boy. The meaning of the
novel never overflows the careful containment of the characterization. The meaning grows quite literally from the language. For this
reason, Huckleberry Finn's 'return to Nature' becomes wholly
acceptable:

It's lovely to live on a raft. We had the sky, up there, all speckled with
stars, and we used to lay on our backs and look up at them, and discuss
about whether they was made, or only just happened.

Soon as it was night, out we shoved; when we got her out to the middle
we let her alone ... then we lit pipes, and dangled our legs in the water and
talked about all kinds of things – we was always naked, day and night, whenever the mosquitoes would let us ...

The sardonic reality of the mosquitoes is of course an essential part of his perception. It withdraws the romantic escape from its ever-attending danger of weakening nostalgia and juvenility. The romanticism of *Huckleberry Finn* is that potent, creative romanticism, which laughs at itself, and survives.

The 'sivilization' against which the book is a 'lived' revolt is given explicitly in the experiences of Huck on the banks of the Mississippi; in such episodes as the Grangerford–Shepherdson feud, the shooting of Boggs, and Huck's relations to those ambiguous villains, the king and the duke. But the true greatness of the novel lies in its exposition of a subtle moral conflict. 'Freedom' and 'sivilization' are confronted within the conscience of the boy himself, in his relationship with the nigger, Jim. Huck's escape is continuously disciplined by the problem of his loyalty to Jim. *Huckleberry Finn* is not a charming novel of boyhood's escape, but a work of the most intricate moral involvement.

Soon after finding Jim on Jackson's Island, Huck has no qualms about accepting the freedom of their relationship. He will not give Jim over:

I said I wouldn't, and I'll stick to it. Honest *injun* I will. People would call me a low-down Ablitionist and despise me for keeping mum – but that don't make no difference . . . and I ain't agoing back there anyways . . .

The subsequent shame of breaking this trust with Jim brings the first triumph of the boy's sympathetic conscience. He hoaxes the nigger, who was so pleased to find him again, after fearing him lost in the fog:

En when I wake up en fine you back agin, all safe en soun', de tears come en I could a got down on my knees en kiss yo' foot I's so thankful. En all you wuz thinkin' 'bout wuz how you could make a fool uv ole Jim wid a lie. Dat truck dah is *trash*; en trash is what people is dat put dirt on de head er day fren's en makes 'em ashamed.

It was fifteen minutes before I could work myself up to go and humble myself to a nigger – but I done it, and I warn't ever sorry for it afterwards, neither. I didn't do him no more mean tricks, and I wouldn't done that one if I'd knowed it would make him feel that way.

But the problem is not so easily resolved. Soon Huck's traditional conscience 'got to stirring' him 'hotter than ever'. Faced with the choice of giving Jim over to authority or lying to conceal him, he lies:

> They went off and I got aboard the raft, feeling bad and low, because I knowed very well I had done wrong. ... Then I thought ... would you felt better than what you do now? ... what's the use you learning to do right, when it's troublesome to do right and ain't no trouble to do wrong, and the wages is just the same? I was stuck. ...

The sympathy between the boy and the nigger grows. It becomes Huck's turn indeed to need Jim, and rejoice at finding him safe:

> It was Jim's voice – nothing ever sounded so good before ... and Jim he grabbed me and hugged me ...

Together they escape to the raft, which Jim has found again, after it had been run down by the steamboat, and the whole meaning of the book focuses:

> I was powerful glad to get away from the feuds ... we said there warn't no home like a raft, after all. Other places do seem so cramped up and smothery, but a raft don't. You feel mighty free and easy and comfortable on a raft.

The force of 'free and easy and comfortable', which in another context might suggest no more than a regressing irresponsibility, derives from the whole context of the friends' relationship, from the moral growth in Huck by which the right to use these words had not easily been acquired. But the acquisition is only temporary. Huck's problem is continuous, and the book conveys him towards the torment of real moral decision. He tries to escape the responsibility of friendship by the prevarication of sending Jim home:

> I tried the best I could to kinder soften it up somehow for myself, by saying I was brung up wicked, and so I warn't so much to blame. ... So I kneeled down. But the words wouldn't come ... I knowed very well why they wouldn't come ... It was because my heart warn't right; it was because I warn't square ... I was letting *on* to give up sin, but away inside of me I was holding on to the biggest one of all. I was trying to make my mouth *say* I

would do the right thing and the clean thing. . . . You can't pray a lie – I found that out.

The morality of the heart is confronted with the morality of social sin, and momentarily Huck's social conscience prevails. He writes the letter revealing Jim's whereabouts:

I knowed I could pray now. But I didn't do it straight off . . . [I] got to thinking over our trip down the river; and I see Jim before me, all the time, in the day, and in the night-time, sometimes moonlight, sometimes storms, and we a-floating along, talking, and singing, and laughing . . . I couldn't seem to strike no places to harden me against him, but only the other kind . . . and see him how glad he was when I come back out of the fog. . . . It was a close place. I took it [the letter] up. . . . I was a-trembling, because I'd got to decide, for ever, betwixt two things, and I knowed it.

He tears the letter up, and decides to 'go to hell'. 'It was awful thoughts, and awful words, but they was said.' The force of Huck's moral decision lies partly, of course, in the irony of Huck's own definition of his virtue in terms of sin and wickedness. In his decision he is absolutely alone, and feels himself alone. There are no social props to sustain him. The absolute antithesis Mark Twain intended between the river and society is focused in the boy's achievement of virtue through the torment of the last test of the individual conscience in considering itself socially 'wicked' and at the same time right.

Huck's tearing up the letter is the moral crux of the novel, and from that point I think the book loses its way. A whole change of tone is introduced with the entry of Tom Sawyer, and more especially with the extended episode about the 'freeing' of what turns out to be the already 'freed' nigger. The book is captured by the tone of the earlier work. The intrusion of Tom Sawyer dissipates the moral intensity of the novel. The freeing of the nigger, which would have been the ultimate test of Huck's moral resolution, is solved by the arbitrary trick of Tom's knowing all along that Jim had been already freed. The moral resolution is neatly side-stepped; the boys return to society, as they returned in *Tom Sawyer*. The conforming factor in Mark Twain's psyche triumphs – except for that last famous assertion from Huckleberry Finn:

But I reckon I got to light out for the Territory ahead of the rest, because Aunt Sally she's going to adopt me and sivilize me, and I can't stand it. I been there before.

This final gesture (signed significantly enough 'yours truly') retrieves but does not wholly redeem the compromise of the final chapters. Huck's rebellion survives, and it has behind it the strength of the whole book, but he is spared the ultimate penalty of his freedom. There are so many layers of meaning in that last deliberate sentence; but one of them is the small boy in the author merely cocking a snook at society.

For Mark Twain himself the sense of compromise continued. The sense of moral dishonesty ('you can't pray a lie') remained with him. 'Am I honest? I give you my word of honour (privately) I am not.' In 1899, he wrote: 'What I have been wanting is a chance to write a book without reserves – a book which should take account of no one's feelings, and no one's prejudices, opinions, beliefs, hopes, illusions, delusions; a book which should say my say, right out of my heart.' He became obsessed with the idea of writing a confessional autobiography, which would be, he said, 'something awful'. Paine writes that he 'confessed freely that he lacked the courage, even the actual ability, to pen the words that would lay his soul bare'.

Everything suggests a repression more personal than a repression inflicted upon his genius by an unsympathetic culture. In one of the unmailed letters he likened his feelings to a volcano – 'sometimes the load is so hot and so great'. Something, whether acutely personal or social, turned his feelings towards such commentaries as this: 'Anybody that knows anything knows that there was not a single life that was ever lived that was worth living.' In *What is Man*, he declared: 'Man originates nothing, not even a thought. . . . Shakespeare could not create. He was a machine, and machines do not create.'

Why had he such an interest in this denigration of humanity and its achievements? To assess the greatness of his work requires no answer. By referring to the man, however, we see how much *Huckleberry Finn* is a remarkable distillate of the various and complex factors which went to the production of Mark Twain's extraordinary sensibility. In the creation of the character of Tom Sawyer, for all its vitality and boyhood exuberance, we see clearly the factors making for weakness. In the creation of Huckleberry Finn we see no less the triumph of Mark Twain the artist over his regressing and weakening impulses. In that one novel of childhood, the personal nostalgia and unbalance of the man expands in an astonishing way into a commentary on American society, and finally on civilization itself.

II

Bevis is very much the English *Huckleberry Finn*. But Coate Reservoir was not the Mississippi. Jefferies was not Mark Twain. Mark Twain was the universal American genius. Jefferies the minor English eccentric, something of a curiosity. Comparisons diminish him; comparisons with any of the great figures he had obvious affinities with. Wordsworth, Lawrence, and, in America, Thoreau and Mark Twain, said very much what he had to say. For all their variety, they all lie within the Romantic tradition of 'Nature' and of 'human instinct'. Yet they were the great professional writers; whilst Jefferies was the amateur at letters, the journalist, the novel-taster, the belles-lettres essayist with the 'fine' style, the purveyor of one major perception, the perception of what Nature had meant to himself. This he purveyed, and this was the force of his integrity, of his strangely intense message. He knew exactly what he wanted to say, and said it; sometimes with garrulous monotony. *Bevis*, it is rightly said, is too long. But somehow his sincerity insists, and he is not to be ignored.

His reputation has belied him. He has had an unfortunate cachet among the sentimentalizers about children. *Bevis* has become, as Mr H. C. Warren says in his *Introduction* to the novel in the uniform edition, the means whereby adults can 'recover the lost world of childhood'. It is a sad epitaph, and one which would have certainly riled Jefferies. He has too an assured place in the urban catalogue of rural nostalgia. He was spokesman for the late nineteenth-century nature-lovers; prophet of the youth-hostellers, the Pennine-walkers, and, less athletically, the country-life columns of the better-class Press.

And all this, to an extent, belies him, the Jefferies who lies behind the minor pieties. The vivid eye, the intensely observed childhood in

Nature, served an essential radicalism, no less intended, if less artistically achieved, than Lawrence's or Mark Twain's. He preached a dynamic revolution by Nature; and to take him for less is to diminish him into something which in fact he was not. There is nothing soft and sentimental about Jefferies's recall of Man to Nature.

The central reference is of course *The Story of My Heart* (1883). Written after both *Wood Magic* and *Bevis*, it is the autobiographical summary of the growth of the man's consciousness. Its passions were seventeen years in fulfilment. It has the urgency, the distilled quality we might expect from a man aware of his powers, already stricken by the disease which killed him four years later. It is the frame into which Jefferies's other works, the child-books, the novels, and the essays, fit. It is an account, in the Wordsworthian sense, of an education by Nature.

Like Wordsworth, Jefferies returned to his childhood and youth as the source of his natural piety. As a child he sometimes went away to 'think unchecked. . . . My thought, or inner consciousness, went up through the illumined sky, and I was lost in a moment of exaltation.' He had a 'deep, strong, and sensuous enjoyment of the beautiful green earth, the beautiful sky and sun'. It seemed to him that he might 'have the inner meaning of the sun, the light, the earth, the trees and grass, translated into some growth of excellence' in himself. As a youth, the sensuous link with Nature became even more intimately strengthened: 'I thought of the earth's firmness – I felt it bear me up; through the grassy couch there came an influence as if I could feel the great earth speaking to me.' Nature took him out of time ('I cannot understand time . . . by no possible means could I get into time if I tried') and out of the limitation of 'history'. The Wiltshire countryside contained for him the totality of all human consciousness. Wiltshire was 'an epitome of the natural world, and . . . if any one has come really into contact with its productions, and is familiar with them, and what they mean and represent, then he has a knowledge of all that exists on earth'.

But for all the emotional luxury and indiscipline of *The Story of My Heart*, there is ultimately no selfishness in Jefferies. The reference is always away from himself towards the general truth. Although he allows himself the indulgence of a poetic prose and never contains his feelings within the discipline of poetry, even so, a wisdom filters through the subjective indulgences of the language. He preached the possibilities open to man through a right relation to Nature. Nature itself he saw as neutral:

Nothing whatsoever is done for us. We are born naked, and not even protected by a shaggy covering. Nothing is done for us. The first and strongest command . . . that nature, the universe, our own bodies give, is to do everything for ourselves. The sea does not make boats for us. . . . The injured lie bleeding, and no invisible power lifts them up. . . . From every human being whose body has been racked with pain . . . there goes up a continually increasing cry. . . . These miseries are your doing, because you have mind and thought, and could have prevented them. . . . It is perfectly certain that all human beings are capable of physical happiness.

The power of man was to make the universe plastic to his will, by understanding Nature, by entering into sympathy with the physical creation:

Let me see the mystery of life – the secret of the sap as it rises in the tree – the secret of the blood as it courses through the vein. . . . Let us become as demi-gods.

Power and knowledge to 'become as demi-gods' could come to Man through Nature. 'The sun was stronger than science; the hills more than philosophy.' Man must go 'straight to the sun'.

For I believe, with all my heart, in the body and the flesh, and believe that it should be increased and made more beautiful by every means. . . . those who stunt their physical life are most certainly stunting their souls . . . I believe all manner of asceticism to be the vilest blasphemy – blasphemy towards the whole of the human race . . . to see a perfect human body unveiled causes a sense of worship.

For Jefferies, the 'outcome and end of all the loveliness of sunshine and green leaf' lay in the perfection of human beauty, in 'the swelling muscle, or the dreamy limb, strong sinew or curve of bust'. 'The surroundings, the clothes, the dwellings, the social status, the pageantry of power, the still more foolish pageantry of wealth', he was indifferent to:

The pettiness of house-life – chairs and tables – and the pettiness of observances, the petty necessity of useless labour, useless because productive of nothing, chafe me the year through. I want to be always in company with the sun, the sea, and earth. These, and the stars by night, are my natural companions.

In a way reminiscent of Lawrence at his least satisfactory, Jefferies's cult of Nature leads to a cult of erotic violence and the quest for the 'hero':

My heart looks back and sympathizes with all the joy and life of ancient time . . . with the extreme fury and feelings, the whirl of joy in the warriors . . . not with the slaughter, but with the passion – the life in the passion. . . . O beautiful human life! Tears come in my eyes as I think of it.

Give me a bow, that I may feel the delight of feeling myself draw the string and the strong wood bending, that I may see the rush of the arrow. . . . Give me an iron mace that I may crush the savage beast and hammer him down . . .'

So deep is the passion of life that, if it were possible to live again it must be exquisite to die pushing the eager breast against the sword.

It is necessary that some far-seeing master-mind, some giant intellect, should arise, and sketch out in bold . . . outlines that grand and noble future which the human race should labour for . . .

These lunatic fantasies are the obverse of the sanity Jefferies sought to convey. They represent him at his very worst. He fell foul of the trap prepared for the prophet of the single vision of the minor truth. He pursued the reason of his awareness into unreason. He succumbs to the common error of thinking in alternatives. He did not see that the alternative to rationalism could be something other than irrationality.

The best of *The Story of My Heart* was already forming in the earlier *Wood Magic* and *Bevis*, in both of which he took the child as the vehicle for the truth that he saw. *Wood Magic* is a fable of the child abroad in Nature. Nature is given through the anthropomorphic vision of the child. The whole Creation is humanized. The wind conversing with the child, educates him to the truths of Nature:

'I can remember everything that ever was. There never was anything that

I cannot remember, and my mind is so clear that if you will but come up here and drink me, you will understand everything.'

But Bevis is a child of a scientific century. He asks:

'Why the sun is up there, and is he very hot if you touch him, and which way does he go when he sinks beyond the wood ... and who painted the sky?'

The wind replies:

'Bevis, my darling, you have not drunk half enough of me yet, else you would never ask such silly questions. ... Why, those are like the silly questions the people ask who live in the houses of the cities, and never feel me or taste me. ... And I have seen them looking through long tubes ...'

'I know,' said Bevis, 'they are telescopes ... and they tell you all about them [the sun and stars].' ...

'How can they know anything of such things who are shut up in houses, dear, where I cannot come in. ... Do not listen, dear, not for one moment, to the stuff and rubbish they tell you down there in the houses. ... Come up to me upon the hills, and your heart will never be heavy, but your eyes will be bright, and your step quick, and you will sing and shout ...'

Bevis gives himself over to the message of the wind:

So Bevis sat down on the thyme, and the wind began to sing. ... The great sun smiled upon him, the great earth bore him in her arms gently, the wind caressed him. ... Now Bevis knew what the wind meant; he felt with his soul out to the far-distant sun just as easily as he could feel with his hand to the bunch of grass beside him ...

'There never was a yesterday,' whispered the wind presently, 'and there never will be tomorrow. It is all one long today.'

Bevis itself was written in the following year, and is probably the best thing Jefferies ever did. It has all his integrity; but it shows convincingly enough that he was not a novelist. It has no organic movement. It points well enough to the failures of *The Dewy Morn* and *Amaryllis*. It is the closest, however, that he ever reached in dramatizing his philosophy.

The strength of *Bevis* is its vivid evocation of Jefferies's own boyhood on the Wiltshire farm with his brother, the friend Mark of the story. But it does not sustain its length. It is very much Wordsworth's 'glad animal movements' without the rest of *The Prelude*. It has singularly little dramatic impulse. It is a strangely static work. But direct it is. Vivid it is. And there is no sweetening nostalgia. The boys are very much there on the page, resilient and robust. There is no feeling that they subserve any compulsion to regression and escape. It is not the work of an adult relishing the creation of boyhood. The feel of the book is in fact the reverse of the neurotic. This passage right at the outset is typical of its tone:

One morning a large wooden case was brought to the farmhouse, and Bevis, impatient to see what was in it, ran for the hard chisel and the hammer and would not be put off the work of undoing it for a moment. . . . The case was very broad and nearly square, but only a few inches deep, and was formed of thin boards.

Away he went with a hatchet to the withy-bed by the brook, to cut some stakes and get them ready. The brook made a sharp turn round the withy-bed, enclosing a tongue of ground which was called in the house at home the 'peninsula'. . . . This piece of land . . . was Bevis's own territory, his own peculiar property, over which he was autocrat and king.

But Bevis is very much Jefferies. Bevis is the child of the man who came to write *The Story of My Heart*:

. . . the swallows had come down from the upper air, and Bevis, as he stood a little apart listening in an abstracted manner to the uproar, watched them swiftly gliding in and out.

But when they had walked up the field and were quite a way from the house . . . he was amazed at the spectacle, for all the meadow was lit up. . . . Bevis became silent and fell into one of his dream states, when, as Mark said, he was like a tree. He was lost – something seemed to take him out of himself.

Bevis lived not only out to the finches and the swallows, to the far-away hills, but he lived out and felt out to the sky. It was living, not thinking. He lived it, never thinking, as the finches live their sunny life in the happy days of June. . . . He did not think, he felt.

The 'philosophy' is in fact a distraction, and with it a falsity descends on the prose. There is a feeling of intrusion in the preciousness of the style. The conscious, heavy alliteration of the following suggests the consciousness of the feeling:

The buttercups rose high above his head, the wind blew and cooled his heated forehead, and a humble-bee hummed along; borne by the breeze from the grass there came the sweet scent of green things growing in the sunshine.

The strength of the book lies in its carefully evoked world of active boyhood, with its vigour and make-believe. The encroaching philosophy stands clear and weak from the book as a whole: 'They bathed in air and sunbeam, and gathered years of health like flowers from the field.' It is in part the success of the work that one feels this as the unnecessary intrusion of the obvious.

His later work reiterated his message. The story of Guido in the collection of essays *The Open Air* returns again to the image of Bevis. Guido is another of Nature's children, wandering in the wood, conversing with flowers, receiving wisdom from the ear of wheat: 'And all the work and labour, and thinking and reading, and learning that your people do ends in nothing – not even one flower!' Sometimes the wheat is sown within earshot of Blake's Schoolboy:

We can hear the hum, hum, all day of the children . . . in the school. The butterflies flutter over us, and the sun shines, and the doves are very, very happy at their nest, but the children go on hum, hum, inside this house, and learn, learn.

All your work is wasted, and you labour in vain. . . . Directly you leave off you are hungry, and thirsty, and miserable. . . . It would not matter about the work so much if you were only happy; the bees work every year, but they are happy; the doves build a nest every year, but they are very, very happy.

There is plenty in Nature, but men will not share the fruits of the earth in love:

How happy your people could be if they would only agree! But you go on teaching even the little children to follow the same silly objects, hum, hum, hum, all the day, and they will grow up to hate each other . . . all the misery is because you have not got the spirit like the wheat, like us; you will not agree, and you will not share, and you will hate each other . . . and you will *not* touch the flowers!

The child in Jefferies lies squarely then in the romantic tradition of Blake, Wordsworth, and Dickens. His work, with all its passionate vehemence, reflects the tension of the human sensibility at the end of the nineteenth century inundated by the dehumanizing town. He heralded a revolution partially successful; but partially forgotten. *Bevis* was the creation of a passionate, virile radicalism. There is no equivocation about Jefferies. It is all a matter of root and branch. We feel a sense of battle in his prose on behalf of childhood which he saw constricted everywhere by the disciplines of learning, destroyed by the death of cities and civilization. The 'humming' school-learning children of Jefferies made their first appearance in the poetry of Blake. He failed, however, to project his vision into the discipline of poetry or the dramatized morality of a great novel. His work points in all its weakness to what Lawrence, with infinitely greater talent, so brilliantly did. He also points unmistakably to the work of Henry Williamson. Willie of *The Flax of Dream* is very clearly Bevis. It takes everything from Jefferies, without of course his anxious radicalism. *The Beautiful Years* is very much *Bevis* without *The Story of My Heart*. It is a minor reflection of something that was already in itself minor art. If the romantic tradition was right in seeing the dissociation of Man and Nature as the urgent problem of modern civilization, with its consequent de-naturing of man, it found a major expression in the boyhood novels of Mark Twain, and, in England, not in the work of Jefferies, but in the novels of D. H. Lawrence.

CHAPTER 10

Escape

I

'. . . the world of the adult made it hard to be an artist'.
William Empson: *Some Versions of Pastoral*

THE purpose and strength of the romantic image of the child had been above all to establish a relation between childhood and adult consciousness, to assert the continuity, the unity of human experience. In their concern with childhood, Wordsworth and Coleridge were interested in growth and continuity, in tracing the organic development of the human consciousness, and, also, in lowering the psychic barriers between adult and child. For Blake, Wordsworth, and, for the most part, Dickens, the image of the child endows their writing with a sense of life, and the same is true of Mark Twain in *Huckleberry Finn*. In writing of the child, their interest was continuously adult; their children function within their total response to adult experience. In talking of the child, they were talking of life.

In the latter decades of the century, however, we are confronted with something entirely other, with a cult of the child wholly different from this. Writers begin to draw on the general sympathy for childhood that has been diffused; but, for patently subjective reasons, their interest in childhood serves not to integrate childhood and adult experience, but to create a barrier of nostalgia and regret between childhood and the potential responses of adult life. The child indeed becomes a means of escape from the pressures of adult adjustment, a means of regression towards the irresponsibility of youth, childhood, infancy, and ultimately nescience itself. The children of Mrs Henry Wood and Marie Corelli, for whom it was better not to grow up, but die, were the commercial expression of something detectably sick in the sensitive roots of English child fiction at the end of the century. The aim of the great Romantics (and for that matter modern psychoanalysis; it is one of the main continuities between them), was to integrate the human personality by surmounting adult insensitivity to childhood. At the end of the century, the insensibility is inverted. It becomes not so much a matter of the adult sensibility barred from awareness of the significance of childhood, but of acute feelings for childhood which do not become integrated into a truly adult response to the significance of human experience as a whole. As Mr Van Wyck Brooks said, very reasonably, of Mark Twain: the writer's consciousness 'flows backward until it reaches a period in ... memory when life still seemed ... open and fluid with possibilities'.

But the 'freedom' in question is of course entirely illusory. It is a regressive escape into the emotional prison of self-limiting nostalgia. The justification of secular art is the responsibility it bears for the enrichment of human awareness, for the extension of the reader's consciousness. The cult of the child in certain authors at the end of the nineteenth century is a denial of this responsibility. Their awareness of childhood is no longer an interest in growth and integration, such as we found in *The Prelude*, but a means of detachment and retreat from the adult world. One feels their morbid withdrawal towards psychic death. The misery on the face of Carroll and Barrie was there because their response towards life had been subtly but irrevocably negated. Their photographs seem to look out at us from the nostalgic prisons they had created for themselves in the cult of Alice Liddell and Peter Pan.

Nostalgia can of course become too easily a blanket term of discredit. It can be as valid a part of human experience as any other. It is the expression and often the necessary solvent of the tension which inevitably exists between any individual and the society he is brought to adjust himself to. It is a product of sensitive adjustment in anyone. It is there in everybody. It is there in every artist. The recurrent nostalgia of romantic literature suggests forcibly enough the particular difficulties involved in that adjustment in the nineteenth century. The insistent nostalgia of the cult of the child at the end of the century suggests that for some the adjustment was unattainable. They indulged nostalgia because they refused or failed to come to sensitive terms with the cultural realities of the times. Regret for childhood takes on the same obsessive emotional quality as the exile's nostalgia for 'home'. Certain artists at the end of the century were clearly very much abroad in an alien world.

The whole impulse of Wordsworth's *Prelude* and *Ode* had been in the exact sense nostalgic. But the resources making for life within the poet's consciousness had been powerful enough to turn the awareness of childhood towards a further creative awareness of life. The movement of Wordsworth's feelings was towards life and growth. His tendency towards nostalgia was contained by the integrating strength of his whole sensibility. In Wordsworth the tendencies to regression had not yet overpowered the response towards life.

The condition of the English sensibility at the turn of the nineteenth century points inevitably to D. H. Lawrence. He is the essential reference. He felt most surely the acute nostalgia inevitable to a rapidly disintegrating culture. His nostalgia was both personal and social. But it did not consume him. He placed his nostalgia within his total response; and whether we accept his diagnosis or his remedies, there is in his work an abiding sense of adult involvement. His awareness of the past nourished his general commentary. *Sons and Lovers* is, again in the exact sense, nostalgic; but one only has to compare it with Barrie's *Sentimental Tommy* to see what 'nostalgia' can mean in on the one hand a healthy and on the other a generally sick sensibility.

II

Barrie is indeed the case of English child nostalgia. *Peter Pan* and *Sentimental Tommy* are the expression of Barrie's personal, nostalgic predicament, which so plainly overcame the artist in him. And in this he is to be compared with Lewis Carroll, whose great impulse was no less nostalgic, but who, through the creativity of his art, in some way fulfilled himself. Carroll's personal predicament was no better than Barrie's; but with him the distinction to be made is between Dodgson the regretful, pathetic man, and Carroll, the triumphant artist.

Everything for Carroll pointed to disaster in his personal life. He was almost the case-book maladjusted neurotic. The tale of the stammering, awkward, spinsterish don, imprisoned within Christ Church, Oxford, from the age of nineteen till his death, has been often enough told, with its dinner-parties in college rooms for little girls, with his obsessive interest in that most nostalgic of all arts, photography. Children were, he confessed, three-fourths of his life. We have it from no less a safe authority than Collingwood that his features remained boyish; some with less interest in preserving a decent memory declare his face became girlish, and that he assumed the embarrassed mannerisms of a young girl. He led perhaps as uneventful a life as anyone possibly could. Everything led to his withdrawal.

As a young man of twenty-one he wrote:

> I'd give all wealth that years have piled,
> The slow result of life's decay,
> To be once more a little child
> For one bright summer-day.

At twenty-three, on seeing a performance of *Henry VIII*, he wrote: 'It was like a delicious reverie, or the most beautiful poetry. This is the true end and object of acting – to raise the mind above itself, and out of its petty cares.' The 'one bright summer-day' became the fixated symbol of Dodgson's living fantasy, with its escape from 'life's decay' and the 'petty cares' of his mind.

The 'cares' were, we suspect, not merely 'petty'. Tormented by insomnia, he wrote in the Preface to *Pillow Problems*:

It is not possible . . . to carry out the resolution, 'I will *not* think of so-and-so'. . . . But it is possible . . . to carry out the resolution, 'I *will* think of so-and-so' . . . the worrying subject is practically annulled. It may recur, from time to time . . . there are unholy thoughts, which torture with their hateful presence, the fancy that would fain be pure. Against all these some real mental work is a most helpful ally.

In the Introduction to *Sylvie and Bruno* he declared his ambition to write a children's Bible, to compile a selection of Biblical quotations for children, and a selection of moralizing passages from other religious works: 'These . . . will help to keep at bay many anxious thoughts, worrying thoughts, uncharitable thoughts, unholy thoughts.'

This sense of sin recurs in his reminiscing account of what he had intended by the creation of Alice. She should have: 'the eager enjoyment of Life that comes only in the happy hours of childhood, when all is new and fair, and when sin and sorrow are but names – empty words signifying nothing.' Alice was then the expression of the romantic pastoral child, the symbol of Blake's innocent Life, but also the expression of Dodgson's frustrated exclusion from Life, the means through which his sense of guilt and sorrow could become for him 'empty words signifying nothing'.

The fusion of the romantic tradition with his own personal nostalgia is so poignantly displayed in that *Easter Greeting* he composed in 1876 to 'Every Child who Loves Alice'. It is as sad an expression of a deeply troubled psyche as one could ever not wish to read. It opens with the middle-aged Dodgson so pathetically seeking the friendship of his child-readers:

Please to fancy, if you can, that you are reading a real letter, from a real friend whom you have seen, and whose voice you can seem to yourself to hear wishing you, as I do now with all my heart, a happy Easter.

The rest is a fantasy of childhood created by the obsessive dreamer, by a psyche dreamily withdrawn from life:

Do you know that delicious dreamy feeling when one first wakes on a summer morning, with the twitter of birds in the air, and the fresh breeze coming in at the open window – when ... one sees as in a dream green boughs waving, or waters rippling in a golden light? ... And is not that a Mother's gentle hand that undraws your curtains, and a Mother's sweet voice that summons you to rise? To rise and forget, in the bright sunlight, the ugly dreams that frightened you so when all was dark?

Were these, he says, strange sentiments to come from the writer of *Alice*? He, however, did not believe that:

God means us thus to divide life into two halves. ... Do you think He cares to see only kneeling figures ... and that He does not also love to see the lambs leaping in the sunlight, and to hear the merry voices of the children, as they roll among the hay? ... And if I have written anything to add to those stores of innocent and healthy amusement ... it is surely something I may hope to look back upon without shame and sorrow (as how much of life must then be recalled!) when *my* turn comes to walk through the valley of shadows.

This Easter sun will rise on you, dear child, feeling your 'life in every limb', and eager to rush out into the fresh morning air – and many an Easter-day will come and go, before it finds you feeble and gray-headed, creeping wearily out to bask once more in the sunlight.

The implied commentary on the Victorian Sabbatarians, the reminiscence of Blake's *Innocence*, the evocation of the romantic symbol of 'life' in childhood, merge into Dodgson's own subjective regret. To grow up is no more than to become 'feeble and gray-headed, creeping wearily'. The 'fresh' innocence of the child is not something, as it was for Wordsworth and Coleridge, to conserve, in order to nourish the fulfilment of the adult; its evocation merely serves to create a sense of poignant contrast. There is no plea for continuity; but an insurmountable barrier of nostalgic regret for the 'eager enjoyment of Life that comes only in the happy hours of childhood', and the forlorn emphasis lies on that one word 'only'.

It was extraordinary that the artist, Carroll, could distinguish from all this, from the 'delicious dreamy feeling', from this 'shame and sorrow', from this self-apologia, the valid emotions which went to the creation of the *Alice* books. Every factor which made for weakness became focused into the astringent and intelligent art of *Alice in Wonderland*, so that, in a strange way indeed, the 'dream', the reverie in Dodgson, becomes in *Alice in Wonderland* the means of setting the reader's senses more fully awake. Lewis Carroll is in fact one of the few cases where Lawrence's famous dictum of trusting the art and not the artist happens to be absolutely true. The *Easter Greeting* with its embarrassing sentimentalities reveals painfully enough all the weakness which the romantic child was heir to, if it subserved a personal regret. The image of the romantic child could become a currency only too easily seized by the writer who had every good reason to seek its comfort in face of a sense of personal failure and shame.

The remarkable fact about Dodgson is that by using the very means of his weakness, by succumbing to his dream and fantasy, he should become so intelligently awake. *Alice in Wonderland* releases the vitality of an intelligent and sensitive commentary on life. It is precisely the opposite of withdrawn. The innocence of Alice casts its incisive, but delicately subtle intelligence upon Victorian society and upon life. But it is not simply that. It is not *simply* anything. Even in this first and greatest work, there is a content not far removed from nightmare. *Alice in Wonderland* has the claustrophobic atmosphere of a children's Kafka. It is the frustrated 'quest' for the 'Garden' which in the event is peopled with such unpleasant creatures. In those poignant lines of Alice's awakening, we feel the work turn towards unfulfilment, and very obviously towards death:

At this the whole pack rose up into the air, and came flying down upon her: she gave a little scream, half of fright and half of anger, and tried to beat them off, and found herself lying on the bank, with her head in the lap of her sister, who was gently brushing away some dead leaves that had fluttered down from the trees upon her face. . . .

The juxtaposition of waking and the image of the dead leaves is no casual coincidence. Carroll's art was too carefully organized for it not to have some special reference of feeling. It has all the force of a poetic continuity, a felt development. With all the vitality and intelligence released within the dream, Carroll becomes very much Dodgson when he wakes. One feels a sense of shock at this sudden, waking reality, of the face of the girl's innocent life blighted with the 'dead leaves'. The whole tone of the work changes from this point. Alice's sister dreams:

First, she dreamed of little Alice herself, and once again the tiny hands were clasped upon her knee, and the bright eager eyes were looking up into hers. . . . Lastly, she pictured to herself how this same little sister of hers would, in the after-time, be herself a grown woman; and how she would keep, through all her riper years, the simple and loving heart of her childhood; and how she would gather about her other little children . . . remembering her own child-life, and the happy summer days.

This idealization introduces a note alien to the work as a whole. The Alice of the ending of the book is in fact not Carroll's Alice, in Wonderland, but Dodgson's Alice Liddell. Already in 1862 we are approaching the world of the *Easter Greeting* of 1876.

Returning to the fantasy of Alice seven years later, Carroll almost achieved the artistic triumph again. But the emotional pressures of seven years' further deterioration had their unmistakable effects. The mood of *Through the Looking Glass* is ominously set by the introductory poem:

A tale begun in other days,
    When summer suns were glowing –
A simple chime, that served to time
    The rhythm of our rowing –
Whose echoes live in memory yet,
Though envious years would say 'forget' ...

Without, the frost, the blinding snow,
    The storm-wind's moody madness –
Within, the firelight's ruddy glow,
    And childhood's nest of gladness.
The magic words shall hold thee fast:
Thou shalt not heed the raving blast.

And though the shadow of a sigh
    May tremble through the story,
For 'happy summer days' gone by,
    A vanish'd summer glory –
It shall not touch with breath of bale
The pleasance of our fairy-tale.

Through the Looking Glass is held between this and the dreaming
denial of the reality of life of the final poem:

A boat beneath a sunny sky
Lingering onward dreamily
In an evening of July ...

Long has paled that sunny sky:
Echoes fade and memories die.
Autumn frosts have slain July ...

Of his readers, he writes:

In a Wonderland they lie,
Dreaming as the days go by,
Dreaming as the summers die.

Ever drifting down the stream –
Lingering in the golden gleam –
Life, what is it but a dream?

Held within this frame, the book retains the intelligence of the *Adventures in Wonderland*. Alice remains the vehicle for Carroll's sensitive commentary. But the tone is perceptibly sharper. The humour is more sardonic. There is more merciless, embittered ridicule. The dream takes on a quality of horror. The note of frustration is struck more insistently; as in the episode in the shop:

The shop seemed to be full of all manner of curious things – but the oddest part of it all was, that whenever she looked hard at any shelf, to make out exactly what it had on it, that particular shelf was always quite empty. . . . 'Things flow about so here!' she said at last in a plaintive tone, after she had spent a minute or so in vainly pursuing a large bright thing . . .

In the sequence among the rushes, the plaintive note makes its meaning clear enough: Alice leaning out of the boat to gather the beautiful rushes exclaims:

'Oh, *what* a lovely one! Only I couldn't quite reach it.' And it certainly *did* seem a little provoking ('almost as if it happened on purpose,' she thought) that, though she managed to pick plenty of beautiful rushes as the boat glided by, there was always a more lovely one that she couldn't reach. 'The prettiest are always further!' she said at last . . . as . . . she . . . began to arrange her new-found treasures.

What mattered it to her just then that the rushes had begun to fade, and to lose all their scent and beauty, from the very moment that she picked them? Even real scented rushes, you know, last only a very little while – and these, being dream-rushes, melted away almost like snow, as they lay in heaps at her feet. . . .

It is as if Carroll in a more self-conscious way than ever in *Wonderland* turns aside from his own fantasy; as if he remains regretfully and painfully awake in his own dream. This may perhaps account for the savagery of so much of the humour, such as in *The Walrus and the Carpenter*. Alice is subjected to a type of subtle cruelty in a way quite alien to the earlier book. The episode in the railway carriage has all the horror of a sadistic nightmare. If life for Carroll was indeed a 'dream', the dream is evidently only too often in *Through the Looking Glass* Dodgson's own personal nightmare. With only the slightest susceptibility to the analysis of literature in psychological terms, it would be difficult not to see both works as psychological fantasies.

They are clearly the works of neurotic genius. The initial rabbit-hole seems to serve as either a birth or copulative symbol. Dodgson's obsession with little girls was both sexual and sexually morbid. His own insistence on the purity of his interest has perhaps a telling, even a morbid undertone. But with Carroll's art, the neurosis is the irrelevance. Even in the clear references one feels to the neurosis, especially in *Through the Looking Glass,* one senses the extraordinary power of artistic sublimation that Carroll brought to the achievement of the two books.

III

It is exactly the reverse with Barrie. With him there is no triumph of sublimation; but almost always one is left with a sense of artistic failure. *Peter Pan* is what *Alice* might very well have been without Carroll's controlling intellectual interests: for Dodgson had all of Barrie's cult of the child that didn't grow up. Barrie's sensibility was not, however, of the complicated order of Carroll's; it did not require the mental, intelligent, and sensitive effort of the *Alice* books to gain the wished-for escape into Kensington Gardens. Barrie's cult was not likely to translate itself into the intelligent exercise of a game of chess. He did not escape through the complex and sardonic awareness of Carroll's involvement with life.

It is not easy now, looking back, to appreciate the cult of J. M. Barrie. Our own tastes lie on the safer side of the astringent criticism of the twenties and thirties. It is safe to assume that nothing quite like the 'institution of J. M. Barrie', as Mr Mackail put it in his official life of Barrie written soon after his death, could ever happen again. The depreciation began long before his death, and the chill reception of *The Boy David* indicated more than a temporary denial of acclaim to the work of an author's senility. One forgets now that Frohman, who had so much to do with the original production of *Peter Pan,* is supposed in generally accepted legend to have fastened his life-belt on the doomed *Lusitania* with Peter Pan's own 'to die will be an awfully big adventure'; and that an American critic of the first production of the play in America could declare it 'one of the most profound, original and universal plays of our epoch'. Mr Mackail says of the play that 'volumes could be written on all that it has meant to generation after generation of playgoers of all ages; on what it has added to English and American imagery, literature and language'. And again: 'hundreds and thousands of [adults] at all kinds of extraordinary ages, fell right into his open trap. . . . They couldn't get away from it. And they, too, suddenly, hated being grown up.' Thomas Moult in a eulogy of Barrie, written in 1928, said that when *Peter Pan* is being played 'all the audience are children'. For him Barrie expressed that 'function of art . . . this . . . opening of barred casements for our human eyes whenever we seek flight, or remoteness, or that most envied thing of all, the state of eternal youthfulness, the Country of the Ever-Young'. Unsuspectingly perhaps, he exactly appreciates what Barrie set out, so unfortunately, to do.

Both Moult and Mr Mackail declare, and there is no reason to doubt them, the universal appeal of *Peter Pan*, not only to children, but to generations of adults. The audience of the first night was almost entirely adult; and it clapped furiously at the line, 'Do you believe in fairies?' to save the life of poor Tinker Bell. For Moult, Barrie had the 'message of Mozart in music . . . the message of the wind, and the flowers of the field'. For Alfred Noyes, *Peter Pan* was an 'exquisite illustration of a very ancient and beautiful phrase about the width and height and wonder of the kingdom of little children'.

But Barrie's 'institutional' stature didn't begin with *Peter Pan*. Already by 1896 his collected works were being produced in a limited edition of fifty sets at 10 guineas a time. *Sentimental Tommy* sold 37,000 copies, and *Margaret Ogilvy* sold 40,000 copies almost at once. Just after the turn of the century, Barrie made some £40,000 in one year, and Mr Mackail tells us that when his agent embezzled some £16,000 of it, Barrie was not aware of the loss.

Barrie's reputation was made on the 'Kailyard' novels. As early as 1895, J. H. Millar, in an article in the *New Review*, called him the *pars magna* of the 'Kailyard' movement. *Auld Licht Idylls* (1888), *A Window in Thrums* (1889), *The Little Minister* (1891), *Sentimental Tommy* (1896), and *Margaret Ogilvy* (1896), were part of the whole movement of Scottish literature in the second half of the century whose aim, as Mr Blake declares in his excellent short study of the Kailyard novelists, was to 'sentimentalize and popularize a merely vestigial and completely unrepresentative Scotland'. They were, Mr Blake says, 'perhaps the victims of the chronic Scots disease of nostalgia, of the urge to escape back into the comprehensible conditions of their original, independent state and away from the new, incomprehensible turmoils of the industrial age'. The whole impetus of the movement was culturally nostalgic. Nicoll, Ian Maclaren, Rutherford Crockett, and Barrie, wrote of a quaint, old-fashioned, rural Scotland, dominated by the Free Church manse, and in this nostalgic school, Barrie served his literary apprenticeship. His receptive London audience thought he wrote of an actual Scotland, contemporary, even though quaint, comic, and endearingly 'odd'. Whereas, in fact, Barrie wrote his early fiction almost entirely about a Kirriemuir he had never himself known, the Kirriemuir of 1840, translated to him in the terms of his own mother's reminiscence, and the hearsay conveyed to her of times before even she was a child there. *Margaret Ogilvy* gives a true account of the young London journalist plaguing his mother to send him copy from her reminiscence to serve for his next article.

It is in every way significant that the first creative impulse of the young author should have been so intimately connected with his mother. Barrie's relation with his mother was the sole but absolute disaster of his artistic life. Mr Blake, with every justice, says the 'complex' was 'more than maternal; it seems to have been positively foetal'. Barrie's story is not even so much the tale of a boy who didn't want to grow up, but, carrying the sentiment to its deadly conclusion, of the boy who wishes so painfully that he need never have been born. Just as it is important to distinguish true art from distracting biographical entanglements; it is none the less important to disentangle the idea of art from the meretricious products which are the exact expression of an author's sickness. It is the very power of Barrie's 'complex' which gives the undeniable, but nevertheless debilitating, power to his writing.

And the great claim to urge against him is that he was at such pains to reveal himself, without the self-discovery affecting him in any way. The revelations, embarrassing as they must be to his readers, merely served as excellent copy. We remember Stevenson's comment about the 'journalist' ever present at his 'elbow'. He was at such odd pains to reveal himself. Everything was grist to the insatiable mill of his successful journalism. Using his mother's maiden name for title, he gave the story of his fixation in *Margaret Ogilvy*:

The reason my books deal with the past instead of with the life I myself have known is simply this, that I soon grow tired of writing tales unless I can see a little girl, of whom my mother has told me, wandering confidently through the pages. Such a grip has her memory of her girlhood upon me since I was a boy of six.

At the end of the novel, he declares that he will not remember a boy,

. . . clinging to his mother's skirt and crying, 'Wait till I'm a man, and you'll lie on feathers', but a little girl in a magenta frock and a white pinafore, who comes towards me through the long parks, singing to herself, and carrying her father's dinner in a flagon.[1]

From the personality Barrie presents of his mother in *Margaret Ogilvy*, it seems that she herself was unbalanced. She insistently conveyed to her imaginative and susceptible son her own obsessive nostalgia for her childhood. She retained the image of herself as the little girl in the magenta frock and white pinafore carrying lunch to her father, and this image obsessed Barrie all his life. He was at no pains to present her for anything but what she was; difficult, petulant, and madly possessive. After the death of Barrie's elder brother, he says: 'Many a time she fell asleep speaking to him, and even while she slept her lips moved and she smiled as if he had come back to her.'

As a dying woman she left her bed to pursue Barrie with the question, 'Am I an auld woman?', and paraded the house gloating at his novels: 'He said every one of them was mine, all mine!' There were few privacies for Barrie's journalism. But unfortunate as she was, he worshipped her:

1. It was most likely Barrie's obsession with his mother as a little girl that led him to create the character of Margaret, and give her his mother's name, in *Dear Brutus*. By a quite extraordinary psychic manoeuvre, his mother seems to materialize in the 'depths of the wood in the enchantment of a moonlight night' as 'an artist's daughter', as Barrie's 'might-have-been'.

For when you looked into my mother's eyes you knew, as if He had told you why God sent her into the world – it was to open the minds of all who looked to beautiful thoughts. And that is the beginning and end of literature.

Everything I could do for her in this life I have done since I was a boy; I look back through the years and I cannot see the smallest thing left undone.

. . . the love of mother and son has written everything of mine that is of any worth.

Of Jess, the heroine of *A Window in Thrums*, he said: 'there never was any Jess, anything in her that was rare and beautiful she had from my mother; the imaginary woman came to me as I looked into the eyes of the real one.'

His books, he said, were written 'to please one woman who is now dead'; and from this relation Barrie never escaped. His novels and plays are full of a sickly glorification of motherhood. Mrs Darling of *Peter Pan* was 'the loveliest lady in Bloomsbury, with a sweet, mocking mouth, and as she is going out to dinner tonight she is already wearing her evening gown because she knows her children like to see her in it'. When she leaves her children at night, for Mrs Darling the night-lights are 'the eyes a mother leaves behind her to guard her children', and she declares: 'Dear night-lights that protect my sleeping babes, burn clear and steadfast tonight.'

In *The Little White Bird*, the prose tale from which *Peter Pan* was ultimately created, we have:

Heaven help all mothers if they be not really dears, for their boy will certainly know it in that strange short hour of the day when every mother stands revealed before her little son. That dread hour ticks between six and seven. . . . He is lapt in for the night now and lies quietly there, madam, with great mysterious eyes fixed upon his mother. . . . I believe that when you [Mary] close David's door softly there is a gladness in your eyes, and the awe of one who knows that the God to whom little boys say their prayers has a face very like their mother's.

Told by Barrie that little boys were birds before birth, the little boy, David, of the story wishes he could have remained so; because 'when she was asleep . . . he would hop on to the frilly things on her nightgown and peck at her mouth'.

The Little White Bird is indeed a wholly preposterous fantasy, full of similar oedipal morbidities. It reveals, in precise terms, the original impulse of the more famous play. Talking to the little boy about his mother, Barrie says he will come and kiss her when she is fifty-two:

She has also said, I learn, that I shall not think so much of her when she is fifty-two, meaning that she will not be so pretty then. So little does the sex know of beauty. Surely a spirited old lady may be the prettiest sight in the world. For my part, I confess that it is they, and not the young ones, who have ever been my undoing. Just as I was about to fall in love I suddenly found that I preferred the mother.

The relation of son and mother was something which horrified Barrie to lose. It is one of the main themes of *The Little White Bird*, and of course *Peter Pan*. Already in *Margaret Ogilvy*, we have the mother's horror at losing her sons: 'Hyde Park, which is so gay by day, is haunted [when night comes] by the ghosts of many mothers, who run, wild-eyed, from seat to seat, looking for their sons.'

But their horror was nothing to Peter Pan's. Returning to his mother's bedside from Kensington Gardens, he watches her asleep:

... glad she was such a pretty mother. ... The hollow in the pillow was like a nest lined with her brown wavy hair. ... He knew he had but to say 'Mother' ever so softly, and she would wake up. They always wake up at once if it is you that says their name. Then she would give such a joyous cry and squeeze him tight. How nice that would be to him, but oh! how exquisitely delicious it would be to her.

He does not wake her, but flies away. When, however, he returns again, the window is closed:

... and there were iron bars on it, and peering inside he saw his mother sleeping peacefully with her arm round another little boy. Peter called, 'Mother! mother!' but she heard him not; in vain he beat his little limbs against the iron bars. He had to fly back, sobbing, to the Gardens, and he never saw his dear again. ... Ah, Peter! we who have made the great mistake, how differently we should all act at the second chance. But Solomon was right – there is no second chance, not for most of us. When we reach the window it is Lock-out Time. The iron bars are up for life.

This is the central image of Barrie's neurosis, with its jealousy and frustrated exclusion. The 'iron bars' were 'up' for Barrie 'for life'; and incidentally they excluded him from creative fulfilment. The image of the loss of his mother drove him to the fixated interest in the boy who would not grow up. Even so early as the novel *Tommy and Grizel*, Tommy, the subjectively motivated hero, declares, 'Oh, that we were boys and girls all our lives.' 'Poor Tommy!' Barrie replies: 'He was still a boy, he was ever a boy, trying sometimes, as now, to be a man, and always when he looked round he ran back to his boyhood as if he saw it holding out its arms to him and inviting him to come back and play. He was so fond of being a boy that he could not grow up.'

In 1898, Barrie met the Davies family in Kensington Gardens, and from then onward the five boys were interwoven into his life. With Michael Davies, who was to die so tragically by drowning in 1921, he corresponded daily throughout his time at Eton and Oxford. He spent his summer holidays with the Davies children, photographing them, and in 1901 actually compiling a book of thirty-five photographs, of which only two copies were made, called the *Boy Castaways of Black Lake Island*. *Peter Pan* was largely made from the five years of story-telling with which he amused the Davies boys. Married in 1894, Barrie was already finding his emotional escape from marriage through the Davies family. Part of his frustration no doubt arose from his own childless marriage. *The Little White Bird* is the account of the love of an ageing man for a child whom he dearly wished could have been his own son, Timothy. Mr Mackail gives us the picture of Mr and Mrs Barrie parading the alleys of Kensington Gardens with their dog Porthos. It is a pathetic picture.

But something more than his own childlessness drove him, in Mr Mackail's words, to find it 'difficult . . . not to play with any little boys whom he met':

Charming, fascinating, elusive, emotional, unconcerned. Who else is all that? Any child, of course; but this one, this strange, lucky, and unlucky child of nearly forty was still searching for a lost mother and lost playfellows; and was making two hundred and fifty pounds a week.

Right at the end of *The Little White Bird*, when the mother asks him if his youth does not 'come swinging back' when he plays with David in the Gardens, he replies: '"Mary A – " I cried, grown afraid of the woman, "I forbid you to make more discoveries today."'

Speaking of his early schoolboy stories in one of his speeches he declared: 'The next best thing to being boys is to write about them.'

Everything, then, for Barrie was to capture, through the vicarious method of his art, the lost world of his childhood. In 1903 his note-book[1] records: 'Play. *The Happy Boy*. Boy who can't grow up – runs away from pain and death – is caught *wild* (and escapes).' The note-book becomes full of dreams of his 'going back to . . . childhood, of starting all over again, or of vanishing and reappearing as someone else'. In January 1907, he records one such dream more fully:

The Lovely Moment. Finest Dream in the World. That it is early morning & I am out on a highland road – dew etc. – it is time before I knew anything of sorrow, pain or death. Everyone I have loved is still alive – it is the morning of life – of the world.

To grow up, for Barrie, was 'sorrow, pain and death'. The age of two he said was 'the beginning of the end'. And in perverse accord with Freud he declared: 'Nothing that happens after we are twelve matters very much.' Living, for Barrie, was a matter of inevitable decay. In relinquishing the fantasy that he had a son, the hero of *The Little White Bird* does so in these terms:

I wished . . . that before he went he could have played once more in Kensington Gardens, and have ridden on the fallen trees, calling gloriously to me to look . . . fain would I have had him chase one hoop a little way down the laughing avenues of childhood, where memory tells us we run but once, on a long summer day, emerging at the other end as men and women with all the fun to pay for. . . .

Childhood for Barrie is not 'innocence' nourishing Blake's 'experience'; but a thing merely for regret. Peter Pan does in fact retain many of the attributes of the romantic Child of Nature. He comes on stage in leaves – but they are autumn leaves, mingled with cobwebs. Peter declares himself: 'I'm youth. I'm joy'; and in the references to Mr Darling there is an echo of the romantic's distaste for society. Mr Darling works in the City 'where he sits on a stool all day, as fixed as a postage stamp, he is so like all the others on stools that you

1. Quoted in *The Story of J. M. B.* by Denis Mackail (London: Peter Davies, 1941).

recognize him not by his face but by his stool'. Later when Peter is offered adoption by Mrs Darling, we have a reminiscence of Mark Twain; but with something of a declension:

PETER: Would you send me to school?
MRS DARLING: Yes.
PETER: And then to office?
MRS DARLING: I suppose.
PETER: Soon I should be a man?
MRS DARLING: Very soon.
PETER (passionately): I don't want to go to school and learn solemn things. No one is going to catch me, lady, and make me a man. I want always to be a little boy and to have fun.

The serious romantic protest is weakened into no more than a wish 'always to be a little boy and to have fun'. Through Huckleberry Finn, Mark Twain did not wish 'always to be a little boy', but through the consciousness of a boy expressed an uninhibited commentary on civilized values, the overthrow of which involved for Huckleberry the precise moral opposite of Barrie's concept of 'to have fun'.

The *leitmotiv* of Barrie's complex had various expression throughout his work; and one always senses the morbidity. When Wendy in *Peter Pan* confronts Peter with his fondness for her, we have:

WENDY: What are your exact feelings for me, Peter?
PETER: Those of a devoted son, Wendy.

In *Sentimental Tommy*, the dying mother takes Tommy 'canny' into her bed to explain to the child the tortuous story of her love for the man she did not marry, and the hatred she held for the depraved man she did marry who was the father of her children. The scene is altogether unhealthy. *The Little White Bird*, strange as it is in its entirety, contains nothing more extraordinary than the following. David's mother has left him with the hero for the afternoon:

I returned to David, and asked him in a low voice whether he would give me a kiss. He shook his head about six times, and I was in despair. Then the smile came, and I knew that he was teasing me only. He now nodded his head about six times. This was the prettiest of all his exploits.

In an access of possessiveness he rushes with the child out of doors and round Kensington Gardens. When his mother finds them, the hero triumphs, for the child wants him and not his mother. Barrie's hero wants to take the child 'utterly from her and make him . . . his'. Whatever the explanation, nothing sane could be taken from such episodes as when the child stays the night in the hero's house. The child is undressed ready for bed:

I took them off [the clothes] with all the coolness of an old hand, and then I placed him on my knee and removed his blouse. This was a delightful experience, but I think I remained wonderfully calm until I came somewhat too suddenly to his little braces, which agitated me profoundly. I cannot proceed in public with the disrobing of David.

Later, after considerable tension, the child reveals his wish to sleep in the man's bed:

'It is what I have been wanting all the time,' said I, and then without more ado the little white figure rose and flung itself at me. For the rest of the night he lay on me and across me, and sometimes his feet were at the bottom of the bed and sometimes on the pillow, but he always retained possession of my finger . . .

Barrie's whole creative life was obsessed with this lust for childhood, and with the pains and penalties of being adult. He knew, painfully enough, the realities of his feelings. Late in his life, he wrote: 'It is as if long after writing *Peter Pan*, its true meaning came to me. Desperate attempts to grow up but can't.' It was not by chance perhaps that after many years of inactivity Elizabeth Bergner should have been able to coax his talents, great as they undeniably were, into life with the suggestion that he write a drama around the Biblical version of Jack the Giant-Killer, David and Goliath, and that the main and eccentric dramatic point of the whole play should reside in David's obsession with acquiring Goliath's spear. After the battle the boy trails the stage disconsolately, because he cannot raise the treasured possession on to his shoulder. In the final scene he confides to Jonathan that he can at last raise it, and the final curtain finds the boy on the highest rock on the stage with the spear shaft as wide as a 'weaver's beam' mounted on his shoulder. From anyone who would deny the phallic character of the symbol (it is to be remembered that Barrie's father was in fact a weaver) it would be interesting to have an explanation of the dramatic point of *The Boy David*.

IV

It might indeed have been *à propos* of Barrie that Hugh Walpole wrote: 'It is the tragedy of childhood that its catastrophes are eternal', as indeed he might well have written it of himself. The particular tragedy of Walpole's childhood was his almost continuous deprivation of affection, and, as a significant part of this, the unhappy experiences of his schoolboy life, especially at Marlow. In his own early life he became very much the 'deprived child', and this is reflected throughout the books in which he deals with children. The four books in which he concerned himself specially with childhood represent a very limited part of his large output: but they point forcibly to the kind of emotional disabilities he had to contend with, and perhaps in part explain that consciousness he himself had of the inadequacy of his emotional experience, and the effect that this had on the quality of his creative work. He came a generation after Barrie, and the degree of self-analysis available to him, as his correspondence and autobiographical pieces show, preserved him perhaps from the indulgence to which, earlier, he might easily have succumbed. *The Golden Scarecrow* is as far as he ever went into the realm of Barrie's whimsy about childhood. Even so, it reveals, as do the *Jeremy* books, his impulse to create a fictitiously 'happy childhood' for himself, to be nostalgic for a childhood which in fact for him had never been there.

Mr Rupert Hart-Davis in his biography of Walpole precisely documents the author's early life, and goes on to display the chief and poignant trait of his subsequent personality, his craving for friendship in compensation for his sense of acute deprivation as a child. Throughout his childhood, his family had had no roots. Soon after marriage his father was sent out on an evangelical mission to New Zealand, and then transferred to New York, his family followed him there, until Hugh was sent back to England to school, first to Truro, then to Marlow, to King's School, Canterbury, and finally to Durham, where he lived at home, attending Durham school as a day-boy. There was no security. His father's professional duties, and his mother's reticent nature gave him little requitement of affection even before he set out at nine to school. He spent his vacations in strangers' homes; and worst fate of all, he fell early into the terror and indecencies of Marlow as he found it just before the turn of the century: his account of his life at Marlow, in *The Crystal Box* (1924), is actual enough:

When I say that it wasn't all that it should be, I mean that the food was inadequate, the morality was 'twisted', and Terror – sheer, stark, unblinking Terror – stared down every one of its passages. I had two years of it, and a passionate desire to be liked, a longing for approval, and a frantic reaction to anybody's geniality have been for me some of the results of that time. I have been frightened since then . . . but I have never, after those days, thank God, known continuous increasing terror night and day. . . . Worst of all was being forced to strip naked, to stand then on a bench before them all while some boy pointed out one's various physical deficiencies and the general company ended by sticking pins and pen-nibs into tender places to see whether one were real or no –

Even so late as 1940, in *Roman Fountain*, he could still write:

There are times when I am sure that life is, in positive reality, a dream, and that I shall wake up any hour and find that I am back in my . . . dormitory again. . . . At such moments my apprehension is exactly the same as it was forty years ago – I am defenceless and naked in a world of hostile enemies . . .

The deprivation forced him into the strong friendships of his life, with A. C. Benson, Henry James, Percy Anderson, James Annand, and with lesser people, though not of lesser importance to him. It also forced him into writing the short stories which he linked tenuously into a novel, *The Golden Scarecrow*, published in 1915, in which he first took up the theme of childhood.

The book is instinct with that atmosphere of whimsy and un-reality which Barrie instilled into so much of his work. It is tradition-ally romantic. The world of childhood's imagination is contrasted with the world of fact and reality as the workaday world under-stands it. There is the implication, never really made explicit, that the child comes from some pre-existent state of wonder, imagination, and make-believe, memories of which he carries into his earthly life. Life itself is the gradual, but continuous loss of the child's memory of his pre-existence. To live, for Hugh Seymour of *The Golden Scarecrow*, is to lose.

At the age of nine, Hugh is sent to school in England. He spends his holidays in exactly the same way as the author as a 'minute and pale-faced . . . paying guest' in houses where 'other children were of more importance than he'. He stays with a Rev. Lasher, a Gradgrind of a man, contemptuous of dreamers, oblivious of Nature. He is a stock romantic figure of 'anti-childhood'. Rev. Lasher receives a visit from a certain Mr Pidgen, and Hugh overhears a quarrel between them, in which Mr Pidgen stands for the life of imagination – 'why shouldn't a fairy-story be as necessary as a sermon?' Hugh hears him declare:

But how do you know who watched over your early years and wanted you to be a dreamy, fairy-tale kind of person instead of the cayenne pepper sort of man you are. There's always someone there I tell you, and you can have your choice, whether you'll believe more than you see all your life or less than you see. Every baby knows about it; then, as they grow older it fades and, with many people, goes altogether. He's never left *me* – St Christopher, you know . . .

This 'St Christopher' becomes the central idea of the book. Hugh recognizes him as 'the Man who comes when you're a baby. . . . He had a beard and I used to think it funny the nurse didn't see Him'. The boy confides to Mr Pidgen that 'one can't be lonely or anything can one if there's always someone about?' Walking together in the country the man and boy see what they both take to be a warrior in a golden helmet. It is in fact no more than an old scarecrow with a tin for a hat, made golden in the sunlight. The 'romantic' imagination of the two sheds its wonder on creation. From this banal translation of the romantic theme, the novel progresses through a series of loosely connected stories about children and their relation to their 'St Christopher', their 'Friend', and the loss of their awareness of the 'Friend's' presence as they become adjusted to life. Their adjustment is harsh. There is a fountain in the Square in which the children live, and they live their lives partly in relation to this symbol of romantic

Life, and partly in relation to the world of their nurses, governesses and parents.

They are all strange children, 'old and serious'; 'deep'; old for their age'; 'a little queer, bless his heart'; 'ready to imagine that people didn't like her'; all in fact very much images of Hugh himself as a child. They are remote, pathetic little creatures on the threshold between the world of their Friend and the world of life's harsh reality. The Friend no doubt exactly symbolizes what Walpole would have wished for himself throughout his own infancy and childhood. For the infant, Henry Fitzgeorge Strether:

How desperate, indeed, would it have been had his Friend not been there, reassuring, pervading him, surrounding him, always subduing those sudden inexplicable alarms.

For Ernest Henry, the Friend:

... always came then [when the room was dark], was there with His arm about Ernest Henry, His great body, His dark beard, His large firm hands. ... His Friend was there, just as always, suddenly sitting there on the bed with His arm round Ernest Henry's body, His dark beard just tickling Ernest Henry's neck, His hand tight about Ernest Henry's hand.

As they grow, the children crave for friendship. Barbara Flint 'must be affectionate. She must demand affection of others. . . . She surveyed her world with an eye to this possible loving'. She walks in the Square hoping to find someone 'it would be possible to worship'. She finds another little girl with 'flaxen hair, blue eyes, and a fine pink-and-white colouring'. The story of Barbara Flint, with its insistent pessimism – 'things are never so good as we hope' – is central to the book. The little 'flaxen-haired' girl-friend she finds, proves unworthy. She merely inveigles the child away from her true Friend: 'Mary took my Friend away – and then she wasn't there herself. There isn't anybody!' That there isn't really 'anybody' is the central assertion of the little book. The last story deals with the boy of nine, setting out to school, forgetting his Friend in the turmoil of leaving home. With school, 'life', Friendless life, had begun.

To accept a psychological reading of the fantasy of the Friend might be to relate it to a birth trauma, accentuated by the author's own acute sense of deprivation as a child. The Friend is always given as someone all-embracing, whom one gradually loses as one grows up. Within the symbol of the Friend, there seems little doubt that Walpole contained everything he himself felt deprived of in childhood.

The book ends with Hugh, now a man, returning to the countryside of his childhood, and for the first time Walpole sketches in the fantasy town of Polchester, which in so many of his later stories became for him the town where he created fictitious roots to compensate for his own rootlessness as a boy. He finds a new incumbent in the Lasher parsonage, another Mr Pidgen; and the book ends with a reassertion of the life of the imagination, symbolized still in the image of the golden scarecrow.

Walpole never attempted another Barriesque fantasy. Though no less a personal fantasy, the *Jeremy* trilogy has none of the deliberate 'unreality', whimsy and make-believe of *The Golden Scarecrow*. Through Jeremy, Walpole lives a vicariously happy childhood. Jeremy is in fact Walpole's own personal what-might-have-been. With the trilogy, the image of Polchester is complete. Jeremy lives in a stable clergyman's home, in a stable town, with actual streets. Polchester is in fact a compound of Truro and Durham. The escapist's fantasy takes on cartographical precision. The dream solidifies. The obsessive concept of the Friend is translated into the *actual* experiences of Jeremy's friendships in Polchester and then at Crale.

Jeremy Cole, like Walpole himself, was born in 1884, and like Walpole's own image of himself, 'he was in no way handsome; his neck, his nose ridiculous . . . and his chin stuck out like a hammer'. The self-identification is unmistakable. The idealized happiness of the boy's home is reminiscent of Dickens's idealization of the Chatham days:

He watched the breakfast-table with increasing satisfaction – the large teapot with the red roses, the dark blue porridge plates, the glass jar with the marmalade a rich yellow inside it, the huge loaf with the soft pieces bursting out between the crusty pieces, the solid square of butter, so beautiful a colour. . . . All these things glittered and glowed in the firelight, and a kettle was singing on the hob . . .

And when the family went on its summer holiday, 'the fields were lit with the glitter of shining glass'. When the boy went on holiday near the Cornish coast in *Jeremy and Hamlet*, 'he lay down among the sea-pinks and the heather and looked up into the cloudless sky'. When Jeremy at length reached school, he embraced an experience entirely the reverse of Walpole's own: 'When he was happy he was tremendously happy. He remembered not past unhappinesses, not the threats of the future overhanging hour. For him there were no future hours.'

When Jeremy meets little girls, they are completely idealized pictures of what little girls might mean to little boys:

She sat under a miniature sunshade of white silk and lace, a vision of loveliness. She was a shimmer of white, a little white cloud that had settled for a moment upon the seat of the carriage to allow the sun to dance upon it, to caress it with fingers of fire . . .

It is the language of complete literary wish-fulfilment. And the same spirit invests Jeremy's meeting with the beautiful woman at the children's dance:

He was staring at the most beautiful lady he had ever conceived of. . . . She was very tall and slender, dressed in white; she had black hair and a jewel blazing in the front of it. But more than everything was her smile, the jolliest, merriest, twinkliest smile he had ever seen

– a woman perhaps the complete reverse of his own mother.

But the idealization leads inevitably to its nostalgic counterbalance of regret. The one would have no force without the other. In his last year before school, the boy spends his last 'magical' Christmas:

After this he was to know too much, was to see Father Christmas vanish before a sum in arithmetic, and a stocking change into something that 'boys who go to school never have' – the last of the Christmases of divine magic, when the snow fell and the waits sang and the stockings were filled and the turkey fattened and the candles blazed and the holly crackled by the will of God rather than the power of man.

But no matter how magical the young boy's life had been, both in the family and later at Crale, Jeremy suffers the slings of childhood's fortunes, and in flight from them, he finds, not the ministrations of some supernatural 'Friend', but the comfort of an actual friend, especially his uncle, Samuel Trefusis.

Jeremy's uncle is a significant creation indeed. He is the 'Friend' of *The Golden Scarecrow* done into human terms. He is the incarnation of Walpole's obsession, the 'uncle-figure'. Like Pidgen, he is a failure, a social misfit. He lives in his brother-in-law's home, painting his unfashionable pictures, in every way the adult who has not grown up; untidy, dilatory, shunning responsibility, without a care in his world; the sympathetic adult who behaves as a boy, who is always there for Jeremy when life presents its difficulties. A typical instance of the man and boy's friendship comes in *Jeremy and Hamlet*, when Jeremy, returning home for Christmas, spends fifteen shillings of his father's money on buying presents for the family. Outlawed by his father, the boy is miserable until Uncle Samuel invites him into the sanctum of his studio, and there explains 'life' to the boy, in tones reminiscent indeed of Marie Corelli:

'If you've got work you like, a friend you can trust and a strong stomach, you'll have enough to be thankful for.' . . . He felt for his uncle's hand and held it. Nothing so wonderful as this had yet happened in his life. . . . All his after life he would look back to it, the dark room, the dog quiet at their feet, the cool strength of his uncle's hand, the strange, heating excitement, the happiness and security after the week of wild loneliness and dismay. It was in that half-hour that his real life began . . .

Later when Jeremy falls foul of both masters and boys at Crale, he is rescued from his misery by a visit from his uncle. On seeing him, Jeremy is aware 'of that curious bond that was between himself and his uncle'. It was 'simply too much for him. He wouldn't have minded if his uncle had kissed him, which, of course, Uncle Samuel would never think of doing.' The experience becomes too much, however, for Uncle Samuel also (although throughout the earlier novels he had carefully simulated a bachelor's dislike for children). He wonders 'why it was that he was more completely at ease with this small boy than with any other human being in the world'.

He took his hat off and sniffed the air, then – because the [railway] platform was dim and there was no one to see – he caught Jeremy and held him and kissed him. He had never kissed him in all their lives before.

The image of the 'Friend' finds other expression in the relations which grow up between Jeremy and his companions, both at home and school. In *Jeremy and Hamlet,* a brief idyll flourishes between Jeremy and a neighbouring lout during a holiday he spends on the Cornish coast. A romantic relation develops between Jeremy and this eldest son of a family he was forbidden to associate with:

One must do Humphrey that justice that he completely respected Jeremy's innocence. . . . They bathed in the pools and ran about naked, Humphrey doing exercises, standing on his head, turning somersaults, lifting Jeremy with his hands as though he weighed nothing at all. Humphrey's body was brown all over, like an animal's. . . . They sat on a little hummock, with a dark wood behind them, and watched the moon rise . . .

'You're a decent kid,' said Humphrey, 'I like you better than my brothers. I suppose you'll forget me as soon as I'm gone.'

'I'll never forget you,' said Jeremy . . .

A similar relation of worship is established at Crale between Jeremy and a senior boy whom he never speaks to until the very close of the trilogy:

At the instant that he saw the boy [Ridley] something happened to him. He stared at him as though he had known him all his life. . . . The boy was considerably older than himself . . . Jeremy felt at once that this boy was everything that he would himself like to be . . .

And again later:

He looked up and there, walking straight towards him, was Ridley. Ridley with that far-away pre-occupied look, slim and straight, *decent*-looking, different, somehow, from everyone else.

Finally, at the end of the book, when Jeremy realizes his childhood is 'over': 'there was Ridley to whom he had never spoken. That would give him what he wanted. He could tell Ridley things.'

The emphasis, significantly, is on the deliberate '*decent*-looking' – on Humphrey's 'respecting Jeremy's innocence'. The emphasis is on a sublimated 'beautiful' friendship, and Walpole recoils from the idea of corruption. Jeremy rejects the friendship of Llewellyn, Captain of his House, because: 'He was afraid, he realized, of something in Llewellyn's liking for him. . . . With Llewellyn there was something "queer". . . . he wasn't comfortable.'

The theme of corruption is treated fully, however, in the character of Charles Morgan, the Dormouse, a child taken from a happy home and exposed to the brutality and filth of his reception by the older boys at Crale:

It is the tragedy of childhood that its catastrophes are eternal. And something, some confidence and pure happiness, departed there and then ... from Charles Morgan's soul, never again to return. . . . But now fear crept on him from every side. He was afraid because there was *no one* to turn to.

It was exactly Walpole's own experience at Marlow. The Dormouse suffers the attentions of Cresson, a 'fully-developed cad'. Cresson 'corrupted with a sure and certain success nearly every boy of his age and size with whom he came into contact'. He does not succeed in corrupting Morgan however: '. . . it takes more . . . than six weeks of misery and bewilderment to contaminate the honour and noble traditions of such a home-life as the Dormouse had known.'

It is this idealization of 'friendship', this unwillingness to look sexual facts in the face, which is the major weakness of Walpole's novels about childhood. He makes a plea for friendship on a level which he fails to establish convincingly. Part of the prevarication of *Jeremy at Crale* lies in his choosing to avoid a meeting between Jeremy and Ridley, leaving the friendship merely on the note of a prospective assignation. The craving for affection which the books reveal seems untenable on the basis of the 'friendship' he describes.

The whole atmosphere of Crale is in fact idealized out of all reality. Except for the minor inflection of the sequence of Morgan's reception and flight, the book is one long wish-fulfilment, of wonderful rugger-matches, dormitory suppers and so forth. Morgan's fate is insufficient to induce Walpole into a condemnation of the public-school system:

This great merit in our public-school system then – it stiffens your back for anything. It is only the too imaginative who are more than temporarily bruised and even they not for ever. There are prizes for those who suffer the severest, unknown to the others, and it is these who often in the end love their school with the finest devotion.

Jeremy and Hamlet had passed through three impressions within the year of its publication, 1923, and a cheap edition sold as early as 1925. *Jeremy at Crale* was a conscious sequel, and it drew no impolitic conclusions. Walpole preferred to praise the public schools for their 'muscularities', and to attack the modern private schools for their over-coddling, suggesting that better results 'perhaps' came from the old system with 'its rough-and-ready indifference'. Although the routine of the public school might catch 'personality by the throat', and 'choke it', when we come to the world of fisticuffs, we are left in little doubt as to where Walpole stands:

Today also I believe the refined feelings and careful supervision of our twentieth-century civilization looks on such exploits as barbarous and immoral. The worse for modern education say I!

In those fine days there were no boxing-gloves and no feeble decision on points.

It was presumably kill or be killed. The fight itself in *Jeremy at Crale* certainly raises some strange images in the boy's mind. When Jeremy goes to hit Stairs in the big fight, he thinks there was 'a big black nigger there instead, naked and shiny and tall as a tree'. At another moment Jeremy imagines Stairs might turn into a rabbit who would hide in his bed at night and bite him. For Jeremy it was 'nice to feel the wet coolness of the blood on the broken skin of his knuckles'.

Jeremy's relation to his rival Stairs, for whom he harbours a completely irrational and unexplained hostility, suggests the considerable degree of repression beneath Walpole's sublimating obsession with 'idealized friendship'. The subconsciously repressed aggression seems unmistakably to out in the sadistic relish of Jeremy's fight with Stairs. The hostility of their relationship gives credence to the suspicion that if one does not love, one hates; or that if one hates, it is because one cannot love.

But for all the vicarious happiness and 'friendship' of his child books, Walpole does not always idealize the child's nature as such. In the treatment of their governess by the children, he describes, in a way reminiscent of Richard Hughes, the 'cruelty' of little children:

Is there any cruelty in after life like the cruelty of a small boy, and is there anything more powerful, more unreasoning, and more malicious than the calculating tortures that small children devise for those weaker than themselves?

And again, in *Jeremy at Crale*, he refers to that 'unthinking cruelty that, let fond parents deny it or no, is contained broadly in the half-savage nature of all normal small boys'. Even with Walpole, the cult of original innocence has started to turn, perhaps through the climate of modern psychological thought, towards something akin to original savagery. The epithet 'noble' has been divorced from 'savage', and with Walpole's 'half', we are perhaps half-way to the 'savagery' of Mr Golding's *Lord of the Flies*.

V

If Walpole's escape came through the creation of a happy childhood he had never known, with Forrest Reid we have an altogether more complex phenomenon. His obsessive interest in children did not, so far as we have evidence to show, arise from any particular deprivation in his own childhood. His deprivation was altogether more total. Forrest Reid is in fact, with Carroll and Barrie, one of the phenomena of modern English child literature. It is the account of a talent, by no means inconsiderable, entirely consumed by an obsession with children, and in particular with boys and youths.

He has been the arch-priest of a minor cult. In his *Portrait of Forrest Reid*, Mr Russell Burlingham declares that 'over all his best work there floats a golden mist of beauty'. Summoning Edmond Pilon's remark about Alain-Fournier that there are books '*d'une fragilité de pastel, et si diaphanes, si douces, si spécialement subtiles et tendres qu'on ne peut pas les toucher du doigt sans les froisser*', he makes out his case for not considering Forrest Reid's work in terms of usual criticism. And, in a sense, of course, Mr Burlingham is right. For to apply anything like an intelligent criticism to Forrest Reid is to deny his work any justification as responsible literature. Such delicacies as M. Pilon and Mr Burlingham talk of make one immediately wary.

And the feeling is confirmed when we remember that Norman Douglas wrote to Forrest Reid about *Demophon* in these terms: 'It stands to reason that a delicate thing like that will not appeal to the general public. Why should it? Thank God it doesn't.' Even Mr E. M. Forster in *Abinger Harvest* has this to say of Forrest Reid: that he concentrated on 'a single point, a point which, when rightly focused, may perhaps make all the surrounding landscape intelligible'. Much depends on the force to be given to 'rightly' in Mr Forster's judgement. It is in fact the absence of focus in Forrest Reid which so often invalidates the 'single point' on which he so deliberately concentrated his creative energies – the 'distress of boyhood changing into man', to use Yeats's words. Regret, nostalgia, consume the light which Reid's vision played upon human experience, until all we are left with is the increasingly brilliant image of a boy. The 'surrounding landscape' remains accordingly blurred. Mr Burlingham accepts that in his work there were 'no plots, no moral lesson, and hardly ever a grown-up'. There was in fact no total emotional focus, shedding light on total adult experience. He celebrated youth, and regretted its transience.

And this, in itself, would scarcely be cavilled at. The transience of human youth and beauty is after all a universal experience. It is a fact, as well as a subject for human complaint. Mr Forster is right to suggest that youth, 'when rightly focused, may perhaps make all the surrounding landscape intelligible'. The impact of the young sensibility and intelligence on the assumptions of a society can be the most suitable subject for a great literature, and one perhaps especially relevant to our own period. One thinks of the German Bildungsroman, of Thomas Mann's *Magic Mountain*, of *Huckleberry Finn*, or to take an example closer to our own time, Mr Salinger's *Catcher in the Rye*. But whereas with these works there is a feeling of expansion at this point of focus of the adolescent world turning into man, with Forrest Reid there is only a sense of emotional constriction, of something the very opposite of growth.

Theoretically he stood well within the romantic tradition of childhood. There is a direct reminiscence of Coleridge in: 'most people have forgotten, lost interest [in their childhood], and their time-consciousness, I think, is less liable to ebb and flow . . . with no overlapping, no swaying backward and forward, no return either in imagination or dream'. And again: 'If I had never written a line . . .

that would not alter my conviction that the years of childhood, boy-hood, and adolescence are the most significant. What follows is chiefly a logical development – the child being father of the man.'

This might be unexceptionable – indeed it has both a 'romantic' and a peculiarly modern ring about it. It is almost one might say Freudian. But his fiction was much more in line with the feeling of Barrie's perverse 'nothing that happens after twelve matters very much'. Mr Burlingham's account is accurate enough:

Everything that happens to a man after he has left the magic confines of childhood and youth becomes, on this view, inessential. With the onset of maturity all that really matters lies behind, all the vividness and colour has ebbed out of life.

For the Romantics, and for Freudian analysis, infancy and childhood have significance only for the power which a knowledge of child-hood gives over mature experience, for only through that knowledge can fully-conscious maturity be attained. Forrest Reid's acute aware-ness, and 'knowledge' of childhood, however, were emotionally very much a cul-de-sac. To read Forrest Reid is to be in the company of a soldier with his eye fixed on the objective, but who remains unconscious of the intervening terrain, the pitfalls and fortifications between. His acute eye for childhood made him, as regards the rest of human experience, singularly blind.

His own infancy does not seem to have been marred by any peculiarity. His father died when he was five; and for his mother he seems to have felt no particularly strong affection. His nurse, Emma, does seem to have been something of a strong influence. But his main reaction to his Northern Irish home was to revolt, in a way reminis-cent of Edmund Gosse, against its Presbyterianism, the account of which he himself gave in *Apostate*. This spiritual antipathy to his home may indeed have given rise to one recurring theme of the novels, the boy or youth developing in an alien, philistine and puri-tanical environment.

Apostate, however, gives another and more important clue. For it reveals that as a small child he experienced the 'vision' which, through the autobiographical character of the novelist Linton in *Brian Westby*, he calls 'some kind of spiritual revelation such as

Wordsworth had in his boyhood among the Cumberland Lakes . . . something which remains ever after as an influence – which creates an ideal – and a longing that it may come again'. This is the account he gives of the experience in *Apostate*. Whilst being read to by his nurse, he sees the perfection of his own dream world:

Here was a bright delicate company, young, beautiful, gay, yet 'sad with the whole of pleasure'. Here were the brown faces, the pouting lips, and naked unspoiled bodies, the slim Pan pipes, the shadowed grass. . . . 'My world! My world!' I could have shouted. . . . It was the only heaven I wanted, or ever was to want.

Continuing the account of the dream he declares, and the passage is central:

The place was a kind of garden. . . . Always when I first awakened (in the dream) I was in broad sunlight, on a low grassy hill that was no more than a gentle incline, sloping down to the shore. A summer sea stretched out below me, blue and calm. . . . I was waiting for someone who had never failed me – my friend in this place, who was infinitely dearer to me than any friend I had on earth. And presently, out from the leafy shadow he bounded into the sunlight . . . a boy of about my own age, with eager parted lips and bright eyes. But he was more beautiful than anything else in the whole world, or in my imagination . . . from the moment I found myself on that hill-side I was happy.

The obsessive images are fixed – the 'garden' – the 'hill-side' – the sea 'blue and calm' – the 'beautiful', sensuously-savoured boy – a world where he declared 'it was always summer, always a little after noon, and always the sun was shining'. *Mutatis mutandis* they are the images of Carroll, Barrie, and Walpole. There is this recurrent fantasy of the escape into the 'garden', into the 'summer sun'. From its origin, the romantic Child was always seen in the context of a falsifyingly benign Nature. It is there even in Blake's *Echoing Green*. Even Blake's astringent 'experience' was almost wholly man-made. It was Wordsworth's pre-eminence to intertwine something of the awe and savagery of Nature into the child's natural education. But generally the Romantics subsumed their child into their 'pathetic fallacy' about Nature's benevolence and sympathy. The personal dreams of Carroll, Barrie and Forrest Reid were the residual conclusions of an entirely illogical premise. It was indeed part of Mark Twain's greatness to take the romantic antithesis of Nature and Society, and discipline his account of Nature with all the physical and moral snares of Huckleberry Finn's Mississippi. The central weakness of the romantic concept of the child lay in its vulnerability to easy wish-fulfilments and indiscipline, of which the escapists, and Forrest Reid was among them, availed themselves.

The dream where 'it was always summer', where 'always the sun was shining' pursued Forrest Reid throughout his childhood and adolescence, and then when he was seventeen or so it faded, never to return. Its recapture remained for him in his art. In fact his novels became for him a dream-substitute:

The primary impulse of the artist springs, I fancy, from discontent, and his art is a kind of crying for Elysium . . . in the most clumsy and bungled work . . . we should doubtless find . . . that same divine homesickness, that same longing for an Eden from which each one of us is exiled . . . all our life is little more than a trying to get back there, our art than a mapping of its mountains and streams.

If the content of this is bared of its easy, mellifluous expression, it reveals itself as a concept of art wholly unacceptable. One does not really detect the 'divine homesickness' in Shakespeare, the 'trying to get back there'. It is a denial of the artist's final responsibility, involvement. It is of course an accurate enough, and revealing enough summation of Forrest Reid's own approach to his particular sort of 'art' and of his work in the novel. Regressing towards the dream, with its lush natural décor of sea and shore and sunlight, and the boy bounding out of the leafy shadow, became the sole impulse of his work.

In *Following Darkness*, he discusses his own requirements in the novel:

In the foreground there must be the portrait of a boy, but painted in the manner of Rembrandt rather than Bronzino. . . . The spirit of youth is not merely bright and vivacious. . . . It is melancholy, dreamy, passionate; it is admirable, and it is base . . . it is healthy, and it is morbid; it is animal, and it is spiritual; sensual, yet filled with vague half-realized yearnings after an ideal – that is to say, it is the spirit of life itself. . . .

All this is true, emotionally, of youth. But to make a cult of it is to make a cult of introversion, indulgence and egotism. The 'portrait of a boy' 'in the foreground' served to connect his work to the dream of the garden, the hill-side, the seashore, and the Friend. Throughout his work there is a disquieting unawareness of external reality. Even in the early novels the descriptions of Belfast exist in an enchanted 'twilight atmosphere', in the words of Mr Burlingham; and the account of the hero's experiences in London in *At the Door of the Gate* is typical of the dangerously topsy-turvy attitude to reality conveyed in his work. The world of Leicester Square is 'unreal and futile'; he talks of London as the 'horror of a dream'. It may indeed be so. But Forrest Reid merely exchanges one dream for another. The hero only finds 'reality' by summoning the image of a 'bare hill-side under the moon, with dark woods below, stretching down to a lonely sea . . . the faint rustle of wind, the smell of heather . . . bringing him back to sanity and peace'.

Forrest Reid had in fact the same lust for Nature as Richard Jefferies. He tells of his experiences in *Apostate*:

I was certainly prepared to join in whatever rites or revels might be required. My body seemed preternaturally sensitive, my blood moved quickly. . . . There was a drumming in my ears; I knew that the green woodland before me was going to split asunder, to swing back on either side. . . .

or again:

. . . here were hours when I could pass *into* Nature, and feel the grass growing and float with the clouds through the transparent air.

Even with Jefferies one feels the erotic indulgence; his enthusiasm for Nature is not always contained within his social commentary. With Forrest Reid there is little more than indulgence, the quest for compensation in Nature for the sense of some inadequacy in himself. Throughout his work there are the carefully constructed agents of escape – Nature – dreams – and the recurring belief in the 'supernatural'. His naturalism, his assertion as to the 'reality' of dreams, the paganism, the cult of youth, all point to his withdrawal.

Everywhere in his work we find the intrusive fantasy of the boy. Griffith Weston of *Spring Song* is typical:

His eyes, beneath their drooping lids, had something of that sleepy gentleness which characterizes the angels and youths of Perugino, but the wide space between them gave the whole countenance, with its beautiful forehead, a kind of grave nobility and innocence.

For the most part, the novels have their only reality where they deal with boyhood and its friendships. Where he attempted adult relationships, they are clearly unreal and unsatisfactory. The only adults who live in his fiction are those, usually middle-aged, men, who have some peculiar relation with the relevant youth of the story. Even in the first novel, *The Kingdom of Twilight*, the danger signs are obvious enough. Its vitality lies in the account of the boyhood friendship between the hero, Willie Trevelyan, and Nick Grayson. The rest, the unrequited love of Trevelyan (a recurring theme of *Following Darkness*, *The Gentle Lover* and *Brian Westby*), fails to establish itself. James in a letter to the young author wrote: 'I confess . . . that *after* the middle, you strike me as *losing* your subject. . . . After the meeting with the woman by the sea . . .' The same could be said of *Following Darkness*, where the reality lies in the evocation of Peter Waring, and not in his unsuccessful *amour* with Katherine Dale.

He was not, however, unconscious of his disability. Writing of the poem he had submitted for the Cambridge Poetry Prize, he declared: 'So perish masterpieces, and so are "inglorious Miltons" blighted, and take to writing prose chronicles of the adventures of small boys.' He had, he said, a 'King Charles's head – the point where a boy becomes a man'. After that, 'my inspiration was cut off, my interest flagged. . . . I supposed it must be some mysterious form of arrested development'. Later he wrote: 'There is a sense in which it would be true to say that Denis and Grif and Peter are mere pretexts for the author to live again through the years of his boyhood, to live those years, as it were, more consciously, if less happily.' It was not only, however, that he re-lived his own childhood; but that through the children of his fiction he acquired friendship with the 'boy' he had first seen in those childhood dreams, the pagan, sensuous image he never escaped from. He pursued his phantom interminably down his own literary cul-de-sac.

Much has been made of the 'reality' of the boys he created in his novels. They were an amalgam of the actual boys he knew and the ideal boy he dreamed of on the slope leading down to the sea. They all bore kinship with the actual Andrew Rutherford, the apprentice in the tea-warehouse where Forrest Reid worked:

Sometimes, indeed, the sunshine, filled with little dancing golden dust specks, touching his hair or his cheek, would set me dreaming of him as a kind of angel who had strayed into this world . . .

and with his friend Kenneth Hamilton, who was 'gay, responsive, affectionate, and with the merriest laugh' he had 'ever heard'. The middle-aged hero of *Brian Westby*, the failed novelist, declares:

And he knew, when he looked deliberately back over the years, just where it had failed. Happiness is only made by affection. Nothing else in the long run matters.

Forrest Reid's concern was in fact with the problem of his affection for these idealized, pagan-imagined boys, an affection he vicariously required of them. At one point in his life he seems to have toyed with the idea of writing a 'realistic' novel. It was to have been called *The Green Avenue*. Mr Burlingham suggests its subject:

The Green Avenue . . . *might* have shocked. Certainly the theme dealt with a moral and emotional problem which requires, even today, great courage to handle; or perhaps it was fear of ridicule, or worse, misunderstanding, which held him back. . . .

In any event, no word of it remains, if any were ever privately written. We can never know what held Forrest Reid back from this act of moral integrity. Instead he reached his fulfilment through the apotheosis of his particular art in the trilogy of Tom Barber and the story of Brian Westby.

Mr Burlingham says that in his novels there was nothing 'overtly sexual', and sees in this perhaps a virtue. It is, however, on grounds of concealed eroticism that most complaint against the novels can be made. Everywhere there are scenes where sexuality is thinly veiled by recourse to naturalism or a kind of Renaissance paganism. The sentiments are never carried through to their real fulfilment. In *The*

Garden God[1] we have the two youths on the seashore. Graham makes Harold stand:

... like the praying boy of the Berlin Museum, the 'Adorante', his face and hands uplifted to the joy of the morning.

'And now what else,' he murmured. 'You are too young for an athlete. Your body is too slender. I will make you a youthful Dionysus instead. Let me put this seaweed in your hair.'

The intrusive references to Greek and Renaissance culture seem to serve as moral support for the evident erotic intention; and in the sensuous description of the young man in *Brian Westby* we have the same thing:

He was very untidy and very attractive, with his flaxen ruffled hair breaking into loose curls over his forehead, and his fair skin. ... He looked as if the cleanness of the sea-wind was in his blood. ... And suddenly Linton found himself thinking of the young horsemen on the Parthenon frieze, riding by in proud humility. ... The boy had reminded him of the world he loved best, the spirit he loved best, the beauty he loved best, the only beauty that had the unspoiled freshness and simplicity of nature.

The central emotion, in itself, is not necessarily embarrassing. The embarrassment arises from the idealizing falsification. Everything safeguards the emotion from its central reality. The whole plot of *Brian Westby*, in which Linton discovers that this boy is his own son, child of his unsuccessful marriage, serves to conceal the emotion from itself. The language, however, gives the reality. In Linton:

... an intense desire grew up within him that this their first meeting should not be their last. Only the strength of that desire, indeed, enabled him to overcome his shyness and the fear of a repulse, and to ask the boy ... if he would come out with him – somewhere – anywhere – in the afternoon.

The given situation is redeemed superficially by the father–son relationship. But this is not the language of a father about his son, but

1. It is interesting that Forrest Reid dedicated the novel to Henry James, and by so doing terminated their literary relationship. The book was unacknowledged, nor did James acknowledge any subsequent volume the author sent him. In *Private Road*, Reid himself suggested that James's attitude seemed prompted 'by a strange moral timidity, which refuses to accept responsibility for what deliberately has been suggested'.

of a lover and his loved one. The situation found final expression in the *Tom Barber* trilogy. In *Uncle Stephen*, perhaps the most succinct expression of what Forrest Reid had to say, through a trick with time, the man, Uncle Stephen, managed to make himself into a boy again, and so find the friendship with Tom Barber that he wanted. Of this book, Reid himself wrote:

> I loved writing this book. . . . During the two years on it Tom grew to be extraordinarily real to me . . . so that sometimes for a few minutes I would stop writing because he seemed to be actually there in the room . . . one evening, after finishing a chapter, I put down my work to go out for a walk with him.

The cult of boyhood in the novel, however, is not given in directly physical terms, but through the symbol of the pagan statue of the boy in the garden of the house where ultimately Uncle Stephen and Tom come together:

> On an island in the middle of the pool stood a naked boy holding an urn tilted forward, though through its weedy mouth no water splashed. . . . A tuft of grass had found a roothold in the hollow of the boy's thigh.

Ultimately Tom goes to the garden, to take his farewell of the statue:

> The stone was warm. The sun had warmed the curved pouting mouth and the smooth limbs and body; but when Tom's lips pressed on those other lips the eyes were looking away from him, and dimly he felt that this was a symbol of life. . . .

Perhaps the best example of the blurred intention of the trilogy comes in *Young Tom*, where Tom goes bathing with James-Arthur, the farmhand. 'Pastoral and Greek influences mingle together,' says Mr Burlingham, in 'sunny unity'. Tom watches the young man bathe:

> . . . the contrast between his fair hair and the golden brown of his body and limbs appeared to the smaller boy as attractive as anything could be. In fact James-Arthur, merely by divesting himself of his clothes, had instantly become part of the natural scene, like the grass and the trees and the river and the sky. . . .

If we really are to have homosexuality treated in the novel, better the directness of Mann's *Death in Venice*, or Gide's *The Coiners*, than the escape into the pagan, pastoral, Greek dream-world of *The Garden God*:

As soon as I fell asleep I saw him – my dream-boy. I awoke, it seemed on the sea-shore, at the very gate of his garden. And I heard his voice calling me – calling, calling. . . . Who he is, what he is; if he indeed be your spirit, or if you only remind me of him, I suppose I shall never know.

But Forrest Reid was, we may imagine, involved in the general taboos of literary taste on sexual matters during the early years of this century. The unacceptability of the emotional realities of his theme was in large measure responsible for creating the idealizing dishonesty of this kind of literature.

CHAPTER II

The End of the Victorian Child

VICTORIAN practice seldom coincided with the romantic protest on behalf of childhood. Rousseau and the other European educational theorists of the late eighteenth and early nineteenth centuries found little acceptance in English educational practice. The European intellect has often had a difficult Channel crossing. The first kindergarten was established in England only so late as 1851, the year before Froebel's own death. The rapid shift away from the naturalism and free expressionism of the Continental reformers is plain enough in the work of the Edgeworths, two of Rousseau's very early English protagonists, who in the very title of their joint educational treatise, *On Practical Education*, laid the stress which educational discussion in England continued to lay throughout most of the century. English theory was in the main concerned with Herbartian method, the technique for the actual conveying of knowledge; with the question of State responsibility for education; with the vexed matter of denominational religious instruction, with the curricular problem of the status of the classics in face of the natural sciences. The great educational controversies of the century were those between Bell and Lancaster, and between the 'classicists' and the reformers who wished to introduce English and science into the public-school curriculum. With all the great Victorian pronouncers on education – the Mills, Ruskin, Arnold, Newman, Huxley, and the contributors to the *Essays on a Liberal Education* of 1868 – there was significantly little, if anything, on the actual nature of the child. For all their importance, Newman, Arnold, and Ruskin discussed a theory of culture and society. There is nothing among the theorists quite like the concern Dickens felt for the influence of education upon the feelings of children. The Prussian Humboldt, with his emphasis on 'State' education and 'organization', was a greater reforming influence in England in the nineteenth century than Rousseau or Froebel or Pestalozzi. The 'negative' idealism of *Emile*, and its romantic protagonists, were most often either denied by severe Puritan morality, or else debased into the ethos of *Little Lord Fauntleroy*. Blake's child that was born for Joy (with all the force that he or Coleridge or Dickens would have given the word) seldom saw very much nurture in practice throughout the greater part of the century. Romantic assertions about childhood remained very much a protest. For all their massive circulations, the nineteenth-century partisans of Feeling only found posthumous fulfilment of their ambitions in the relaxations of the present century. The circulations of Dickens's novels, for example, remain something of a mystery of nineteenth-century taste; that a society should concede celebrity to a writer who poured such ridicule and anger upon values which in practice it sedulously cultivated. In spite of the sentiment expressed on behalf of the child – and the sentimentality – the *status quo* of the Victorian child was most often the actual miseries and unkindnesses which Dickens deplored, or the moral severities of Mrs Sherwood, or the placid domesticities of Charlotte Yonge. The enormous success of Charlotte Yonge's novels testifies that she conveyed an Anglican respectability acceptable to a large reading public. But whether in the terms of the moral strait-jacket of the Fairchild family, or the mellowing terms of Charlotte Yonge's *The Heir of Redclyffe* and *The Daisy Chain*, with their gentle morals and adolescent emotional and ethical problems, the Victorian child was held fast within the family.

This is not to say, however, that Rousseauism had no influence in the Victorian period. Arnold's reforms at Rugby did as much to suppress public-school brutality as to improve morality and prefectorial organization. Successive Factory Acts removed children from the worst outrages of early industrial exploitation. The development of children's literature during the century shows the gradual intrusion of 'gaiety'. John Harris and Catherine Sinclair, writing in the manner of Lamb's *Tales from Shakespeare*, wrote to please and attract children themselves. Marryat, and the Americans – Hawthorne, Cooper, Harriet Beecher Stowe, and Mark Twain himself – gave children books written for themselves, in which the shadow of Satan did not fall across every conceivable pathway. Lear and Carroll added their own solvent of nonsense and parody – perhaps the most disrespectful and powerful solvent of all to the régime of adult rigidity and pomposity. Ruskin's *King of the Golden River*, MacDonald's *At the Back of the North Wind*, and Kingsley's *Water Babies* nourished the child's imagination and fantasy. Carroll, Kingsley, and Stevenson diffused a sedition of nonsense, wonder, and adventure within the strict confines of the Victorian nursery. If Dombey were still secure in his drawing-room, Paul was already in 'wonderland', or 'through the looking glass', or dreaming on 'Treasure Island'. One important aspect of the growth of children's literature was the gradual differentiation made in the market between boys and girls, and between boys and girls of different ages, which suggests that both writers and parents were becoming more conscious of the particular identity of the child.

A sign of the coming revolution in the approach to the family was the publication of Anstey's *Vice Versa* in 1882. Making use of a variation of a common fantasy of children that their parents will grow small as they themselves grow big, the tyrant father is subjected to the tyrannies he had previously imposed upon his son. It is a comic foreshadowing of the overthrow of the 'father' and of his values expressed in so much of the literature of the early twentieth century, a process accelerated by the evident exposure of the inadequacy of those values in the cynicism and moral squalor of the First World War. The 'parent' had been a figure of constraint for Blake. Dickens had attacked parental tyranny and insensitivity in Dombey and Gradgrind. During the century, the 'family' seemed to many to have become a microcosmos within which all the forces in opposition to the romantic child were freely at work. It was Samuel Butler at the end of the century who really attempted to give the case against the 'family' and its *pater familias*.

Butler's 'Way of All Flesh'

Written between 1872 and 1884, *The Way of All Flesh* was not published until 1903, a year before Butler's death. It was one of the great literary solvents of the Victorian family régime. It is not easy now to appreciate fully the impact of the piece upon publication. The picture of family behaviour which it portrays may seem to us almost incredible. But it created stir enough to suggest that Butler had put a finger on the public conscience where something hurt. Preposterous as the novel seems, it would have been literally so if Butler had been creating a myth, or sensationalizing his own experiences. Its very incredibility seems to argue for its acceptance as a depressingly accurate account of the treatment of children during the nineteenth century, within homes of a certain religious pattern. Closely concerned with the idea of heredity and the influences of environment on human behaviour, the action of the novel covers three generations, stretching from the middle of the eighteenth century to the close of the nineteenth. It was conceived as a dramatic morality (one is tempted to wonder what Dickens might have done with the theme). It is the tale of the redemption of a child, Ernest Pontifex, from the influences of his family environment. The villains of the piece are George Pontifex, and his son Theobald, whom he corrupts into maintaining his own harsh paternal practices, and Theobald's snobbish and weak-headed wife. Their victim, Theobald's son Ernest, is saved through the influence of Overton, the narrator, and his Aunt Alethea. With remarkable grasp, intellectual rather than sensitive, the book contains a whole phase of English family development, and stands as an indictment of a whole epoch of English behaviour towards children.

The Pontifex family had its roots in the rural craft society of eighteenth-century domestic industry. The original George Pontifex, Ernest's great-grandfather, was a modest, unambitious man, a craft carpenter, and it is to his tolerant and unpretentious values that the regenerate Ernest returns at the end of the novel. The corruption of the family begins with the adoption of the second George Pontifex by his London uncle, owner of a publishing house. The boy relinquishes the unassuming country life of his parents, and by the turn of the century inherits his uncle's business. He assumes the ethics of early nineteenth-century business, reforming the unaggressive methods of the old-fashioned firm. The point is tellingly made by reference to the introduction of the young man's 'modern' advertising methods. He marries and begets children, and we are at once at the centre of what Butler had to say:

Yet when a man is very fond of his money it is not easy for him at all times to be very fond of his children also. The two are like God and Mammon.

It must be remembered that at the beginning of the nineteenth century the relations between parents and children were still far from satisfactory. . . . In the Elizabethan time the relations between parents and children seem on the whole to have been more kindly. The fathers and the sons are for the most part friends in Shakespeare, nor does the evil appear to have reached its full abomination till a long course of Puritanism had familiarized men's minds with Jewish ideals as those which we should endeavour to reproduce in our everyday life. . . . Puritanism restricted natural pleasures; it substituted the Jeremiad for the Paean, and it forgot that the poor abuses of all times want countenance.

Mr Pontifex may have been a little sterner with his children than some of his neighbours, but not much. He thrashed his boys two or three times a week and some weeks a good deal oftener, but in those days fathers were always thrashing their boys. . . . St Paul had placed disobedience to parents in very ugly company . . .

'In the popular phrase,' George Pontifex saw to it that the 'wills' of his children were 'well-broken' in their childhood. They swiftly become victims of his Puritan Anglicanism. Eliza and Maria are the exemplary, vacuous products of their father's system. John, the elder son, soon learned that every family is divided into hares and hounds, and decides early to humour his father by hunting the particular hare, his younger brother, Theobald, a child of considerable energy and passion, who under the repressions of the system becomes 'reserved and shy, and, I should say, indolent in mind and body'. One child only escapes, his sister Alethea, with her 'lively, affectionate disposition'. Like her grandfather, she had a great 'love of fun', a fund of 'life'. She is clearly within the Romantic tradition. She is very much a central influence of the novel, in her nephew's salvation; a convenient figure perhaps, for it is never explained how she survived her environment. It is merely necessary to the novel that she should have done so.

Morally destroyed, in Butler's sense, Theobald becomes a clergyman, through parental influence. He begets his own children, and one especially. Ernest Pontifex is subjected to all the barbarities his own father had endured at the hands of George Pontifex:

Before Ernest could well crawl he was taught to kneel; before he could well speak he was taught to lisp the Lord's prayer. . . .

If his attention flagged . . . here was an ill weed which would grow apace, unless it were plucked out . . . and the only way to pluck it out was to whip him, or shut him up in a cupboard, or dock him of some of the small pleasures of childhood . . .

This, Butler says, was done from 'love, anxiety, timidity, stupidity, and impatience'. He castigates Theobald for his 'ignorance and stupidity' – indeed the whole force of the book seems to fall on this word 'stupidity'. A keener analysis might see Theobald caught within the repressions and consequent aggressions of his own emotions, a man reduced inevitably to the recourse of thrashings, whippings, and every resort of calculated physical, mental, and emotional cruelty. The picture given by Butler suggests obviously neurotic characteristics. It might be more acceptable now to see the aggression in Theobald Pontifex as inherent in the severities of the Puritan ethic, so cruelly enforced against his children. Butler makes none of the allusions we might feel justified in making to the relation between the restrictions of the morality and the restrictions it placed so cruelly on the very heart of life itself, on its children. In dealing with the Pontifex family, we may perhaps suspect that Butler was in fact dealing with the emotional superstructure of an acquisitive and repressive society. The family severities of *The Way of All Flesh* raise indeed the whole pattern of psychological relationships between the politics, the economics, the religion, and the family *mores* of the period. The aggression towards children seems part of a much larger cultural whole. The religious treatment of Ernest Pontifex seems part of a whole cultural and psychological way of life. If the pursuit of culture itself involves repression, some cultures we feel seem to involve more repression than others.

In an ironic passage Butler gives the facts of the cruelty clearly enough:

To parents who wish to lead a quiet life I would say: Tell your children that they are very naughty. . . . Point to the young people of some acquaintances as models of perfection and impress your own children with a deep sense of their own inferiority. You carry so many more guns than they do that they cannot fight you. This is called moral influence. . . . You keep the dice and throw them both for your children and yourself. Load them then, for you can easily manage to stop your children from examining them. . . . You hold all the trump cards, or if you do not you can filch them. . . . True, your children will probably find out all about it some day. But not until too late . . .

In a baleful, rather Shavian tone, he makes his case against Puritan Christianity:

I think the Church Catechism has a good deal to do with the unhappy relations which commonly even now exist between parents and children. . . . the person who composed it did not get a few children to come in and help him; he was clearly not young himself, nor should I say it was the work of one who liked children. . . . The general impression it leaves upon the mind of the young is that their wickedness at birth was but very imperfectly wiped out at baptism, and that the mere fact of being young at all has something with it that savours more or less distinctly of the nature of sin . . .

One need not suggest the genealogy of this. The central antithesis of the book lies in this opposition between Puritan restriction and romantic freedom. Butler expresses his values in a way reminiscent of Dickens himself. When Ernest was ill: 'His mamma had told him he need not be afraid of dying, for he would go straight to heaven, if he would only be sorry for having done his lessons so badly and vexed his poor papa.' Ernest, however, was overjoyed to recover, for, as a romantic child indeed, he says: 'There were no kittens in heaven, and he did not think there were cowslips to make cowslip tea.' And again when Ernest is redeemed through his godfather's, the narrator's, influence, he becomes a child, enjoying an adult childhood, with all its pleasure in romantic sensation:

It pleased me to see the delight he took in all about him; the fire-place with a fire in it; the easy chairs . . . the red geraniums in the window. . . . Everything was pregnant with the most exquisite pleasure to him. . . . The plane trees were full of leaf still . . . never till now, he said, had he known what the enjoyment of these things really was . . .

and when, after his disastrous marriage, he goes abroad:

. . . not a bank opening cowslips as we passed through the railway cuttings, but he was drinking it all in with an enjoyment too deep for words.

Both the narrator, and Ernest's Aunt Alethea, stand for the Joy of life – for music, for physical beauty, for Nature, for craft-work with the hands, against the harsh restrictions of Roughborough and Dr Skinner's Latin and Greek. The central antithesis of the novel lies between the image of the Pontifex children and the image of Ernest's own children at the end of the novel. The Pontifex children 'might not cut out things, nor use their paintbox on a Sunday'. The description of them continues:

Their cousins might play with their toy train on Sunday, but though they had promised that they would run none but Sunday trains, all traffic had been prohibited. One treat only was allowed them – on Sunday evenings they might choose their own hymns.

For his own children, Ernest had learned to want something different:

He wanted his children to be brought up in the fresh pure air, and among other children who were happy and contented.

Overton himself comments on their education:

They were still so young that it did not much matter where they were, so long as they were with kindly decent people, and in a healthy neighbourhood.

These romantic assertions – 'fresh pure air' – 'happy and contented' – 'kindly decent people' – 'in a healthy neighbourhood' – are flaccid in expression; they do not contain the force to counterbalance the negative image of Roughborough and the Pontifex family. In the last image of these children, when Ernest and Overton visit them on the farm near Gravesend, there is an air of the stock image too easily resorted to:

While we were still a quarter of a mile off we heard shouts and children's laughter, and could see a lot of boys and girls romping together and running after one another. We could not distinguish our own two, but when we got near they were soon made out, for the other children were blue-eyed, flaxen-pated little folks, whereas ours were dark and straight-haired. . . . They were like a lot of wild young colts . . .

The prose is flat and careless (one might, for example, ask what 'young' adds to 'colt' in the last sentence).

The Way of All Flesh is not only a novel *à thèse*, but very much a novel with a negative thesis, and this is brilliantly enough dramatized. The failure lies in its definition of positive virtue. Butler, through the narrator Overton, conveys a casual hedonism:

All animals, except man, know that the principal business of life is to enjoy it.

He has spent his life best who has enjoyed it most; God will take care that we do not enjoy it any more than is good for us.

In his revised Catechism, he would instil into the child 'the duty of seeking all reasonable pleasure and avoiding all pain that can be honourably avoided'.

A whole world of political, social and ethical problems, however, lies in the definition to be given to 'reasonable' and 'honourably' in the above. In his rejection of Puritan antagonism to human pleasure, and in particular childhood's pleasure, Butler leaves unexplored the debatable ethic of unrestrained hedonism. To reject unreasonable and cruel restraint is only to begin the discovery of the best adjustment between uninhibited Joy and the individual's social obligation. With Butler as with many others who were critical of the values of the century, the negative complaint is usually more convincing than the positive remedies proposed. Arnold's castigations of the Philistines has an edge which his proposal of 'sweetness and light' has not. Lawrence's negative dissection of society's ills has a power which his positive of 'blood' has not. *The Way of All Flesh* is an interesting case of a romantic assertion of freedom which does not continue to define itself in terms of its attendant disciplines. The book slides out by asserting an easy philosophy of tolerance. In the matter of his children's education, the regenerate Ernest merely echoes the sentiments his Aunt Alethea had expressed about his own:

Don't scold him . . . if he is volatile. . . . Let him go here and there, and learn his truest liking by finding out what, after all, he catches himself turning to habitually – then let him stick to this.

Ernest echoes this by asserting the same kind of tolerance for his own children:

Why should I take them from where they are . . . to send them to schools where they will not be one-half so happy. . . . Georgie wants to be a barge-

man, let him begin as one, the sooner the better . . . then if he shows developments I can be on the look-out to encourage them and make things easy for
him; while if he shows no desire to go ahead, what on earth is the good of
trying to shove him forward . . .

One remembers what Coleridge said to Thelwall. Butler's intention
is that Ernest should be seen to return to the tolerant, unambitious
values of his eighteenth-century great-grandfather; but there are
worlds of social difference between the values of the rural carpenter
and the values of Ernest become a man of enormous private fortune,
as a result of his aunt's bequest and its subsequent speculative invest-
ment in the hands of his godfather, settling to a life of dilettante
authorship, with strikingly little actual relation to society. It is a
resolution wholly enervating. The arch with which Butler intended
to frame his novel sinks in the dilettantism and casual tolerance of
the novel's end:

Then he saw – that it matters little what profession, whether religion or
irreligion, a man may make, provided only he follows it out with charitable
inconsistency.

And Overton says of Ernest:

I mean that he was trying to give up father and mother for Christ's sake. He
would have said he was giving them up because he thought they hindered
him in the pursuit of his truest and most lasting happiness. Granted, but what
is this if it is not Christ? What is Christ if he is not this? He who takes the
highest and most self-respecting view of his own welfare which it is in his
power to conceive . . . is a Christian whether he knows it and calls himself
one, or whether he does not . . .

This is nothing but perverse reduction of terms where words no
longer mean anything. Ultimately the novel begs the very question it
raises, the question fundamental to any philosophy of human liberty
– the subtlety of adjustment between the free individual and his
obligation to his society.

This sense of deficiency in the positives in Butler comes I think
from the cerebrated quality of the novel. For although one may
cavil at the whole romantic tradition for its frequent failure to pursue
the implications of its assertions on behalf of freedom for the child,

and, through the image of the child, for humanity itself, there is a nourishment of feeling enriching the positive assertion for Life in Blake, Dickens, and Mark Twain. Butler's thesis, however, was not sensitively perceived. The novel's only real escape of emotion comes, significantly, in the portrayal of the father's cruelty, and in this we sometimes feel something of a relish in Butler, a disquieting reminder that he himself was so painfully involved in just such an upbringing:

Certainly there is no inherent love for the family system on the part of nature herself. . . . The fishes know it not, and they get along quite nicely. The ants and the bees, who far outnumber man, sting their fathers to death as a matter of course!

Why cannot we be buried as eggs in neat little cells with ten or twenty thousand pounds each wrapped round us in Bank of England notes, and wake up, as the sphex wasp does, to find that its papa and mamma have not only left ample provision at its elbow, but have been eaten by sparrows . . .

One suspects the acutely personal reference of this sort of thing. Shorn of its humour, it seems in fact rather repellent; and in any case denies the force of something he was trying to say. The Pontifex children were 'white and puny', because he says they 'were suffering from *home-sickness*'. The italics are Butler's own. One feels perhaps that his own injured and uncontrolled feelings have betrayed him into this contradiction of his more accurate and reasonable analysis of the condition of the Pontifex children.

But to notice its major weaknesses (its plot is almost absurd in the way it manages everything for Ernest's salvation) is not to deny its courage, or diminish its influence. It remains the most energetic exposure of Puritan practice in rearing the child. It stands among a whole corpus of late nineteenth- and early twentieth-century literature concerned with the emancipation of childhood and adolescence from the family and religion – notably Edmund Gosse's *Father and Son* (1907), and, earlier, *The Autobiography of Mark Rutherford* (1881), both of which, in autobiographical form, dealt with the very religious problems which exercised Butler, although both Gosse and Rutherford were more concerned than Butler with intellectual emancipation, with the narrow-mindedness of 'religion', rather than with the emotional cruelty of its professors towards their children.

Freud's Essay on Infantile Sexuality

The Pontifex family of *The Way of All Flesh* was, however, only one aspect of the Victorian attitude to the child. Its savagery contrasted constantly with the other and entirely opposite tradition of the sentimentalized Romantic attitude. Nonconformist and Low Church 'original sin' jostled perpetually with the residue of Rousseau's 'original innocence' to be found in the popularized expression the Victorians enjoyed of the Romantic concept. Wordsworth's child trailed his 'clouds of glory', and William Carlyle of *East Lynne* returned clearly enough to the 'imperial palace' of 'Paradise' which he inherited by nature. With Mrs Henry Wood, and even more so with Marie Corelli, Christianity itself became romanticized. Throughout the century, literature, from the mature to the banal, expressed this conflict between restraint and romantic freedom. Industrialism, utilitarian 'facts', Puritan morality, and the institution of the Victorian family, were the engines of restraint; Nature, Imagination, Wonder, and Feeling were the symbols of the child's emancipation. Through the symbol of childhood's 'original innocence', expression was given to one of the major problems of modern culture, the plight of humanity in a harshly de-humanizing society, and the urgent conflict of Reason with Feeling. But in making the humanist protest on behalf of innocent childhood, Romantic literature, even as we have seen the greatest, served to disseminate a world-picture of childhood which led to a very widely accepted falsification of its nature. The angry protest became in general acceptance nothing more than a convenient vehicle for stagnating pathos, or, in so far as it remained active, a potent means for withdrawal, for regression away from the very problems it had been created to express. So that, at the turn of the century, the child needed emancipation, not only in Butler's sense, from the Puritan family, but from the careless and very widely accepted falsification of the myth of its 'innocent' nature. Both 'original sin' and 'original innocence' in their general acceptance had become impediments to an objective assessment of the nature of the child, and the significance to be attached to his education and experience. This emancipation from both innocence and sin was very much the product of the new techniques discovered by psycho-analysis for the observation and investigation of the child's nature.

In discussing the relation between literature and psychology, and especially Freudian psycho-analysis, it seems advisable to set out from the beginning the chosen limits of discussion. The whole field of psychology, and especially its relation to the arts, is so frequently bedevilled by prejudice and misunderstanding that it becomes necessary to clarify what exactly one is intending to do: namely, to put down in as precise a way as possible the major positions of Freud, in particular, with reference to the child, and to see how the whole climate of psycho-analytical thought, not always necessarily deriving precisely from his own theories, may be seen to have influenced the post-Freudian literature of childhood.

The terminology of psycho-analysis has already passed into the intellectual jargon of our age. Whether from the enthusiasms of Freud's own later followers, or from the seemingly inescapable tendency of the non-specialist mind to think in terms of cliché, and inexact cliché at that, the subtle and gentle quality of much of Freud's own analysis has often been lost in popularization. His own shaft of analytic light has been too often spread through the prism of infinite popularizing, only to be focused again into a dogmatism which he himself would have been perhaps the last to wish to convey. For this reason it is important to lay out in some detail the essentials of Freudian analysis, with its account of mental structure, energy, and the mechanisms through which that energy is conveyed into actual conscious human behaviour. It is essentially relevant to our interest to do this, since for psycho-analysis, more than for any other major school of modern psychology, the child was, from the outset, of such great importance.

Freud considered himself as extending into a largely undiscovered field, the nineteenth-century tradition of scientific analysis and rational discussion. His own early work was conducted on the ambiguous frontier between neurology and psychology, and it was only after becoming convinced that a purely physical account of the origins of mental illness was untenable that he turned his scientific intelligence to the elaboration of what became psycho-analysis. He was at first one of many – Janet, Charcot, Bleuler, Havelock Ellis, William James – who were directing the Western mind towards the discoveries with which in time he became so intimately associated. Pursuing the logic of the intellectual moment, he made his fundamental distinction between the physical and the psychic, and between the conscious and the unconscious, by positing the reality of the unconscious and its relation, first to mental disorder, and thence to the whole field of human behaviour. Although he laid such stress on the unconscious motivation of human activity, and devoted his life to its analysis, the popular conception, frequently met with, that his was in some way a plea for 'irrationality', is entirely wrong. He sought rather to establish through psycho-analysis the control which alone he felt could permit of true freedom; or the emotional freedom which alone could permit of valid human control. Without an understanding of the unconscious and its interaction with conscious behaviour, to attempt to affect either personal or social restraint for humanity was for him something akin to attempting to restrain the bull in the mental china shop by offering a piece of Dresden porcelain to its consideration.

Freud established the concept of the unconscious, and directed his analytic attention especially towards the period in the individual's development when the conscious was in its most dynamic and tender relationship with the unconscious, during infancy and childhood. He conceived of the Ego as a mediating agency of the mind, standing between the innate pleasure-impulses of the Id and the demands of external reality. It was for him during the period of infancy and early childhood that the Ego is called upon to make the first and fundamental adjustments between these conflicting demands. The stable personality would be the personality which through the consciousness of the Ego had resolved the conflict between the impulses of the Id seeking satisfaction, and the demands of external existence, and also that other conflict between the instincts and the unconsciously inhibiting pressures of the Super-Ego, that agency in the unconscious which through parental and social influences assumes the power of an unconscious moral 'conscience'. Stability, in so far as it could ever be attained, would lie in the resolution achieved by the Ego of these conflicts within the mental structure. This stability could be upset by failure to achieve a conscious resolution, particularly in the case of the infantile Ego.

To the erotic energy of the Id, Freud gave the name of 'libido', and it was for him the unresolved impulses of the libido, particularly in its exact sexual expression, that worked such havoc upon the mental stability of his patients. During his period as a student under Charcot in Paris, and later in association with Breuer in Vienna, he became himself convinced that mental illness was most often neither neurological in origin, nor susceptible to neurological therapy. Everything seemed to indicate that mental disorder derived from some repressed sexual factor, and in time, with the element of parental seduction so suspiciously frequent among the stories of his patients, he 'stumbled upon', as he put it, the Oedipus complex. He realized that the neurotic patient might be constructing wish-fulfil-ments of his infantile impulses through the medium of fantasies of parental seduction. In the neurotic symptoms of the adult he saw reflected the failure of the infantile Ego to control the impulses of the Id; and, in this way, the whole concept of 'infantile sexuality' was formulated.

It was, then, to the developmental factor of the individual during his earliest infancy and childhood that Freud was to devote so much of his analytic attention. The suspiciously convenient, resistant amnesia of most adults towards their childhood suggested to Freud a clear intrusion of the factor of unconscious 'repression', beyond which the conscious memory of the adult could not, without analysis, and would not, without necessity, go. The aim of psycho-analysis would be to discover for the rational purposes of the Ego the factor in infantile sexuality which had been repressed into the unconscious, and which lay there as a disturbing quantity of greater or lesser extent in everyone's psyche. For, in this view, the distinction between normality and abnormality becomes essentially a matter of quantity and gradation. The neurotic patient is, in the strict sense, a casualty of the fundamental conflict between the conscious and unconscious, and, to the Freudian, they are few who emerge into adult conscious-ness without fairly distinguishable battle-scars.

Without asserting a rigid chronology, Freud considered infantile sexuality as di-phasic. He suggested that the first phase begins at birth and extends until about the end of the fifth or sixth year. A period of 'latency' then ensues, which continues until, with the onset of puberty, sexuality becomes focused in genital interests, leading to the accomplished sexuality or unaccomplished neurosis of the adult. It may be that, in internal detail, Freud's analysis is more specifically relevant to the chronology of maturation in Western bourgeois cultures, where the environmental factor of sexual segregation at school must particularly be taken into account, than to other cultures where the sexual pressures of environment are frequently very different indeed. But arguments, mainly chronological, about developments within the system detract little from the acceptability of the concept of 'infantile sexuality'; and it is perhaps a sign of the widespread acknowledgement of his basic premise that few would now assert the *non*-sexual character of the child without fear of being considered either ignorant or perverse – though many would of course qualify the definition of Freud's 'sexuality'. Much of the hostility his theories aroused arose in part from the frequent misunderstanding of what may very well have been an unfortunate and misleading descriptive term. In everyday language 'sexuality' suggests something rather different from the continuities of libidinal energies, in childhood and maturity, which, primarily, he was seeking to establish.

For Freud, the adult's life would in great part be determined by the adjustments achieved, or not achieved, by the Ego during the earliest phase of infantile development. The quantity of later maladjustment would depend to a great extent upon the rearing of the child during his very earliest years, and the redirection he could effect with the aid of parents and teachers of the impulses arising from his infantile unconscious, redirecting them into sublimated and socially-acceptable forms. He saw the child, when the apparatus for adjustment, the Ego, was weakest, faced with enormous problems of accommodation to reality – through birth itself, through weaning, through the necessity to adopt clean bodily habits, and to accept the existence of other brothers and sisters in respect of the affection demanded from the loved parent, through the prohibition on infantile masturbation, and, most important for Freud, through the frustration of the child's oedipal impulse towards sexual satisfaction with the parent of the opposite sex. For him, serious danger lay in too early and strict inhibition of natural impulses. The child could only be brought safely to maturity with the utmost care. Too crude a transition at any stage of the child's development, too sudden a prohibition of the gratification of its earliest oral, anal, and oedipal impulses would lead to the repression of such impulses into the unconscious, engendering fear, anxiety, and guilt in the child's and adult's conscious behaviour, and thus preventing, through the unconscious obstacle of repression, the continuous development of the psyche towards adult maturity. In his *Outline of Psycho-Analysis*, written towards the end of his life, Freud declared:

It seems that neuroses are only acquired during early childhood (up to the age of six), even though their symptoms may not make their appearance until much later. . . . We can easily account for this preference for the first period of childhood. Neuroses are, as we know, disorders of the Ego; and it is not to be wondered at that the Ego, while it is weak, immature, and incapable of resistance, should fail in dealing with problems which it could later manage with utmost ease.[1]

An essential pre-condition of prophylaxis against neurosis lay in the enlightened treatment of the child. In the *Outline*, he returned to the problem:

We cannot escape the conclusion that neuroses could be avoided if the child's ego were spared this task, that is, if the child's sexual life were allowed free play, as happens among many primitive races.[2]

This is not to say, however, that he advocated the gratification of the child at the expense of his social obligation. It has been a frequent complaint against his system that educationally his ideas lead to moral licence and coddling in the schools. The whole purpose of education, however, for him, lay in the possibility of redirecting libidinal energy, through its control – 'most of our most highly-valued cultural heritage', he suggested, 'has been acquired at the cost

1. *An Outline of Psycho-Analysis*, by Sigmund Freud, Ch. 7, p. 51. Translated by James Strachey (London: Hogarth Press, 1949).
2. ibid., Ch. 8, p. 71.

of sexuality and by the restriction of sexual motive forces'.[1] His concern was that the transition from the free gratification of the infant's sexual impulses towards the higher purposes of education and his social fulfilment was too often too crudely enforced. He counselled a relaxation in the demands made upon the infantile Ego in order to create the basis for ultimately a more satisfactory control. Civilization could be bought, so to say, at too high an emotional price for the individual, and at too high a price for society itself, for the repression of libidinal and aggressive instincts could at best only lead to a fitful and unproductive accommodation between the individual and society, and at worst could frequently lead to chronic instability, delinquency and mental breakdown. The central problem of human existence, the conflict between individual satisfaction and man's gregarious necessity, lies at the heart of Freud's thought, and he hoped that psycho-analysis would be a further weapon in the human struggle towards a viable theory of human freedom. The whole plea of psycho-analysis was that the individual's adjustment to society should not be imposed so harshly during childhood as to prevent his development towards a stable, self-fulfilling relation between his instinctive satisfactions and the demands of social necessity in adulthood.

It is of interest that Freud's insistence on the importance of repressed infantile sexuality played so important a part in the defection of what were to become the main, dissident schools of early modern psychological theory. Most of these schools indeed came to stress some other factor than the infantile, if not, as with Jung, actually to deny its significance altogether. Adler found the origin of adult neurosis in frustrated aggression consequent upon the 'inferiority complex'. Rank suggested the fundamental agency of the 'birth trauma'. The tendency of Freud's opponents was, in fact, to short-circuit the route his own analysis took through the phase of the individual's infantile sexual development.

1. ibid., Ch. 8, p. 72. A suggestion which may in part explain the significant 'activity' of the Puritan nations in the modern era, where the sexual restraints required of the individual have been most marked, and the comparative 'decadence' of activity of the Latin nations, where the restraints have at least been less severely enforced.

It is a common acceptance that 'modern psychology' has implied some special concern with the psychology of the child. It is important, however, that in one of the other systems of psychological theory, in significant dissent from Freud's, in Jung's Analytical Psychology, the emphasis shifted away from the Freudian centre of analysis in the child, with all its complex investigation of unconscious, repressed infantile factors in the adult, to a central interest in the conscious adult himself. For Jung, the origin of neurosis most often lies in a conflict of the Conscious with the Collective Unconscious. 'I no longer', he declares, in a significant sentence, 'find the cause of neurosis in the past, but in the present. I ask what the necessary task is which the patient will not accomplish.'[1] Neurotic symptoms for Jung are the 'suffering of a human being who has not discovered what life means to him'.[2] It is 'an act of adaptation that has failed',[3] an 'escape from the inner voice and so from vocation'.[4] 'Behind the neurotic perversion is concealed vocation, destiny, the development of personality, the complete realization of the life-will that is born with the individual.'[5] Therapy for the neurotic lies not in Freud's investigation of the infantile period of psychic development, but in refreshing the psyche through recourse to the mythology of the universally inherited Collective Unconscious. For Jung, in one phrase, the child 'has no real problems';[6] for he lives within the psychic ambience of his parents until he achieves individuality of his Ego at puberty.

Perhaps the fundamental opposition of the two systems with regard to the child cannot be better demonstrated than by comparing their attitudes to the Oedipus complex. Freud based so much on its sexual character. For him it was everything:

1. *Freud or Jung*, by Edward Glover, p. 122 (London: Allen and Unwin, 1950).
2. *Modern Man in Search of a Soul*, by C. G. Jung, p. 260 (London: Kegan Paul, 1945).
3. *Freud or Jung*, by Edward Glover, p. 122.
4. *The Integration of the Personality*, by C. G. Jung, p. 300 (London: Kegan Paul, 1940).
5. ibid., p. 301.
6. *Modern Man in Search of a Soul*, by C. G. Jung, p. 115. See also pp. 113 and 131.

I venture to assert that if psycho-analysis could boast of no other achieve-ment than the discovery of the repressed Oedipus complex, that alone would give it a claim to be counted among the precious new acquisitions of man-kind.[1]

Jung, however, evacuates the Oedipus impulse of any specifically sexual content. For him it is merely the desire for re-birth, part of Man's universally inherited mythology. The 'incest-fantasy', he declares:

... is most especially the totality of the sun myth which proves to us that the fundamental basis of the 'incestuous' desire does not aim at cohabitation, but at the special thought of becoming a child again, of turning back to the parent's protection, of coming into the mother once more in order to be born again. . . . But here the incest prohibition interferes . . .[2]

There were of course many factors involved in the opposition which Freud encountered. The fact that he was pleased to consider himself with Copernicus and Darwin as dealing a blow to Man's inflated self-esteem makes him an uncomfortable prophet. He under-mined not only the façade of man's rational behaviour, but investi-gated the origins of his most valued possessions, his religion, his ethics, his jurisprudence, and his art. His therapy was scarcely notorious for its excessive optimism. His theories cannot easily be abused as a form of substitute religion. Concerning himself with the rational means for alleviating actual mental disorder, and indicating the means by which men might reach towards viable emotional freedom, he did not seek to explain the purposes of human existence. To minds hungry for religion, his theories were a cold repast.

But, in this matter of the hostility he aroused, it seems significant to note that his *Interpretation of Dreams* met with singularly little popular interest, let alone hostility. The storm broke with the publication of the *Three Essays* in 1905, and in particular with the Essay on Infantile Sexuality. In his biography of Freud, Dr Ernest Jones puts it this way:

Naturally the main opprobrium fell on his assertion that children are born with sexual urges, which undergo a complicated development before they

1. *An Outline of Psycho-Analysis*, by Sigmund Freud, Ch. 7, p. 61.
2. *Psychology of the Unconscious*, by C. G. Jung, p. 138 (London: Kegan Paul, 1919).

attain the familiar adult form, and that their first sexual objects are their parents. This assault on the pristine innocence of childhood was unforgivable. In spite of the contemporary furor and abuses, however, which continued for perhaps twenty years, time worked its way with the book, and Freud's prediction that its conclusions would before long be taken for granted is approaching fulfilment.[1]

In assaulting the 'pristine innocence of childhood' it has been sometimes suggested that Freudian analysis bears some relation to the concept of 'original sin', that the religious idea of the child's 'corrupt' nature bears a striking resemblance to the Freudian idea of the child as the heir of libidinal impulses and the father of adult neurosis, that the Power of Darkness seen by the Christian in the 'fallen' nature of Man resembles the dark, unconscious impulses of the Id, forcing themselves into and subverting his conscious behaviour, that in fact Freud was merely describing the mechanisms through which Evil works itself out in the human consciousness, that the Freudian Id is no more than a descriptive synonym for the whole concept of religious Evil.

Such comparisons ignore, of course, the whole attitude from which Freud made his investigation of mental structure and organization. Concepts of 'corruption', 'innocence' and 'sin' were wholly alien to his scientific approach. He had indeed a fundamental distaste for the traditional Christian theory of human consciousness, which treated the child's nature as corrupt, and saw the function of 'character-training' as the bending of its froward, evil will to the moral requirements of religion and society. He hoped to bring no preconceptions to his investigations of the human consciousness; he aspired only to deal in its 'facts'. This was germane to his central position that the only hope for humanity lay in bringing the unconscious into rational human control. If ever an accommodation were to be effected between religious concepts and psycho-analysis, between 'original sin' and 'original complex' in the child, it would (if his plea that the utmost care should be exercised in bending the child to his social adjustment were to be respected) necessitate a very different

1. *Sigmund Freud. Life and Work*, by Ernest Jones, Vol. 2, pp. 13–14 (London: Hogarth Press, 1955).

treatment of childhood's 'wickedness' than, until his discoveries, the concept of 'original sin' had often been responsible for. Even if, among the many metaphysical sophistications of the mid-twentieth century, the Freudian Id can be subsumed into the doctrine of Man's original Fall, it in no way blurs the fact that Freud's theories were the primary agent in destroying the religious attitude to childhood expressed in the family of Theobald Pontifex of *The Way of All Flesh*. For all his destruction of the idea of childhood's innocence, Freud's ideas were in fact in fundamental sympathy with the original romantic assertion of childhood's importance, and its vulnerability to social victimization. He discussed, in a way reminiscent of Blake himself, the acute damage that could be inflicted on the child's innocent sexuality through the mindless prohibitions of parents, teachers, and priests.

But just as his theories subverted the savageries to which the doctrine of 'original sin' had often led, so too his assertion of infantile sexuality subverted the vacuous image of childhood to which the romantic symbol had itself become reduced. He was, in this sense, doubly under fire, and no more passionately than from the partisans of childhood's innocence. The religious idea of the child's 'fallen nature' (which, if taken seriously, is a much more total denial of innocence than Freud's) never roused such popular hostility as the idea of the child's 'sexual' nature.[1] The implication is that 'infantile sexuality' subverted a 'myth of childhood' which many found it necessary to retain. Nineteenth-century science was notorious for its unpalatable and disturbing discoveries about the nature and environment of Man. One of the most disturbing of all was Freud's assault upon childhood's innocence. The very special and continuing hostility that he aroused over this suggests that a concept of childhood's innocence may in fact have been an emotional convenience to an age decreasingly able to find satisfaction for guilt in universally-accepted religious forms. The nineteenth century was especially fearful of sexuality. It maintained a strict taboo on its discussion in literature and polite society. Is it entirely fanciful to suppose that a myth of

1. Possibly because of society's long cultural-conditioning to the idea over the centuries, and the emotional counter-balance provided by the ritual of baptism and the whole concept of Man's 'redemption'.

childhood's innocence was a convenient means of emotional absolu-
tion from guilt in a society in which natural instinct was an unmen-
tionable vice, and in which the religious means for expiation of
guilt were decreasingly sought? Was the romantic symbol of childhood's purity and innocence, which the Victorians held to so
dearly, and defended, when it came under suspicion, so passionately,
a symbol of what one might term secular expiation? Did a sexually-
fearful society create a myth of childhood as a period in life when the
Devil, in the guise of Sex, could not assail the purity of Man? Is this
in part the explanation of why so many adults, in the manner of
Theobald Pontifex, employed the faith of what is after all a charitable
religion to deal so uncharitably with the 'symbol' whenever it
failed to act up to the mythological 'purity' they demanded from it
for their own deeper satisfaction? In the psychology of sexual repression and its ever-attendant guilt we may indeed find part of the
explanation of the popularity of the myth of innocent childhood and
the savagery towards children in practice, which seem to have
existed so astonishingly – otherwise – side by side. We have seen in a
previous chapter how the symbol of happy, carefree childhood became for certain authors a means for escape from sexual immaturity.
There seems good reason to wonder whether, on a much wider
scale, the popularized myth of childhood's innocence provided a
means for coming to terms with the guilt created by a widely-
imposed repressive sexual morality, as an escape from a very widespread immaturity towards sexuality.

One would not be so clearly directed towards psychological
explanations, if the Victorian image of childhood had not become so
clearly involved with sexuality when Freud began his investigation of
the unmistakable facts of the child's sexual character. The Romantic
image of the child started with Blake's free acceptance of its innocent
sexuality. It is ironic indeed that a literary image initiated in this way
should have become one of the most powerful obstacles to the acceptance of the sexual character of the child a century later. In his verses,
Blake foresaw some of the opprobrium which Freud and his associates faced in their analysis of the child's nature, an analysis which, in
time, revolutionized the whole attitude of Western society to its
children.

CHAPTER 12

Joyce: Virginia Woolf: D. H. Lawrence

I

ONE speaks of revolution; but one does so knowing the danger of the distortions which usually accompany the idea. Psycho-analysis in its wide, if sometimes inaccurate, acceptance could scarcely have obtained such acceptance if it had not been in a general sense representative. Freud's theories nourished a dissatisfaction with conventional attitudes towards human nature, a dissatisfaction widely felt by many, and particularly by literary minds of his period. 'On or about December 1910 human character changed,' Virginia Woolf declared in the twenties, and we know fully what she meant. *The Way of All Flesh*, Shaw's plays, Tchekov, Dostoievsky, the novels of H. G. Wells, *Sinister Street*, and *Sons and Lovers* were all to be read in England between 1900 and 1914. It is not long, of course, in citing a succession of names before one is obliged to discriminate. But taking the period indiscriminately, *en masse*, one sees how Freud's theories merge into the whole shift of intellect and sensibility through which he lived. *Sons and Lovers*, *Ulysses*, and *To the Lighthouse* would have been written, one suspects, had Freud never lived, or if his theories had never been known to their authors. The relation between modern literature and Freudian analysis is perhaps best expressed as a cross-fertilization between intellects and sensibilities working in parallel fields for the most part; but sometimes the fields coincide.

The first impact of psycho-analysis outside purely clinical spheres was significantly in literature; before it made its effect in education, criminology, and the other fields in which it has since had such influence. The references of Freud's work were closely related to those of nineteenth-century literature, with its concern with the emotional realities behind the façade of everyday appearances, and the tensions it frequently discovered between the individual and his adjustment to society. The terms, the descriptive language might change, but the central interests were often very similar. Hailed as the 'discoverer of the unconscious' at the celebration of his seventieth birthday, Freud disclaimed the title, adding that 'poets and philosophers before me discovered the unconscious. What I discovered was the scientific method by which the unconscious can be studied.' His theories were in this sense the pursuit of romantic subjectivity in the field of science and rational codifying analysis. His own statement testifies to the similarity between his own interests and those of literature; but none the less firmly sets down the fundamental dissimilarity of his method. His interest, however, moved in the world of the dream, the fantasy, the myth, and the analysis of motivation and feeling. It is no coincidence that Wordsworth's most celebrated pronouncement of the child's 'fatherhood' of the Man should seem to us so close to Freud's own thought; and it is not surprising that Freud should have been so great an admirer of *Middlemarch*, considering it one of the greatest novels ever created.

The most immediately obvious influence of psychology in literature lies in the novels we associate with the idea of the 'stream of consciousness', in the work of Dorothy Richardson, May Sinclair, and more importantly James Joyce and Virginia Woolf. Although as a term, it may have been first used by May Sinclair in 1918, in reviewing Dorothy Richardson, the phrase derived from William James's *Principles of Psychology* (1890):

Every definite image in the mind is steeped and dyed in the free water that flows round it. The significance, the value of the image is all in this halo or penumbra that surrounds and escorts it. . . . Consciousness does not appear to itself chopped up in bits. . . . It is nothing jointed; it flows. . . . Let us call it the stream of thought, of consciousness, or of the subjective life.

This is reminiscent indeed of Virginia Woolf's own celebrated reaction away from the 'jointed' (and therefore dis-jointed) techniques of the late Victorian and Edwardian novel. In her *Common Reader*, we have:

Look within and life, it seems, is very far from being 'like this'. Examine for a moment an ordinary mind on an ordinary day. The mind receives a myriad impressions – trivial, fantastic, evanescent, or engraved with the sharpness of steel. From all sides they come, an incessant shower of innumerable atoms. . . . Life is not a series of giglamps, symmetrically arranged; life is a luminous halo, a semi-transparent envelope surrounding us from the beginning of consciousness to the end.

Such an attitude to experience we might suspect to have certain limitations as the basis for the awareness of an artist; limitations which are apparent enough in the work of Virginia Woolf herself. It places the accent where with a creative sensibility the accent should not lie, except at the utmost danger to itself, namely on the introverted sensibility towards sensations in utter disunity. The precarious equilibrium in any sensitive artist between the acute awareness of his responses and the relation of that awareness outside itself is, in this view, in acute danger of unbalance. With such an attitude to experience, the novelist is in danger of evacuating sensibility of its significance. A sensibility, no matter how acute, subtle, and tenderly aware, only has significance at the point of integration, where experience coheres. The 'stream of consciousness', with its revolutionary desire to say everything, was frequently in danger of saying nothing. If the frame which Wells, and Galsworthy, and Bennett imposed upon experience was false as they conveyed it, with their workaday time-sequence and Balzacian concern with the minutiae of physical description, it does not cure the falsity necessarily by suggesting that there is no clock on the wall. It does not argue against a 'frame', if framed experience can only be obtained by the kind of effort of integration which Lawrence brought to his achievement in the novel. Even if it *is* difficult to *say*, one harbours the old-fashioned requirement that the novelist should at least try to say something: he must not entirely blame us if we look on him as something of a secular priest.

But if in its ultimates, the 'stream of consciousness' should seem sterile, it effected its catharsis. It rejected the short-circuit of experience purveyed by the novel with the 'plot'. In keeping with the whole climate of psychological thought, it delved to reach its psychic realities. It cleared the encumbrances, and even though its heroes and heroines might sometimes convey the disconnexion with reality of neurosis itself, it could, with a major talent such as Joyce's, convey a sense of integration. It attempted to see human experience and human nature for what it conceived it to be. There would be no taboos between the experience and its description; no impediments, least of all sexual ones, between fact as it was apprehended and its expression. Experiences which the Victorian novel had frequently relegated to the attic were brought down, and it was not surprising that to many they may not always have seemed suitable as drawing-room furniture.

Among them of course we find the experiences of childhood. The child would no longer be used for a romantic 'message', or as the vehicle for self-pity, indulgent pathos, or escape. If he were 'impure', malicious, cruel, tender, kind, painfully sensitive – and most often an amalgam of all these qualities – then he would be presented in his reality. He would no longer be used as the guiltless 'angel' of a romantic, moralizing idyll; or the child of the Puritans' sin and the Devil; a child neither of 'purity' nor 'wrath', nor necessarily 'happy' in a fallacious, romanticized Nature, nor poignantly and inevitably 'unhappy' as the 'victim' of industrial society. He would be conveyed as a child, with his awareness conveyed as it was experienced, from within. A foremost early example of the method was the childhood of Stephen Dedalus in Joyce's *A Portrait of the Artist as a Young Man*.

II

Joyce was not of course in any sense a 'child' novelist. The child does not occupy either a very frequent or really important place in his work. Nevertheless his treatment of childhood is typical of his general treatment of character and experience, and the boyhood of Stephen in the *Portrait* is an interesting example of the new approach to the child. Before *A Portrait of the Artist as a Young Man*, Joyce had already written about children in *Dubliners*, which, although written as early as 1904, was not published until 1914. The first three of this first collection of stories centre in the consciousness of a boy. In the first, *The Sisters*, Joyce deals with the relation between a boy and a recently deceased priest, Father Flynn. Everything is given as through the child's eyes, especially the description of the two sisters mourning the dead priest. The account of the child's vision has

306

something of Dickens in it, and this is more especially so in the most remarkable of the three stories, *An Encounter*. It is the tale of an encounter between two boys and a grotesque stranger. It is an excellent example of the precision and objectivity of Joyce's art. There are no sentimentalizing undertones in the account of the friendship of the two boys, no importations from the adult author such as we might have had from Walpole: 'We were serious to the point of solemnity, but once during the short voyage our eyes met and we laughed.' Within their mutual truancy, the boys exist as separate individuals; and the 'encounter' ultimately takes place between them and the monstrous figure of the stranger.

The stranger talks to the boys lasciviously:

He began to speak to us about girls, saying what nice soft hair they had and how soft their hands were and how all girls were not so good as they seemed to be if only one knew.

And again:

When a boy was rough and unruly there was nothing would do him any good but a good sound whipping. . . . What he wanted was to get a nice warm whipping. I was surprised at this sentiment and involuntarily glanced up at his face. As I did so I met the gaze of a pair of bottle-green eyes peering at me from under a twitching forehead.

The whole feeling of the piece conveys precisely the phantasmagoric world of childhood. It has a grotesque quality not unlike some of *Oliver Twist*, or the early chapters of *Great Expectations*.

The other story in the volume dealing with childhood, *Araby*, deals with the disenchantment of a child, without, however, declining into self-pity and regret. The child looks forward to visiting a bazaar, to buy a present for his friend's sister. His father returns home late, and the boy does not have the money soon enough to reach the bazaar before closing time. Its conclusion has all the pain of childhood turning into life:

I heard a voice call from one end of the gallery that the light was out. The upper part of the hall was now completely dark. Gazing up into the darkness I saw myself as a creature driven and derided by vanity; and my eyes burned with anguish and anger.

A Portrait of the Artist as a Young Man, published two years later in 1916, develops the inwardness of the writing, and lies, in style, exactly between *Dubliners* and *Ulysses*. Everything is given from within the developing consciousness of the boy and adolescent. It is almost clinical in the directness of its psychological approach. The childhood of Stephen is a brilliant instance of Joyce's technique. It conveys the disconnected, sporadic quality of the infant's sensations, the grotesque, exaggerated and passionate appearance to the child of the world of adults, and the deep and painful impression of that adult world upon the child's emotions. The prose has an easy movement, and even where the style is most deliberately childlike, there is no sense of straining after effect:

Once upon a time and a very good time it was there was a moocow coming down along the road and this moocow that was coming down along the road met a nicens little boy named baby tuckoo. . . . His father told him that story: his father looked at him though a glass: he had a hairy face. He was baby tuckoo. The moocow came down the road where Betty Byrne lived: she sold lemon platt. . . . When you wet the bed first it is warm then it gets cold. His mother put on the oilsheet. That had the queer smell. His mother had a nicer smell than his father.

The Vances lived in number seven. They had a different father and mother. They were Eileen's father and mother. When they were grown up he was going to marry Eileen.

It conveys the consciousness of the very young child as one essentially of sensation, of smell and touch, only gradually distinguishing its own identity and its own family from other people and other children's fathers and mothers. One need scarcely comment on the fact that when the child was 'grown up he was going to marry Eileen'.

In dealing with Stephen's school-life, Joyce continues the same technique. He makes no attempt to re-create an external school. The school is felt through Stephen's consciousness of it. It is very much 'there', in the sense in which it is not in many of the more deliberate, described accounts of 'school' novels. Stephen is still self-involved, with that acute egotism and self-reference of childhood, but at the same time he is brought to the first painful adjustments with the external reality of the school:

He crept about from point to point on the fringe of his line, making little runs now and then. But his hands were bluish with cold. He kept his hands in the side pockets of his belted grey suit. That was a belt round his pocket. And belt was also to give a fellow a belt . . .

It gives exactly the half-involved consciousness of the boy, playing the game required of him, but pondering privately on the ambiguities of words.

Then Jack Lawton's yellow boots dodged out the ball and all the other boots and legs ran after. He ran after them a little way and then stopped. It was useless to run on. Soon they would be going home for the holidays. After supper . . . he would change the number pasted up inside his desk from seventy-seven to seventy-six.

For a moment the image of another being, Jack Lawton, becomes precise within the boy's consciousness. But another moment and the other children are merely 'other boots and legs'; the boy's egocentric consciousness returns to its own thoughts of homesickness and holidays. Everyone else is outside him: and the horror of the school's gregariousness descends upon him:

He drank another cup of hot tea and Fleming said:
What's up? Have you a pain or what's up with you?
I don't know, Stephen said.
Sick in the breadbasket, Fleming said, because your face looks white. It will go away.
O, yes, Stephen said.
But he was not sick there. He thought that he was sick in his heart if you could be sick in that place. Fleming was very decent to ask him. He wanted to cry. He leaned his elbows on the table and shut and opened the flaps of his ears. Then he heard the noise of the refectory every time he opened the flaps of his ears. It made a roar like a train at night.

The dry movement of the conversation gives the rawness, the resentment of the child at even Fleming's well-intentioned intrusion into his private misery. We have the same even more strikingly conveyed in this:

. . . And one day he had asked:
What is your name?
Stephen had answered: Stephen Dedalus.

Then Nasty Roche had said:

What kind of a name is that?

And when Stephen had not been able to answer Nasty Roche had asked:

What is your father?

Stephen had answered:

A gentleman.

What might seem at first a deliberate mannerism is in fact used to convey the disembodied quality of the boy's relation to his outside environment. Conversation itself is felt as an intrusion. The sadism of the following presents for the boy a very particular kind of intrusion:

Tell us, Dedalus, do you kiss your mother before you go to bed?

Stephen answered:

I do.

Wells turned to the other fellows and said:

O, I say, here's a fellow says he kisses his mother every night before he goes to bed.

The other fellows stopped their game and turned round, laughing. Stephen blushed under their eyes and said:

I do not.

Wells said:

O, I say, here's a fellow says he doesn't kiss his mother before he goes to bed.

Was it right to kiss his mother or wrong to kiss his mother? What did that mean, to kiss. You put your face up like that to say goodnight and then his mother put her face down. That was to kiss. His mother put her lips on his cheek; her lips were soft and they wetted his cheek; and they made a tiny little noise: kiss. Why did people do that with their two faces?

At home on vacation, the boy is initiated into the central religious theme of the novel, in the quarrel between his nationalist father and Mr Casey with Dante, over the treatment Parnell suffered at the hands of his Catholic supporters after his divorce:

At the door Dante turned round violently and shouted down the room, her cheeks flushed and quivering with rage:

Devil out of hell! We won! We crushed him to death! Fiend!

The door slammed behind her.

Mr Casey, freeing his arms from his holders, suddenly bowed his head on his hands with a sob of pain –

Poor Parnell! he cried loudly. My dead king!

He sobbed loudly and bitterly.

Stephen, raising his terrorstricken face, saw that his father's eyes were full of tears.

In time, the family meets ill-fortune. Stephen is not sent back to Clongowes. His consciousness slowly grasps the insecurity of the approaching adult world:

For some time he had felt the slight change in his house; and those changes in what he had deemed unchangeable were so many slight shocks to his boyish conception of the world.

Experiencing in turn the feverish and morose solitude of adolescence, he finds his childhood at an end:

... a strange unrest crept into his blood. Sometimes a fever gathered within him and led him to rove alone in the evening along the quiet avenue. ... The noise of children at play annoyed him and their silly voices made him feel, even more keenly than he had felt at Clongowes, that he was different from others.

Sexuality enters feverishly into his growing awareness. Taken by his father to Queen's College, he sees the word 'foetus' carved on a desk:

It shocked him to find in the outer world a trace of what he had deemed till then a brutish and individual malady of his own mind. His monstrous reveries came thronging into his memory. ... He had soon given in to them and allowed them to sweep across and abase his intellect, wondering always where they came from, from what den of monstrous images. ... The letters cut in the stained wood of the desk stared upon him ... making him loathe himself for his own mad and filthy orgies.

With Stephen's childhood at an end, Joyce conveys brilliantly the egocentricity of the adolescent consciousness, cut off from its own childhood, and unrelated to the adult world:

The memory of his childhood suddenly grew dim. He tried to call forth some of its vivid moments but could not. ... A little boy had been taught geography by an old woman who kept two brushes in her wardrobe ... he had made his first communion and eaten slim jim out of his cricket cap and watched the firelight leaping and dancing on the wall of a little bedroom in the infirmary and dreamed of being dead . . .

Stephen listens to his father and an old man talking of their youth:

No life or youth stirred in him as it had stirred in them. He had known neither the pleasure of companionship with others nor the vigour of rude male health nor filial piety. Nothing stirred within his soul but a cold and cruel and loveless lust. His childhood was dead or lost and with it his soul capable of simple joys and he was drifting amid life like the barren shell of the moon.

There is in Joyce no tone of nostalgic regret for the passage of child-hood's 'simple joys'. The vivid re-creation of Stephen's childhood merely serves as prologue to the central conflict of the 'young man' with his Catholic and unsympathetic environment. The movement of the book is towards the involvement of Stephen with manhood. The psychological realism of the boy's childhood serves indeed to strengthen the total 'portrait' of the developing consciousness of the 'young man'.

III

To turn to the novels of Virginia Woolf from Joyce's Stephen Dedalus is to turn to a wholly different sensibility. There was no doubt of the similarity of intention between the two writers. She herself praised Joyce for his concern 'at all costs to reveal the flicker-ings of that innermost flame which flashes its messages through the brain. . . . If we want life itself, here surely we have it . . .' But considering the massive achievement of *Ulysses*, with its wholeness, its complex integration of experience, few would now perhaps consider Virginia Woolf within Joyce's class. In delineating the individual consciousness, Joyce conveys something universal to human experience. In this respect, it is interesting to note Mrs Bennett's comment, in a not in any way depreciatory study of Virginia Woolf's work:

Her range is limited in so far as she sees most clearly, because she sympathizes most fully, with men and women who are either sensitive or intelligent or both, and the dimmer wits and, above all, blunter sensibilities are further removed from her centre of vision.

For her central characters she limits herself to one large social class, the class of those who have incomes or earn salaries.

This is not of course to raise the issue of 'class' in the novel; or to suggest that preoccupation with a particular class involves inevitable limitations, for how then could one support Jane Austen's claim to universality as a novelist? But the life of the eighteenth-century gentry class was perhaps altogether a different thing from the life of the 'class of those who have incomes or earn salaries' which, for good or ill, was in a state of decadence throughout the period Virginia Woolf wrote of them. In any event Mrs Bennett's comment seems to lay a finger on one cause for the sense of limited experience conveyed in so much of Virginia Woolf's fiction. She was of course herself aware of her rarefied predicament, that she wrote within a cultural vacuum:

At the present moment we are suffering, not from decay, but from having no code of manners which writers and readers accept as a prelude to the more exciting intercourse of friendship.

As Mr Daiches says in his study of her novels, she was continually preoccupied with 'reality' and its definition. 'Art without belief,' he says, 'without, that is, community belief – is not easy to write.' It was this, he suggests, which forced her into such a concern with the definition of 'reality'. It seems a significant anxiety, and this was her own answer:

'What is meant by reality? . . . It would seem to be something very erratic, very undependable – now to be found in a dusty road, now in a scrap of newspaper in the street, now in a daffodil in the sun. . . . It overwhelms one walking home beneath the stars and makes the silent world more real than the world of speech. . . . Now the writer, as I think, has the chance to live more than other people in the presence of this reality. . . .

It was to this inner 'reality' of the artist's sensibility, to the conveying of the 'reality' of the 'semi-transparent envelope' of the psyche that she disposed her art.

313

And within that 'envelope' her children exist. She concerned herself, more than Joyce, with attempting to convey the inward sensibilities of the child. One might indeed suggest that her work very often displays the consciousness of the child where she was not in fact writing of children. As Joyce suggests in *A Portrait of the Artist as a Young Man*, the consciousness of the child, and more particularly of the adolescent, is sensuous, dreamy, non-intellectual, and unrelated to external realities, and it is this sort of consciousness which her novels as a whole so persistently convey.

Was it perhaps for this reason that one of her most moving evocations was the relation between Mrs Ramsay and her son in *To the Lighthouse*? It is an exquisitely painful book, in the exact meaning of those words. It purveys an atmosphere of cool, resigned pessimism. Its central idea lies in the frustration symbol of the visit to the lighthouse, which the child is fated never to make, until as an adolescent he makes the visit in company with his father and sister, with that terrible sense of unfulfilment and anti-climax. For all its writing from within, for all its effort to convey the psychological reality of James Ramsay's feelings, the book conveys a pessimism about childhood, even though the regret is done with restraint. Its theme of childhood's disenchantment continues a familiar theme:

'Yes, of course, if it's fine tomorrow,' said Mrs Ramsay. 'But you'll have to be up with the lark,' she added.

To her son these words conveyed an extraordinary joy, as if it were settled the expedition were bound to take place, and the wonder to which he had looked forward, for years and years it seemed, was, after a night's darkness and a day's sail, within touch. Since he belonged, even at the age of six, to that great clan which cannot keep this feeling separate from that, but must let future prospects, with their joys and sorrows, cloud what is actually at hand . . . James Ramsay, sitting on the floor cutting out pictures from the illustrated catalogue of the Army and Navy Stores, endowed the picture of a refrigerator as his mother spoke with heavenly bliss. It was fringed with joy.

His private, romantic 'joy' is immediately shattered by his father:

'But,' said his father, stopping in front of the drawing-room window, 'it won't be fine.'

Had there been an axe handy, a poker, or any weapon that would have gashed a hole in his father's breast and killed him, there and then, James would have seized it.

The novel does not in fact draw any Freudian conclusions, does not choose to see an oedipal relation between Mrs Ramsay and her son, destroyed by the intrusion of the father, so murderously resented by the son. Mr Ramsay is seen much more as the romantic villain, cruel and careless of childhood's joy and wonder. The book creates a romantic tension between the compassionate mother and the heartless nature of the father-philosopher. Mr Ramsay is content that his children should 'be aware from childhood that life is difficult . . . and the passage to that fabled land where our brightest hopes are extinguished, our frail barks founder in darkness . . . one that needs, above all, courage, truth, and the power to endure'. This harsh, unpalatable reality is countered by Mrs Ramsay's reply: 'But it may be fine – I expect it will be fine.' But her sympathy for the child is again countered with this from the 'atheist Tansley':

'It's due west,' said the atheist Tansley, holding his bony fingers spread so that the wind blew through them. . . .
'There'll be no landing at the Lighthouse tomorrow. . . .'

The antithesis between the children and their father's and Mr Tansley's unsympathetic regard for 'truth' develops:

When they [the children] talked about something interesting, people, music, history, anything, even said it was a fine evening so why not sit out of doors, then what they complained of about Charles Tansley was that until he had turned the whole thing round and made it somehow reflect himself and disparage them, put them all on edge somehow with his acid way of peeling the flesh and blood off everything, he was not satisfied.

This reminiscence of a romantic theme is sustained when Mrs Ramsay goes into the town with Tansley, and sees a circus advertisement. Tansley thinks only of a possible professorial appointment. Mrs Ramsay, however, exclaims:

'Let us all go!' she cried, moving on, as if all those riders and horses had filled her with childlike exultation and made her forget her pity.

Mrs Ramsay retains the child's capacity for the enjoyment of life; but she is aware enough of life's 'reality'. She watches her children grow into disenchantment:

Strife, divisions, difference of opinion, prejudices twisted into the very fibre of being, oh that they should begin so early, Mrs Ramsay deplored.

In the presence of her son at night:

'Perhaps you will wake up and find the sun shining and the birds singing,' she said compassionately, smoothing the little boy's hair, for her husband, with his caustic saying that it would not be fine, had dashed his spirits she could see.

Gradually Mrs Ramsay's attitude to childhood emerges – and she is of course the sympathetic centre of the novel. James is a fragile, expectant being, with his hopes easily dashed and disenchanted. She feels her own disenchantment lived again through the life of her children:

'. . . And even if it isn't fine tomorrow,' said Mrs Ramsay . . . 'it will be another day.'

She measures the stocking she is knitting against her son's leg:

And the result of it was, she sighed, taking in the whole room from floor to ceiling, as she held the stocking against James's leg, that things got shabbier and got shabbier summer after summer.

The juxtaposition of the furniture and the leg has unmistakable meaning. Of her husband's heartless pursuit of truth, she thinks:

To pursue truth with such astonishing lack of consideration for other people's feelings, to rend the thin veils of civilization so wantonly, so brutally, was to her so horrible an outrage of human decency that . . . she bent her head as if to let the pelt of jagged hail . . . bespatter her unrebuked. . . .

She represents the humanist virtues of tolerance, of consideration for other people's feelings, even at the cost of denying truth. Like Mrs Wilcox of *Howards End*, she stands for the sympathetic virtue of good manners. But it is a diminishing resemblance. Mrs Wilcox would never have spoken like this of childhood:

Oh but she never wanted James to grow a day older or Cam either. These two she would have liked to keep for ever just as they were, demons of wickedness, angels of delight, never to see them grow up into long-legged monsters. Nothing made up for the loss. When she read just now to James . . . and his eyes darkened, she thought, why should they grow up, and lose all that? . . . And, touching his hair with her lips, she thought, he will never be so happy again. . . . They were happier now than they would ever be again. . . . They came bustling along the passage. Then the door sprang open and in they came, fresh as roses, staring, wide awake, as if this coming into the dining-room after breakfast, which they did every day of their lives, was a positive event to them. . . . And so she went down and said to her husband, Why must they grow up and lose it all? Never will they be so happy again . . . for the most part, oddly enough, she must admit that she felt this thing that she called life terrible, hostile, and quick to pounce on you if you gave it a chance. . . . For that reason, knowing what was before them – love and ambition and being wretched alone in dreary places – she had often the feeling: Why must they grow up and lose it all? And then she said to herself, brandishing her sword at life, nonsense. They will be perfectly happy.

The emphasis is clear enough, and the last gesture seems, and was perhaps intended to seem, no more than a politeness, a well-mannered self-mockery.

The resolution of the novel comes when Mrs Ramsay is dead, and James, grown older, goes to the Lighthouse:

So it was like that, James thought, the Lighthouse one had seen across the bay all these years; it was a stark tower on a bare rock. It satisfied him.

The novel never attaches any conscious significance to the Lighthouse as a sexual symbol; and I think it would be difficult to read any continuously unconscious sexual meaning into it. But here, with James's attainment of the symbol, there is a sense of desolation and evacuation suddenly, of greyness and emptiness at a disenchanting discovery, such as human beings usually associate with unsatisfying sexuality.

For all its limiting refinement, *To the Lighthouse* reveals an astonishingly intense sensibility, such as a greater novelist might indeed envy. The sensibility, however, is placed at the disposal of an ambiguously pessimistic philosophy of life. The sense of children conveyed within the sensibility is one of fragility, enchantment, joy, and painful vulnerability to the disenchantment of experience. For Virginia Woolf, no less than for Walpole, the catastrophes of childhood are 'eternal':

But he kept looking back over his shoulder as Mildred carried him out, and she was certain that he was thinking, we are not going to the Lighthouse tomorrow; and she thought, he will remember that all his life. . . . No, she thought, . . . children never forget. . . .

It was to this fragile sensitivity of childhood that she returned in *The Waves*, perhaps the most ambitious and ruthless of her attempts to convey the idea of the 'stream of consciousness'. It is generally accepted now that the attempt was unfulfilled. Six characters are traced from birth to maturity, using the symbol of sunrise and sunset seen across moving water to convey the sense of the plastic development of their human consciousness. She employs exclusively the method of the interior monologue. There is no descriptive frame supplied by the author's distorting intrusion from without. The sense of time is obtained by interludes written in a lush poetic-prose linking the monologues of the characters. The early episodes deal with the sensations of the children in their garden near the sea, and then when they go to school. There is no attempt at rendering their sensations into a child-language; the diction is in fact heavily stylized. Everything lies in the sensuous responses of the children to their environment. But there is not enough differentiation made (at least if it is there, it is not easily to be perceived) between the characters; there is only the highest common factor of their sensitivity. There is little sense of their development. They all seem, even as children, to start as highly sensitive adolescents, and remain so. Their sensibilities never become nourished with conceptual thought; nor vice versa. The work has a static feeling about it; a sense of emotional constriction, almost of emotional suffocation. The children describe their perception of the sunrise:

'I see a ring,' said Bernard, 'hanging above me. It quivers and hangs in a loop of light.'
'I see a slab of pale yellow,' said Susan, 'spreading away until it meets a purple stripe.'

'I hear a sound,' said Rhoda, 'cheep, chirp; cheep, chirp; going up and down.'

'Now they have all gone,' said Louis, 'I am alone . . . I am left standing by the wall among the flowers. . . . Flower after flower is specked on the depths of green. The petals are harlequins. . . . The flowers swim like fish made of light upon the dark, green waters. . . . Up here my eyes are green leaves. . . . I am a boy in grey flannels with a belt fastened by a brass snake up here. Down there my eyes are the lidless eyes of a stone figure in a desert by the Nile.'

Compared with the psychological realities of Joyce's portrait of Stephen Dedalus's infancy and childhood, one senses that the author here is imposing upon the feelings of these children the responses of her own sensibility. Joyce integrates the intensity of his own psychological awareness into establishing a sense of the growth of Stephen's development, into the organic development of the book. The sensitive intensities of *The Waves* are static, in the sense that they exist for themselves. The movement of the work is discontinuous. The book finds no resolution. The sensations of its characters remind one of T. S. Eliot's 'trailing consequence of further days and hours'. *The Waves* represents in fact a kind of emotional nihilism. Once the feeling moves outside its awareness into a commentary on the meaning of its sensations, we sense the thinness. If life is annihilated into sensitivity, it is no wonder that the resultant appreciation of 'life' should so frequently become in Virginia Woolf, in the words of Mrs Dalloway:

All the same, that one day should follow another; Wednesday, Thursday, Friday, Saturday; that one should wake up in the morning; see the sky; walk in the park; meet Hugh Whitbread; then suddenly in came Peter; then these roses; it was enough. After that how unbelievable death was! . . .

To a sensibility concerned with life, that alone perhaps might serve as a sufficient definition of death. With Virginia Woolf one is brought, in a way reminiscent of Henry James, to reflections on the adequacy of the experience nourishing the undeniably 'fine' sensibility. One recalls the following from *The Voyage Out*:

I really respect some snuffy old stockbroker who's gone on adding up column after column all his days, and trotting back to his villa at Brixton with some old pug dog he worships, and a dreary little wife sitting at the end of the table, and going off to Margate for a fortnight.

The passage is full of social hearsay, and one remembers Mrs Bennett's observations, quoted earlier, and her own comment on Jane Austen, if she had 'stayed in London, dined out, lunched out, met famous people, made new friends, read, travelled, and carried back to the quiet country cottage a hoard of observations to feast upon at leisure . . . she would have been the forerunner of Henry James and Proust'. It is of course a statement of a certain cultural *curriculum vitae*, which we might think bears slender relation to the social basis of experience which has generally informed great fiction.

This annihilation of the significance of life into terms of sensation is nowhere more convincingly felt than at the moment when the children in *The Waves* leave school:

'Now we are off,' said Louis. 'Now I hang suspended without attachments. We are nowhere. We are passing through England in a train. England slips by the window, always changing from hill to wood, from rivers and willows to towns again . . . Bernard and Neville, Percival, Archie, Larpent and Baker go to Oxford or Cambridge, to Edinburgh, Rome, Paris, Berlin, or to some American University. I go vaguely, to make money vaguely. . . . This is the first day of a new life, another spoke of the rising wheel. But my body passes vagrant as a bird's shadow. I should be transient as the shadow on the meadow, soon fading, soon darkening . . .'

It would be terrible enough, if it were an acute indictment. But the edge of commentary, of satire, is surprisingly absent. Defensive recourse instead is made to the vaguenesses of a 'new life', the 'spoke of the rising wheel', the body passing 'vagrant as a bird's shadow'. It seems no wonder that for these children the 'waves' merely 'broke on the shore'.

IV

It would be an easy matter to juxtapose half a dozen passages from Lawrence, similar in situation to this from Virginia Woolf – a geographical inspection, if you like, of the cultural-emotional landscape – for it was something to which the peculiar nature of his awareness constantly directed him. But at these points in Lawrence there is usually a sense of acute involvement between the character concerned and his social perception; and even when he conveys a sense of disconnexion between psyche and environment, as in *St Mawr* when Lou Witt sails from Europe for the last time, the disconnexion is definite, in the sense that it develops from a complex analysis of the society within which Lou had, in every way, previously been involved. It was in fact just this combination of his intense psychological insight with his social grasp which made of him the very great novelist he was. The two qualities have often existed in separation. It is when they exist together and nourish one another within a sensibility that we are confronted with a novelist of really major significance. In a way very closely resembling Dickens, he was intensely concerned with the psychic relation between the individual and his society, the psychic death or life resulting from the social values and acceptances an individual is called upon to live within. The sense of individuality he conveys most often arises from the disentanglement of the individual from the deadening influences of false emotional values in a society. This is very much the 'message', the central 'wisdom' he sought to establish in his work. It is not in any way extraordinary that in one of his great novels, *The Rainbow*, this central concern with social values and individual integrity, the two polarizing interests of his art, should be very closely related to a concern with childhood and its development.

His art was, as we know, very differently conceived from that of Joyce and Virginia Woolf. It reflected less consciously the psychological preoccupations of his time; and, superficially, his work was less revolutionary in method. The resemblances of his early work to George Eliot have been sufficiently remarked; and there is a close affinity between his own attitude to the novel and that of the mature Dickens, both in what he wanted to do through the novel, and in the methods he adopted. To psychological theory as such he was at times ardently hostile for what he considered its emotional Newtonianism. The letter of 1913, the year of *Sons and Lovers*, in which he declares: 'I never did read Freud, but I have heard about him since I was in Germany', has its significance. He praised Trigant Burrow's *Psychoanalysis in Theory and in Life*, because 'it's the first thing I've read for a long time that isn't out to bully somebody in some way or other.

It is true, the essential self is so simple.' In a letter of 1927 he speaks of this 'scientific jargoning' of psycho-analysis. But it is in the letter to Katherine Mansfield of 1919 that he really shows his actual hostility to Jung and Freud: recollecting the sight of the stars at night, he writes:

Then, I said, 'That's Jupiter' – but I felt that it wasn't Jupiter – at least not the everyday Jupiter. Ask Jung or Freud about it? Never! It was a star that blazed for a second on one's soul.

In view of this, it is not surprising that we should find this in *St Mawr*:

If anatomy pre-supposes a corpse, then psychology pre-supposes a world of corpses. Personalities, which means personal criticism and analysis, pre-supposes a whole world-laboratory of human psyches waiting to be vivisected. If you cut a thing up, of course it will smell. Hence, nothing raises such an infernal stink, at last, as human psychology.

He disliked psychology for what he conceived to be its reduction of the integrity of man. To him psychology was not integrative, but a destructive agent of the 'mental, cognitive mode' in fundamental antagonism to the 'naïve or physical or sexual mode of consciousness', as he once declared. The emotional, psychological if you like, investigations of his novels were done with the purpose (one is not necessarily talking of achievement) of establishing a sense of integrity and wholeness in the individual. He was himself insistently concerned with the emotional relationships which concerned so much psychological theory, the relation between child and parent, the relation between mother and son, between man and wife; these were after all the psychological heart of his interest. It was one particular attitude of psychological analysis which he deplored, when it became, in his definition, a mental agency for the depersonalization of humanity.

It was inevitable that a sensibility so intensely concerned with emotional values should concern itself with childhood; not of course as an exclusive interest, but as part of his general perceptions. Children figure within his general conspexus. They exist in the short stories; in for example *The Rocking-Horse Winner*, which is a miniature analysis of the psychic ruin of a child through the money-consciousness of his parents. There are what might be called 'Lawrence' children – vital, self-willed, intense, passionate creatures. There is Joyce, in *England, My England*: 'a lovely little blonde daughter with a head of thistle-down . . . a quicksilver little thing of six years old', and Annabel in the same story was 'another blonde, winsome touching little thing'. Anna in *The Rainbow* is a 'brown elfish-mite dancing about'. She was: '. . . a child with a face like a bud of apple-blossom, and glistening fair hair like thistle-down sticking out in straight, wild, flamy pieces, and very dark eyes . . .' and again: 'She was a little oddity, with her fierce, fair hair like spun glass sticking out in a flamy halo round the apple-blossom face and the black eyes, and the men liked an oddity.' These descriptions are not, as they might seem in extraction, casual, word-spinning clichés. The intensity and vitality of his children represent important qualities he intended to express through them.

The first important children in Lawrence are the children of the clearly autobiographical *Sons and Lovers*. Everything might have seemed set for fairly certain artistic failure. But the central relationship between the son and mother is presented without either equivocation or sensationalism. Considering his personal involvement, the touch is remarkably sure. It deals, in fairly simple terms, with a central theme of Lawrence's work, the stultification of the life of an individual through entanglement in a false emotional relationship. The early part of the book conveys the hostility between two incompatible parents, and the impression this makes upon the feelings of their children. There is no apportionment of blame – although the warm-hearted, 'physical' Mr Morel suggests a wholly more sympathetic personality than Mrs Morel with her tendency to snobbery and egocentric refinements. The interest is to display the emotional influence upon her children of a woman who 'casts off' her husband:

. . . half regretfully, but relentlessly; casting him off and turning now for love and life to the children. Henceforward he was more or less a husk. And he half acquiesced, as so many men do, yielding their place to their children.

The children sense the psychic deadness about them:

There was a feeling of misery over all the house. The children breathed the air that was poisoned, and they felt dreary. They were rather disconsolate, did not know what to do, what to play at.

In front of the house was a huge old ash-tree. The west wind, sweeping from Derbyshire, caught the houses with full force, and the tree shrieked again. . . . To Paul it became almost a demoniacal noise. . . . Having such a great space in front of the house gave the children a feeling of night, of vastness, and of terror. This terror came in from the shrieking of the tree and the anguish of the home discord. Often Paul would wake up, after he had been asleep a long time, aware of thuds downstairs. Instantly he was wide awake. . . . And then the whole was drowned in a piercing medley of shrieks and cries from the great, wind-swept ash-tree. . . . There was a feeling of horror, a kind of bristling in the darkness, and a sense of blood. . . . The wind came through the tree fiercer and fiercer. All the cords of the great harp hummed, whistled, and shrieked. And then came the horror of the sudden silence. . . .

Out of this the children develop their keen sense of intimacy with the mother:

The sense of his sitting in all his pit-dirt, drinking . . . made Mrs Morel unable to bear herself. From her the feeling was transmitted to the other children. She never suffered alone any more: the children suffered with her.

The emotional relations are never theorized on. They are presented through the dramatic detail of the novel:

Then Paul ran anxiously into the kitchen. The one candle still burned on the table. . . . Mrs Morel sat alone. . . . All the room was full of the sense of waiting. . . . Paul stood in the doorway.

'Has my dad come?' he asked.

'You can see he hasn't,' said Mrs Morel, cross with the futility of the question.

Then the boy dawdled about near his mother. They shared the same anxiety. . . . Not many words were spoken. Paul almost hated his mother for suffering because his father did not come home from work.

The book develops into the central oedipal relationship between Paul and his mother. It is a remarkable account of the complex, magnified, as it usually is, by the emotional requirements of both participants. Paul 'launches into life', but is retained, enmeshed by the relation to his mother, which is only to be resolved by her death.

But there is more than this oedipal theme to *Sons and Lovers*. Paul is very much a creation of what Lawrence came to intend by 'life'; and the poignancy of the novel is the sense it conveys of the boy's sensitive vitality caught and devitalized by the relation with his mother. The children all convey this sense of vitality, particularized in the character of Paul:

> Mrs Morel going into her parlour, would hear the children singing away.
> ... They sounded so perfectly absorbed in the game as their voices came out of the night, that they had the feel of wild creatures singing. It stirred the mother; and she understood when they came in at eight o'clock, ruddy, with brilliant eyes, and quick, passionate speech.

It is in this sort of thing that one sees the close relationship of Lawrence's work to the whole Romantic protest on behalf of 'humanity' and 'life', and here he specially lies within the Romantic tradition of the child. At fourteen, Paul usually looked:

> ... as if he saw things, was full of life, and warm; then his smile, like his mother's, came suddenly and was very lovable; and then, when there was any clog in his soul's quick running, his face went stupid and ugly. He was the sort of boy that becomes a clown and a lout as soon as he is not understood, or feels himself held cheap; and, again, is adorable at the first touch of warmth.

It is very much the description of Tom Brangwen in the early chapters of *The Rainbow*. The central approach is forming, the central interest lies at the point where the individual psyche is in its first contact with society, the 'man's world'. *Sons and Lovers* deals in, then, the two main interests of Lawrence's whole work, the individual spoiled by possessive and false affection, and the individual vitality bruised by its contact with society, and very clearly, with industrial society. Paul grows up in a landscape with all its poignant juxtapositions of countryside and industry. The juxtaposition remained the central reference for Lawrence's whole career. When Paul looks through the advertisements in the Public Library for a job:

> ... He looked wistfully out of the window. Already he was a prisoner of industrialism. Large sunflowers stared over the old red wall of the garden

opposite, looking in their jolly way down on the women who were hurrying with something for dinner. The valley was full of corn, brightening in the sun. Two collieries, among the fields, waved their small white plumes of steam. Far off on the hills were the woods of Annesley, dark and fascinating. Already his heart went down. He was being taken into bondage. His freedom in the beloved home valley was going now.

This sense of the 'bondage' to come is only subsidiary to the central 'bondage' of his relation to his mother. But with that bondage broken by her death, he does not turn away from the other potential 'bondage', of launching, in his independence, towards the 'town':

But no, he would not give in. Turning sharply, he walked towards the city's gold phosphorescence. His fists were shut, his mouth set fast. He would not take that direction, to the darkness, to follow her. He walked towards the faintly humming, glowing town, quickly.

It is an astonishing forecast of his own literary development. No author of the modern period walked with such determination, towards – and away.

One speaks of two main interests; but it was not the character of his sensibility to see them as in any way separate; the personal, emotional relationships are always seen within their social context, and society was significant for Lawrence at its point of impact upon the feelings of the individual. His interest contained the psychology of his characters at every level of their accommodation to their personal and social environment. Culture was under continuous inspection for its psychic influences upon the individual; and the quality of individual emotion was continuously judged within its social context. It is this interest which led him to the complex organization of individual and social experience which became *The Rainbow*. Taking the movement of a culture through three generations it was inevitable that much of its concern should lie in the childhood of its characters. In one aspect it is a tale of the conflict between two cultures, lived through the experience of its children as they become adults. The children are in fact integral to the whole meaning of the work.

The opening chapter sets the theme:

The Brangwens had lived for generations on the Marsh Farm. . . . So the Brangwens came and went without fear of necessity, working hard because of the life that was in them . . . heaven and earth was teeming around them, and how should this cease? They felt the rush of the sap in spring, they knew the wave which cannot halt, but every year throws forward the seed to begetting, and, falling back, leaves the young-born on the earth.

The women were different. On them too was the drowse of blood-intimacy, calves sucking and hens running together in droves. . . . But the women looked out from the heated, blind intercourse of farm-life, to the spoken world beyond . . . they heard the sound in the distance, and they strained to listen . . . the woman wanted another form of life . . . something that was not blood-intimacy. Her house faced out from the farm-buildings and fields, looked out to the road and the village . . . and the world beyond . . . she strained her eyes to see what man had done in fighting outwards to know-ledge . . . her deepest desire hung on the battle that she heard, far off, being waged on the edge of the unknown. She also wanted to know, and to be of the fighting host.

The whole weight of the novel rests on this questing outward of the women, of first Anna and then Ursula Brangwen. In a very deep sense, it is the logic of their lives to take the influences of their childhood environment, as the basis of their values when, inevitably, they move beyond it, into the 'battle' that they had heard 'far-off'. They always 'wanted to know, and to be of the fighting host'. The novel reveals its commentary on civilized values through the feelings of the two women who experience within themselves the conflict between the world of the 'Marsh' and the 'man's world' beyond.

Both the children, first Anna and then her daughter Ursula, represent the quick of life itself, receptive, intense, and acutely aware of their own integrity. When Tom Brangwen first becomes aware of the Polish widow, her four-year-old daughter, Anna, is given in this way:

The child beside her watched everything with wide, black eyes. She had an odd little defiant look, her little red mouth was pinched shut. She seemed to be jealously guarding something, to be always on the alert for defence.

She has a fine self-confidence:

She loved driving with Brangwen in the trap. Then, sitting high up and bowling along, her passion for eminence and dominance was satisfied. She was like a little savage in her arrogance.

The description is by no means casual. 'Like a little savage' conveys exactly what Lawrence wished to express through her, the self-confident sense of her inviolate self. With the marriage between her mother and Tom Brangwen she becomes free from the close, unnatural intimacy she had previously lived with her mother:

Gradually the child was freed. She became an independent, forgetful little soul, loving from her own centre.

She has the freedom, independence and peace of her parents' relationship:

Anna's soul was at peace between them. She looked from one to the other, and she saw them established to her safety, and she was free. She played between the pillar of fire and the pillar of cloud in confidence, having the assurance on her right hand and the assurance on her left. She was no longer called upon to uphold with her childish might the broken end of the arch. Her father and her mother now met to the span of the heavens, and she, the child, was free to play in the space beneath, between.

Her situation is indeed exactly different from that of Paul in *Sons and Lovers*, and it shows how far Lawrence had freed himself from the preoccupations of the earlier novel. The peace of Cossethay, however, is no wish-fulfilment; and if the quotations might suggest a certain theorizing, in fact the life of Cossethay is convincingly established in the dramatic detail and experience of the novel.

Anna grows up inviolate and self-willed. At school, she has a strong 'indifference to respectability', and shows a general 'lack of reverence':

She deeply hated ugliness, or intrusion, or arrogance, however. As a child she was proud and shadowy as a tiger, and as aloof. . . . Like a wild thing, she wanted her distance. She mistrusted intimacy.

Sent to the young ladies' school in Nottingham, she finds the girls 'petty and mean'. There is never anything simplifying in Lawrence's cultural analysis, and part of the greatness of *The Rainbow* lies in the discipline he imposes upon the central emotion of the women's looking 'to the spoken world beyond' by continually evaluating the quality of that 'world', by reference to the values he adumbrates in the first chapter. Both Anna, and later Ursula, look to the 'world beyond' and find it 'petty and mean':

> She had a curious shrinking from commonplace people, and particularly from the young lady of her day. . . . She wanted to respect them. Still she thought the people she did not *know* were wonderful. Those she knew seemed always to be limiting her, tying her up in little falsities that irritated her beyond bearing.

The petty-bourgeois world of the ladies' college was one of the worlds 'beyond', and its 'pettiness' leads her to an acute awareness of the Marsh's superiority in its human values:

> After the loose, generous atmosphere of her home, where little things did not count, she was always uneasy in the world, that would snap and bite at every trifle.

> For at the Marsh life had indeed a certain freedom and largeness. There was no fret about money, no mean little precedence, nor care for what other people thought. . . . So Anna was only easy at home, where the common sense and the supreme relation between her parents produced a freer standard of being than she could find outside. . . . The people . . . outside seemed to begrudge her her very existence. . . . There was over the house a kind of dark silence and intensity . . . There was in the house a sort of richness, a deep, inarticulate interchange which made other places seem thin and unsatisfying.

Anna finds resolution from 'thinness' (it is, if anything is, the central assertion of Lawrence's work) through seeking fulfilment with another '*person*'. As a girl, it is significant that 'the first *person* she met, who affected her as a real, living person, whom she regarded as having definite existence' was the Baron Skrebensky. This description of the Baron defines the quality of the personal relationship she thought she could find in her love for her cousin, Will. But the relationship with him is a failure on the level she required. Will is not a 'real, living person'. The mentalized, idealizing, unphysical quality of his 'feelings' is brilliantly conveyed in their visit together to Lincoln Cathedral. She feels encased by the beauty. She does not want to be 'roofed in'; her own feelings strive out to the heavens and stars 'wheeling in freedom'.

She achieves a partial resolution, however, through maternity, within the home she establishes and the children she bears. But it is only a momentary pause in the development of the novel. It is the withdrawal of one generation, to prepare the creation of another. In the person of Anna's daughter Ursula, the progression continues from the one culture towards the other, from the culture of the Marsh to the 'world beyond':

If she were not the wayfarer to the unknown, if she were arrived now, settled in her builded house, a rich woman, still her doors opened under the arch of the rainbow, her threshold reflected the passing of the sun and moon, the great travellers, her house was full of the echo of journeying.

She was a door and a threshold, she herself. Through her another soul was coming, to stand upon her as upon the threshold, looking out, shading its eyes for the direction to take.

This 'shading its eyes for the direction to take', defines very closely Lawrence's whole interest, and it is not surprising that in considering childhood he should convey it in these terms.

In one sense Ursula repeats the experience of her mother. The movement of the novel is not repetitive, however, but intensifying. With Ursula we are within Lawrence's own contemporary society, his account of which, for all its being written some forty years ago, retains an essential modernity. The 'direction' for Ursula is wholly more difficult for her to distinguish, and from the outset she is given in terms of the most extreme vulnerability:

One evening, suddenly, he saw the tiny, living thing rolling naked in the mother's lap, and he was sick, it was so utterly helpless and vulnerable and extraneous; in a world of hard surfaces and varying altitudes, it lay vulnerable and naked at every point. Yet it was quite blithe. And yet, in its blind, awful crying, was there not the blind, far-off terror of its own vulnerable nakedness, the terror of being so utterly delivered over, helpless at every point.

It is very much Lawrence's perception of the 'human condition' – and the 'Yet it was quite blithe' also conveys something very typical of his resilience. The sensitivity of childhood in Lawrence is not something cultivated for itself, but for what it might sensitively become.

Ursula's vulnerability and living intensity is dramatized in such an episode as this:

Then Brangwen coming up the steep round of the hill, would see before him on the brown of the path a tiny, tottering, wind-blown little mite with a dark head, who, as soon as she saw him, would come running in tiny, wild, windmill fashion, lifting her arms up and down to him, down the steep hill.

and also her inviolate integrity:

The child ran about absorbed in life, quiet, full of amusement. She did not notice things, nor changes, nor alterations. One day she would find daisies in the grass, another day, apple-blossoms would be sprinkled white on the ground, and she would run among it, for pleasure because it was there. . . . She did not remember what had been nor what would be, the outside things were there each day. She was always herself, the world outside was accidental . . .

It is this integrity which she struggles to sustain when, with the inevitable movement of life, she becomes involved with the 'world beyond' Cossethay. For all the evocation of the values of the Marsh and Cossethay, however, there is no sense of regressive nostalgia. Her childhood experience endows Ursula with the criteria for evaluating the 'Man's world' and in establishing for her the sense of her own integrity as the only means for her spiritual salvation.

At twelve, she goes to school in Nottingham, as her mother had. Like her mother she seeks to avoid the same 'belittling circumstances' of life, the 'little jealousies, the little differences, the little meannesses. . . . She had an instinctive fear of petty people, as a deer is afraid of dogs.'

She measured by the standard of her own people. . . . Her beloved father, so utterly simple in his demeanour, yet with his strong, dark soul fixed like a root in unexpressed depths . . . her mother, so strangely free of all money and convention and fear, entirely indifferent to the world, standing by herself . . .

331

But Lawrence was not concerned with simplifying juxtapositions, between the valid and the invalid. For all the rightness of the past, it was a limiting rightness, serving only as a basis for further advance. The sense of the past merely creates the criteria to judge and control the inevitable future. The impulse of the work is dynamic: it is not deadened with cultural regret:

So even as a girl of twelve she was glad to burst the narrow boundary of Cossethay, where only limited people lived. Outside, was all vastness, and a throng of real, proud people whom she would love.

But the self-indulgent vaguenesses of this 'vastness', of these 'real, proud people whom she would love', are immediately disciplined by the experiences to which she is painfully subjected. She falls a victim to 'romantic poetry'; she bursts the 'narrow boundary' of Cossethay by day-dreaming fantasies: she imagines that by becoming a schoolmistress she can find a vehicle for her 'love'. With intense self-honesty, Lawrence parodies what his own attitude might so easily have become: when Ursula is made to dream of teaching at Gillingham:

Gillingham was such a lovely name, and Kent was the Garden of England. So that, in Gillingham, an old, old village by the hopfields, where the sun shone softly, she came out of school in the afternoon into the shadow of the planetrees by the gate. . . .

She dreamed how she would make the little, ugly children love her. She would be so *personal*. Teachers were always so hard and impersonal. There was no vivid relationship. She would make everything so personal and vivid. . . .

A 'cloud of self-responsibility' gathers about Ursula; but that responsibility is not to be resolved by the facility of the 'love' which she thought the school would allow her to display towards the 'little, ugly children'. Her development is in fact one of continuous self-enlightenment. The schoolteaching section of *The Rainbow* was not a haphazard episode Lawrence happened to include from copy acquired from his own experience at Croydon. It disciplines Ursula into an awareness that 'love' itself needs definition, and crystallizes into one fully experienced symbol, the 'mechanical' inhumanity of the world 'beyond' Cossethay. Again, it is not by chance that Lawrence should take the world of the school to display the sickness which he diagnoses throughout modern society.

Ursula's journey to the school in Ilkeston is given with continuous reference to the past, with all the values the earlier sections of the novel had established around it:

As she waited at the tram-terminus she reverted swiftly to her childhood; her teasing grandfather, with his fair beard and blue eyes, and his big, monumental body . . . the little church school. . . . With a passion she clung to the past.

. . . behind her was the little church school she had attended when she was a child. . . . Behind her was Cossethay, and blackberries were ripe on the hedges.

The images of 'the little church school' and the 'blackberries ripe on the hedges' draw the meaning of the past together both for Ursula and for the reader, at the moment when they are to be placed beside their cultural antithesis, the Ilkeston school.

The school is conveyed through imagery which establishes its own emotional values, by a method very close indeed to Dickens's own. With this section of *The Rainbow* we are very clearly back in the world of *Dombey and Son* and *Hard Times*:

She was walking down a small, mean, wet street, empty of people. The school squatted low within its railed, asphalt yard, that shone black with rain. The building was grimy, and horrible, dry plants were shadowily looking through the windows . . .

Each epithet evokes its poetic response. The 'horrible, dry plants' have the same intention as those in Mrs Pipchin's establishment. The same method continues throughout the chapter – 'There was a great heap of curled white-and-scribbled sheets on the table.' One of the teachers was 'about thirty or thirty-three years old, thin, greenish'. Another was a 'neutral-tinted woman of about twenty-eight'. In the 'rigid' class-rooms, there was a 'long silence . . . official and chilling'. 'Half-way down was a glass partition . . . A clock ticked re-echoing.' In this way he expresses Ursula's intuition of the school's sterility.

The prison was round her now! She looked at the walls, colour washed, pale green and chocolate, at the large windows with frowsy geraniums against the pale glass. . . . This was a new world, a new life, with which she was threatened. But still excited, she climbed into her chair at her teacher's desk. . . . How different it was from the mist of rain blowing over Cossethay. As she thought of her own village, a spasm of yearning crossed her, it seemed so far off, so lost to her.

She was here in this hard, stark reality – *reality*. It was queer that she should call this the reality, which she had never known till today. . . . This was the reality, and Cossethay, her beloved, beautiful, well-known Cossethay, which was as herself unto her, that was minor reality. This prison of a school was reality. . . . Here she would realize her dream of being the beloved teacher, bringing light and joy to her children! But the desks before her had an abstract angularity that bruised her sentiment . . .

It is an art in which nothing is thrown to loss. The movement of the feeling is in exact relation to Ursula's own response – at once nostalgic, ironic, accepting, and still idealizing – until the 'abstract angularity' 'bruises' her 'sentiment' and 'she felt rebuffed'.

She could always hear Mr Brunt. Like a machine, always in the same hard high, inhuman voice he went on with his teaching. . . . And before this inhuman number of children she was always at bay. . . . There it was, this class of fifty collective children. . . . It made her feel she could not breathe; she must suffocate, it was so inhuman . . . they were not children. They were a squadron. She could not speak as she would to a child, because they were not individual children, they were a collective, inhuman thing.

Ursula felt her heart fail inside her. . . . The first great task was to reduce sixty children to one state of mind, or being. This state must be produced automatically, through the will of the teacher . . . imposed upon the will of the children. . . . So there existed a set of separate wills, each straining itself to the utmost to exert its own authority. . . . Whereas Ursula thought she was going to become the first wise teacher by making the whole business personal, and using no compulsion. She believed entirely in her own personality.

So that she was in a very deep mess.

She could feel the ghastly necessity. She must become the same – put away the personal self, become an instrument, an abstraction, working upon a certain material, the class, to achieve a set purpose. . . . And she could not submit. . . . The sun was being blocked out. Often when she went out at playtime and saw a luminous blue sky with changing clouds, it seemed just a fantasy, like a piece of painted scenery.

Not 'submitting', however, lands her in the 'very deep mess' of her class's indiscipline; and the conflict between her 'feeling' and the children's 'will' is dramatized in the extended account of her misery in dealing with the boy, who rejects her authority:

So that, pale, shut, at last distant and impersonal, she saw no longer the child, how his eyes danced, or how he had a queer little soul that could not be bothered with shaping hand-writing so long as he dashed down what he thought. She saw no children, only the task that was to be done. And keeping her eyes there, on the task, and not on the child, she was impersonal enough to punish where she could otherwise only have sympathized, understood, and condoned . . .

The situation is resolved in the final lunacy of her fighting the child. The sun *is* blocked out, and she thrashes him.

If *The Rainbow* has a weakness, it lies, I think, in the terms in which Lawrence defines the other world towards which Ursula still yearns:

For once she were free she could get somewhere. Ah, the wonderful, real somewhere that was beyond her, the somewhere that she felt deep, deep inside her.

Sometimes she still manages to think of the children as 'flowers, birds, little bright animals, children, anything'. These feelings, even after the catharsis of her experience at Ilkeston, remain dangerously close to the emotions the novel itself had earlier parodied; and their tone takes the concluding section of the novel through Ursula's relation with Skrebensky, and to the unsatisfactory and too easy optimism of its last chapter:

Why should she give her allegiance to this world, and let it so dominate her, that her own world of warm sun and growing, sap-filled life was turned into nothing.

One wonders, if in spite of the novel's experience, these assertions have in fact become adequately refined. The school-teaching section

is only partial to the central interest of the novel, which is the fulfilment of Ursula's 'sap-filled' world in relation with a man; which she
seeks but does not find in Skrebensky. The problem is left unsolved
except for the rather applied optimisms of the last chapter. The
complexities which the previous chapters had diagnosed in its solution suggested that he would take up the problem again, in *Women
in Love*, and, yet again, in *Lady Chatterley's Lover*.

Epilogue

To take this study further would be to engage oneself in another volume. The hope is that it will have at least suggested some of the criteria upon which the immense proliferation of literature concerned with children in more recent times may be assessed. The fusion of psychological and social interests which we find in Lawrence has not elsewhere been very much developed. The general influence of Freudian analysis has been mainly to direct literary interest towards the investigation and presentation of the child's consciousness, towards an objective account of the child's emotions. The frequent reference backward to childhood in the characterization of many twentieth-century novels suggests a literary reflection of Freud's assertion of the significance of the child's development to the adult personality. *Sinister Street*, *Death of a Hero*, *Dusty Answer*, and the novels of Aldous Huxley, all tried to convey something at least of the whole psychology of their characters.

In novels where the central interest lay in the child, the post-Freudian influences have been even more clearly detectable, with their stress (one thinks of Richard Hughes and Ivy Compton Burnett) on the complications of the child's nature, its disconcerting cruelties, its being the very opposite of paste-board innocence. The emphasis of uninhibited analysis has often been on the child's sexual complexities. There has been a whole gamut indeed of twentieth-century novels stressing childhood and early adolescence as periods of acute sexual torment and potential trauma – such as James Hanley's *Boy*, and the novels and stories of Denton Welch. The painful initiation of the child to society which we find in earlier Romantic literature is translated into the more intimate terms of emotional and sexual spoliation. But, just as in the nineteenth century, concern with childhood often suggested powerful subjective motives, so too the freer discussion of childhood sexuality in the modern novel need not necessarily imply any greater objectivity. Uninhibited discussion and portrayal is itself susceptible of a variety of sophisticated emotional indulgences. The sort of thing one means can, I think, be seen clearly enough in, say, Denton Welch's *When I was Thirteen*. A little psychological gold can go a long way when one wants to debase the literary currencies.

In more recent literature of the child, it remains true that an exclusive interest in childhood in an author most often leads to an impoverishment of general responses. Two of the most important novels about childhood in recent times have been Mr L. P. Hartley's trilogy, beginning with *The Shrimp and the Anemone*, and Mr Salinger's American *Catcher in the Rye*. It is not entirely by chance perhaps that they also happen to be works of fairly wide reference. The sensitive account of Mr Hartley's children, Eustace and Hilda, develops through the psychic tragedy of their adult lives. Mr Salinger's *Catcher in the Rye*, a more interesting novel, I think, written self-consciously in the 'tradition' of Mark Twain, contains within its humour at least a seriously-intended commentary on American contemporary values.

To have ended with *The Rainbow* enables one to make certain concluding judgements. Very clearly, Lawrence's children do not carry with them any importations from the escapist, nostalgic attitudes towards the child of the late nineteenth century. They are not regretful symbols wriggling on the pin of their author's own escape. It is astonishing when one remembers that the division in time between Peter Pan and Paul Morel, Ursula Brangwen, and, for that matter, Stephen Dedalus, was no more than that which separates us from the middle fifties. Remembering the success of Barrie's nostalgic whimsy (and Marie Corelli's best-selling romanticism) is to get some gauge of one's admiration for the sort of things Lawrence and Joyce did with the English novel, for damming some at least of the polluted streams.

Both Lawrence and Joyce investigated the consciousness of the child. Their children develop within the whole psychological interest of their novels. They were important to them as figures of developing life, and with Lawrence, especially, his interest in them leads to involvement with the problems of human development within society as he, rightly or wrongly, conceived them. At this point, one is much more concerned with distinguishing motive and intention than with evaluing achievement. And in this one sees the continuity of a tradition developed through Blake, Wordsworth, Coleridge, Dickens, and Mark Twain. For them, as for Lawrence, the child was a symbol of their concern with the individual humanity of Man in relation to the influences, most often the encroachments, of modern, industrial, urban society upon it. The situation in which they found themselves, where so many of the former religious and social sanctions were gone, or were, at best, a matter of intense debate (one recalls Wordsworth's predicament), seems to have impelled them towards a continuous discussion of social values, and of the proper relation of the sensitive individual to, for them, an insensitive society; and finally towards the formulation of a Romantic philosophy of the integral Self, not as a static philosophy for withdrawal, but as the basis for the discovery and establishment of the individual's re-integration with society. For them, at least, 'alienation' only describes the initial state of their feelings.

The cultural predicament Lawrence diagnosed at the beginning of *Lady Chatterley's Lover* comes at the end of a whole tradition of 'romantic' analysis. Famous as it is, it might be as well to remind ourselves of it:

Ours is essentially a tragic age, so we refuse to take it tragically. The cataclysm has happened, we are among the ruins, we start to build up new little habitats, to have new little hopes. It is rather hard work: there is now no smooth road into the future: but we go round, or scramble over the obstacles. We've got to live, no matter how many skies have fallen.

For Wordsworth it had been the 'skies' of the Revolution and the Enlightenment. For Lawrence they were the 'skies' of nineteenth-century values brought down in the cataclysm of the First World War. The predicament was continuous, and, for them, continuously worsening. The response – 'we've got to live' – was very much the same. And it is within this response that they directed their interest towards the child, as a symbol of sensitive growth towards viable maturity. For them the child was, if you like, a creative symbol; a focal point of contact between the growing human consciousness and the 'experience' of an alien world, about which they could

339

concentrate their disquiet, and, importantly, their hopes for human salvation. We see just how significant Blake's initial definition of 'innocence' and 'experience' became to the long tradition of Romantic protest through the symbol of the child, and how closely it serves as a definition for the interest which Lawrence brought to the character of Ursula Brangwen in *The Rainbow*.

But, as we have seen, it was not always a matter of 'growth'. The Romantic image once established became as frequently a powerful means for withdrawal; not only a cult of 'life', but, to use the language of its logical antithesis, a cult of 'nescience' and 'death'. This inversion of the image often enough arose from some essentially personal factor in the emotions of the authors concerned – with Dickens, self-pity – with many, the clear, if painful, result of emotional immaturity. But it may be excused perhaps if, in establishing this distinction between the two contrary attitudes to the child so frequently met with, the impulse towards life, and the impulse towards escape and death, we draw some more general conclusions. The various literary attitudes towards the child in the nineteenth and early twentieth centuries mingled in a very wide, and clearly popular acceptance; the Romantic symbol of growth, the innocence, the pathos, the nostalgia, the regret, the withdrawal, the 'death' – the child-image contains not only the response of the artist to his condition, but the response of a whole society, to itself. It is not remarkable perhaps when major authors see the child as a symbol of growth, life, and fertility, as a means for establishing human values in an increasingly secular age. It is, however, remarkable when a society sees the child as a symbol of dying, as life that is 'better dead'. I have already suggested a possible relation between the psychology of a repressive morality and the image of the 'dying child', and this seems to me a significant part of the Victorian morbidity towards children. *East Lynne* was not untypical of its age. It was perhaps the most popular novel of the whole century. One wonders if, in that very 'moral' work, the death of William Carlyle, with all its intensely envisaged luxuries of 'Paradise', is something of a non-fertility rite, an immolation of the instinctual self performed through the drama of the death of a child. One says 'performed', because the whole episode has very much the atmosphere of religious ritual:

By the side of William Carlyle's dying bed knelt the Lady Isabel. The time was at hand, and the boy was quite reconciled to his fate. Merciful indeed is God to dying children! ... We *can* bear death; it is not the worst parting that the earth knows. He will be quit of this cruel world; sheltered in heaven. I wish we were all there!

We remember the following from that other best-selling novelist of the later century:

We may ask whether for many a child it would not have been happiest never to have grown up at all. Honestly speaking, we cannot grieve for the fair legions of beloved children who have passed away in their childhood, – we know, even without the aid of Gospel comfort, that it is 'far better' with them so.

We remember also Wordsworth's child that 'brings hope with it, and forward-looking thoughts'. With all their variety of definition and statement, these are the two fundamental polarities of the modern literature of the child.

Bibliography

THE following are the works which I have found most useful in making this study:

Adamson, J. W. *The Educational Writings of John Locke*. London: Longmans, 1922.

Allen, Walter. *The English Novel. A Short Critical History*. London: Phoenix, 1954.

Archer, R. L. *Rousseau on Education: Selections, edited with an introduction by R. L. Archer*. London: Arnold, 1928.

Aydelotte, W. O. 'The England of Marx and Mill as Reflected in Fiction': *Journal of Economic History, Supp. viii*, 1948.

Ayres, H. M. *Carroll's Alice*. New York: Columbia University Press, 1936.

Babenroth, A. C. *English Childhood. Wordsworth's Treatment of childhood in the light of English poetry from Prior to Crabbe*. New York: Columbia University Studies in English and Comparative Literature, 1922.

Balint, Alice. *The Psycho-Analysis of the Nursery*. London: Kegan Paul, 1953.

Bateson, F. N. *Wordsworth. A Re-Interpretation*. London: Longmans, 1954.

Batho, Edith C. (with Dobrée, Bonamy). *The Victorians and After, 1830–1914*. Second Revised Edition. London: Cresset Press, 1950.

Battiscombe, G. *Charlotte Mary Yonge: a biography with an introduction by E. M. Delafield*. London: Constable, 1943.

Baudoin, L. C. *The Mind of the Child*. London: Allen & Unwin, 1933.

Beatty, A. *William Wordsworth, his doctrine and art in their historical relations*. University of Wisconsin Studies in Language and Literature. Second Edition. Madison, 1927.

Bennett, Joan. *Virginia Woolf. Her Art as a Novelist*. Cambridge University Press, 1945.

Besant, Walter. *The Eulogy of Richard Jefferies*. London: Chatto & Windus, 1888.

Bewley, M. 'Appearance and Reality in Henry James': *Scrutiny*: Summer, 1950.

Blackstone, B. *English Blake*. Cambridge University Press, 1949.

Blake, G. *Barrie and the Kailyard School*. London: Arthur Barker, 1951.

Boyd, W. *The Educational Theory of Jean Jacques Rousseau*. London: Longmans, 1911.

Boyd, W. *The History of Western Education*. Sixth Edition. London: Black, 1952.

Branch, E. M. *The Literary Apprenticeship of Mark Twain*. University of Urbana: Illinois Press, 1950.

Bronowski, J. *A Man Without a Mask. William Blake, 1757–1827*. Harmondsworth: Pelican Books, 1954.

Brooks, Van Wyck. *The Ordeal of Mark Twain*. New York: Dutton, 1933.

Buer, M. C. *Health, Wealth and Population in the Early Days of the Industrial Revolution*. London: Routledge, 1926.

Burlingham, Dorothy (with Anna Freud). *Infants without Families*. London: Allen & Unwin, 1943.

Burlingham, Russell. *Forrest Reid. A Portrait and Study*. London: Faber, 1953.

Buxbaum, Edith. *Your Child Makes Sense. A Guidebook for Parents*. London: Allen & Unwin, 1951.

Cazamian, Louis. *Le Roman social en Angleterre, 1830–1850*. Paris, 1904.

Chambers, E. K. *Samuel Taylor Coleridge*. Oxford: Clarendon Press, 1938.

Chancellor, E. B. *Dickens and his Times*. London: Richards, 1932.

Chesterton, G. K. *Charles Dickens*. London: Methuen, 1906.

Clark, Cumberland. *Charles Dickens and the Yorkshire Schools*. London: Chiswick Press, 1918.

Clarke, Isabel C. *Maria Edgeworth, her Family and Friends*. London: Hutchinson, 1950.

Coleridge, S. T. *Letters: edited by E. H. Coleridge*. London: Heinemann, 1895.

Coleridge, S. T. *Inquiring Spirit. A new presentation of Coleridge from his published and unpublished prose writings: edited by Kathleen Coburn*. London: Routledge & Kegan Paul, 1951.

Collingwood, S. D. *The Life and Letters of Lewis Carroll – Rev. C. L. Dodgson*. London: T. Fisher Unwin, 1898.

Cooper, T. P. *With Dickens in Yorkshire*. London: Ben Johnson & Co., 1923.

Daiches, D. *Virginia Woolf*. London: Editions Poetry, 1945.

Darton, F. J. H. *Children's Books in England*. Cambridge University Press, 1932.

De Voto, Bernard. *Mark Twain's America*. Boston, 1932.

De Voto, Bernard. *Mark Twain at Work*. Cambridge, Mass.: Harvard University Press, 1942.

Dupee, F. W. *Henry James*. London: Methuen, 1951.

Edel, Leon. *Henry James. The Untried Years (1843–70)*. London: Hart-Davis, 1953.

Edel, Leon. *The Psychological Novel, 1900–1950*. London: Hart-Davis, 1955.

Ellis, H. Havelock. *From Rousseau to Proust*. London: Constable, 1936.

Empson, William. *Some Versions of Pastoral*. London: Chatto & Windus, 1935.

Engels, F. *The Condition of the Working Class in England in 1844: translated by F. K. Wischnewetzky*. London: Allen & Unwin, 1926.

Fairchild, H. N. *The Noble Savage. A study in romantic naturalism*. New York: Columbia University Press, 1928.

Forster, J. *The Life of Charles Dickens*. London: Dent, 1927.

Fotheringham, J. *Wordsworth's 'Prelude' as a Study of Education*. London: Horace Marshall, 1899.

Freud, Sigmund. *The Interpretation of Dreams* and *On Dreams*. Vols. 4 and 5 of the Standard Edition of the Complete Works of Sigmund Freud: translated under the general editorship of James Strachey. London: Hogarth, 1953.

Freud, Sigmund. *Three Essays on the Theory of Sexuality: translated by James Strachey*. London: Imago Publishing Company, 1949.

Freud, Sigmund. *The Ego and the Id: translated by Joan Rivière*. London: L. & V. Woolf, Institute of Psycho-Analysis, 1927.

Freud, Sigmund. *An Outline of Psycho-Analysis: translated by James Strachey*. London: Hogarth Press, 1949.

Freud, Anna. *The Psycho-Analytical Treatment of Children: translated by Nancy Procter-Gregg*. London: Imago Publishing Company, 1946.

Frye, Northrop. *Fearful Symmetry. A Study of William Blake*. Princeton: Princeton University Press, 1947.

Garrod, H. W. *Wordsworth*. Oxford: Clarendon Press, 1927.

Gilchrist, A. *Life of William Blake: edited by Ruthven Todd*. London: Dent, 1942.

Gissing, G. *Charles Dickens. A Critical Study*. London, 1898.

Glover, E. *Freud or Jung*. London: Allen & Unwin, 1950.

Green, F. L. *Jean-Jacques Rousseau. A Study of his Life and Writings*. Cambridge University Press, 1955.

Haldane, E. S. *Mrs Gaskell and her Friends*. London: Hodder & Stoughton, 1930.

Halévy, Elie. *A History of the English People in the 19th Century: translated by E. I. Watkin and D. A. Barker*. London: Benn, 1949–52.

Hammond, J. L. and Barbara. *The Town Labourer, 1760–1832*. London: Longmans, 1925.

Hammond, J. L. and Barbara. *The Age of the Chartists, 1832–1854. A Study of Discontent*. London: Longmans, 1930.

Hanson, L. and E. H. *Marian Evans and George Eliot*. Oxford University Press, 1952.

Harding, D. W. 'A Note on Nostalgia': *Determinations*. London: Chatto & Windus, 1934.

Hart-Davis, Rupert. *Hugh Walpole. A Biography*. London: Macmillan, 1952.

Hazard, Paul. *European Thought in the Eighteenth Century from Montesquieu to Lessing: translated by J. Lewis May*. London: Hollis & Carter, 1954.

Hoff, F. J. *Freudianism and the Literary Mind*. Louisiana State University Press, 1946.

Hopkins, A. B. 'Dickens and Mrs Gaskell': *Huntington Library Quarterly*, August, 1946.

House, Humphry. *The Dickens World*. Oxford University Press, 1941.

Hughes, J. L. *Dickens as an Educator*. Appleton, 1900.

Jackson, T. A. *Charles Dickens: the Progress of a Radical*. London: Lawrence and Wishart, 1937.

Jarrasch, W. *Das Problem der heranwachsenden Jugend im Spiegel des zeitgenossischen englischen Romans (1900–1933)*. Doctorate Thesis: Giessen University, 1939.

Johnson, Edgar. *Charles Dickens. A Biography*. 2 vols. London: Gollancz, 1951.

Jones, Ernest. *Sigmund Freud. Life and Work*. 2 vols. London: Hogarth Press, 1953 and 1955.

Jung, C. G. *Psychological Types, translated by H. Godwin Baynes*. London: Kegan Paul, 1920.

Jung, C. G. *Psychology of the Unconscious, translated by B. M. Hinkle*. London: Kegan Paul, 1919.

Jung, C. G. *The Integration of the Personality, translated by S. Dell*. London: Kegan Paul, 1940.

Jung, C. G. *Modern Man in Search of a Soul, translated by C. F. Baynes*. London: Kegan Paul, 1933.

Keynes, G. *Blake Studies*. London: Hart-Davis, 1949.

Knights, L. C. 'Henry James and the Trapped Spectator': *Explorations*. London: Chatto & Windus, 1946.

Langton, R. *The Childhood and Youth of Charles Dickens*. London: Hutchinson, 1891.

Leavis, F. R. *Revaluation: Tradition and Development in English Poetry. Chapter 5. 'Wordsworth'*. London: Chatto & Windus, 1936.

Leavis, F. R. *The Great Tradition. George Eliot: Henry James: Joseph Conrad*. London: Chatto & Windus, 1948.

Leavis, F. R. 'James's *What Maisie Knew*: A Disagreement': *Scrutiny*, Summer, 1950.

Leavis, F. R. *Introduction to Pudd'nhead Wilson, a Tale by Mark Twain*. London: Zodiac Press, 1955.

Leavis, F. R. *D. H. Lawrence. Novelist*. London: Chatto & Windus, 1955.

Lennon, F. B. *Lewis Carroll*. London: Cassell, 1947.

Mackail, Denis. *The Story of J.M.B. (Sir James Barrie, Bart., O.M.)*. London: Peter Davies, 1941.

Mare, M. L. (with Alicia C. Percival). *Victorian Best-Seller. The World of C. M. Yonge*. London: Harrap, 1947.

Margoliouth, H. M. *William Blake*. Oxford University Press, 1951.

Martin, L. C. 'Henry Vaughan and the Theme of Infancy': *Seventeenth Century Studies presented to Sir Herbert Grierson*. Oxford University Press, 1938.

Mill, J. S. *Mill on Bentham and Coleridge. With an introduction by F. R. Leavis*. London: Chatto & Windus, 1950.

Morley, Lord. J. *Rousseau*. London: Chapman & Hall, 1873.

Moult, Thomas. *Barrie*. London: Cape, 1928.

Muir, P. H. *English Children's Books, 1600–1900*. London: Batsford, 1954.

Niblett, W. R. 'Wordsworth and the Child': *Educational Papers, King's College Education Society, No. 3, Vol. 5, p. 61*.

Orwell, George. 'Charles Dickens': *Critical Essays*. London: Secker & Warburg, 1946.

Paterson, A. *George Eliot's Family Life and Letters*. London: Selwyn & Blount, 1928.

Plowman, Max. *An Introduction to the Study of Blake*. London: Dent, 1927.

Pons, Jacques. *L'Education en Angleterre entre 1750 et 1800: aperçu sur l'influence pédagogique de J. J. Rousseau en Angleterre*. Paris, 1919.

Read, Sir Herbert. *Wordsworth. The Clark Lectures*. London: Cape, 1930.

Reed, Langford. *Life of Lewis Carroll*. London: Foyle, 1932.

Roddier, H. *J. J. Rousseau en Angleterre au XVIIIᵉ siècle. L'oeuvre et l'homme*. Paris, 1950.

Russell, A. G. B. *The Letters of William Blake. Together with a Life by F. Tatham: edited with an introduction by A. G. B. Russell*. London, 1906.

Saurat, Denis. *Blake and Modern Thought*. London: Constable, 1929.

Sélincourt, E. de. *The Letters of William and Dorothy Wordsworth: arranged and edited by E. de Sélincourt*. Oxford: Clarendon Press, 1935–9.

Seward, G. H. *Sex and Social Order*. Harmondsworth: Penguin Books, 1946.

Shaw, G. B. *Introduction to Hard Times*. London: Waverley, 1912.

Stephen, Leslie. *George Eliot*. London, 1902.

Thomas, Edward. *Richard Jefferies*. London: Dent, 1938.

Tillotson, K. *Novels of the 1840's*. Cambridge University Press, 1954.

Trilling, L. *The Liberal Imagination*. London: Secker & Warburg, 1951.

Trilling, L. *Freud and the Crisis of our Literature*. Boston: The Beacon Press, 1955.

Walsh, W. 'Coleridge's Vision of Childhood': The *Listener*, 24 Feb. 1955.

Wecter, Dixon. *Sam Clemens of Hannibal*. Boston: Houghton Mifflin, 1952.

Whitehead, A. N. *Science and the Modern World: The Lowell Lectures for 1925*. Cambridge University Press, 1929.

Whitney, Lois. *Primitivism and the Idea of Progress in English Popular Literature of the Eighteenth Century*. Baltimore: John Hopkins Press, 1934.

Wicksteed, J. H. *Blake's Innocence and Experience. A Study of the Songs and manuscripts etc*. London: Dent, 1928.

Willey, Basil. *The Eighteenth Century Background*. London: Chatto & Windus, 1940.

Willey, Basil. *Nineteenth Century Studies. Coleridge to Matthew Arnold*. London: Chatto & Windus, 1949.

Wilson, Edmund. *The Triple Thinkers*. Oxford University Press, 1938.

Wilson, Edmund. 'Dickens: The Two Scrooges': *The Wound and the Bow*. Boston: Houghton Mifflin, 1941.

Witcutt, W. P. *Blake. A Psychological Study*. London: Hollis & Carter, 1946.

Wodehouse, Helen. *A Survey of the History of Education*. London: Arnold, 1929.

Index

Index

Abbeychurch (Yonge), 92
Abinger Harvest (Forster), 270
Adam Bede (George Eliot), 165-6, 178
Addison, Joseph, 37
Alder, Alfred, 297
Aikin, Anna Letitia. *See* Barbauld, Mrs Anna Letitia
Aikin, John, 50
Alcott, Louisa May, 218
Aldington, Richard, 337
Alice in Wonderland (Carroll), 243-5
Alton Locke (Kingsley), 92, 100-105, 150
Anstey, F., 282
Apostate (Reid), 271-2, 274
Arlequin Sauvage (La Drévetière), 42
Arnold, Matthew, 68, 114, 288
Arnold, Thomas, 280, 281
Art and Nature (La Drévetière), 42
Associationism, 38, 39, 40, 54, 69, 74, 85
At the Back of the North Wind (Mac-Donald), 282
At the Door of the Gate (Reid), 274
Auld Licht Idylls (Barrie), 250
Austen, Jane, 71 n., 91, 106, 162, 175-6, 177, 320
Autobiography of Mark Rutherford, The, 290
Awkward Age, The (James), 195, 196, 200, 206-9

Bage, Robert, 48
Barbauld, Mrs Anna Letitia, 48, 49, 50, 57, 103

Barrie, Sir James, 32, 242, 249-59, 260, 263; Elizabeth Bergner and *The Boy David,* 258; G. Blake on, 250-51; Carroll compared with, 242, 249; childless marriage of, 255-6; cult of, 249-50; Davies family and, 255; Dickens compared with, 32; the Kailyard School, 250-51; Mackail on, 250-51; Millar on, 250; mother complex of, 251-5; morbidity of, 256-8; Moult on, 249-50; nostalgia for childhood in, 256, 257; Noyes on, 250; Stevenson on, 251-2; compared with Mark Twain, 257
Barrie and the Kailyard School (Blake), 250-51
Bateson, Francis N., 71
Batho, Edith Clara, 111, 123
Beaconsfield, Benjamin Disraeli, 1st Earl. *See* Disraeli, Benjamin, 1st Earl Beaconsfield
Beattie, James, 53
Beatty, Arthur, 71
Beaurieu, Gaspard Guillard de, 48
Beautiful Years, The (Williamson), 239
Bell, Andrew, 280
Bennett, Arnold, 337
Bennett, Mrs Joan, 313, 320
Bentham Jeremy, 39-40
Bergner, Elizabeth, 258
Bevis (Jefferies), 232, 236-8
Bildungsroman, 270

351

Blake, George, 250, 251

Blake, William, 29, 33, 40, 51, 52–67, 114, 240, 245, 280–81, 290, 339; attitude to religion, 53, 64; child a symbol of innocence for, 52, 192, 340; concern with 'Vision', 40, 51, 54–5; criticism of industrialization, 59, 60, 64–6; T. S. Eliot on, 56; humanism of, 55, 64–5; Imagination and, 55; relation to D. H. Lawrence, 340; meaning of Free Love, 61; opposition to Rationalism, 54–5; Palmer on, 56; rescue of Astley's circus-boy, 64–5; Mark Twain compared with, 222–3; views on Education, 66; on Wordsworth, 54

Bleak House (Dickens), 93, 114, 124

Bowes Academy, 134, 136

Boy (Corelli), 184, 190–92, 341

Boy (Hanley), 337

Boy Castaways of Black Lake Island (Barrie), 255

Boy David, The (Barrie), 249, 258–9

Brian Westby (Reid), 271, 275, 276, 277

Brontë, Charlotte, 91, 92, 105–10

Brontë, Emily, 91

Brooke, Mrs Frances, 48

Brooks, Van Wyck, 215, 216, 241

Bruce, Michael, 53

Burke, Edmund, 40

Burlingham, Russell, 269, 271, 274, 276

Burnett, Ivy Compton, 337

Burrow, Trigant, 321

Butler, Samuel, 34, 282–90

Cambridge Platonists, 42

Carroll, Lewis, 242–9, 281; Barrie compared with, 242, 249; Neurotic obsession with children, 242, 246, 248; nostalgia for childhood, 243, 244, 245; the Romantic tradition and, 244, 245, 246; sadistic humour of, 248; sense of sin in, 243; views on religion, 244

Catcher in the Rye, The (Salinger), 270, 338

Centuries of Meditation (Traherne), 56

Charity-children, 59, 65

Child: as theme in literature before the Romantics, 29, 52–3; choice of, as literary theme, 34–5; concern with social conditions of, 92; death of, as literary theme, 140, 161, 181–5, 189–90, 191, 192, 340–41; debasement of Romantic tradition of, 34, 161, 192, 240–41, 302, 339–40; Freud and the Romantic tradition of, 34, 291–2, 301–2; Freud's account of, 291–302; genesis of the Romantic child, 29, 37, 41, 51; literature written for the, 49–51, 281–2; nineteenth-century Puritan treatment of, 34–5, 245, 282–91; 'original innocence', 32–4; Realistic treatment of in literature, 305–6; Romantic tradition of, 29, 30, 32–3, 42–3, 91, 92, 192, 238–9, 240, 244, 272–3, 290; treated by Rationalists as small adult, 40, 43; used as commentator on adult society, 92, 112, 194, 230, 240, 245, 271, 306, 338–9. *See also under the name of individual writers.*

Clayhanger (Bennett), 337

Clemens, Samuel, *See* Twain, Mark.

Climbing-boys, 57, 59

Coleridge, Samuel Taylor, 37, 40, 50–51, 84–90, 102, 240, 270, 339; on education, 87–90; on eighteenth-century philosophy, 85–6; friendship of, with Wordsworth, 84; on Hartley, 84; on Imagination and Reason, 40, 86–7; influence of, 37; Mill on, 37, 84; on moralizing literature for children, 50–51; on Wordsworth, 69, 87

Commission on the Employment of Young Persons and Children, 1842, 93, 94, 96, 97

Common Reader, The (Woolf), 304

Compton Burnett, Ivy. See Burnett, Ivy Compton.

Cooper, Anthony Ashley, 3rd Earl Shaftesbury. See Shaftesbury, Anthony Ashley Cooper, 3rd Earl

Cooper, James Fenimore, 281

Cooper, Thomas Parsons, 134

Corelli, Marie, 184–92, 193, 240, 265–6, 291, 340

Cowper, William, 52

Crockett, Rutherford, 251

Crystal Box, The (Walpole), 260

Culture and Anarchy (Arnold), 114

Daiches, David, 313

Daisy Chain, The (Yonge), 281

Daniel Deronda (George Eliot), 175–8

David Copperfield (Dickens), 106–7, 110, 126, 127, 158, 159, 160

Davies family, Barrie and the, 255

Davis, Rupert Hart-. See Hart-Davis, Rupert

Day, Thomas, 47, 49, 50

Dear Brutus (Barrie), 252 n.

Death of a Hero (Aldington), 337

Death of children as literary theme, 140, 161, 181–4, 188–9, 191, 193, 340–41

De La Drévetière, Louis de Lisle. See La Drévetière, Louis de Lisle de

De Staël, Anne Louise Germaine, Madame. See Staël Anne Louise Germaine, Madame de

Dickens, Charles, 33, 41, 91, 92, 93, 111–61, 179, 240, 263, 280, 281, 282, 286, 290, 307, 339, 340; Arnold compared with, 114; Barrie and, 32; Batho and Dobrée on, 111, 123; Charlotte Brontë compared with, 106–7, 110; Butler compared with, 286; the child as symbol of sensitive feeling in, 111–12, 114; child's sense of isolation, theme in, 122–3; concern with influence of environment, 124–5; concern with social reform, 93, 123–4; Marie Corelli and, 186–7, 188–9; dramatic sense, 33, 114–15, 157; early life, 116–19; on education, 41, 126, 133–4, 146, 151–2; George Eliot compared with, 162; T. S. Eliot compared with, 114; Joyce compared with, 306, 307; Lawrence compared with, 113–14, 138, 321, 333; nostalgia in, 32; reading public, 31, 281; on religion, 126–7; the Romantic tradition and, 110, 114, 160–61, 179, 192, 240, 339; self-identification with his characters, 159, 340; sense of industrial and social change in, 94, 118–22; sentimentality, 112, 147, 158; symbolic technique of, 129–31, 156; and

Dickens, Charles – *cont.*
Mark Twain, 221; visit to York-shire schools, 133–4; Edmund Wilson on, 119
Dickens World (House), 119, 124
Discours (Rousseau), 43
Disraeli, Benjamin, 1st Earl Beacons-field, 94–7, 100, 105
Dobell, Sidney, 110
Dobrée, Bonamy, 111, 123
Dodgson, Charles Lutwidge. *See* Carroll, Lewis
Dombey and Son (Dickens), 51, 91, 114, 120–21, 122, 125, 135, 140–50, 157, 158, 160, 179
Dostoievsky, Feodor, 303
Douglas, Norman, 269
Drévetière, Louis de Lisle de la. *See* La Drévetière, Louis de Lisle de
Dubliners (Joyce), 306–8
Dusty Answer (Lehmann), 337

Early Lessons (Mrs Barbauld), 49
Easter Greeting (Carroll), 244
East Lynne (Mrs Henry Wood), 179–84, 291, 340
Edgeworth, Maria, 47–8, 50, 280
Edgeworth, Richard Lovell, 47–8, 280
Education, 40, 42–6, 47–8, 66, 82–3, 87–90, 106, 125, 133–4, 145, 151–2, 184–6, 188–9, 191, 280–81, 296
Elève de la Nature (Beaurieu), 48
Eliot, George, 91, 93, 162–78, 179; Jane Austen compared with, 175, 177; Dickens compared with, 162; Lawrence compared with, 176, 321; Lawrence on, 163; memories of earlier social order, 162–3, 165,

170; nostalgia in, 167–71; psycho-logical perception of, 171–2; Romantic concept of Innocence and, 171; self-involvement in children's characters, 162–3, 166, 171; sentimentality, 162, 163–4, 165, 172–3; Wordsworth's in-fluence on, 83, 169–70, 172, 173
Eliot, Thomas Stearns, 56, 92, 114, 319
Elizabeth, Charlotte, 93
Emile (Rousseau), 42–7, 280
Emma (Jane Austen), 175
Empson, William, 32, 71, 240
England, My England (Lawrence), 323
Essay Concerning the Human Under-standing (Locke), 37, 39
Essay on Coleridge (Mill), 37, 38–9, 84
Essays on a Liberal Education, 280
Essays on Practical Education (Richard and Maria Edgeworth), 47–8, 280
Evans, Mary Ann. *See* Eliot, George

Father and Son (Gosse), 290
Felix Holt (George Eliot), 93, 174
Fielding, Henry, 91
Fields, Mrs James T., 219
First Principles of Government (Priest-ley), 40
Fitzgerald, F. Scott, 93
Flax of Dream, The (Williamson), 239
Following Darkness (Reid), 273, 275
Forster, E. M., 270, 316
Fotheringham, James, 68
Franklin, Benjamin, 220
Freud, Sigmund, 34–5, 219, 291–302, 303–4, 337; development from, of dissident schools of psychological theory, 297–8; on education, 296;

Freud, Sigmund – *cont.*
enlightened treatment of children advocated, 295–6; effect of, on sentimentalizing Victorian view of the child, 33–6, 291–2, 301–2; on humour, 219; infantile sexuality, 294–5, 301, 302; on influence of childhood experience on adult life, 294, 295; on innocence, 300, 302; Lawrence on, 321, 322; the libido, 294; not advocate of irrationality, 293; Oedipus complex, 294; relation to nineteenth-century scientific tradition, 293; and religion, 299, 300, 301; theories distorted in popularization, 292; the unconscious, 293–4
Friend, The (Coleridge), 84, 88
Froebel, Friedrich, 280
Frohman, Charles, 249

Garden God, The (Reid), 276–7, 279
Gaskell, Mrs Elizabeth, 93, 97–9, 100, 105
Gentle Lover, The (Reid), 275
Godwin, William, 39, 40, 70, 72
Golden Scarecrow, The (Walpole), 259, 260, 261–3, 265
Golding, William, 269
Gosse, Edmund, 271, 290
Graham, Mrs Catharine Macaulay. *See* Macaulay, Mrs Catharine
Gray, Thomas, 52
Great Expectations (Dickens), 125, 139, 158, 160, 307
Guillard de Beaurieu, Gaspard. *See* Beaurieu, Gaspard Guillard de
Guthrie, Thomas Anstey. *See* Anstey F.

Hanley, James, 337
Hard Times (Dickens), 41, 51, 114, 123, 125–6, 150–57, 160
Harris, John, 281
Harrison, Frederic, 187
Hart-Davis, Rupert, 259
Hartley, David, 39, 69, 71, 73–4, 75, 76, 84
Hartley, L. P., 338
Hawthorne, Nathaniel, 281
Heir of Redclyffe, The (Yonge), 281
Helen Fleetwood (Charlotte Elizabeth), 93
Herbart, Johann Friedrich, 280
Heredity and environment, 124–5, 283
History of Emily Montague, The (Mrs Brooke), 48
History of Julia Mandeville, The (Mrs Brooke), 48 n.
Hobbes, Thomas, 42
Home, Henry, Lord Kames. *See* Kames, Lord Henry Home
House, Humphry, 119, 124
Howards End (Forster), 316
Huckleberry Finn (Mark Twain), 215, 221, 225–32, 240, 270, 273
Hughes, Richard, 268, 337
Humboldt, Friedrich Heinrich Alexander, Baron von, 280
Hume, David, 41
Hutcheson, Francis, 41
Huxley, Aldous, 337
Huxley, Thomas, 280

Inchbald, Mrs Elizabeth, 48
Interpretation of Dreams, The (Freud), 299
Intimations Ode (Wordsworth), 29, 76–81, 87, 190, 242, 291

James, Henry, 31, 194–214, 275, 277 n., 319–20
James, William, 304
Jane Eyre (Charlotte Brontë), 91, 92, 105–10
Janeway, James, 44
Jefferies, Richard, 233–9, 274
Jeremy books (Walpole), 259, 263–9
Jerusalem (Blake), 57, 64
Jones, Ernest, 299
Joyce, James, 303, 304, 305, 306–12, 312, 314, 319, 321, 338
Jung, Carl Gustav, 298–9, 322

Kailyard novelists, 250–51
Kames, Lord Henry Home, 46
Keats, John, 51
Kindergartens, 280
King of the Golden River, The (Ruskin), 282
Kingdom of Twilight, The (Reid), 275
Kingsley, Charles, 93, 100–105, 150, 282

La Drévetière, Louis de Lisle de, 42
Lady Chatterley's Lover (Lawrence), 336, 339
Lamb, Charles, 50–51, 56
Lancaster, Henry Hill, 280
Lawrence, David Herbert, 92, 93, 239, 288, 303, 305, 320–36, 338, 339; relation to Blake, 340; compared with Dickens, 113–14, 138, 333; compared with George Eliot, 175–6; on George Eliot, 163; and Mark Twain on Benjamin Franklin, 220; fusion of social and psychological interests, 321, 326, 337; compared with Joyce, 321; nostalgia in, 242; on psychological theory, 321–2; compared with Virginia Woolf, 267–8
Lear, Edward, 281
Leavis, Frank Raymond, 69, 197–8
Lehmann, Rosamond, 337
Letters on Education (Mrs Macaulay), 46
Liberal Imagination, The (Trilling), 77, 80
Life on the Mississippi (Mark Twain), 216, 217
Lines Written above Tintern Abbey (Wordsworth), 74, 76, 79
Literature and society, 29–32, 93, 105, 288–9, 339–40
Little Dorrit (Dickens), 107, 113, 126
Little Minister, The (Barrie), 250
Little White Bird, The (Barrie), 253–4, 255, 256, 257–8
Little Women (Alcott), 218
Lochleven (Bruce), 53
Locke, John, 37, 39, 40, 54
Loose Hints on Education (Kames), 46
Lord of the Flies (Golding), 269
Lost Girl, The (Lawrence), 138
Lyrical Ballads, Preface to the (Wordsworth), 73

Macaulay, Mrs Catharine, 46
MacDonald, George, 282
Mackail, Denis, 249, 250, 255–6
Mackenzie, Sir Compton, 303, 337
Mackenzie, Henry, 51
Maclaren, Ian, 251
Magic Mountain, The (Mann), 270
Man of Nature, The (Beaurieu), 48
Mann, Thomas, 270
Mansfield Park (Jane Austen), 106, 162, 177

Margaret Ogilvy (Barrie), 251, 252, 254

Mark Twain. *See* Twain, Mark

Marryat, Frederick, 92, 105

Mary Barton (Mrs Gaskell), 93, 97–100, 105

Memoirs (Richard Lovell Edgeworth), 47

Michael Armstrong (Frances Trollope), 93

Middlemarch (George Eliot), 93, 162, 175, 304

Mighty Atom, The (Corelli), 184–90

Mill, John Stuart, 37, 38–9, 41, 84, 280

Mill on the Floss, The (George Eliot), 162, 166–72, 174, 175, 178

Millar, J. H., 250

Minstrel, The (Beattie), 53

Montagu, Mrs Elizabeth, 57

Moral Tales for Young People (Maria Edgeworth), 50

More, Hannah, 50

Morley, John, Viscount Morley of Blackburn, 43

Moult, Thomas, 250

Nature and Art (Mrs Inchbald), 48

New System of Education (Coleridge), 89

Newman, John Henry, 280

Newton, Sir Isaac, 37, 38, 54

Nicholas Nickleby (Dickens), 115–16, 119, 134–40

Nicoll, Sir William Robertson, 251

North and South (Mrs Gaskell), 100

Nostalgia for childhood, 32–3, 46, 52, 167–71, 222, 241–2, 243, 244, 245, 256, 260, 263–4, 340

Nouvelle Héloïse, La (Rousseau), 43

Novel as literary form, 91–3, 105, 273, 304–5

Noyes, Alfred, 250

Observations on Man (Hartley), 39

Ode: Intimations of Immortality from recollections of Early Childhood (Wordsworth), 29, 76–80, 87, 190, 242, 291

Ode on a Distant Prospect of Eton College (Gray), 52

Ode to Dejection (Coleridge), 86

Old Curiosity Shop, The (Dickens), 122–3, 157, 159–60

Oliver Twist (Dickens), 91, 92, 106–7, 127–33, 138, 139, 140, 307

On the receipt of my Mother's Picture out of Norfolk (Cowper), 52

Open Air, The (Jefferies), 238–9

Ordeal of Mark Twain, The (Brooks), 215

Original sin, 42, 44, 291, 300–301. *See also* Religion.

Paine, Albert Bigelow, 217, 219, 231

Palmer, Samuel, 56

Parent's Assistant (Maria Edgeworth), 50

Pestalozzi, Johann Heinrich, 280

Peter Pan (Barrie), 32, 242, 249–50, 253–5, 256–8

Peter Simple (Marryat), 92, 105

Picaresque novels, 91 n.

Pickwick Papers, The (Dickens), 91, 119, 127

Pillow Problems (Carroll), 243

Plato's educational theory, Coleridge on, 89

Poor Law Amendment Act, 1834, 127

Popular Tales (Maria Edgeworth), 50

Portrait of a Lady, The (James), 194–5, 196, 198–9

Portrait of Forrest Reid (Burlingham), 269–70, 271

Portrait of the Artist as a Young Man, A (Joyce), 306, 308–12, 314, 319

Practical Education (Richard and Maria Edgeworth), 47–8, 280

Prelude, The (Wordsworth), 50, 68, 74, 75, 76, 82, 92, 242

Priestley, Joseph, 39, 40

Princess Casamassima, The (James), 196

Principia (Newton), 37

Principles of Psychology (James), 304

Private Road (Reid), 277 n.

Psychoanalysis in Theory and in Life (Burrow), 321

Pupil, The (James), 199

Rainbow, The (Lawrence), 198, 321, 323, 325, 326–36, 338, 340

Rainbow, The (Wordsworth), 84

Rank, Otto, 297

Read, Sir Herbert, 72

Reading public, 30–31, 281

Reflections on the Revolution in France (Burke), 40

Reid, Forrest, 269–79; concealed eroticism in, 276–9; cult of, 269–70; Norman Douglas on, 269; E. M. Forster on, 270; and Henry James, 275, 277 n.; and Nature, 274; obsessive interest in youth, 269–73; on writing, 273, 275, 278; project for a realistic novel, 276; 'vision' of, 272

Religion, 42, 63, 103, 126–7, 183, 187–8, 189, 244, 283, 284, 290, 299, 300. *See also* Original Sin

Richardson, Dorothy, 304

Richardson, Samuel, 37, 48

Rocking-Horse Winner, The (Lawrence), 322

Roddier, Henri, 46

Roman Fountain (Walpole), 260

Rousseau, Jean Jacques, 37, 40, 41, 42, 43–9, 50; influence of, 47–9, 280, 281, 290; Morley on, 43; 'original innocence', 33, 43–4, 290

Rousseau en Angleterre (Roddier), 46

Royal Commission on the Employment of Young Persons and Children, 1842, 93, 94, 96, 97

Ruskin, John, 280, 282

Rutherford, Mark, 290

St Mawr (Lawrence), 175, 321

Salinger, J. D., 270, 338

Sandford and Merton (Day), 49–50

Scenes from Clerical Life (George Eliot), 163, 164, 166, 178

Scott, Sir Walter, 52, 91

Scott Fitzgerald, F. *See* Fitzgerald, F. Scott.

Sense and Sensibility (Jane Austen), 71 n., 177

Sentimental Tommy (Barry), 242, 250, 257

Sex, 59, 60, 61–3, 249, 258, 276–9, 302, 306

Shaftesbury, Anthony Ashley Cooper, 3rd Earl, 37, 42

Shakespeare, William, 30

Shaw, George Bernard, 303

Sherwood, Mrs Mary Martha, 50, 287

Shrimp and the Anemone, The (Hartley), 338

Sigmund Freud: Life and Work (Jones), 300

Silas Marner (George Eliot), 83, 172–4, 178, 179

Sinclair, Catherine, 281

Sinclair, May, 304

Sinister Street (Mackenzie), 303, 337

Smith, Charlotte, 48

Smollett, Tobias, 91

Some Versions of Pastoral (Empson), 240

Songs of Experience (Blake), 53, 56, 57, 60–66, 114

Songs of Innocence (Blake), 29, 53, 56, 57, 58–61, 114, 245, 272

Sons and Lovers (Lawrence), 242, 303, 323–6, 328

Southey, Robert, 52

Spender, Stephen, 204

Spring Song (Reid), 274–5

Staël, Anne Louise Germaine, Madame de, 50, 51

Sterne, Laurence, 37, 48

Stevenson, Robert Louis, 251, 282

Story of J.M.B., The (Mackail), 249

Story of My Heart, The (Jefferies), 232–6, 237

Stowe, Harriet Beecher, 281

Stream of consciousness, 304–5, 318

Sunday School movement, 49, 50

Sybil (Disraeli), 93–7, 105

Sylvie and Bruno (Carroll), 243

Task, The (Cowper), 52

Tchekov, Anton, 303

Tennyson, Alfred, 1st Baron Tennyson, 92

Thoughts concerning Education (Locke), 40

Three Essays on the Theory of Sexuality (Freud), 299

Through the Looking Glass (Carroll), 246–9

To Childhood (Scott), 52

To Margaret Hill (Southey), 52

To the Lighthouse (Woolf), 303, 314–18

Token for Children, A (Janeway), 44

Tom Barber trilogy (Reid), 278–9

Tom Sawyer (Mark Twain), 217, 221–5

Tommy and Grizel (Barrie), 255

Tragedy, 167–8

Traherne, Thomas, 42, 56

Treatise of Human Nature (Hume), 41

Trilling, Lionel, 77, 80

Trimmer, Mrs Sarah, 50, 57, 103

Trollope, Anthony, 91 n.

Trollope, Mrs Frances, 92

Turn of the Screw, The (James), 195, 196, 198, 209–14

Twain, Mark, 215–32, 240, 257, 270, 273, 281, 290, 338; compared with Barrie, 257; Arnold Bennett on, 215; compared with Blake, 222; Van Wyck Brooks on, 215–16, 241; despair of, 215–16; and Dickens, 221; Mrs Fields on, 219; and Lawrence on Franklin's maxims, 220; 'illiterate' prose of, 227–8; compared with Jefferies, 232; as national humorist, 218; the National Lie, 219; nostalgia for piloting days, 32, 215, 216, 217, 221; Paine on, 217, 219, 231;

Mark Twain – *cont.*
relations with mother, 216–17; relations with wife and daughters, 217, 219, 226; self-contempt of, 215, 218, 219, 231; snobbery of, 218

Ulysses (Joyce), 303, 312

Van Wyck Brooks, *See* Brooks, Van Wyck
Vaughan, Henry, 42
Vice Versa (Anstey), 282
Victorians and After (Batho and Dobrée), 111, 123
Voltaire, François Marie Arouet de, 38

Walpole, Sir Hugh, 259–69, 307; compared with Barrie, 260, 263; the figure of the Friend in, 262–3, 265–6; Rupert Hart-Davis on, 259; compared with Richard Hughes, 268; nostalgia for imagined childhood, 260, 262–4; and public schools, 260, 266–7, 268–9; unhappy childhood of, 259–60; whimsy in, 260–63
Warren, H. C., 232
Waste Land, The (T. S. Eliot), 92, 114
Water Babies, The (Kingsley), 103, 282
Waves, The (Woolf), 317–19
Way of All Flesh, The (Butler), 34–5, 282–91, 303
Welch, Denton, 338
Wells, H. G., 303
What is Man (Mark Twain), 231

What Maisie Knew (James), 195, 196, 198, 199–207
When I was Thirteen (Welch), 337
White, William Hale. *See* Rutherford, Mark
Whitehead, Alfred North, 71
Willey, Basil, 41, 81, 85
Williams, Helen Maria, 51
Williamson, Henry, 239
Wilson, Edmund, 119, 197, 209, 210
Window in Thrums, A (Barrie), 250, 253
Wings of the Dove, The (James), 196
With Dickens in Yorkshire (Cooper), 134
Women in Love (Lawrence), 336
Wood Magic (Jefferies), 235
Wood, Mrs Henry, 179–84, 193, 240, 291, 340
Woolf, Virginia, 303, 304, 305, 312–20, 321
Wordsworth, Dorothy, 71
Wordsworth, William, 29, 33, 50, 68–83, 92, 102, 114, 240, 241–2, 304, 339, 341; Anglicanism of, 81; Arnold on, 68; and associationism, 69, 71, 72–3, 85; compared with Jane Austen, 71 n.; balance between eighteenth-century and Romantic sensibilities in, 70; Bateson on, 71; Beatty on, 71; Blake on, 54; friendship with Coleridge, 84–5; Coleridge on, 69, 84, 87; disillusion with Godwinian Enlightenment, 72; early life, 71; on education, 81–2; George Eliot and, 83, 168–9, 173; Empson on, 71; Fotheringham on, 68; and Hartley, 69, 71,

Wordsworth, William – *cont.*
73–4, 75, 84; influence of, 80,
83–4, 190, 291, 304; Leavis on,
69; on moralizing literature for
children, 50; nostalgia in, 242;
philosophy and poetry, 68–9, 75–
6; Read on, 72–3; Whitehead on,
71

Wound and the Bow, The (Wilson),
119
Wuthering Heights (Emily Brontë),
91
Wyck Brooks, Van. *See* Brooks,
Van Wyck

Yonge, Charlotte, 92, 281

MORE ABOUT PENGUINS
AND PEREGRINES

If you have enjoyed reading this book you may
wish to know that *Penguin Book News* appears
every month. It is an attractively illustrated maga-
zine containing a complete list of books published
by Penguins and still in print, together with details
of the month's new books. A specimen copy will
be sent free on request.

Penguin Book News is obtainable from most book-
shops; but you may prefer to become a regular
subscriber at 3s for twelve issues. Just write to
Dept. EP, Penguin Books Ltd., Harmondsworth,
Middlesex, enclosing a cheque or postal order, and
you will be put on the mailing list.

Some other books published by Penguins are
described on the following pages.

Note: *Penguin Book News* is not
available in the U.S.A., Canada or Australia

The Penguin English Library

JONATHAN SWIFT

GULLIVER'S TRAVELS

With an Introduction by Michael Foot

Swift published *Gulliver's Travels* in 1726 ' to vex the world rather than divert it'. If the world has often replied by expurgating the book and presenting it to children to read, it has never quite succeeded in extracting the sting from this scornful and incisive satire of man. 'Gulliver' is a book to which the adult reader comes back with surprise and a fresh respect. Whether it is seen as the product of an embittered mind or profound comment on the Age of Reason and Nature, there is all the fascination of distorting mirrors in Swift's accounts of Lilliput and Brobdingnag, and far more than mere spleen in the *saeva indignatio* with which he lashes human passions and institutions.

The Penguin English Library

CHARLES DICKENS

DAVID COPPERFIELD

Edited by Trevor Blount

David Copperfield (1849/50) was Dickens's 'favourite child' and the book in which he revealed most of himself and particularly of his early life. But, as Trevor Blount writes in his introduction, Dickens 'did more than transliterate autobiography. He fashioned himself anew in what he wrote, and in so doing achieved simultaneously the sanity and distinction of art, and the warmth and quickness of joyous life'. Above all in this novel he created some of his most famous characters – Micawber, Uriah Heep, Steerforth – creatures whom, in Chesterton's words, 'we would not forget if we could, creatures whom we could not forget if we would, creatures who are more actual than the man who made them'.

The Penguin English Library

CHARLES DICKENS

OLIVER TWIST

With an Introduction by Angus Wilson

Oliver Twist, Dickens's second novel, has recognizable antecedents in the Gothic Romance and the Newgate Novel and in popular melodrama. But out of these elements the 25-year-old writer created an entirely new kind of novel, scathing in its exposure of contemporary cruelties, always exciting, and clothed in an unforgettable atmosphere of mystery and pervasive evil. Its major characters – Fagin, Bill Sykes, the Artful Dodger – have become creatures of myth, and its great scenes have lost none of their power to terrify and move.

MARK TWAIN

THE ADVENTURES
OF HUCKLEBERRY FINN

Edited by Peter Coveney

Of all the contenders for the title of The Great American Novel, none has a better claim than *The Adventures of Huckleberry Finn*. This idyll, intended at first as 'a kind of companion to *Tom Sawyer*', grew and matured under Mark Twain's hand into a work of immeasurable richness and complexity. Critics have argued over the symbolic significance of Huck's and Jim's voyage down the Mississippi: none has disputed the greatness of the book itself. It remains a work that can be enjoyed at many levels; as an incomparable adventure story, as a classic of American humour, and as a metaphor of the American predicament.